THE DIVINE
Feminine

*A
Treatise
on the
Female
in Christian
Spirituality*

DR. LEE ANN B. MARINO,
PH.D., D.MIN., D.D.

THE DIVINE FEMININE

A Treatise on the Female in Christian Spirituality

DR. LEE ANN B. MARINO, PH.D., D.MIN., D.D.

Published by:
PHOTINI PRESS
(An imprint of the Righteous Pen Publications Group)
www.righteouspenpublications.com

Unless otherwise noted, all Scripture quotations are taken from **The Expanded Bible.** Copyright © 2011 by Thomas Nelson. Used by permission. All rights reserved.

All Scriptures marked KJV are taken from **The Holy Bible, Authorized King James Version,** Public Domain.

All Scriptures marked NIV are taken from **The Holy Bible, New International Version ®, NIV®,** Copyright © 1973, 1978, 1984, 2011 by Biblica, Inc. ™ Used by permission of Zondervan. All rights reserved worldwide.

All Scriptures marked ASV are from **The American Standard Version of the Holy Bible,** 1901. Public domain.

All Scriptures marked AMPC are taken from the **Amplified® Bible Classic,** Copyright © 1954, 1958, 1962, 1964, 1965, 1987 by The Lockman Foundation Used by permission. (www.Lockman.org)

All Scriptures marked CSB are taken from **The Christian Standard Bible**. Copyright © 2017 by Holman Bible Publishers. Used by permission. Christian Standard Bible®, and CSB® are federally registered trademarks of Holman Bible Publishers, all rights reserved.

All Scriptures marked CJB are taken from **The Complete Jewish Bible** by David H. Stern. Copyright © 1998. All rights reserved. Used by permission of Messianic Jewish Publishers, 6120 Day Long Lane, Clarksville, MD 21029. www.messianicjewish.net.

All Scriptures marked ESV are taken from **The Holy Bible, English Standard Version®,** Copyright © 2001 by Crossway, a publishing ministry of Good News Publishers. All rights reserved. Used by permission.

All Scriptures marked NRSV are taken from **The New Revised Standard Version Bible®,** Copyright © 1989 National Council of the Churches of Christ in the United States of America. All rights reserved. Used by permission.

Book classification: Books > Religion & Spirituality > Religious Studies > Gender & Sexuality.

Cover photo: Photo by Klara Kulikova on Unsplash. All images found throughout this book are either the property of the author or are in the Public Domain.

ISBN: 1-940197-54-6
13-Digit: 978-1-940197-54-8

Printed in the United States of America

I' WOMAN, AM THAT WONDER-BREATHING ROSE
THAT BLOSSOMS IN THE GARDEN OF THE KING.
IN ALL THE WORLD THERE IS NO LOVELIER THING,
AND THE LEARNED STARS NO SECRET CAN DISCLOSE
DEEPER THAN MINE — THAT ALMOST NO ONE KNOWS.
THE PERFUME OF MY PETALS IN THE SPRING
INSPIRATION TO ALL BIRDS THAT SING
OF LOVE, THE SPIRIT'S LYRIC UNREPOSE.

UNDER MY VEIL IS HID THE MYSTERY
OF UNACCOMPLISHED AEONS, AND MY BREATH
THE MASTER-LOVER'S LIFE REPLENISHETH,
THE MORTAL GARMENT THAT IS WORN BY ME
THE LOOM OF TIME RENEWS CONTINUALLY;
AND WHEN I DIE — THE UNIVERSE KNOWS DEATH.
(ELSA BARKER, 1917)

TABLE OF CONTENTS

Introduction

Shall call me mad, the great God's prophetess,
For He showed me what happened formerly
To my ancestors; what things were the first
Those God made known to me; and in my mind
Did God put all things to be afterwards,
That I might prophesy of things to come,
And things that were, and tell them unto men.
(Sibylline Oracles 3:1018-1020[1])

WHEN I first thought about writing this book back in 2004, I had no idea it would take me almost 14 years to discipline myself enough to sit down and actually do it. The idea came from two seemingly unconnected events. The first was by accident: I was looking for a new book to read that would discuss Biblical issues from a female perspective. As a result, I surveyed the contents of popular books for Christian women. The books I discovered all reflected similar, if not exactly the same, themes: overcoming abuse, emotional healing, managing households and parenting, and, of course, relationship advice (because where would we be without it, right?). As I stood there, surrounded by an array of books that were all alike, I realized I wasn't interested in anything they offered. Even books that were about Biblical women still held certain overtones that related to the more general themes found in the other books one could buy.

- Eve was about submission (relationships).
- Ruth was about finding your Boaz (relationships).
- Jezebel was the wrong way to be a wife (relationships).
- The woman with the issue of blood was about finding your emotional needs completely met in Jesus (healing).
- The Proverbs 31 woman was about time and home management (managing households and parenting).
- The book about Esther was about sexual purity (relationships).

1

Much of the content in these books related the personal experiences and perspectives of the author in their own circumstances that related to the topic. Reading the back of the books revealed the authors probably didn't know how to be objective about the topics at hand, and they probably didn't have a lot of experience with the subject matter from an objective, or ministerial, point of view. Whether or not they were objective, however, quickly became a side point. The writing styles, topics, and issues were all the same, and they didn't interest me. They weren't what I was looking for. I was looking for a study, a look, a search for issues as pertained to women, and I personally wanted something that would change the way I saw myself in relationship to the Word...and none of these were it.

The second event came in like a flood, as I was doing a Bible study of my own and realized how much of the Scriptures related certain words, phrases, and terminology to the feminine. Use of feminine language in the Scriptures was not something I was taught to think about, so I never thought about it. The most I ever remember discussing language usage and word terminology was the issue of gender-inclusive terminology in the Bible (using "brothers and sisters," for example, rather than the traditional "brothers"), when I was a teenager in the Catholic Church. The efforts they went through to eliminate gender and gender identity seemed overwhelming at the time, not to mention highly controversial. They changed song lyrics and released new missals and translations of the Bible, making a point not to refer to God by any pronouns, because it was believed to do as such would imply gender. When I started attending Pentecostal churches in the late 1990s, I found the total opposite – not only was God referred to with male pronouns, but God's identity also was perceived as decidedly "male," in a literal sense. Because the Scriptural language surrounding God was often male, that meant God was a man, and this notion went unchallenged. Challenging such a notion was to challenge the Bible, which was regarded as infallible, and was equal to challenging the notion of God, Himself.

Even though I identify as a radical feminist (which, for those who are unfamiliar with the term, means that I believe equality for women starts as we challenge and change the idea of traditional roles and relationships) even though my relationship has changed with feminism over the years, I suppose it's safe to say I never thought much about the overwhelming male dominance present in much of Christianity as relates to God, even to this very day. I have always been comfortable using male pronouns in relation to God, and I have never felt the need to abandon my faith identity. I've struggled over the years with many of the concepts and ideas that were presented, and it has been an experience of transformation and growth to move away from the patriarchy that has often overshadowed the truth about God. There were things I believed, but I didn't always understand how to explain them from a spiritual perspective, and as scholarship on this topic and others related to it is often lacking, I set out to discover these matters, once and for all, for myself.

The problem with such a resolution is that these are not matters that are settled "once and for all." We continue to learn and grow, and come to new understandings, and that is what has happened to me over this 14-year period. What I was looking for might not have been out there in terms of accessible, published material, but it was in the Scriptures, and the more I have learned, the more I have discovered that shows me why I have never felt like I am missing something as a Christian. All it took was for someone to point out to me that the church is always spoken of in feminine form to set me on the course we see now, and that is a resolution that never runs dry. All throughout the Scriptures, the people of God were always spoken of in feminine terms when referring to the general group. We might have heard the church referred to as "her" before (especially in hymns), but I bet it's safe to say that most of us have never, ever thought about what it means to be "her" as the Body of Christ. We might have turned God inside out to make Him one gender or another, we commonly overlook the clear feminine forms of the divine experience that are found in the Bible, and why they are clearly feminine. Just as we think on God in terms of Himself, we, too, must think about the question and identity of her – and just what her is meant to mean for all of us.

Finding writing or accessible scholarship to think on such things, starting that process of growth and understanding, is not easy. If you aren't interested in reading about emotional healing and forgiveness for the rest of your life, then it isn't easy to find writing that will suit your identity and understanding of self. While emotional healing and forgiveness are certainly of importance at points in everyone's spiritual walk, they aren't sufficient reading material for the remainder of one's Christian life. There is much for us to learn, develop, and seek as believers, beyond this, however, and we should seek to move beyond immediate and elementary things to discover a whole new aspect of our identity and being.

It is most disturbing to me that while we see other areas of the church change and morph into new areas, men's and women's ministry never seems to change. I've watched the church pass through the Y2K phase, the Messianic phase, the Brownsville Revival re-creation phase, the Purpose Driven Life phase, the Todd Bentley phase, the 7-7-07 phase, the seeker-friendly phase, the modern numerology phase, and now the "make nice with everyone" phase, which we still seem to be in. Yet women's ministry seems to always remain ordinary, and as I am not one comfortable with ordinary, I've spent a lot of time resisting ennui. We don't seem to grow out of safe and traditional teachings that don't push women to do more or be more than might be culturally acceptable, and time and time again, these teachings never seem to change. Women's ministry teachings always seem to be about being wives and mothers, getting married, keeping your husband happy, healing from your past, not being too aggressive sexually, what you are allowed to do during sex (apparently there are rules), not being too bold, not being too loud, how to give your husband his way all the time (whether he is right or wrong), what church rules still apply to women (on wearing pants we went from yes, to no, to yes, to no, to yes again), and being satisfied with the "ordinary" of life. If we were not satisfied with such, disagreed with the teaching, or wanted more for ourselves, then we went back to "forgiveness" and "emotional healing" again.

It was also not beyond my scope that most of these programs, supposedly designed and customized for women, were written by, taught by, or assessed as suitable by men. Even when women taught these courses created by men, they still had the same sound, sting, and impression – the same words, ideas, and concepts we hear all the time, imposed upon us from the pulpit. The long list of dos and don'ts somehow changed, but did not change, all the time, and the burden was always on us. If the men in our lives weren't Christians, that was regarded as being our fault. If the man someone was dating wouldn't marry her, that was regarded as being her fault. If a woman's husband had an affair, that was regarded as being her fault. If a woman was raped, she was told it was how she dressed, how short her skirt was, or that she had on make-up. If a spouse was displeased, it was regarded as being our fault. If a woman was single, that was automatically seen as being wrong, and it was often expressed that a woman was single because she was somehow displeasing to God and men, at the same time. The constant role of blame for everything was always, either expressly or indirectly, placed upon women.

What we never heard about was where we were in Scripture. Bible women and female Biblical figures were made out to be models of the ideals we heard in the teachings we received. They never had bad days, said any bad words, and sat around as supposedly ordinary women who happened to live free of any and all imperfections. Women, like Eve and Jezebel, were women who were bad to the bone and negatively influenced men. We never discussed anything feminine about the Word, even though the Scriptures themselves are feminine. In one form or another, we always focused on men, and how we should, or should not, interact with them. The more we heard, the more we listened, the more impossible it seemed to achieve anything other than what was presented to us.

This leads many women to assume the Bible is inherently sexist. There are still an overwhelming number of women who believe the Scriptures encourage a subordinate position for women, and being a Christian means that you have to accept a position of subordination. Many are resistant to embrace the images of women in the Bible, if for no other reason, women are considered with such little regard in church settings.

When I started studying an honest survey of everything female in the Bible, I was able to come to a better understanding of why exactly such teachings are unbiblical. Even though literalists and traditionalists might throw the book at me, what literalism shows us is a complete and total failure to understand the Scriptures in any kind of context. The result was what I call Female Apologetics, my school of apologetical research pertaining to all things female as applies to Scripture. It was born out of the realization that if we are treating and portraying women incorrectly, we aren't understanding the feminine perspectives as exist within the Scriptures, either. This means we can't embrace essential aspects of Scripture, and we do not recognize who we are as a church body, either. For our survival as a church, it is entirely necessary for us to change our perspectives on these matters.

The reality is that the way we perceive the feminine – and women – in the Word has everything to do with a right and proper understanding of the Scriptures in the life of a believer. If we don't uphold women in favor of an unbalanced perspective biased toward the male believer, it causes us to distort the perception we have of women in the Bible. This equates to an improper perspective about ourselves, and how we, as women, see ourselves in God's plan.

It is also a point, though might have been discovered in a secondary way, that much of the feminine revelations of Scripture also overlap with non-binary and genderqueer entities, as well. Including these revelations helps bridge the gender gap and promote a sense of inclusion, one that better helps us see gender across a spectrum, rather than as a binary.

The inspiration of this book now, all these years later, has been confirmed time and time again as I watch women in ministry and Christian women as a group suffer discrimination for no other reason than they are women. Being women is not grounds for exclusionary discrimination, nor is it an automatic indicator that we do not need to know ourselves or our place in the Kingdom. Through this book, it is my greatest hope to introduce the church to Female Apologetics in a larger way: to realize that, contrary to what some believe, gender does matter, even if it's not in the sense we often think it does; being female is an extraordinary thing in the eyes of God; and that the relevance of the female in spirituality is one of the most important understandings for the church of our day.

CHAPTER ONE
Does Gender Matter?

BUT THE LORD SAID TO SAMUEL, "DON'T LOOK AT HOW HANDSOME ELIAB IS
[HIS APPEARANCE] OR HOW TALL HE IS [HIS HEIGHT], BECAUSE I HAVE NOT CHOSEN
[REJECTED] HIM. GOD DOES NOT SEE THE SAME WAY [AS] PEOPLE SEE.
PEOPLE LOOK AT THE OUTSIDE OF A PERSON [APPEARANCES; THE OUTWARD APPEARANCE],
BUT THE LORD LOOKS AT [ON] THE HEART."
(1 SAMUEL 16:7)

"GENDER doesn't matter."

These words haunted my mind for over 12 hours as I laid awake after the conference call ended. The conference was supposed to be about "female apostles," but somehow, it spiraled out of control, like everything seems to nowadays. A discussion on women in the apostolic turned into burying the past, it being a new day, and arguments about gender and whether gender mattered at all. It turned into the mire of puffing up that everything turned into as always, no matter what the topic at hand might have been. Everything always winds up about leaving the past behind, emotional healing, and new days, even though we wake up the same exact way the next day.

But I digress.

Every time someone on that line said, "gender doesn't matter," I cringed. I was, most likely, the only woman on the line who couldn't get myself into the cheerleading phase as we lauded a principle that most on that line don't even embrace themselves. There was something about their words that didn't seem honest to me. If gender didn't matter, why was it specified as a conference for women? What were we there to talk about, if gender doesn't matter? If gender doesn't matter, why is it such a focal point in the life of the church? And if gender doesn't matter, where does that leave those who identify as women in the concept of church identity and understanding?

What bothered me about the whole incident boiled down to

one simple, little thing: it seems impossible to have a discussion on matters anymore without dragging gender into the conversation. No matter what people believe about gender, it seems like gender is used one way or the other, either to support something or suppress it, or to argue one way or the other.

It might seem odd for me to speak on gender in this matter, especially given I work openly with communities that embrace the world of gender non-binary and have also documented many Christians throughout history who were on the non-binary spectrum. When I talk about gender and whether it matters, I think the issue remains in understanding, rather than in specific identities. I am not here to talk about "gender matters" as considers roles or regulations, but in the essential question: when trying to understand Christianity, Christian history, and in this specific context, the Bible, is it right to entirely throw out any and all reference to gender, if that is what was understood in the context of time?

Language and gender

In terms of universal language, English doesn't take on the characteristics of several other languages. One of the major things we lack are gender-specific articles and identities for our words. Most of the time, we translate all these articles the same way – we indicate them to be "a," "an," or "the." In other languages, they do more than just point to a thing – they also are the first indicator of their gender identity. In most languages, all words are identified as either masculine or feminine, and in some cases, there is also the incorporation of a neuter tense, or one that is identified as neither masculine nor feminine (and this tense will come up later in this book). Most plural words are masculine when in a mixed group (masculine and feminine) and there is a separate form of a pluralized word for a group that is entirely female.

French
- Le – masculine
- La – Feminine
- Les – plural

German
- Der – masculine
- Die – Feminine
- Das – neuter

Italian
- Il – masculine
- La – Feminine
- Lo – neuter

Spanish
- El – masculine
- La – Feminine
- Lo – neuter

Portuguese
- O – masculine
- A – feminine

Hawaiian
- Ka – masculine
- Ke – feminine

Hungarian
- A – masculine
- Az - feminine

Some consider the evolution of gender in language to be arbitrary. In some ways, it certainly does appear to be as such. There's no solid reason why some objects are associated with a feminine identity and some with a masculine identity, and that these things vary from culture to culture. In one language, an item might be identified as female, and in others, it is male, or neuter still in others. The complexities of language evolve over time, without simplistic answers as to why things are identified in certain ways. The simplest explanation probably relates to cultural association; words were identified as male or female as people saw and understood them, recognizing the use, work, or purpose behind something to be closely related to the gender with which they were identified, with neutral words evolving out of a tradition that either embraced both genders or neither gender.

Hebrew and Greek are both languages that evolved to identify words as masculine or feminine, and Greek also identifies certain words in the neuter tense. This means when the Bible was written, words were used in association with what was familiar and known to the writers. There were also words that evolved over time, often associated because of the words themselves and their meanings. If we are to take things to a slightly deeper level, this also means that when the Bible was written, the words given by inspiration were given to illustrate certain points and associations, those that would be easily understood by those who heard the stories told and those who would later read the writings that stemmed from different oral traditions.

If words were a part of a language tradition that embraced these different traditions of language and identity, the use of certain words in certain instances has relevance. It is not to say that we always have to understand things as pertain to gender literally (such as the use of the word "brothers" to refer to the entire Christian community, rather than seeing the term as exclusive to men), but that we do have to understand gender usage within the Scriptures as a part of the language that existed in Biblical times. To understand the Bible, we must understand the use of gender language, and why such language becomes relevant for key spiritual themes. We do not have space to examine every single word that is female in the Bible, and discuss why it is, indeed, feminine, so we will be looking at major themes, ideas, and words present therein.

Gender and the Bible

Over the many years I have spent as a Christian, I have been party to many different theories as pertain to gender and the Bible. I've met those who believe the Bible is completely gender specific, and those who believe the Bible is completely gender neutral. There is a never-ending debate, fight, and railing cry, either for or against gender understanding in our churches today. Some want it to be of no consequence; others want it to be the only consequence. Considering modern society, as we try to interpret the Bible for our times, it is overly tempting to try and fall into extremes to comfort our own upheld understandings, rather than truly understand what the Bible is telling us.

The problem with this battle is two-fold. Yes, I agree that the Spirit is alive and active, and the Bible has something to say to us that is neither outdated, nor impossible to understand for our modern times. This does not mean that we don't seek to understand, as much as is possible, the original context of the Scriptures. To use the Bible to say that gender is irrelevant is as problematic as it is to say that gender is all that matters. If we understand gender as having no relevance, we don't understand key things the Scriptures are trying to tell us, and if all we see when we look at the Bible is gender, then we are failing to understand deeper spiritual truths that exist, so we can transcend the natural and move to a deeper understanding of the spiritual.

As a feminist, I find myself in an interesting position within the debate. While I do not believe gender is everything and I do not ascribe to the belief that it assigns us to roles within our lives, I certainly can't subscribe to the belief that the Bible has no take on gender whatsoever, either. Both perspectives seem to miss the essence of the Scriptures, of important things that reveal history and context to us, and I also feel they deny us the discomfort of overcoming ourselves and forcing ourselves to accept others, however they may be. While yes, we may get the message that gender is not everything and should not assault the essential ideas of unity present in Scripture, we can't ignore the many other passages which seem to suggest something different considering gender and the Bible.

Neither gender as nothing nor gender as everything are accurate portrayals of the Bible's take – and usage – on matters of gender. The Bible is not gender neutral, nor is it always gender specific. It is something in the middle, a mixture of ideas and concepts that relate to eternal salvation and the way that salvation impacts our everyday lives and interactions with others. To label the Bible all one way when it comes to gender is misleading, but that doesn't mean that we, as Christians, should not take a specific approach over another when it comes to gender understanding from a spiritual perspective.

The Bible was not written in a time where people were "gender neutral." Ancient cultures were far rawer and more unfiltered than we are today, and gender neutrality was simply not a part of the world of the Bible's authors. The sensitivities we have evolved down to modern time were not a part of the Bible's language, and they were not even a consideration in the thoughts and lives of ancient peoples. These realities explain to us much about the culture of Bible times, as well as the realities of the time and tone the of which the Bible was written. Statements that might seem insensitive to us within our modern rendering did not sound that way to those who first received those words, because they were speaking out of their cultural understanding and their cultural ideals. The goal was not to offend or create gender wars, as we have today; it was just to show that God reached His people, right where they were, with the issues they had and the complications that came with their everyday lives. No one was trying to offend modern sensibilities; they simply did not exist yet.

Whenever we, as women (and especially as female scholars) read the Bible, we must consider the patriarchal viewpoint present within the culture of the day and the ways that such patriarchy would have influenced the way that women, children, and general society interacted with one another. This doesn't mean this was the way it should be for all eternity, the way that it is in heaven, or the way that it will be once Jesus comes back. We can't ignore the cultural issues women faced, nor can we ignore the way that women were often treated. What we can do is look at Scripture and see deeper purpose and understanding, and find a sense of ourselves in the types and shadows of ultimate inclusivity spoken of in the church and in the existence of the Body as we see later in the New Testament.

If the Bible writers were not deliberately trying to offend people of this era, they also were not trying to impose gender straits, either. The ultimate promise, the ultimate work of the New Covenant is liberation, and we either understand that to be a radical, life-changing thing, or we only understand it in a limited sense. It is obvious from New Testament passages that the writers struggled with their own realities, of believing in this radical liberation while seeing it manifest in limited ways due to cultural restrictions and governmental impositions, but it doesn't mean they didn't believe that ultimate liberation was to come and would be a true reality for the people of God. When women are mentioned and things that pertain to women are mentioned in the context of their culture, they were never intended to imply that patriarchy was the correct way to go and society should never evolve past where they were at that time in history.

If the Bible's evident patriarchal worldview is not a statement of proper literal spiritual implementation, then it proves to us, beyond a shadow of the doubt, that human beings perceive spiritual understanding through cultural limitations. It is a part of reaching out to the divine, and seeing the divine through what we know, perceive, and understand with our own limited influences. We experience God through what we best understand, and in ways that are best to our understanding, and ultimately, those biases influence the way we understand God at times. This means that when God conveys a message, He is going to convey it in a way that breaks through our biases and is understandable to us, at the same time. So what does God do? He uses those biases to challenge us and to turn our understanding of spiritual matters right on their heads. The catch is, we have to break through the bias to fully understand just what it is that God is seeking to do.

Is the Bible gender neutral?

We use the term "gender neutral" today to indicate a disposition against gender imposition or ideal on an individual. It is also used as an orientation of identity, a way that people see themselves that is neither male nor female, but something else, either crossing both genders or embracing ideals from neither. As a principle, the concept of gender neutrality is an aspiration, a concept that many aspire to today when raising children or when operating in a workplace or general society. Gender neutrality seems to many to be an object of reality, in which people act as if gender and its societal constructs do not exist.

I believe that gender neutrality sounds like a good idea, because it sounds like the opposite of the incredible fuss and strain that people make as pertains to gender. If all we do is force gender roles on people, then a neutral concept of gender and what gender means seems to be the solution, right?

Gender neutrality sounds good in the ears of many, but I don't believe it is a viable solution. The concept of gender neutrality is to erase gender, and all concepts associated with it, and to pretend that gender of any sort does not exist. In the first place, such a concept is unrealistic. Gender, while a societal construct, does exist in the world in which we live. It is a part of the human experience for most people, as well. This doesn't mean that the concept we have of gender is always proper or biological, nor does it mean that we always have the right ideas about gender and what gender should mean, but it does mean that we cannot, with any reason of understanding, pretend that gender does not exist.

The answer for us, as humanity, is not to erase gender; it's to change the way we look at it. Whenever we start neutralizing the existence of gender, we also neutralize the great things that come along with gender, and we ignore wonderful opportunities to help girls feel good about being female and about becoming strong, independent women. Negating gender also means we ignore the many abuses and ways that gender bias has been misappropriated throughout the ages, and somehow, at least in my sight, gender neutrality minimizes those realities that many women worldwide still deal with, even today.

It is with this in sight that anyone reading the Bible must take a deep breath and accept the fact that God is not blind to gender, nor to gender struggles, and neither is the Bible. Gender neutrality implies a certain oversight to gender and gender issues, and there is nothing to suggest that God ever did such in history. If we made God gender neutral, it would imply He is ignorant and insensitive to the various issues that we, as humans face, because of gender. Such is incompatible with at Scriptural view of God, because the Bible tells us God is attentive to our very cry, to the injustices we face, and to the cruelty that sin has caused.

Gender neutrality also cannot exist as a sole theory in Scriptural understanding because if we understand the Scriptures, God created male, female, and every other expression in His image. Gender identity does not render one lesser in God's sight, but equal before Him, as a representation of qualities and attributes that He has within Himself and His identity within eternity. Neither does such force a binary view of gender, because much of gender association is cultural, rather than Biblical. For women, our creation as female is a part of God's nature. It is not diminished, and it is important, a raising up and a representation that is needed both practically and spiritually. Such does not limit what we can do or who we can be for God, but it does represent an important aspect of what God calls all of us, as believers, to be.

What the Bible teaches us about gender

Contrary to popular belief, the Bible doesn't give us a static list on the history and issues pertaining to gender. I would define it as gender ambivalent. This means the Bible acknowledges the existence of such, but such is not exclusive nor limiting in the way we often see it now. It might have defined cultural expectation, but God has a history of defying cultural expectations through His people. For as much as there seems to be one "rule" about gender, there's another passage that seems to break that rule.

It also means the Bible's perceptions of gender aren't exclusive, by any means. To limit the Bible as having one constant perspective on gender is unrealistic. The Bible was written over thousands of years by several different writers, and if we understand gender to exist as part of our understanding of culture and cultural norms, different writers had different perspectives on just what gender meant from a spiritual perspective. This means what the Bible teaches on gender needs to be examined from a New Covenant perspective, from the ideal that God sets forth for us and for an inclusive principle. Keeping this in mind, that means when we read the Bible, particularly passages that seem troublesome for us today, we need to maintain the perspective of what it can reveal to us about gender and gender disparity in our day and age.

- **All gender expressions reflect the image of God**: Being created in the image of God is a spiritual statement on behalf of humanity, rather than a limitation. It reflects that even in our humanity, we still have connection to the divine, and no matter how that gender expresses itself, it still reflects the creation and image of God.

- **Gender changes the way we relate to God**: The back story behind the books of Esther and Ruth is an unfortunate one. Many of the male Reformers felt they had no purpose and place in the Bible canon. Why is this? It is because Ruth and Esther reveal a uniquely feminine perspective of God, which the men did not relate to, nor understand. Esther and Ruth did not receive direct visits from prophets, they didn't hear a grand voice bellow to them from above, and we don't have any indication they ever had a dream or a vision. They knew instinctively the right thing to do, and they did it.

- **Gender does not change our purpose in God's sight, i.e., it is not prohibitive**: The Bible is full of women who worked alongside men, worked in place of men, or whose positions were superior or of greater character than those of men. As much as a specific Biblical injunction might seem one way, there are examples of women who broke those rules as well as other passages and statements that contradict that role. Gender is not prohibitive, nor is it all-imposing.

- **Gender, as a separate concept from biological sex, does serve biological function, but is not limited to biology**: It takes male and female to populate the species, as simple biological reality. This doesn't mean reproduction is what or all what gender is about, nor does it mean that biology is a spiritual or social restriction upon us. It means that while gender can connect to biology, it is more about the way cultures and concepts form ideas, and the ideas people have about things related to gender and social interactions.

- **The sexes are antithetical; gender, in its very reality, causes conflict**: When God told Eve that "Your desire would be for your husband, and he will rule over you," there is nothing in that statement to indicate such was God's design for order or the way God intended things to be. It was a statement; one of fact, one looking far into the future for what life would be like. What God pointed out was one of the consequences for sin was relationship desire, with an antithetical and controlling nature, not to mention a real look into the future at the way gender often creates conflict.

- **Gender matters are complicated**: There is nowhere else that exemplifies the truly complicated issues of gender better than the Bible. From archaic laws that limited the way women were viewed, to realities that showed the way women were treated as property, to liberated ideals of women in positions of authority and as equals in the church, gender has never been a simple idea that societies have been able to sort out with consistent, pat answers.

- **Gender matters "down here;" culturally, maybe too much**: The mere fact that women are given time and attention in the Bible in ways that liberate and elevate women to an equal status of men shows us that the emphasis we have on gender is over the top. It doesn't mean we should ignore gender, but it does mean that it should not dictate the codes of society and societal conduct in quite the way it does.

- **Gender dictates how we interact with each other**: As more of the societal aspect of our construct, gender dictates (perhaps too much) of how we interact with each other, not just as women and men, but also as women with other women and men with other men. We also have societal constructs that demand women interact a certain way with children, with animals, and within cultural roles, such as a First Lady or subordinate position to man.

- **In meeting us where we are, the Bible gives us spiritual associations with gender**: The spiritual associations made between male and female reflect the nature of God, not as one or the other, but as non-competing, understanding that both have a purpose and one is not superseding the other. It also doesn't mean that gender associations in the spiritual realm are a statement on the accuracy of society's gender guidelines or that such spiritual things are literally rendered by gender, but it exists to show us important things about ourselves in a way we can both understand and relate.

The messages we convey about gender

If we are looking at what the Bible teaches about gender, we also must look at the cultural messages we receive about gender, and why those messages are conflicting with spiritual ideas about these matters. This probably seems a contradictory statement to some, because to many, their concepts about gender are regarded as spiritual principles. Embracing one's birth-assigned gender, for example, is considered a fundamental aspect of defining the aspirations and goals one can, or cannot, have throughout their lives. We assume boys like dark colors and girls like frilly, lacy things. Girls want to play with dolls and boys with trucks, and girls will never want to roughhouse. When boys and girls get older, we assume they will take on adult gender roles in their lives: males as providers, females as wives and mothers, and never the twain shall meet. We've made it impossible for husbands and wives to embrace any sense of understanding of one another, and that has caused us to feel as if gender dominates and controls our entire identities. In that singular message, we learn one thing: being female, in any form, is bad.

I think the best way I can summarize this issue is simple: years ago, Kitty Wells sang the line, "Ain't it a shame that all the blame is on us women." In essence, this is the very heart of where many stand when it comes to female matters in church, even today. The constant messages women receive against being female manifest in a number of ways. We don't see holiness codes imposed upon men anymore (although, at one time, they were for men and women). It is still questionable just what "women can do" in church and home settings. Women are still given the message that they are incomplete without a man, because men are seen as offering authority, leadership, and guidance that women need in order to survive. Women are seen as incomplete if they are single or do not have children. Whenever something goes wrong in the world, feminists, independent women, or those who don't follow the rules, always get the blame.

These obvious messages that cast women in a negative light don't end in direct statements and questions, posed such as these. There are many other ways the messages are conveyed, often in manner we wouldn't suspect. One such way is the way homosexuality, gender identity, or presuppositions of such are argued. Often these issues are not reasoned Biblically (all relate to idolatry and hygiene and can be understood to relate to pagan practices rather than the understanding often applied in a modern context), but imply within their understanding that there is something inherently wrong with being female. The stereotype is that homosexual relationships consist of effeminate men or two overly masculinized women, and that in such a state, no one is in "charge." If there's no man to lead a woman or if men are perceived as somehow taking on a feminine nature, such is understood to be an assault on the very fabric of societal viewpoints about male-female relationships. Yet what we fail to understand is in such, we are degrading through the messages we give about such relationships and identities. It is implied that being a woman is a bad thing, both from a sexual perspective and an identifying one in terms of society. Whether a woman is perceived as being extremely feminine or overtly masculine, or if a man is perceived as being feminine, something is implied to be inherently wrong within one's being.

What people have done, especially in modern times when gender and sexuality have stood front and center, is read Biblical passages in the light of their desired cultural adaptation, added their own spin, and placed dozens and dozens of cultural rules in between the lines of the Bible. They are not just reading the Bible; they are reading the message that being a woman is bad, being female is bad, resembling a woman is bad, and that gender is an inherently spiritual issue, beyond the natural, into the eternal.

We already know that there are cultural associations with the feminine that are decidedly problematic. Such assertions create theological problems as well as cultural ones. If we keep imposing culture in Biblical interpretation, we will never truly understand what the Scriptures have to say to us. At the same time, this is a pervasive issue that has existed throughout history. The imposition of culture and cultural desire on Biblical interpretation isn't a new problem and has seriously damaged the way people viewed the divine and their relationship therein. But there is a difference between understanding that God reaches us right where we are and loves us regardless and not taking the time to understand God's revelation to us in a way that is comprehensive, purposed, and captures the heart of what God has wanted to teach us, all along.

When it comes to the issue of women, we have not, as a church, been particularly apt to take the time and learn what God desires to say to us about such. We've gone along, aggrandizing our personal viewpoints to those of the divine, and overlooked an entire message that is there, for us. The message we intend to convey of gender isn't the one God often desires to convey, and that means we must start looking at gender differently to understand the fullness He has for us in spiritual perspective.

Going beyond our bodies

If we are attempting to re-examine how we look at gender, then we must make the leap to go beyond our bodies and consider Biblical precepts on male and female. I've heard it said that we are never more in touch with the divine than when we are most human. Have we ever considered why this kind of statement might bear with a certain level of truth, even from a spiritual perspective? It might seem odd to us, but if we think about it with any sort of veracity, we are most in touch with our need for God when we accept our humanity. Accepting our limitations as human beings – we are not divine, but human – sparks us to connect with the divine.

I believe this foundation is what grounds us in Galatians 3:26-28:

[FOR] YOU ARE ALL CHILDREN OF GOD THROUGH FAITH IN CHRIST JESUS [OR IN CHRIST JESUS YOU ARE ALL CHILDREN/SONS OF GOD THROUGH FAITH]. [FOR] ALL OF YOU WHO WERE BAPTIZED INTO CHRIST HAVE CLOTHED YOURSELVES WITH CHRIST. IN CHRIST, THERE IS NO DIFFERENCE BETWEEN JEW AND GREEK [NEITHER JEW NOR GREEK], SLAVE AND FREE PERSON, MALE AND FEMALE. YOU ARE ALL THE SAME [OR UNITED; ONE] IN CHRIST JESUS.

The Bible tells us there is neither "male nor female" in Christ, because we have died to ourselves – our humanity – to discover a greater connection with God. In church, it is not our gender that is to define us. At the same time, we are to rise to the occasion and come to a different understanding of these things that we have put such emphasis on in culture. What has defined us in society is not to define us in the Kingdom, because now we are in Christ. We are something different, and our perspectives on everything that is a part of this world radically changes and alters, to bring us to a place where God increases within us, and we decrease within ourselves (John 3:33). This includes our concepts of gender, as much as anything else. Gender matters down here. God speaks to us in gender-specific language so we can understand while we are down here, but that doesn't mean such is where gender begins and ends. In all things, we seek to understand greater who God calls us to be, and that transcends the limitations we place on ourselves.

This book is a challenge to both the standard gender models and our call to understand something higher, something greater than ourselves, as we examine different female models and examples of spiritual identities throughout these pages. God is speaking to us, in every example and message given through the Scriptures, and it is now up to us, to listen to His voice echoing about the feminine in spirituality as we walk through this call we have to allow Him to increase within us, and us to decrease within ourselves.

Eve tempted by the Serpent alongside the tree of Knowledge. Adam is sleeping in the background (William Blake)

CHAPTER TWO
Types of the Church to Come

I WILL THANK [PRAISE] THE LORD WITH ALL MY HEART
IN THE MEETING OF HIS GOOD PEOPLE [COUNCIL OF THE UPRIGHT/VIRTUOUS,
IN THE ASSEMBLY].
THE LORD DOES GREAT THINGS [DEEDS OF THE LORD ARE GREAT];
THOSE WHO ENJOY THEM SEEK [STUDY] THEM.
WHAT HE DOES IS [HIS DEEDS ARE] GLORIOUS [BEAUTIFUL] AND SPLENDID [MAJESTIC],
AND HIS GOODNESS [RIGHTEOUSNESS] CONTINUES [STANDS] FOREVER.
(PSALM 111:1-3)

WHENEVER we talk about or study typology, we often speak about the types of Christ that exist in the Old Testament. From the water in the rock to the Passover lamb, we are quick – and eager – to find reflections of Christ as are present in the ways and movements of the Old Covenant. It inspires our faith and proves the Scripture to be Christ-centric, the experience of spirituality and the purpose of Christ to exist, even if invisible to those who experienced those spiritual moments for the first time, revealed to us. Salvation has never been far from or out of God's plan, and typology proves this. As we look over the various types and shadows that point to Christ and to His reality, we see God's love and His hand, even when we don't expect it.

There is nothing wrong at all with looking at types and shadows of Christ in typology. There is something wrong, however, with thinking our efforts and educations in typology end with Christ. All throughout salvation history, there are types and shadows of all things that relate to the spiritual realm, to the work of the Kingdom of God, the church, the Ephesians 4:11 ministry, and the work of Christianity, even before Christ was born. Everything revealed in the New Testament is found in the Old Testament, but we, unfortunately, have not always been taught how to properly discern the types of the New Testament of things beyond Christ as present in the Old Testament. There is much for us to learn, especially as it applies to the feminine

23

and the promise of all spiritual things feminine, within the work of the Old Testament.

To see these things, we must retrain ourselves to recognize them. We have spent so many years learning to only see one thing; we must expand our minds to see beyond what we have been taught and realize the promise that lies in the feminine for every believer.

The principle of typology

For those who are less familiar with the concept of types and shadows, it is when something is used as a type, or "shadow" or "illustration" in place of something else. The terms "type" and "shadow" are used interchangeably, as pointing to someone or something else, as a stand-in or representation, even though it is not the person or thing itself. Just as a shadow cast by the sun represents that someone or something else is there, even if we can't see whatever or whomever that may be, so a spiritual shadow does the same thing. It points us to a reality, without being that same reality. In all things, God is always pointing us to something greater, something beyond where we are right now, and what is to come.

Christian theologians and apologists have spent hundreds of years studying the Bible for types and shadows of Christ, present in the Old Testament and then revealed in the New Testament. Typology relates to prophecy and its importance, seeing that God has revealed the details of His plan even in places we might not consider to be noteworthy or relevant. God cares about everything, from the largest detail to the smallest one. In types and shadows, we see these pictures of God and His plan, manifesting as real to us, right before our eyes.

The only thing we have done with typology is paid attention to the bigger things of Scripture – such as the revelation of Christ Himself – and paid lesser attention to the supporting roles of the church, the Spirit, and other Biblical figures. They often don't seem as relevant, and without proper training, they are harder to find. We recognize the Passover lamb and water from the rock as types of Christ (Exodus 12:21, Exodus 17:1-6), but we ignore the Kingdom of God, typified by Israel, in that same passage (Psalm 7:7, Psalm 22:2-5, Psalm 89:5). We recognize the prophets of old in speaking of Christ, but we miss their powerful prefigure as types of the New Testament Ephesians 4:11 ministry offices (Genesis 12:1-6, Judges 4:4-16, 1 Samuel 1:1-2:11, Malachi 4:5-6, the books of Isaiah, Jonah, and Hosea, Jeremiah 3:15, the book of Amos, Exodus 18:13-26, Ezra 7:1-10:44, the books of Proverbs and Ecclesiastes). In combining these different issues, and as we shall see here, we also see Christ and His redemptive work (Genesis 28:12, Exodus 12, Leviticus 23), but we fail to see the church, and her agents (Genesis 47:2, Leviticus 26:8, Numbers 27:1-11, Judges 18:2, 1 Chronicles 2:4).

In a bigger sense than just an illustration, typology is the way God shadows Himself, His very being, upon the world. God reveals Himself to us in bits and pieces, here and there, so we can see and recognize Him as a part of our everyday existence. It is a way that spirituality transcends the distant, and brings the eternal to a practical level, one that any of us can understand and experience in our everyday lives. In typology, we find the message of salvation present in the most unexpected and understated places, seeing creation as subject to God, and the world and all contained therein as a part of a bigger, divine plan. In looking at types and shadows this way, they reveal more to us than just theology; they reveal God, they reveal us, and they reveal the way that all these things come together to produce God's plans.

One of the most difficult things for theologians to admit – and readily see – is the role of the feminine in typology. Embracing patriarchy means embracing a male-dominated view, and that means if we are looking for shadows of Christ, Who is male, we are looking exclusively for types that can be interpreted through a masculine lens. In so doing, we are overlooking other experiences and forms of typology that can help teach us important things about the work of the church, the nature of the Kingdom, and of God and Christ, as well.

Why the feminine is present in typology

If we understand God to be omnipresent and omniscient, then we recognize God knew humanity would fall into sin. Nothing that has happened in the duration of human history comes as a shock or surprise to Him, and that means that while He knew sin would most definitely be a problem, it also means that God made provision for the results of sin within His plan. We do not understand people to be the pre-destined aspect of salvation history, but the plan itself, recognizing nothing is ever, at any point in time, beyond God's reach.

We don't tend to think of the social implications of sin, but the reasons for feminine representations in typology are a direct result of the way that sin has impacted the sexes. It's not a big secret that men and women are frequently opposed to one another, and that has taken no bigger seat than placing itself right in the religious realm. The way we understand our theology tends to look negatively upon the female while uplifting the male. There has even been question throughout history as to whether women can be legitimately saved. Some have believed salvation is exclusive for men, and some have taken the position that women can be exclusively saved through childbearing, or even through their husbands or fathers. In every era, there have always been people who have sought to raise the competitive nature between men and women to new heights and have chosen selectively to ignore the obvious when it comes to salvation. Yes, it is for everyone, and yes there is proof in there, but we must understand typology to see it, up front, for real.

If it were not for God's display through types, salvation (and its accompanying concepts) would be nearly impossible for us to fathom in our limited human understanding. Types make God and God's realities real to us, visible and understandable. They show us salvation in a way that makes it real and applicable to us, in ways we can comprehensively understand. Male types point us to the promise of redemption for men. Female types point us to the promise of redemption for females. Group types are for both, inclusively, and display the truly inclusive nature of God's plan, even for those who may not identify exclusively in a biological context, but in a broader gender understanding. The promise of the Gospel includes all of us, and that is part of why identifying the female in typology is so essential. Salvation is for "whosoever," as in whosoever desires to receive it for themselves. It's not gender restrictive. It is important women see themselves as a part of God's salvation plan, and we cannot do that if we only see male reflections in theological musing.

The church in Eve, the Mother of all Living

EVE[1]

- *CHAVVAH:* "LIFE," THE FIRST WOMAN
- ORIGINAL WORD: חַוָּה
- PART OF SPEECH: PROPER NAME FEMININE
- TRANSLITERATION: CHAVVAH
- PHONETIC SPELLING: (KHAV-VAW')
- SHORT DEFINITION: EVE

Here is a memory recall for all the women out there. When you were a girl, how did your mother feel about herself? Did she often make comments about needing to lose weight, feeling she was fat or unattractive, negative remarks about her aging process (such as wrinkles or fine lines), or maybe just a general sense of feeling badly about things in her life? As you got older, especially once you hit your teens, how did hearing your mom's self-criticisms make you feel? A part of you probably felt bad for your mom, but part of you internalized that self-criticism, didn't you? You started to look at yourself and wonder if what was wrong with her was also wrong with you. Fast-forward to today, that same critical, self-abashing assessment tends to come out, if not all the time, at least part of the time.

Studies have shown the way mothers view themselves influences the way daughters also view themselves. The concept is simple: if our role model, the person we identify with, has all these issues, then we, surely, must have them, too. If we can understand this to be true, then that means the way we view the first mother, Eve, also relates to how all of us, as women, view ourselves...and also how we view the church. If our first mother was fallen, bad-to-the-bone, inherently evil, a troublemaker, and a problem, so too do we receive that message, loud and clear, repeatedly, as Christian women.

Whenever anyone has something negative to say about women, it usually stems back, in some form, to Eve:

- Women can't preach because Eve was deceived.
- Women can't minister because Adam was created first.
- Women can't preach because they are mothers.

- Women can't work outside the home because Eve listened to the serpent. (Not sure what this has to do with anything, but moving on.)
- Women are responsible for what happens to them (rape, sexual abuse, spousal abuse), because of Eve.
- Women aren't capable of good decisions because of Eve.

If you are a woman, you've heard something like this uttered within your Christian experience, especially to this extent. Yet doesn't this create a dichotomy in understanding the nature of Eve? Both Adam and Eve were created in a perfect state, and both fell into different things – deception and sin – within their experience in paradise. The Bible tells us it was Adam who sinned, not Eve, and we still seem to find redemption for him, but not for her:

[THEREFORE, JUST AS] SIN CAME INTO THE WORLD BECAUSE OF WHAT ONE MAN DID [THROUGH ONE MAN], AND WITH SIN CAME DEATH. THIS IS WHY [...AND SO; *OR* AND IN THIS WAY] EVERYONE MUST DIE [DEATH SPREAD/PASSED TO ALL PEOPLE]—BECAUSE EVERYONE SINNED. SIN WAS IN THE WORLD BEFORE THE LAW OF MOSES [THE LAW], BUT SIN IS NOT COUNTED AGAINST US AS BREAKING A COMMAND [CHARGED TO ONE'S ACCOUNT; RECORDED AS SIN] WHEN THERE IS NO LAW [4:15]. BUT FROM THE TIME OF ADAM TO THE TIME OF MOSES, EVERYONE HAD TO DIE [DEATH REIGNED/RULED], EVEN THOSE WHO HAD NOT SINNED BY BREAKING A COMMAND, AS ADAM HAD [IN THE LIKENESS OF ADAM'S DISOBEDIENCE/TRANSGRESSION].

ADAM WAS LIKE [A TYPE/PATTERN/PREFIGUREMENT OF] THE ONE WHO WAS COMING IN THE FUTURE. BUT GOD'S FREE GIFT [THE GIFT] IS NOT LIKE ADAM'S SIN [VIOLATION; TRANSGRESSION]. [FOR IF] MANY PEOPLE DIED BECAUSE OF THE SIN [VIOLATION; TRANSGRESSION] OF THAT ONE MAN. BUT THE GRACE FROM GOD WAS MUCH GREATER, SINCE MANY PEOPLE RECEIVED GOD'S GIFT OF LIFE [...HOW MUCH MORE DID GOD'S GRACE AND GIFT ABOUND/MULTIPLY TO THE MANY] BY THE GRACE OF THE ONE MAN, JESUS CHRIST [THE DEATH OF THE "ONE" SAVED THE "MANY"; SEE V. 19; IS. 53:11]. BUT THE GIFT OF GOD IS DIFFERENT FROM ADAM'S [THE ONE MAN'S] SIN. AFTER ADAM SINNED ONCE, HE WAS JUDGED GUILTY [HIS JUDGMENT BROUGHT CONDEMNATION]. [BUT] GOD'S FREE GIFT CAME AFTER MANY SINS [VIOLATIONS; TRANSGRESSIONS], AND IT MAKES PEOPLE

RIGHT WITH GOD [BROUGHT JUSTIFICATION]. [FOR IF] ONE MAN'S SIN [VIOLATION; TRANSGRESSION] CAUSED DEATH TO RULE OVER ALL PEOPLE [REIGN; RULE] BECAUSE OF THAT ONE MAN. HOW MUCH MORE, THEN, WILL THOSE PEOPLE WHO ACCEPT [RECEIVE] GOD'S FULL GRACE [THE ABUNDANCE OF GRACE] AND THE GREAT GIFT OF BEING MADE RIGHT WITH HIM [RIGHTEOUSNESS] HAVE TRUE LIFE AND RULE [OR RULE IN THE FUTURE LIFE; REIGN/RULE IN LIFE] THROUGH THE ONE MAN, JESUS CHRIST. [JUST AS DEATH "RULED" IN ADAM, SO BELIEVERS "RULE" OVER DEATH THROUGH CHRIST.]

SO AS ONE SIN OF ADAM [VIOLATION; TRANSGRESSION] BROUGHT THE PUNISHMENT OF DEATH [CONDEMNATION] TO ALL PEOPLE, SO TOO ONE GOOD ACT THAT CHRIST DID [RIGHTEOUS ACT/DEED] MAKES ALL PEOPLE RIGHT WITH GOD, BRINGING THEM TRUE LIFE [BRINGS JUSTIFICATION OF LIFE TO ALL PEOPLE]. [FOR JUST AS...] ONE MAN DISOBEYED GOD, AND MANY BECAME SINNERS. IN THE SAME WAY, [...SO ALSO] ONE MAN OBEYED GOD, AND MANY WILL BE MADE RIGHT [RIGHTEOUS]. THE LAW CAME TO MAKE SIN WORSE [OR TO REVEAL THE TRUE EXTENT OF SIN; TO INCREASE THE VIOLATION/TRANSGRESSION]. BUT WHEN SIN GREW WORSE [INCREASED; MULTIPLIED], GOD'S GRACE INCREASED [MULTIPLIED/ABOUNDED ALL THE MORE]. SIN ONCE USED DEATH TO RULE US [JUST AS SIN REIGNED IN DEATH...], BUT GOD GAVE PEOPLE MORE OF HIS GRACE SO THAT GRACE COULD RULE [...SO GRACE WILL REIGN] BY MAKING PEOPLE RIGHT WITH HIM [THROUGH JUSTIFICATION/RIGHTEOUSNESS]. AND THIS BRINGS LIFE FOREVER [ETERNAL LIFE] THROUGH JESUS CHRIST OUR LORD. (Romans 5:12-21)

If God's omnipresence was present at the creation of Adam to see Christ's redemption down the line, then God's omnipresence was also present at the creation of Eve to see the redemption of the church. If we can find respite from Adam's sin, then we can also find respite for Eve's deception. There isn't one present without the other. Instead of viewing her as the one woman that all of history pays the consequences for, unredeemed, we need to see her considering the covenant...and that is as a prefigure of the church.

IN CHRIST WE WERE CHOSEN TO BE GOD'S PEOPLE [HAVE RECEIVED/WERE GIVEN OUR PART OF AN INHERITANCE], BECAUSE FROM THE VERY BEGINNING GOD HAD DECIDED THIS [HAVING BEEN PREDESTINED] IN KEEPING WITH HIS PLAN. AND HE IS THE ONE WHO MAKES EVERYTHING AGREE [OR ACCOMPLISHES EVERYTHING IN ACCORD] WITH WHAT HE DECIDES AND WANTS. WE ARE THE FIRST PEOPLE WHO HOPED IN CHRIST [THE MESSIAH], AND WE WERE CHOSEN SO THAT WE WOULD BRING PRAISE TO GOD'S GLORY. SO IT IS WITH YOU. WHEN YOU HEARD THE TRUE TEACHING [MESSAGE/WORD OF TRUTH]—THE GOOD NEWS ABOUT [GOSPEL OF] YOUR SALVATION—YOU BELIEVED IN CHRIST. AND IN CHRIST, GOD PUT HIS SPECIAL MARK OF OWNERSHIP ON YOU BY GIVING YOU [...HAVING BEEN SEALED WITH] THE HOLY SPIRIT THAT HE HAD PROMISED. THAT HOLY SPIRIT IS THE GUARANTEE [DOWN PAYMENT; DEPOSIT] THAT WE WILL RECEIVE WHAT GOD PROMISED FOR HIS PEOPLE [OF OUR INHERITANCE] UNTIL GOD GIVES FULL FREEDOM TO THOSE WHO ARE HIS [OR WE ACQUIRE POSSESSION OF IT; THE REDEMPTION OF THE POSSESSION; V. 7]—TO BRING PRAISE TO GOD'S GLORY. (Ephesians 1:11-14)

CHURCH[2]
- *EKKLÉSIA*: AN ASSEMBLY, A (RELIGIOUS) CONGREGATION; CHURCH; THE CHURCH, THE WHOLE BODY OF CHRISTIAN BELIEVERS.
- ORIGINAL WORD: ἐκκλησία, ας, ἡ
- PART OF SPEECH: NOUN, FEMININE
- TRANSLITERATION: EKKLÉSIA
- PHONETIC SPELLING: (EK-KLAY-SEE'-AH)
- SHORT DEFINITION: AN ASSEMBLY, CONGREGATION, CHURCH

If we see the church as a part of God's plan – not a replacement plan, not a back-up plan, not a secondary plan, not something that came along to replace something else – then the church was present at the beginning of time, typed and shadowed in the life of Eve. God knew Adam and Eve were going to sin before they were created, and God's plan for salvation was bigger than their immediate sin. If there was no sin, there would have been no need for Christ, and for Christ's purpose to be fully revealed, Adam and Eve must be realities of the fall into sin, as well as prefigures of Christ and the church to come. This becomes even more relevant when we consider the words spoken to Eve, as Eve received a promise within God's words to her:

I WILL MAKE YOU AND THE WOMAN
    ENEMIES TO EACH OTHER [PLACE HOSTILITY/ENMITY BETWEEN YOU
AND THE WOMAN].
YOUR DESCENDANTS [SEED] AND HER DESCENDANTS [SEED]
    WILL BE ENEMIES.
ONE OF HER DESCENDANTS [HE] WILL CRUSH YOUR HEAD,
    AND YOU WILL BITE [STRIKE; BRUISE; CRUSH] HIS HEEL [ROM.
16:20; REV. 12:9]."

THEN GOD SAID TO THE WOMAN,
"I WILL CAUSE YOU TO HAVE MUCH TROUBLE [OR INCREASE YOUR
PAIN]
    WHEN YOU ARE PREGNANT [IN CHILDBEARING],
AND WHEN YOU GIVE BIRTH TO CHILDREN,
    YOU WILL HAVE GREAT PAIN.
YOU WILL GREATLY DESIRE [THE WORD IMPLIES A DESIRE TO
CONTROL; 4:7] YOUR HUSBAND,
    BUT HE WILL RULE OVER YOU." (EXB)

THE MAN NAMED HIS WIFE EVE [THE NAME DERIVES FROM AN EARLY
FORM OF THE VERB "TO LIVE"], BECAUSE SHE WAS THE MOTHER OF ALL
THE LIVING. (GENESIS 3:15-16, 20)

Through Eve, God promised the Redeemer would come – not through Adam. The reason for this is simple: the promise of Christ was given to the church, to the called-out believers who have agreed to become a new nation, a chosen people, a royal priesthood through Him. Just as belonging to the church was a choice, so, too, was Eve a choice, presented to Adam. Through the church, we find the Redeemer, who was promised to the type of the church, Eve. The woman was not just to be redeemed but would be the catalyst for the Redeemer. While mankind officially moved into sin, and by proxy, humanity moved away from God, God made a promise to Eve and all who would come after her. While mankind has officially stayed in sin, both Adam and Eve moved away from God via sin and deception. Yet God declared He would not leave humanity in a sorry, alienated state, but that

He had something better to come, that would come forth from a woman. Yet God's words to Eve were not just about Eve, but also revealing as to the church, who is hiding within Eve in the text. The prophecy reveals a few key things to us about the church, because as with many Biblical prophecies, she is hiding in the words of the text:

- **<u>The primary concern of the church is falling into deception, because deception leads to sin</u>**: If we read numerous issues raised about the church, especially in the New Testament, there is a constant cry against being led astray into deception (Luke 21:8, 1 Corinthians 6:9, 2 Corinthians 11:3, Galatians 6:7, 1 Timothy 2:14, 2 Timothy 3:13, James 1:16). This is an obvious type, tying the church back to Eve, her experience, and her identity, from the very beginning. Eve was led astray by Satan; so is the church. We, as the church, required a Savior, because we were found in a fallen state. The only way to avoid this long-term predicament is to avoid deception, because as we can see through the experience of Adam and Eve, deception precedes sin.

- **<u>The woman and the serpent are automatic enemies from this point on</u>**: All that is represented within Eve and those who are the descendants of this woman, have an automatic response to evil and to manipulation. The hostility placed there, between Eve and the serpent and the church and Satan, is God-designed.

- **<u>The descendants of the woman are automatic enemies with the serpent</u>**: I shall discuss this in detail, paralleling with the next point.

- **<u>One descendant shall come from the woman, who shall be begotten without the assistance of a natural man, the "seed" of a woman</u>**: Biology tells us it takes a biological man and woman to reproduce and create life, with the man offering seed. This prophecy speaks of a child's birth from the seed of a woman, Who will crush the head (or authority) of the enemy, and the enemy shall bruise His heel. We know this to be a prophecy of the birth, death, and resurrection of Jesus Christ, all in a few words. By His birth, Jesus would be born via a divine conception that did not involve a man; by His death, the serpent struck the heel of Christ, bruising or wounding him; by His resurrection, Christ crushed the head of the serpent, destroying his power, influence, and authority.

- **The woman, Eve, is not just a representation of women, but of the church, as well**: The church herself is feminine, as was Eve. Even though those in the church may be beguiled and charmed by Satan, the ultimate authority goes to her new Adam, Christ, because the church is the new Eve. Her descendants, those that are produced by the church, fight the battle and war with Satan, experiencing the intense odds and occasional bruising attacks that he brings our way. The ultimate victory, however, shall belong to the descendants (the members of the church, who are protected and guarded by the church).

- **The labor of the church shall be difficult**: The term "labor" in Genesis 3 does not exclusively imply childbirth in the original Hebrew language. It is automatically associated with birth, however, because it is spoken of in terms of women. The "labor" spoken of in Eve's prophecy and the "work labor" spoken of in Adam's prophecy are the same exact word and indicate a difficulty in life. This side of heaven, the work of the church will be difficult and will be done in a labor of love. It will require a toil and a trouble, as we, in a certain sense, birth Christ on the world. We will experience the pain and stigma of betrayal and persecution, and what we do in the Name of Christ will not be easy, not as we labor in this world.

- **The church shall desire her husband (Christ) and He will lead and guide us**: The natural aspect of this prophecy that men would rule over women is not spoken of as being the ideal relationship or of a relationship built on godly principles. Nothing in the passage indicates that it would be the way God intended it to be. It simply states that this is what would happen, and this distortion causes us to misunderstand the relationship and love that the church would have with Christ. In looking at it like this, it is obvious that our relationships would, too require a redemption. The control and confusion that has resulted from abuse of power and vying for control has caused us to miss the powerful submission that Christ extended toward His bride in His death on the cross. In Eve, we see the promise to come: that we will desire our Lord, we desire the fullness of all He can offer and all that He is, and He will rule in His rightful authority over the church, leading us into all truth, as is present in Ephesians 5:21-33.

- **Every time we do something in connection with the church, we are connected all the way back to our original roots of Adam and Eve**: In the life and experience of Eve, as a mother, as the Mother of all Living, Eve shows us a powerful picture of the church. We can see its struggles, difficulties, challenges, temptations, losses, empowerments, and gains. No one, not even the gates of hell, could overcome it. Not even sin could keep Eve away from her position as the mother of all living. She was the first to prefigure the church, the first to teach us about it, and was one of the first to believe and hope for a promise that even she didn't understand within her life experience.

- **Eve, as the Mother of all Living, is a living type of the church, which also serves as the mother of all living**: The name "Eve" literally means "life, living." In church, we are the redeemed, those who are alive, snatched back from death. The church, as a female, as the Bride of Christ, represents the haven, the protector, the guide and font, our mother, for those who are alive spiritually. This rightly places the church as the new Eve, alongside the new Adam, Christ.

Eve was more than just a fallen woman; she was the ultimate promise of what we are all to become when we are in Christ. To be redeemed, we must first be fallen, knowing our humble estate. Only in humility can we be restored, and beyond restoration, placed in an eternal position of beauty and prestige. To haven those who would find life, Eve had to first learn what it was like to lose position, to lose status, to experience loss, to experience sin. We talk about having a High Priest Who understands what we go through (Hebrews 4:15); we also have a spiritual type, a promise, of the church who also understands, through her own experience, and the spiritual reality of her redemption in the new Adam, who was desired from the beginning.

That which is far off has come near

Sarah and Hagar are a much-explored theme throughout the Scriptures, particularly as pertains to promise and just who inherits the promise. The one consistency we tend to see in scholarly interpretation, however, is the elevation of Sarah and the denunciation of Hagar. That sounds just like the church as we understand it, doesn't it? We denounce the seemingly lesser promise because the more obvious promise seems to resonate larger than life in our minds. We exclude those who are brought near, because they were not there in the first place, at least in our minds' eye view of the "first place."

Several years ago, I was on a mission trip to the Netherlands when my host made the comment that she had more "understanding" of the Torah than I did, because I could only have "little knowledge" of the revelation, as I was not a Jew (and had no Jewish lineage that I was aware of). To be honest, the statement astounded me. It made me feel like I was less relevant, less important than she was, by virtue of something I could not control. In her statement, and the thinking behind the statement, I was never going to be able to understand, nor comprehend, anything on her level, no matter how much I studied, believed, or even sought God. I wasn't a Jew, and that meant I was done. The truth was that when it came to actual Scripture study and knowledge, I knew quite a bit more than her, but she was not apt to listen. I wasn't what she felt I should have been, and she was vying for control of my ideas and concepts, simply because she felt hers were superior. Rather than sharing, the entire experience broke down into one big, long, control battle with superiority overtones.

I am so thankful we do not serve a God Who feels that way.

PETER BEGAN TO SPEAK [OPENED HIS MOUTH]: "I REALLY [TRULY] UNDERSTAND NOW THAT TO GOD EVERY PERSON IS THE SAME [GOD DOES NOT SHOW FAVORITISM/PARTIALITY]. (Acts 10:38)

I have related this story for one reason: even though we might not think in terms of the Jew/Gentile divide that much in church anymore (the woman in this story was a part of the Hebrew Roots Movement, thus the Jewishness issue), there are still a lot of people who hold similar sentiments of superiority. They have been in that church their whole lives, their relatives were in church their whole lives, for so many generations, and that means they are closer to God, or know more, than someone who comes in from the outside. Even though that outsider might be called of God and have an incredible experience with God that parallels those of an "insider," the discrimination many feel in church does not go away, no matter how long they have been in covenant.

SARAI, ABRAM'S WIFE, HAD NO CHILDREN, BUT SHE HAD A SLAVE GIRL FROM EGYPT NAMED HAGAR. SARAI SAID TO ABRAM, "LOOK, THE LORD HAS NOT ALLOWED ME TO HAVE [PREVENTED/RESTRAINED ME FROM HAVING] CHILDREN, SO HAVE SEXUAL RELATIONS WITH [GO TO] MY SLAVE GIRL. IF SHE HAS A CHILD, MAYBE I CAN HAVE MY OWN FAMILY [REPRODUCE; HAVE A CHILD; BUILD] THROUGH HER [TAKING A SECOND WIFE OR CONCUBINE WAS COMMON FOR A CHILDLESS COUPLE AT THE TIME]."

ABRAM DID WHAT SARAI SAID. IT WAS AFTER HE HAD LIVED TEN YEARS IN CANAAN THAT SARAI GAVE HAGAR TO HER HUSBAND ABRAM AS A WIFE [*OR* CONCUBINE]. (HAGAR WAS HER SLAVE GIRL FROM EGYPT.)

ABRAM HAD SEXUAL RELATIONS WITH [WENT IN TO] HAGAR, AND SHE BECAME PREGNANT [CONCEIVED]. WHEN HAGAR LEARNED SHE WAS PREGNANT [CONCEIVED], SHE BEGAN TO TREAT [LOOK ON] HER MISTRESS SARAI BADLY [WITH CONTEMPT]. THEN SARAI SAID TO ABRAM, "THIS IS YOUR FAULT [MAY THE WRONG/VIOLENCE DONE TO ME BE ON YOU]. I GAVE MY SLAVE GIRL TO YOU [INTO YOUR EMBRACE; INTO YOUR LAP], AND WHEN SHE BECAME PREGNANT [CONCEIVED], SHE BEGAN TO TREAT [LOOK ON] ME BADLY [WITH CONTEMPT]. LET

THE LORD DECIDE WHO IS RIGHT—[JUDGE BETWEEN] YOU OR ME."
(Genesis 16:1-5)

It's important for us to embrace all Biblical figures, especially the ones that make us uncomfortable or make us look at things differently. Hagar was a slave, brought into Sarai and Abram's (later Sarah and Abraham) relationship when the child of promise, Isaac, didn't come quickly into the picture. It was Sarah's desire that Hagar could have a child for her, on her behalf, that would be half Hagar's and half Abraham's, and they could raise that child as their own. It doesn't take a genius to see where this situation will go south quickly, yet they moved ahead with their plans, and the result was Ishmael.

Hagar was the "outsider" in the relationship between Sarah and Abraham. She was brought in, through no choice of her own. Today, we would classify Hagar as a sex slave, as a victim of human trafficking. Commentaries vary on just where Hagar came from, but many believe she had been acquired as a female attendant for Sarah during their stint in Egypt. She entered their mess without choice, and then she remained in it, throughout her life. Yet something incredible happened to Hagar, that merits note, that recognizes her standing before God. If Hagar did indeed come from Egypt, this would mean she was not originally of promise or standing within promise. She knew a pagan way of living, and while Sarah and Abraham were not properly a part of the Hebrew system yet, she was still now a part of another family, another identity, that should have introduced her to something more than she knew before.

HAGAR[3]
- *HAGAR*: SARAH'S EGYPTIAN MAID, THE MOTHER OF ISHMAEL
- ORIGINAL WORD: הָגָר
- PART OF SPEECH: PROPER NAME FEMININE
- TRANSLITERATION: HAGAR
- PHONETIC SPELLING: (HAW-GAWR')
- SHORT DEFINITION: HAGAR

Like Ruth and Naomi (who we will talk more in-depth about later in this book), Sarah and Hagar have a common link in terms of spiritual redemption. Ruth married Boaz, and had Obed, which connected her back to Naomi biologically, and into the linage of Israel's spiritual heritage. Sarah and Hagar's common link was they both bore children for Abraham. While Hagar's son does represent disobedience to God on the part of Abraham and Sarah, that is not Hagar's fault, and such is evident in the incredible spiritual revelation Hagar received. Hagar is the first of only six people who received a personal appearance of the angel of the Lord in the Old Testament, and one of only two women. Hagar had an experience with God, one that was direct and powerful, and life-transforming, to echo to her that no matter what she went through, she, too, had a child of promise, and God would care for her, and for him, throughout their lives.

BUT ABRAM SAID TO SARAI, "YOU ARE HAGAR'S MISTRESS [YOUR SLAVE GIRL IS IN YOUR HAND/POWER]. DO ANYTHING YOU WANT [WHAT IS GOOD IN YOUR EYES] TO HER." THEN SARAI WAS HARD ON [AFFLICTED; ABUSED] HAGAR, AND HAGAR RAN AWAY [FLED FROM HER PRESENCE].

THE ANGEL [MESSENGER] OF THE LORD [THE ANGEL OF THE LORD WAS EITHER A REPRESENTATIVE OF THE LORD OR THE LORD HIMSELF; V. 13; JUDG. 6:11, 14] FOUND HAGAR BESIDE A SPRING OF WATER IN THE DESERT [WILDERNESS], BY THE ROAD TO SHUR [LIKELY A LOCATION IN SOUTHERN CANAAN; 20:1; 25:18; EX. 15:22; 1 SAM. 15:7]. THE ANGEL [HE] SAID, "HAGAR, SARAI'S SLAVE GIRL, WHERE HAVE YOU COME FROM? WHERE ARE YOU GOING?"

HAGAR ANSWERED, "I AM RUNNING AWAY [FLEEING] FROM MY MISTRESS SARAI."

THE ANGEL [MESSENGER] OF THE LORD [16:7] SAID TO HER, "GO HOME TO YOUR MISTRESS AND OBEY [SUBMIT TO] HER." THE ANGEL OF THE LORD ALSO SAID, "I WILL GIVE YOU SO MANY DESCENDANTS [GREATLY MULTIPLY YOUR SEED SO THAT] THEY CANNOT BE COUNTED."

THE ANGEL [MESSENGER] ADDED,
"YOU ARE NOW PREGNANT [HAVE CONCEIVED],
 AND YOU WILL HAVE [GIVE BIRTH TO] A SON.

YOU WILL NAME HIM ISHMAEL [SOUNDS LIKE THE VERB "TO HEAR"],
BECAUSE THE LORD HAS HEARD YOUR CRIES [OF YOUR AFFLICTION].
ISHMAEL WILL BE LIKE A WILD DONKEY [A WILD DONKEY/ASS OF A
MAN].
HE [HIS HAND] WILL BE AGAINST EVERYONE,
AND EVERYONE [EVERYONE'S HAND] WILL BE AGAINST HIM.
HE WILL ATTACK [DWELL AGAINST] ALL HIS BROTHERS."

THE SLAVE GIRL GAVE A NAME TO THE LORD WHO SPOKE TO HER:
"YOU ARE 'GOD WHO SEES ME [OR GOD OF SEEING; HEBREW EL-
ROI]'" BECAUSE SHE SAID TO HERSELF, "HAVE I REALLY SEEN GOD
WHO SEES ME?" SO THE WELL THERE, BETWEEN KADESH [ALSO
KNOWN AS KADESH BARNEA IN NORTHEAST SINAI] AND BERED
[LOCATION UNKNOWN], WAS CALLED BEER LAHAI ROI [THE WELL OF
THE LIVING ONE WHO SEES ME].

HAGAR GAVE BIRTH TO A SON FOR ABRAM, AND ABRAM NAMED HIM
[HIS SON WHICH HAGAR BORE HIM] ISHMAEL. ABRAM WAS EIGHTY-
SIX YEARS OLD WHEN HAGAR GAVE BIRTH TO ISHMAEL. (Genesis
16:6-16)

ISAAC GREW, AND WHEN HE BECAME OLD ENOUGH TO EAT FOOD [WAS
WEANED], ABRAHAM GAVE A GREAT FEAST [ON THE DAY OF HIS
WEANING]. BUT SARAH SAW ISHMAEL [THE SON OF HAGAR THE
EGYPTIAN] MAKING FUN OF ISAAC [LAUGHING; OR PLAYING]. SO
SARAH SAID TO ABRAHAM, "THROW [DRIVE] OUT THIS SLAVE WOMAN
AND HER SON. HER SON SHOULD NOT INHERIT ANYTHING; MY SON
ISAAC SHOULD RECEIVE IT ALL [GAL. 4:21—5:1]."

THIS TROUBLED [DISTRESSED; UPSET] ABRAHAM VERY MUCH BECAUSE
ISHMAEL WAS ALSO HIS SON. BUT GOD SAID TO ABRAHAM, "DON'T BE
TROUBLED [DISTRESSED; UPSET] ABOUT THE BOY AND THE SLAVE
WOMAN. DO WHATEVER [ALL] SARAH TELLS YOU. THE DESCENDANTS I
PROMISED YOU WILL BE FROM [THE SEED WILL BE NAMED FOR YOU
THROUGH] ISAAC. I WILL ALSO MAKE THE DESCENDANTS OF ISHMAEL
[THE SON OF YOUR SLAVE WOMAN] INTO A GREAT NATION BECAUSE HE
IS YOUR SON [SEED], TOO."

EARLY THE NEXT MORNING ABRAHAM [GOT UP AND] TOOK SOME FOOD
AND A LEATHER BAG FULL [SKIN] OF WATER. HE GAVE THEM TO
HAGAR AND SENT HER AWAY. CARRYING THESE THINGS AND HER SON

[ON HER SHOULDER], HAGAR WENT AND WANDERED [THE VERB MAY IMPLY MOVING AIMLESSLY AND WITHOUT HOPE] IN THE DESERT [WILDERNESS] OF BEERSHEBA [AN AREA IN THE NORTHERN PART OF THE NEGEV, SOUTHERN CANAAN].

LATER, WHEN ALL THE WATER WAS GONE [FINISHED] FROM THE BAG [SKIN], HAGAR PUT HER SON UNDER A BUSH. THEN SHE WENT A GOOD WAY OFF, THE DISTANCE OF A BOWSHOT, AND SAT DOWN ACROSS FROM HIM. SHE THOUGHT, "MY SON WILL DIE, AND I CANNOT WATCH THIS HAPPEN." SHE SAT THERE ACROSS FROM HIM AND BEGAN TO CRY.

GOD HEARD THE BOY CRYING [SOUND/VOICE OF THE BOY], AND GOD'S ANGEL [MESSENGER; 16:7] CALLED TO HAGAR FROM HEAVEN. HE SAID, "WHAT IS WRONG, HAGAR? DON'T BE AFRAID! GOD HAS HEARD THE BOY CRYING [THE SOUND/VOICE OF THE BOY] THERE. HELP [GET UP AND LIFT] HIM UP AND TAKE HIM BY THE HAND. I WILL MAKE HIS DESCENDANTS [HIM] INTO A GREAT NATION." [ISHMAEL IS CONSIDERED THE ANCESTOR OF THE ARAB PEOPLE.]

THEN GOD [OPENED HER EYES AND] SHOWED HAGAR A WELL OF WATER. SO SHE WENT TO THE WELL AND FILLED HER BAG [SKIN] WITH WATER AND GAVE THE BOY A DRINK.

GOD WAS WITH THE BOY AS HE GREW UP. ISHMAEL LIVED IN THE DESERT [WILDERNESS] AND BECAME AN ARCHER. HE LIVED IN THE DESERT OF PARAN [A REGION IN THE EASTERN SINAI PENINSULA], AND HIS MOTHER FOUND A WIFE FOR HIM IN EGYPT [HAGAR'S ORIGINAL HOMELAND]. (Genesis 21:8-21)

Sarah and Abraham were the forerunners for Israel, and Hagar was the outsider. Still, God appeared first to the outsider, rather than those who were of the promise. Why is this? Yes, Hagar certainly needed a revelation, and she needed to know this God, Who saw her and would take care of her. But Abraham and Sarah were already supposed to have knowledge of this God, and they still disobeyed, leading a new promise, a new revelation, to come unto the one whom they dragged into this situation. She was still a part of the promise, and she needed to recognize that. Hagar was accepted by God, even though she was the outsider, and it came through her child, the one she was to protect and guard (Ishmael), because he was a part of the family of promise.

This is why in Genesis 17 he was circumcised, according to the regulation of the covenant. Hagar came into the promise, outsider and all, and received a nearly identical promise to that of Sarah, because she, too, was now a part of the promise.

This proves that God is not a respecter of persons, even way back in the book of Genesis. Even though Hagar entered the situation against her will, she still tapped into the promise of God, through the lineage she was now a part. The far off now was near (Ephesians 2:13), all because of the promise. Hagar and Sarah are also a type of the church, one that is a bit more uncomfortable for all of us, because even though Hagar received the promise, Sarah didn't want her to have it. She wanted her mistake, her issues, to take precedence over Hagar's, because she was there first. Because Hagar was a slave, Sarah received her way in the natural, but not in the spiritual. The promise superseded Sarah's natural wishes, and Hagar remained in the promise of God, a type of the Gentile coming into the church, and receiving spiritual promise, no matter how much those on the inside might reject the outsider coming to receive.

This is the way it often is in church: those who are natively placed there, be it by birth or positional seniority, often lord over those who come in from the outside. This isn't God's view, however. Hagar proves to us that those who are different than we are can become a part of the church and have great and powerful revelation of God. The evidence of such is found in a passage we would often not consider, Galatians 4:21-31:

SOME OF YOU STILL WANT TO BE UNDER THE LAW. TELL ME, DO YOU KNOW WHAT THE LAW SAYS? [FOR] THE SCRIPTURES SAY THAT ABRAHAM HAD TWO SONS. THE MOTHER OF ONE SON WAS A SLAVE WOMAN, AND THE MOTHER OF THE OTHER SON WAS A FREE WOMAN. ABRAHAM'S SON FROM THE SLAVE WOMAN WAS BORN IN THE NORMAL HUMAN WAY [OR THROUGH HUMAN EFFORT/PLAN; ACCORDING TO THE FLESH; ISHMAEL; GEN. 16]. BUT THE SON FROM THE FREE WOMAN WAS BORN BECAUSE OF THE PROMISE GOD MADE TO ABRAHAM [THROUGH THE PROMISE; ISAAC; GEN. 17; 21].

THIS STORY TEACHES SOMETHING ELSE [OR MAY BE READ ALLEGORICALLY/FIGURATIVELY/AS AN ILLUSTRATION]: THE TWO WOMEN ARE LIKE THE TWO AGREEMENTS BETWEEN GOD AND HIS PEOPLE [TWO COVENANTS]. ONE IS THE LAW THAT GOD MADE ON

MOUNT SINAI [FROM MOUNT SINAI; THE MOUNTAIN IN ARABIA WHERE GOD DELIVERED HIS LAW TO ISRAEL THROUGH MOSES; EX. 19—31], AND THE PEOPLE WHO ARE UNDER THIS AGREEMENT ARE LIKE SLAVES [...BEARING CHILDREN FOR SLAVERY]. THE MOTHER NAMED HAGAR IS LIKE THAT AGREEMENT [THIS IS HAGAR]. SHE IS LIKE MOUNT SINAI IN ARABIA AND IS A PICTURE OF [CORRESPONDS TO; REPRESENTS] THE EARTHLY CITY OF [PRESENT] JERUSALEM. THIS CITY AND ITS PEOPLE [HER CHILDREN] ARE SLAVES TO THE LAW [SLAVES]. BUT THE HEAVENLY JERUSALEM, WHICH IS ABOVE [JERUSALEM ABOVE], IS LIKE THE FREE WOMAN. SHE IS OUR MOTHER. [FOR] IT IS WRITTEN IN THE SCRIPTURES:

"BE HAPPY [REJOICE], BARREN ONE [JERUSALEM].
  YOU ARE LIKE A WOMAN WHO NEVER GAVE BIRTH TO CHILDREN.
START SINGING [BURST OUT] AND SHOUT FOR JOY [CRY OUT].
  YOU NEVER FELT THE PAIN OF GIVING BIRTH [*OR* WENT INTO LABOR],
BUT YOU WHO ARE CHILDLESS [DESOLATE; *OR* DESERTED] WILL HAVE MORE CHILDREN
  THAN THE WOMAN WHO HAS A HUSBAND [IS. 54:1]."

MY BROTHERS AND SISTERS, YOU ARE GOD'S CHILDREN BECAUSE OF HIS PROMISE [CHILDREN OF THE PROMISE], AS ISAAC WAS THEN. [FOR JUST AS] THE SON WHO WAS BORN IN THE NORMAL WAY [*OR* THROUGH HUMAN EFFORT/PLAN; ACCORDING TO THE FLESH] TREATED THE OTHER SON BADLY. IT IS THE SAME TODAY [A REFERENCE TO JEWISH PERSECUTION OF CHRISTIANS]. BUT WHAT DOES THE SCRIPTURE SAY? "THROW OUT THE SLAVE WOMAN AND HER SON. THE SON OF THE SLAVE WOMAN WILL NOT SHARE IN THE INHERITANCE WITH THE SON OF THE FREE WOMAN [GEN. 21:10]." SO, MY BROTHERS AND SISTERS, WE ARE NOT CHILDREN OF THE SLAVE WOMAN, BUT OF THE FREE WOMAN.

Often used against Hagar, have we considered what it is rightly teaching us? Only two covenants are spoken of in Galatians 4, not three. One is clearly the Old Covenant, that of the Mosaic Law, and the New Covenant, the covenant of grace, we find under Christ. There is no special, nor separate, covenant mentioned between Hagar and God; there is only one covenant, made with two people, because an outsider came into the family. Hagar was a part of that covenant, because otherwise, the passage makes no sense. Hagar existed in Biblical experience before the law, so how can she be compared to or as part of a law if she had nothing to do with it? Hagar, as the slave woman, still became a part of that lineage, and a part of that Old Covenant system, because she was grafted in through family and biology, otherwise the comparison makes no sense, whatsoever. Those who still, after Christ, desire to follow the law, become the product of Hagar, because they adhere to an older promise, rather than the reality of that promise. Hagar became a type of the church, while now, we have the reality, thanks to the One we protect and guard, Christ. Sarah and Hagar are a picture of how church often is, rather than the more ideal portraits found in other places, of how it should be.

As church, and especially as women, who face far more spiritual discrimination than men, should be aware of the Sarah/Hagar type and how such interferes with and can hurt people, in the natural. While position before God is always secure, it is not always so simple to say that how God feels about us matters, while no one else's opinion does. Hagar proves that the way others treat us in church can have a lasting impression on our lives and our self-perceptions, and that it can take nothing short of a miracle for our self-image to experience restoration after the degrading nature of a judgmental, holier-than-thou, person.

[THEREFORE] IF YOU THINK YOU CAN JUDGE OTHERS, [O MAN,] YOU ARE WRONG [WITHOUT EXCUSE]. [FOR] WHEN YOU JUDGE THEM, YOU ARE REALLY JUDGING YOURSELF GUILTY, BECAUSE YOU [WHO ARE JUDGING] DO THE SAME THINGS THEY DO. GOD JUDGES THOSE WHO DO WRONG [SUCH] THINGS, AND WE KNOW THAT HIS JUDGING IS RIGHT [JUST; JUSTIFIED; BASED ON TRUTH]. YOU JUDGE THOSE WHO DO WRONG [SUCH THINGS], BUT YOU DO WRONG [THE SAME THINGS] YOURSELVES. DO YOU THINK [O MAN,] YOU WILL BE ABLE TO ESCAPE THE JUDGMENT OF GOD? YOU [DO YOU...?] THINK NOTHING OF [DESPISE; HAVE CONTEMPT FOR; DISREGARD] HIS KINDNESS, TOLERANCE [FORBEARANCE] AND PATIENCE. PERHAPS YOU DO NOT UNDERSTAND THAT GOD IS KIND TO YOU SO YOU WILL CHANGE YOUR HEARTS AND LIVES [REPENT]. BUT BECAUSE YOU ARE STUBBORN AND REFUSE TO CHANGE [HAVE AN UNREPENTANT HEART], YOU ARE MAKING YOUR OWN PUNISHMENT EVEN GREATER [STORING UP WRATH FOR YOURSELF] ON THE DAY HE SHOWS HIS ANGER [OF (GOD'S)

WRATH]. ON THAT DAY EVERYONE WILL SEE [...AND THE DAY OF THE REVELATION OF] GOD'S RIGHT [RIGHTEOUS; JUST] JUDGMENTS. GOD WILL REWARD OR PUNISH [GIVE BACK TO; REPAY] EVERY PERSON FOR WHAT THAT PERSON HAS DONE. SOME PEOPLE, BY ALWAYS CONTINUING [PERSEVERING] TO DO GOOD, LIVE FOR [SEEK AFTER; AIM FOR] GOD'S GLORY [GLORY], FOR HONOR, AND FOR LIFE THAT HAS NO END [IMMORTALITY]. GOD WILL GIVE THEM LIFE FOREVER [ETERNAL LIFE]. BUT OTHER PEOPLE ARE SELFISH [SELF-SEEKING], REFUSING TO FOLLOW [DISOBEYING; *OR* DISBELIEVING] TRUTH AND INSTEAD FOLLOWING [OBEYING; *OR* BELIEVING] EVIL. GOD WILL GIVE THEM HIS PUNISHMENT [WRATH] AND ANGER. HE WILL GIVE [*OR* THERE WILL BE] TROUBLE [AFFLICTION; TRIBULATION] AND SUFFERING [DISTRESS] TO EVERYONE WHO DOES EVIL—TO THE JEWS FIRST AND ALSO TO THOSE WHO ARE NOT JEWS [THE GREEK; HERE MEANING ALL GENTILES; SEE 1:13, 14, 16]. BUT HE WILL GIVE [*OR* THERE WILL BE] GLORY, HONOR, AND PEACE TO EVERYONE WHO DOES GOOD—TO THE JEWS FIRST AND ALSO TO THOSE WHO ARE NOT JEWS [THE GREEK; V. 9]. FOR GOD JUDGES ALL PEOPLE IN THE SAME WAY [THERE IS NO PARTIALITY WITH GOD].

PEOPLE [*OR* FOR ALL THOSE] WHO DO NOT HAVE THE LAW [GENTILES WITHOUT THE WRITTEN LAW OF MOSES] AND WHO ARE SINNERS WILL BE LOST [PERISH], ALTHOUGH THEY DO NOT HAVE THE LAW. AND, IN THE SAME WAY, THOSE WHO HAVE THE LAW [JEWS WHO HAVE THE LAW OF MOSES] AND ARE SINNERS WILL BE JUDGED BY THE LAW. HEARING THE LAW DOES NOT MAKE PEOPLE RIGHT WITH [RIGHTEOUS/JUSTIFIED BEFORE] GOD. IT IS THOSE WHO OBEY THE LAW WHO WILL BE RIGHT WITH [JUSTIFIED/DECLARED RIGHTEOUS BEFORE] HIM. (THOSE WHO ARE NOT JEWS [GENTILES] DO NOT HAVE THE LAW, BUT WHEN THEY FREELY [BY NATURE; INSTINCTIVELY] DO WHAT THE LAW COMMANDS, THEY ARE THE LAW FOR THEMSELVES [*OR* REVEAL THEIR AWARENESS OF GOD'S LAW]. THIS IS TRUE EVEN THOUGH THEY DO NOT HAVE THE LAW [THE WRITTEN LAW OF MOSES]. THEY SHOW THAT IN THEIR HEARTS THEY KNOW WHAT IS RIGHT AND WRONG, JUST AS THE LAW COMMANDS [THE REQUIREMENTS OF THE LAW ARE WRITTEN ON THEIR HEARTS]. AND THEY SHOW THIS BY THEIR CONSCIENCES [BEARING WITNESS]. SOMETIMES THEIR THOUGHTS TELL THEM THEY DID WRONG [ACCUSE THEM], AND SOMETIMES THEIR THOUGHTS TELL THEM THEY DID RIGHT [DEFEND THEM].) ALL THESE THINGS [*OR* THIS] WILL HAPPEN ON THE DAY

WHEN, ACCORDING TO MY GOSPEL [THE GOOD NEWS I PREACH], GOD, THROUGH CHRIST JESUS, WILL JUDGE PEOPLE'S SECRET THOUGHTS.

WHAT ABOUT YOU? YOU CALL YOURSELF A JEW. YOU TRUST IN [RELY ON] THE LAW OF MOSES [LAW] AND BRAG THAT YOU ARE CLOSE TO GOD [BOAST IN GOD]. YOU KNOW WHAT HE WANTS YOU TO DO [HIS WILL] AND WHAT IS IMPORTANT [CAN DISCERN/TEST WHAT IS BEST/SUPERIOR], BECAUSE YOU HAVE LEARNED [BEEN INSTRUCTED IN] THE LAW. YOU THINK [ARE CONVINCED/CONFIDENT THAT] YOU ARE A GUIDE FOR THE BLIND AND A LIGHT FOR THOSE WHO ARE IN DARKNESS. YOU THINK YOU CAN SHOW FOOLISH PEOPLE WHAT IS RIGHT [ARE AN INSTRUCTOR TO THE FOOLISH] AND TEACH [A TEACHER FOR] THOSE WHO KNOW NOTHING [THE IMMATURE/IGNORANT; *OR* CHILDREN/INFANTS]. YOU HAVE THE LAW; SO YOU THINK YOU KNOW EVERYTHING AND HAVE ALL TRUTH [HAVE THE EMBODIMENT/FORMULATION OF KNOWLEDGE AND TRUTH]. YOU TEACH OTHERS, SO WHY DON'T YOU TEACH YOURSELF? YOU TELL [PREACH TO] OTHERS NOT TO STEAL, BUT DO YOU STEAL? YOU SAY THAT OTHERS MUST NOT COMMIT ADULTERY, BUT DO YOU COMMIT ADULTERY? YOU HATE [ABHOR; DETEST] IDOLS, BUT DO YOU STEAL FROM TEMPLES [PERHAPS (1) PROFITING BY SELLING STOLEN IDOLS TO GENTILES; OR (2) WITHHOLDING WHAT IS DUE TO GOD AND SO "ROBBING" HIS TEMPLE]? YOU BRAG [BOAST] ABOUT HAVING GOD'S LAW [THE LAW], BUT DO YOU BRING SHAME TO [DISHONOR] GOD BY BREAKING HIS LAW? IT IS JUST AS THE SCRIPTURES SAY: "GOD'S NAME IS BLASPHEMED AMONG THE GENTILES BECAUSE OF YOU [IS. 52:5; EZEK. 36:20]."

IF YOU FOLLOW THE LAW, YOUR CIRCUMCISION [A KEY DISTINCTIVE OF JEWISH IDENTITY; GEN. 17] HAS MEANING [VALUE; BENEFIT]. BUT IF YOU BREAK [TRANSGRESS; DISOBEY] THE LAW, IT IS AS IF YOU WERE NEVER CIRCUMCISED. IF THOSE WHO ARE NOT CIRCUMCISED DO [KEEP; OBEY] WHAT THE LAW SAYS [*OR* THE LAW'S RIGHTEOUS REQUIREMENTS], IT IS AS IF THEY WERE CIRCUMCISED. THOSE WHO ARE NOT CIRCUMCISED IN THEIR BODIES, BUT STILL OBEY [FULFILL; CARRY OUT] THE LAW, WILL PASS JUDGMENT ON [CONDEMN] YOU WHO, THOUGH HAVING THE WRITTEN LAW AND CIRCUMCISION, BREAK [TRANSGRESS; DISOBEY] THE LAW. THEY CAN DO THIS BECAUSE A PERSON IS NOT A TRUE JEW IF HE IS ONLY A JEW ·IN HIS PHYSICAL BODY [BY (PHYSICAL) APPEARANCE]; TRUE CIRCUMCISION IS NOT ·ONLY ON THE OUTSIDE OF THE BODY [THE APPEARANCE OF THE

FLESH]. A PERSON IS A JEW ONLY IF HE IS A JEW INSIDE [INWARDLY]; TRUE CIRCUMCISION IS DONE IN THE HEART BY THE SPIRIT, NOT BY THE WRITTEN LAW. SUCH A PERSON GETS PRAISE FROM GOD RATHER THAN FROM PEOPLE. (Romans 2:1-29)

The New Testament teaches us that self-righteousness is just as bad as idolatry, thus everyone, no matter where they come from, is just as bad as the next when it comes to sin, no matter how close or far they might have been to the origin of the promise. If we are in Christ, then we belong to Him, and attuning ourselves to the Hagars around us brings us closer to the unity of the promise He seeks for us to have.

The nation of Israel

In keeping with types of the church, the nation of Israel is a frequently overlooked type because theologians and scholars have spent so many years trying to distance themselves with the failings and faults of Old Testament Israel. There are many different theories about the church and just what position the church is to take into relation of Israel: Is the church a continuation, a replacement, a second covenant, or something else, all together?

ISRAEL[4]
- YISRAEL: DESCENDANT OF JACOB
- ORIGINAL WORD: יִשְׂרָאֵל
- PART OF SPEECH: PROPER NAME MASCULINE
- TRANSLITERATION: YISRAEL
- PHONETIC SPELLING: (YIS-RAW-ALE')
- SHORT DEFINITION: ISRAEL

The confusion as to who Israel is in relation to the church is simple: I think the church (particularly our scholars) in general doesn't like the idea of our spirituality being compared, in any form, with that of Israel. The Old Testament shows the failings of Israel, time and time again, in many graphic and hard-to-swallow ways. We like the idea of being free from the law, because the law convicts of sin, and we don't want to think that we, too, are guilty of looking in the "law mirror" and seeing all the things we have done wrong.

The problem with ignoring or overlooking Israel is that in doing so, we are ignoring and overlooking human behavior. No matter how much we might not want to deal with our own faults and failings through the lens of Israel, those faults and failings are still present. The Bible itself clarifies that Israel was not selected by God because it was the biggest nation, or most moral nation, or because it was full of sinless people (Deuteronomy 7:7), but because God intended to do something great through it. In essence, Israel's relationship with God is a fascinating study into the struggles people have with God, with others, and with themselves, no matter how many rules or regulations may exist to curtail negative tendencies. Israel proves that no matter how much we might want to try, we can't do this spiritual walk with God by ourselves.

That is the essence of why understanding Israel as a type of the church is so vitally important. If we want to have a right relationship with God, we must learn from the types that went before the realities, in order to see where we, as God's people, are, in our rawest form, and learn from that.

In keeping with the essence of understanding, it is also essential for us to understand the nature of Israel as relates to gender identity. Israel presents to us a unique gender-queer, non-binary situation. While Jacob was male and the name "Israel" itself is also male in grammatical form, the identity that came forth for the nation of Israel is feminine. Everything spoken of about Israel, as a nation, was feminine in identity, yet the name was masculine in definition.

This probably sounds confusing, but there are a few perfectly theological reasons why this is. The first is that the name Israel literally means, "Contender with God," or more literally, "He who perseveres or persists with God." The name came to Jacob after wrestling with the angel of the Lord all night:

THAT NIGHT JACOB GOT UP AND TOOK HIS TWO WIVES, HIS TWO FEMALE SERVANTS AND HIS ELEVEN SONS AND CROSSED THE FORD OF THE JABBOK. AFTER HE HAD SENT THEM ACROSS THE STREAM, HE SENT OVER ALL HIS POSSESSIONS. SO JACOB WAS LEFT ALONE, AND A MAN WRESTLED WITH HIM TILL DAYBREAK. WHEN THE MAN SAW THAT HE COULD NOT OVERPOWER HIM, HE TOUCHED THE SOCKET OF

Jacob's hip so that his hip was wrenched as he wrestled with the man. Then the man said, "Let me go, for it is daybreak." But Jacob replied, "I will not let you go unless you bless me."

The man asked him, "What is your name?"
"Jacob," he answered.

Then the man said, "Your name will no longer be Jacob, but Israel, because you have struggled with God and with humans and have overcome."

Jacob said, "Please tell me your name."

But he replied, "Why do you ask my name?" Then he blessed him there.
So Jacob called the place Peniel, saying, "It is because I saw God face to face, and yet my life was spared."

The sun rose above him as he passed Peniel, and he was limping because of his hip. Therefore to this day the Israelites do not eat the tendon attached to the socket of the hip, because the socket of Jacob's hip was touched near the tendon. (Genesis 38:22-32, NIV 2011)

Persisting, contending, and persevering with God are not just attributes unique to Jacob and his experience. Even though some try to gloss over Jacob's failings, Jacob was far from perfect. He spent much of his early life deceiving others, causing hurt, heartache, and loss, only to experience the same. Jacob paid a heavy price for being who he was; his clever ways came home to roost when he, too, was deceived by his father-in-law. Jacob spent the better part of his life in a complicated relationship triangle between two sisters, their own existing rivalries, and their battle to outdo each other in the child-bearing department. He saw this same type of sibling rivalry in his own children, who sold their own brother into slavery. This was after losing one of his wives in childbirth. Jacob forever contended with himself, who he was in his nature, and who he needed to become to be the man his family needed.

Jacob became Israel as he prepared to meet his brother Esau, a man he had played downright dirty earlier in their lives, for the first time after their extensive separation. In other words, Jacob became Israel at a point in time where he had to confront himself. Going out to meet his brother and giving him many gifts wasn't going to be enough; Jacob had to offer a sign of recompense, a genuine and sincere aspect of transformation. In the process, Jacob had to contend with God. He had to confront himself and what he did to his brother. The result – the process – was a struggle. It required Jacob to persevere and persist with God, contending with the character God sought him to realize and embrace.

I've been asked many times, who does Jacob typify? Imperfect or not, he does not bear the mark as a type of Christ, nor does he seem to fit in play with the criteria for five-fold ministry or appointment. The answer is simple; so simple, in fact, we don't often recognize it right in front of us. Jacob, as the masculine counterpart of Israel, typifies each and every one of us, because each and every one of us must contend, persevere, and persist with God. We are all Jacob in our fallen, untransformed state, trying to scheme and deceive with our ways through this world. Every one of us wrestles with God, and reaches a point where we, hopefully, overcome the haunts and trials of our pasts to move into a new identity. We wrestle with God, and God puts us in a body, the church. Jacob wrestled with God, and through him came Israel. He was Israel; and he was also part of Israel. Thus, down the line, we have all adopted his nature of contending, and striving, to get to a place where we do things right.

As Jacob faltered, so, too, did Israel falter. That same nature, that same inclination to get lost, meant Israel failed too, more of the time, than not. They spent years wrestling, contriving with God, and failing to get it right, time and time again. The origin of Israel, in Jacob, was seen in those who came after him. No matter how much they hoped to get it right, they didn't.

Jacob was in Israel, and Israel was in Jacob, just as Christ is in us, and we are in Christ. We are His Body, just as Israel was from Jacob's body; and we are in Him, and He is in us. This displays the poignant and powerful unity of the church, a mystery that theologians and scholars have tried to expound and understand for ages. We are many, but one; we are in Christ, Who is represented as masculine, yet in His body, we are feminine. We are identified as female, but not in a gender binary context.

Israel's relationship shadows our relationship with Christ. In a certain sense, at least in terms of spiritual lineage, however, they are more than just a type. They are a type because we are not literally Israel, but they are us, a reality of us, and of the issues and struggles we, too, have with our originator.

In a bigger sense, Israel's type parallels being the bride of God, as belonging to God in a special way, having a special relationship with Him, one that represented a unique bond between the two. This special relationship was known as covenant and reflected the belief that for a spiritual relationship to properly work with the divine, both those in the natural realm and the being in the spiritual realm had to agree to meet certain conditions. We recognize the covenant with Israel to be the written law, and in the instance of the church, we recognize the New Covenant, God's grace, enabling us to stand as the bride of Christ, thanks to the work of Christ on the cross.

THE LORD TOLD MOSES, "YOU, AARON, NADAB, ABIHU, AND SEVENTY OF THE ELDERS OF ISRAEL MUST COME UP TO ME AND WORSHIP [BOW DOWN TO] ME FROM A DISTANCE. THEN MOSES ALONE MUST COME NEAR ME; THE OTHERS MUST NOT COME NEAR. THE REST OF THE PEOPLE MUST NOT COME UP THE MOUNTAIN WITH MOSES."

MOSES TOLD [WENT AND RECOUNTED TO] THE PEOPLE ALL THE LORD'S WORDS AND LAWS FOR LIVING [REGULATIONS; JUDGMENTS]. THEN ALL OF THE PEOPLE ANSWERED OUT LOUD TOGETHER, "WE WILL DO ALL THE THINGS THE LORD HAS SAID." SO MOSES WROTE DOWN ALL THE WORDS OF THE LORD. AND HE GOT UP EARLY THE NEXT MORNING AND BUILT AN ALTAR NEAR THE BOTTOM OF THE MOUNTAIN. HE SET UP TWELVE STONES [PILLARS], ONE STONE [PILLAR] FOR EACH OF THE TWELVE TRIBES OF ISRAEL. THEN MOSES SENT YOUNG ISRAELITE MEN [YOUTH OF THE SONS/ CHILDREN OF ISRAEL] TO OFFER WHOLE BURNT OFFERINGS AND TO SACRIFICE YOUNG BULLS AS FELLOWSHIP [OR PEACE; LEV. 3] OFFERINGS TO THE LORD. MOSES PUT HALF OF THE BLOOD OF THESE ANIMALS IN BOWLS [BASINS], AND HE SPRINKLED [OR DASHED] THE OTHER HALF OF THE BLOOD ON THE ALTAR. THEN HE TOOK THE BOOK OF THE AGREEMENT [COVENANT; TREATY REFERRING TO THE LAWS FOUND IN 20:2– 23:19] AND READ IT SO THE PEOPLE COULD HEAR HIM. AND THEY

SAID, "WE WILL DO EVERYTHING THAT THE LORD HAS SAID; WE WILL OBEY."

THEN MOSES TOOK THE BLOOD FROM THE BOWLS [THE BLOOD] AND SPRINKLED [DASHED] IT ON THE PEOPLE, SAYING, "THIS IS THE BLOOD THAT BEGINS [OF] THE AGREEMENT [COVENANT; TREATY], THE AGREEMENT [COVENANT; TREATY] WHICH THE LORD HAS MADE [CUT] WITH YOU ABOUT [OR IN ACCORD WITH] ALL THESE WORDS." (Exodus 24:1-8)

THE GOD WHO MADE YOU IS LIKE [FOR YOUR MAKER IS] YOUR HUSBAND.
  HIS NAME IS THE LORD ALL-POWERFUL [ALMIGHTY; OF HEAVEN'S ARMIES; OF HOSTS].
THE HOLY ONE OF ISRAEL [1:4] IS THE ONE WHO SAVES YOU [YOUR REDEEMER].
  HE IS CALLED THE GOD OF ALL THE EARTH. (Isaiah 54:5)

"GO AND SPEAK TO THE PEOPLE OF JERUSALEM [ANNOUNCE/PROCLAIM IN THE EARS OF JERUSALEM], SAYING: THIS IS WHAT THE LORD SAYS:
'I REMEMBER HOW FAITHFUL YOU WERE TO ME WHEN YOU WERE A YOUNG NATION [YOUR LOYALTY/DEVOTION AS A YOUTH/GIRL/CHILD].
  YOU LOVED ME LIKE A YOUNG BRIDE.
YOU FOLLOWED [WENT AFTER] ME THROUGH THE DESERT [WILDERNESS; AS THEY TRAVELED FROM EGYPT TO THE PROMISED LAND],
  A LAND THAT HAD NEVER BEEN PLANTED [SOWN]. (Jeremiah 2:2)

"IF A MAN DIVORCES [SENDS AWAY] HIS WIFE
  AND SHE LEAVES HIM AND MARRIES ANOTHER MAN,
SHOULD HER FIRST HUSBAND COME BACK TO HER AGAIN?
  IF HE WENT BACK TO HER, WOULDN'T THE LAND BECOME COMPLETELY UNCLEAN [DEFILED; POLLUTED; IN A RITUAL SENSE; SUCH A THING WAS FORBIDDEN BY THE LAW; DEUT. 24:1–4]?
BUT YOU HAVE ACTED LIKE A PROSTITUTE WITH MANY LOVERS,
  AND NOW YOU WANT TO COME BACK TO ME?" SAYS THE LORD [HOS. 2:7]. (Jeremiah 3:1)

JUDAH SAW THAT I DIVORCED [SENT AWAY WITH A CERTIFICATE OF DIVORCE] UNFAITHFUL ISRAEL BECAUSE OF HER ADULTERY [IN THE

ASSYRIAN EXILE OF 722 BC], BUT THAT DIDN'T MAKE ISRAEL'S WICKED [TRAITOROUS; TREACHEROUS] SISTER JUDAH AFRAID. SHE ALSO WENT OUT AND ACTED LIKE A PROSTITUTE! (Jeremiah 3:8)

"LOOK, THE TIME IS [DAYS ARE] COMING," SAYS THE LORD,
    "WHEN I WILL MAKE [CUT] A NEW AGREEMENT [COVENANT; TREATY]
WITH THE PEOPLE [HOUSE] OF ISRAEL
    AND THE PEOPLE [HOUSE] OF JUDAH.
IT WILL NOT BE LIKE THE AGREEMENT [COVENANT; TREATY]
    I MADE [CUT] WITH THEIR ANCESTORS [FATHERS]
WHEN I TOOK THEM BY THE HAND
    TO BRING THEM OUT OF EGYPT [THE MOSAIC COVENANT; EX. 19–24].
I WAS A HUSBAND [*OR* MASTER] TO THEM [2:2],
    BUT THEY BROKE THAT AGREEMENT [MY COVENANT/TREATY],"
SAYS THE LORD. (Jeremiah 31:31-32)

"'WHEN I PASSED BY AND SAW YOU KICKING ABOUT IN YOUR BLOOD, I SAID TO YOU AS YOU LAY IN YOUR BLOOD [IN YOUR BLOOD], "LIVE!" I MADE YOU GROW [FLOURISH] LIKE A PLANT IN THE FIELD. YOU GREW UP AND BECAME TALL [*OR* MATURED; DEVELOPED] AND BECAME LIKE A BEAUTIFUL JEWEL [*OR* ENTERED PUBERTY; REACHED WOMANHOOD]. YOUR BREASTS FORMED, AND YOUR HAIR GREW, BUT YOU WERE NAKED AND WITHOUT CLOTHES [BARE; EXPOSED].

"'LATER WHEN I PASSED BY YOU AND LOOKED AT YOU, I SAW THAT [BEHOLD] YOU WERE OLD ENOUGH FOR LOVE. SO I SPREAD MY ROBE [THE CORNER OF MY GARMENT; DEUT. 22:30; RUTH 3:9] OVER YOU AND COVERED YOUR NAKEDNESS. I ALSO MADE A PROMISE [SWORE; MADE A VOW] TO YOU AND ENTERED INTO AN AGREEMENT [COVENANT; TREATY; EX. 19:5] WITH YOU SO THAT YOU BECAME MINE, SAYS THE LORD GOD.
"'THEN I BATHED YOU WITH WATER, WASHED ALL THE BLOOD OFF OF YOU, AND PUT OIL ON YOU [ANOINTED YOU WITH OIL/OINTMENT]. I PUT BEAUTIFUL CLOTHES MADE WITH NEEDLEWORK [EMBROIDERED CLOTHING] ON YOU AND PUT SANDALS OF FINE LEATHER ON YOUR FEET. I WRAPPED YOU IN FINE LINEN AND COVERED YOU WITH SILK. I PUT JEWELRY ON YOU: BRACELETS ON YOUR ARMS, A NECKLACE [CHAIN] AROUND YOUR NECK, A RING IN YOUR NOSE, EARRINGS IN YOUR EARS, AND A BEAUTIFUL CROWN [TIARA] ON YOUR HEAD. SO YOU

WORE [WERE ADORNED WITH] GOLD AND SILVER. YOUR CLOTHES WERE MADE OF FINE LINEN, SILK, AND BEAUTIFUL NEEDLEWORK [EMBROIDERY]. YOU ATE FINE FLOUR, HONEY, AND OLIVE OIL. YOU WERE VERY BEAUTIFUL AND BECAME A QUEEN [ROYALTY]. THEN YOU BECAME FAMOUS [YOUR FAME SPREAD] AMONG THE NATIONS, BECAUSE YOU WERE SO BEAUTIFUL. YOUR BEAUTY WAS PERFECT, BECAUSE OF THE GLORY [SPLENDOR] I GAVE YOU, SAYS THE LORD GOD.'" (Ezekiel 16:6-14)

"PLEAD WITH [OR REBUKE; OR ACCUSE; BRING CHARGES AGAINST] YOUR MOTHER [THE NATION ISRAEL].
    PLEAD WITH [OR REBUKE; OR ACCUSE; BRING CHARGES AGAINST] HER, BECAUSE SHE IS NO LONGER [NOT] MY WIFE,
    AND I AM NO LONGER [NOT] HER HUSBAND.
TELL HER TO STOP ACTING LIKE A PROSTITUTE [OR TAKE OFF HER PROSTITUTE'S MAKE-UP; SET ASIDE HER HARLOTRIES FROM HER PRESENCE/FACE],
    TO STOP BEHAVING LIKE AN UNFAITHFUL WIFE [AND SET ASIDE UNFAITHFULNESS FROM BETWEEN HER BREASTS]." (Hosea 2:2)

THE LORD SAYS, "IN THE FUTURE SHE WILL CALL ME 'MY HUSBAND';
    NO LONGER WILL SHE CALL ME 'MY BAAL ["BAAL" CAN MEAN "HUSBAND," "MASTER," OR "BAAL" (THE CANAANITE GOD); IN THIS WORDPLAY, ISRAEL HAS REPLACED ONE HUSBAND (THE LORD) WITH ANOTHER (BAAL)].' (Hosea 2:16)

It is this concept of covenant that helped the nation of Israel to adapt a female identity and character. While most nations are identified by female character (even today), the relationship between Israel and God was to be unique, for them. Nor was it uncommon for the ancient realm to believe a human being could have such a special relationship with their deity, as specific demands or conditions were met. Certain aspects of Israel's relationship with God, however, did make their relationship, and its dynamics, unique to their circumstances and situation. The way we understand this is to understand the pagan world, the world from which Israel first came.

    It might sound horrifying to describe Israel as coming forth from the pagan world, but that's exactly what happened. There was a time in history when the religion of the ancient Hebrews did not exist, and in that frame of reference, there were ancient religions that reflected indigenous and pagan principles. Before Israel was a nation, the fathers who chose to pursue a religion with the Most High God were pagan men, those who followed different pagan precepts and beliefs. This means they pursued the gods of their ancestors, performed various pagan rituals, and they called on beings they did not know. They saw the world from the pagan viewpoint: intimate with nature, acknowledging and recognizing times and seasons, and knowing what was most problematic and familiar to them, attributing all difficulties and victories to spiritual causes.

A subheading of polytheism is a belief known as henotheism, whereby a group of people worship a specific deity as their personal chief deity, but do not believe their deity is the only deity in existence. Different regions tended toward different gods, as different conditions existed in different places, and the result were pockets of cult devotion, with the same basic themes and emphasis. The people in that region would feel a special connection to the god they sought out above other gods, and they would offer an exclusive sense of devotion to that god, creating a special alliance with them.

It is for this reason that people came to devote themselves to their gods, in one form or another, unto the point of seeing themselves as espoused to them. The name "Ba'al" popular in the Bible as a common source of idolatrous temptation for Israel means, by extension, "husband." The ancients rallied around their special deities, offering all to keep them happy, and usher in favor and good fortune because they were willing to, and often did, offer anything to those deities, whether crops, human beings, or adoration.

There were a couple of differences between these systems and Israel's systematic relationship with God, however. The major difference was the role that God played with Israel. Whereas other groups might have encouraged or adhered to a devotion of a singular deity, that deity wasn't required to exclusively take care of them. Actually, the deity (or deities) they served wasn't required to do anything for them. In what can only be described as a dysfunctional relationship (we could say the original abusive relationships were found in spiritual origin), the people of a given nation sought to honor a deity repeatedly, with wishy-washy results. They might get good results for their offerings, but more often than not, they wouldn't get the results they desired. They would have to up the ante and offer more and more, hoping to win the favor of their deity, and end whatever string of bad luck, bad weather, or bad circumstances befell them. They did not have a relationship with their deity that stemmed from love; only obligation. Their gods were not required to extend themselves in any way, and while the cycles of life manifested year after year, the demands and requirements of their gods did not improve, nor benefit, through time.

Marriage customs of old involved a purchase. Women were considered the property of their fathers, and marriages were arranged between families, sometimes at birth or when girls were of pre-marrying age. The arranged dowry, or bridal price, exchanged hands, and after a girl started her first period, she was transferred to her husband's property, including his family name and identity. While yes, it is without question that in the west we find such practice to be horrifying and inappropriate, it is the world that imagery of Israel and God, and Christ and the church, emerged. Understanding this dynamic is essential to understand the perspective of various spiritual writers throughout the ages, and to see ourselves in place within view. It is from this system that the spiritual relationship between God and His people is best understood: God paid the price for His people, something other deities were unwilling to do, and as a result, the people of God belong to God, and He to them.

SHECHEM ALSO TALKED TO JACOB [HER FATHER] AND TO DINAH'S BROTHERS AND SAID, "PLEASE ACCEPT MY OFFER [LET ME FIND GRACE/FAVOR IN YOUR EYES]. I WILL GIVE ANYTHING YOU ASK. ASK AS MUCH AS YOU WANT FOR THE PAYMENT FOR THE BRIDE [BRIDAL PAYMENT AND GIFT; TRADITIONAL PAYMENTS TO THE FAMILY], AND I WILL GIVE IT TO YOU. JUST LET ME MARRY DINAH [GIVE ME THE GIRL AS A WIFE]." (Genesis 34:11-12)

"SUPPOSE A MAN FINDS A WOMAN WHO IS NOT PLEDGED [ENGAGED] TO BE MARRIED AND HAS NEVER HAD SEXUAL RELATIONS WITH A MAN [IS A VIRGIN]. IF HE TRICKS [OR SEDUCES] HER INTO HAVING SEXUAL RELATIONS WITH HIM, HE MUST GIVE HER FAMILY THE PAYMENT TO MARRY [THE BRIDE-PRICE FOR] HER, AND SHE WILL BECOME HIS WIFE. BUT IF HER FATHER REFUSES TO ALLOW HIS DAUGHTER TO MARRY HIM, THE MAN MUST STILL GIVE THE USUAL PAYMENT FOR A BRIDE WHO HAS NEVER HAD SEXUAL RELATIONS [BRIDE-PRICE FOR A

VIRGIN]. (Exodus 22:16-17)

IF A MAN MEETS A VIRGIN WHO IS NOT ENGAGED TO BE MARRIED AND FORCES HER TO HAVE SEXUAL RELATIONS WITH HIM [GRABS HER AND LIES WITH HER] AND PEOPLE FIND OUT ABOUT IT [IS DISCOVERED], THE MAN WHO HAD SEXUAL RELATIONS [LAY] WITH HER MUST PAY THE GIRL'S FATHER ABOUT ONE AND ONE-FOURTH POUNDS [FIFTY SHEKELS] OF SILVER. HE MUST ALSO MARRY THE GIRL, BECAUSE HE HAS DISHONORED [HUMILIATED; RAPED] HER, AND HE MAY NEVER DIVORCE HER FOR AS LONG AS HE LIVES [EX. 22:16–17]. (Deuteronomy 22:28-29)

THEN DAVID SENT MESSENGERS TO SAUL'S SON ISH-BOSHETH, SAYING, "GIVE ME MY WIFE MICHAL. SHE WAS PROMISED [ENGAGED; BETROTHED] TO ME, AND I KILLED A HUNDRED PHILISTINES TO GET HER [FOR ONE HUNDRED PHILISTINE FORESKINS]." (2 Samuel 3:14)

God created a covenant with Israel, which meant that He agreed to do certain things for them, and they were to do certain things for Him. This unique aspect of their spiritual relationship with God entitled Him to be their God, their spiritual husband, and Israel, His bride, and His people. By redeeming Israel from slavery under Pharaoh, God pledged to do for Israel, and Israel pledged to do for Him. The unique points of their relationship include:

- **Demand of exclusive devotion**: Monotheism was a rarity in the ancient world. Most understood the various deities and powers to bring certain luck, favor, or purpose into one's life. Even though some groups did practice henotheistic spiritual value, it was understood that another deity might offer what one needed at any given time. In that instance, one would offer to the god that was most suitable. In Israel's walk, worshiping or offering to other gods was classified as idolatry, because it drew them away from the One True God, Who was their spouse. They were to express their special relationship with God as they engaged in worship, adoration, and detail of relationship with their one God, not deviating, nor pursuing, false gods. (Exodus 20:3, Exodus 34:14, Deuteronomy 5:7, Psalm 96:4-5, Philippians 2:9-11)

- **The promise of a Redeemer**: The promise of the One to come, Who would redeem humanity from sin, was first prophesied to Eve. That promise was kept alive through the prophets of Israel, who often echoed the words of the Redeemer to come in periods where Israel was at its lowest, and most disobedient. (Genesis 3:15, Genesis 12:2-3, Numbers 24:17, 2 Kings 7:13, Psalm 71:10, Jeremiah 31:15, Daniel 2:44)

- **The written law**: Known as the "Mosaic covenant," it is Israel's part of commitment in covenant. As God's people, they were to be a different people, and their differences were to show in their conduct as a nation. The 613 laws and codes extended into their spiritual belief and conduct, personal codes of hygiene and diet, and interactions with one another and foreign nations. It was never kept in totality and proves the reason why the promised Redeemer was so desired, and so needed. (Romans 3:19-20)

Like the church, Israel is always spoken of as feminine, as being the spouse of God, and as being bought by God through Christ (John 3:29, 2 Corinthians 11:2, Ephesians 5:22-33, Revelation 19:7-9). Israel took on the feminine counterpart of the relationship, not just because she was a nation, and not just because she had a national identity, but because she was the one God bought and sacrificed, to make His own, just as is the same case with the church. We will look at this more specifically later in this book, but the major question is, why was Israel chosen as a type of the church, especially in light of the fact that Israel seemed to fail and falter so many times in that relationship with God. This has nothing to do with the feminine identity of Israel, but the gender non-binary understanding of Israel's femininity has everything to do with her spirituality. No, Israel didn't get it right, and within that, we are able to see the reality of remnant, which is all God has ever had. Israel did fall, and did fail, just as Eve did; but in Israel is the promise of life, the carrier of the Redeemer, of the Redeemer Who would be born of God, without human male intervention. There is no promise of a perfect woman to bring that male into this world, but of the image of woman, of the image of the guardian of God, of His bride, who no matter how fallen and imperfect without history, had the ability to bring forth something incredible, and something powerful, that we protect and stand upon today: the Redeemer, Christ.

Guarding the Redeemer

The book of Jeremiah isn't one we typically think of when it comes to types and shadows as pertain to the feminine aspects of spirituality. Jeremiah was an intense prophet; young, emotional, and passionate about the reality of Israel in his day. His own ministry is a type of the pastoral office, and it's no mistake that many of the only prophecies and descriptions of pastors are found in his words (Jeremiah 3:15-16, Jeremiah 10:19-25, Jeremiah 12:10-17, Jeremiah 17:13-27, Jeremiah 23:1-4).

Jeremiah's lament, however, was not without its unique gender non-binary, feminine touch. While in a seemingly unimportant passage to most who read Jeremiah, the truth is that its few words reveal something important to us about both the vision of Jeremiah and the church, herself.

It is important to understand that the Scriptures are Christocentric, meaning that Christ is the central figure of salvation history. We can see this in what we have already seen, thus far: wherever there are women present, there are types of the church, and in those types of the church, we also see a pointing to Christ. Where Christ is, there is the Kingdom, and where the Kingdom is, we find the church, herself, because the church is the Kingdom. We can't have one without the other. This means that whenever we are looking for Christ in the Scriptures, we should also be looking for the Kingdom, in one form or another, to see our positioning with Christ. Whether looking for the Kingdom shows us what to do or what not to do, we have something to learn from the relationship between Christ and the Kingdom, and something powerful for our own concepts of Christ and the role that the church is to play in salvation history.

One of the major (and often forgotten) roles of the church is that of guarding the Redeemer. Prior to Christ's incarnation, it was Israel's job to prepare for and herald His coming. Now that He has come, it is our job to guard His work, protect the revelation and support the work of salvation. Surrounding the

Messiah, compassing His spiritual purpose and work, we find the church, the Kingdom, Israel, which means in terms of role and identity, we always find a woman, doing works that are not perceived to be so feminine: guarding, positioning, and protecting the man.

Society has positioned us to believe that men are hunters, protectors, gatherers and directors, and women are followers and helpers. We don't ever look at the work that women do and see (even in traditional gender roles) the leadership that is inherent and purposed in women. You can't take care of children, run a household (whether it is your own or you lead someone else's as a servant), or work in professions often stereotyped as being feminine (such as nursing or teaching) without having some leadership ability. Yet throughout history, women have seldom been given the attention they deserve as leaders, and we have seen female abilities put down or criticized, as seeing women in that capacity seems to be beyond society's viewpoints for its females.

Yet Jeremiah 31 gives a different perspective, speaking of a "new thing" to come, as pertains specifically to women and to the female type present in the church. This particular passage of Jeremiah refers to a time of restoration in Israel, when Israel would be captive no more and the nation would receive its natural redemption, freedom from the oppression of captivity which continually befell Israel, due to its disobedience and idolatry. Every time Israel was swayed away from her spiritual Husband, she fell into the hands of the cultures that worshiped the gods always so pervasively tempting for her. Falling into the hands of captivity was to bring Israel to the realization that following these idols was not right for them. None of these gods had their best interests at heart, and none had loved, nor adored, nor married Israel, as Jehovah had. The results of captivity are the results of idolatry, and those results are to bring anyone who falls into the trap of idolatry back to their Creator, Redeemer, and Sustainer, Who shall never leave, nor forsake them.

Jeremiah 31 heralds a time when Israel will be restored from this negative period in history, and things shall reach a place of shalom, or wholeness and completion. Instead of standing as an adulteress, wayward wife, Israel will find peace. The beauty of the passage echoes the everlasting love and kindness God has extended to Israel, and that those who are lost will return, coming back, bringing hope in a place of reality amidst their idols and idolatrous ways.

In verse 22, we see a most interesting verse:

HOW LONG WILT THOU GO ABOUT, O THOU BACKSLIDING DAUGHTER? FOR THE LORD HATH CREATED A NEW THING IN THE EARTH, A WOMAN SHALL COMPASS A MAN. (KJV)

HOW LONG WILT THOU GO HITHER AND THITHER, O THOU BACKSLIDING DAUGHTER? FOR JEHOVAH HATH CREATED A NEW THING IN THE EARTH: A WOMAN SHALL ENCOMPASS A MAN. (ASV)

HOW LONG WILL YOU WAVER *AND* HESITATE [TO RETURN], O YOU BACKSLIDING DAUGHTER? FOR THE LORD HAS CREATED A NEW THING IN THE LAND [OF ISRAEL]: A FEMALE SHALL COMPASS (WOO, WIN, AND PROTECT) A MAN. (AMPC)

HOW LONG WILL YOU TURN HERE AND THERE,
FAITHLESS DAUGHTER?
FOR THE LORD CREATES SOMETHING NEW IN THE LAND—
A FEMALE WILL SHELTER A MAN. (CSB)

YOU ARE AN UNFAITHFUL DAUGHTER.
HOW LONG WILL YOU WANDER BEFORE YOU COME HOME [WAVER]?
THE LORD HAS MADE [CREATED] SOMETHING NEW HAPPEN IN THE LAND:
A WOMAN WILL GO SEEKING [*OR* PROTECT; *OR* EMBRACE; SURROUND] A MAN."

BLACKSLIDING DAUGHTER[5]
- *SHOBEB*: TURNING BACK, APOSTATE
- ORIGINAL WORD: שׁוֹבֵבָה
- PART OF SPEECH: ADJECTIVE
- TRANSLITERATION: SHOBEB
- PHONETIC SPELLING: (SHO-BABE')
- SHORT DEFINITION: APOSTATE

The "backsliding daughter" is Israel in its idolatrous state. Considering the wonderful prophecy of restoration, what is

Israel waiting for? Why will they continue to remain in their spiritually fallen state? Their backslidden state was problematic, because God had created something new in the earth – the woman would woo, win, guide, protect, and lead – a man – and He wanted it to materialize. As long as Israel remained backslidden, this incredible prophecy had to wait for its fruition.

Surely this passage is not just about Israel, however. Remember, if Israel is a type of the church, that means God is speaking to the church, as well. There are so many different ways we are carried off by various idols into a place of captivity. The passage parallels both natural and spiritual realities, and the hope – and promise – is that instead of being carried in so many directions, we can be brought to God, in full, through Christ. In Christ, we find the respite, the peace, the completeness we look for, we seek, and we strive to discover.

Just what is this "new thing" the passage is speaking of? The concept of a woman guarding and protecting isn't new in terms of reality. Women guard and protect their children, their families, and their very lives. It is new, however, as a new thing in the earth, because it is not "work" thought of as being for a woman. Guarding and protecting are regarded as roles for men, because they are considered leadership positions. For women to assume such a role indicates a side-step of authority and would be (and has been) frequently frowned upon. Regardless, Israel had the responsibility of guarding, protecting, and preparing the world for the Redeemer, and every time Israel fell into idolatry, Israel was not doing its job.

It is new in the sense of the redemption of the woman, unto the position of authority. Ever since Eve, women had to hear of the sins of Eve as passed down to them. The "new thing" is the redemption of woman – and Israel – unto the position of not just guarding the Redeemer, but compassing Him – wooing Him, winning the victory with Him, guiding Him, protecting Him, and leading His way in this world. A time would come when, in restored spiritual state, the woman, the church, would have the responsibility to shelter the Redeemer, would fight for Him and protect Him, would pursue Him and seek Him out, and would embrace Him as her own.

Ever since the redemption of Christ, the restored woman has been a part of this new thing in her own identity. It takes on the literal form in our spiritual entity but also takes on a typology in each and every restored woman who assumes leadership. It is the woman's position to be the pursuer, the one who seeks out the Lord, and who finds rest in Him as she leads others to Him. She is to have the courage of her faith, the solidness of her spirituality, and to assume her position, whatever that position is, within the church, within her state of serenity and peace. Yes, this new thing hasn't just been done once; it has been done throughout history and is new every time – it is new on earth, clearly, but is not a new thing in heaven. The woman compasses every time someone comes to faith, to hear of and receive Jesus Christ, and comes to pass every time a woman assumes her position in ministry, her position in leadership within the church, and assumes the role of authority over earthly men, because she has pursued a greater man – the Son of Man – Who has equipped her to lead, guide, and protect in this era of redemption.

The promise of a restored woman

The Bible constantly speaks of Israel's need for restoration, found only in the Redeemer. The written law could not save, thus a Redeemer, spoken of first to Eve in Genesis 3:15, was the One Who could come and set things right. In the meantime, Israel fell, over and over again, into a state of needed restoration. Seeing Israel as a wayward bride, the typology of a lost female brought back to sanity and position by a redeemer, was seen nowhere better than Hosea's prophecy.

Hosea is a powerful book, one that is not studied nearly enough, nor considered for its spiritual realities. The Prophet Hosea was a man called by God to literally live his prophecy, which was Israel's wayward path into idolatry, away from God. Told to marry a prostitute, Hosea and Gomer have children while married, separate and ultimately divorce, and then God instructs Hosea to go after his wayward wife, who is living with someone else at the time. He is to pay the price (the bridal price) for her, and bring her back home, to resume their married life.

WHEN THE LORD BEGAN SPEAKING THROUGH HOSEA, THE LORD SAID TO HIM, "GO, AND MARRY [TAKE FOR YOURSELF] AN UNFAITHFUL WOMAN [OR PROSTITUTE; WOMAN/WIFE OF PROSTITUTION/HARLOTRIES] AND HAVE UNFAITHFUL CHILDREN

[CHILDREN OF PROSTITUTION/HARLOTRIES], BECAUSE THE PEOPLE IN THIS COUNTRY [THIS LAND] HAVE BEEN COMPLETELY UNFAITHFUL TO [PRACTICED PROSTITUTION/HARLOTRY AGAINST] THE LORD [THEY HAVE BEEN SPIRITUALLY UNFAITHFUL; GOMER MAY HAVE BEEN A PROSTITUTE OR PROMISCUOUS WOMAN BEFORE THE MARRIAGE, OR ONLY AFTERWARD]." SO HOSEA MARRIED [WENT AND TOOK] GOMER DAUGHTER OF DIBLAIM, AND SHE BECAME PREGNANT [CONCEIVED] AND GAVE BIRTH TO HOSEA'S SON.

THE LORD SAID TO HOSEA, "NAME HIM JEZREEL [HEBREW: "GOD SOWS"], BECAUSE SOON I WILL PUNISH THE FAMILY [HOUSE] OF JEHU FOR THE PEOPLE THEY KILLED AT [BLOOD OF] JEZREEL [JEHU SLAUGHTERED THE FAMILY OF KING AHAB; 2 KIN. 9:7—10:28]. IN THE FUTURE [THAT DAY] I WILL PUT AN END TO THE KINGDOM OF [THE HOUSE OF] ISRAEL AND BREAK THE POWER OF ISRAEL'S ARMY [BOW OF ISRAEL] IN THE VALLEY OF JEZREEL."

GOMER BECAME PREGNANT [CONCEIVED] AGAIN AND GAVE BIRTH TO A DAUGHTER. THE LORD SAID TO HOSEA, "NAME HER LO-RUHAMAH [HEBREW: "NO PITY/MERCY" OR "NOT LOVED"], BECAUSE I WILL NOT PITY [HAVE MERCY ON; SHOW LOVE TO] ISRAEL ANYMORE, NOR WILL I FORGIVE THEM. BUT I WILL SHOW PITY [MERCY; LOVE] TO THE PEOPLE OF JUDAH. I WILL SAVE THEM, BUT NOT BY USING BOWS OR SWORDS, HORSES OR HORSEMEN, OR WEAPONS OF WAR [OR BATTLE; WAR]. I, THE LORD THEIR GOD, WILL SAVE THEM."

AFTER GOMER HAD STOPPED NURSING LO-RUHAMAH, SHE BECAME PREGNANT [CONCEIVED] AGAIN AND GAVE BIRTH TO ANOTHER SON. THE LORD SAID, "NAME HIM LO-AMMI ["NOT MY PEOPLE"], BECAUSE YOU ARE NOT MY PEOPLE, AND I AM NOT YOUR GOD. (Hosea 1:2-9)

"PLEAD WITH [OR REBUKE; OR ACCUSE; BRING CHARGES AGAINST] YOUR MOTHER [THE NATION ISRAEL].
  PLEAD WITH [OR REBUKE; OR ACCUSE; BRING CHARGES AGAINST] HER, BECAUSE SHE IS NO LONGER [NOT] MY WIFE,
    AND I AM NO LONGER [NOT] HER HUSBAND.
TELL HER TO STOP ACTING LIKE A PROSTITUTE [OR TAKE OFF HER PROSTITUTE'S MAKE-UP; SET ASIDE HER HARLOTRIES FROM HER PRESENCE/FACE],
    TO STOP BEHAVING LIKE AN UNFAITHFUL WIFE [AND SET ASIDE UNFAITHFULNESS FROM BETWEEN HER BREASTS].

IF SHE REFUSES, I WILL STRIP HER NAKED
　AND LEAVE HER BARE [EXPOSE HER] LIKE THE DAY SHE WAS BORN.
I WILL MAKE HER DRY LIKE A DESERT,
　　LIKE A LAND WITHOUT WATER [PARCHED LAND],
　　AND I WILL KILL HER WITH THIRST.
I WILL NOT TAKE PITY [HAVE MERCY/COMPASSION] ON HER CHILDREN,
　　BECAUSE THEY ARE THE CHILDREN OF A PROSTITUTE [OR ADULTERY;
HARLOTRY].
THEIR MOTHER HAS ACTED LIKE A PROSTITUTE [BEEN UNFAITHFUL;
COMMITTED ADULTERY];
　　THE ONE WHO BECAME PREGNANT WITH [CONCEIVED] THEM HAS
ACTED DISGRACEFULLY [SHAMEFULLY].
SHE SAID, 'I WILL CHASE [SEEK; GO] AFTER MY LOVERS [THE IDOL-
WORSHIPING NATIONS AROUND ISRAEL],
　　WHO GIVE ME MY FOOD [BREAD] AND WATER,
WOOL AND FLAX, WINE [DRINKS] AND OLIVE OIL.'
SO I WILL BLOCK HER ROAD [OR FENCE/HEDGE HER IN] WITH
THORNBUSHES;
　　I WILL BUILD A WALL AROUND HER [WALL HER IN]
　　SO SHE CANNOT FIND HER WAY.
SHE WILL RUN AFTER [PURSUE] HER LOVERS,
　　BUT SHE WON'T CATCH THEM.
SHE WILL LOOK FOR THEM,
　　BUT SHE WON'T FIND THEM.
THEN SHE WILL SAY, 'I WILL GO BACK TO MY FIRST HUSBAND [GOD],
　　BECAUSE LIFE WAS BETTER THEN FOR ME THAN IT IS NOW.'
BUT SHE DOES NOT KNOW [ACKNOWLEDGE] THAT I WAS THE ONE
　　WHO GAVE HER GRAIN, NEW WINE, AND OIL.
I GAVE HER MUCH [LAVISHED ON HER] SILVER AND GOLD,
　　BUT SHE [THEY; THE NATION] USED IT FOR BAAL.

"SO I WILL COME BACK AND TAKE AWAY MY GRAIN AT HARVEST TIME
[IN ITS TIME]
　　AND MY NEW WINE WHEN IT IS READY [IN ITS SEASON/APPOINTED
TIME].
I WILL TAKE BACK MY WOOL AND LINEN [FLAX]
　　THAT COVERED HER NAKEDNESS.
SO I WILL SHOW HER NAKEDNESS [UNCOVER HER
LEWDNESS/SHAMELESSNESS] TO HER LOVERS,
　　AND NO ONE WILL SAVE [RESCUE] HER FROM ME [MY HAND].
I WILL PUT AN END TO ALL HER CELEBRATIONS [MERRYMAKING]:

HER YEARLY FESTIVALS, HER NEW MOON FESTIVALS, AND HER
SABBATHS.
  I WILL STOP ALL OF HER SPECIAL [APPOINTED] FEASTS.
I WILL DESTROY HER VINES AND FIG TREES,
  WHICH SHE SAID WERE HER PAY FROM HER LOVERS.
I WILL TURN THEM INTO A FOREST [OVERGROWN THICKET],
  AND WILD ANIMALS [BEASTS OF THE FIELD] WILL EAT THEM.
I WILL PUNISH HER FOR ALL THE TIMES [DAYS; PAGAN FEAST DAYS]
  SHE BURNED INCENSE TO THE BAALS [THE LOCAL GODS OF THE
CANAANITES WORSHIPED BY THE ISRAELITES].
SHE PUT ON HER [ADORNED HERSELF WITH] RINGS [OR EARRINGS]
AND JEWELRY
  AND WENT CHASING AFTER [OUT TO] HER LOVERS,
BUT SHE FORGOT ME!"
  SAYS THE LORD.

"SO I AM GOING TO ATTRACT [ALLURE; WOO] HER;
  I WILL LEAD HER INTO THE DESERT [WILDERNESS; AS IN THE
EXODUS, WHEN GOD RESCUED ISRAEL FROM SLAVERY AND CARED FOR
HER; EX. 12–17]
  AND SPEAK TENDERLY TO HER.
THERE I WILL GIVE HER BACK HER VINEYARDS,
  AND I WILL MAKE THE VALLEY OF TROUBLE [ACHOR; SEE JOSH.
7:1–26] A DOOR OF HOPE.
THERE SHE WILL RESPOND [OR SING] AS WHEN SHE WAS YOUNG [IN
THE DAYS OF HER YOUTH],
  AS WHEN SHE CAME OUT OF EGYPT."

THE LORD SAYS, "IN THE FUTURE SHE WILL CALL ME 'MY HUSBAND';
  NO LONGER WILL SHE CALL ME 'MY BAAL ["BAAL" CAN MEAN
"HUSBAND," "MASTER," OR "BAAL" (THE CANAANITE GOD); IN THIS
WORDPLAY, ISRAEL HAS REPLACED ONE HUSBAND (THE LORD) WITH
ANOTHER (BAAL)].'
I WILL NEVER LET HER SAY [REMOVE FROM HER LIPS] THE NAMES OF
BAAL AGAIN;
  PEOPLE WON'T USE [UTTER; INVOKE; OR REMEMBER] THEIR NAMES
ANYMORE.
AT THAT TIME I WILL MAKE AN AGREEMENT [COVENANT; TREATY] FOR
THEM
  WITH THE WILD ANIMALS [BEASTS OF THE FIELD], THE BIRDS [BIRDS
OF THE SKY/HEAVENS], AND THE CRAWLING THINGS [CREEPING

THINGS OF THE GROUND].
I WILL SMASH [SHATTER; ABOLISH] FROM THE LAND
    THE BOW AND THE SWORD AND THE WEAPONS OF WAR [OR WAR; BATTLE],
    SO MY PEOPLE WILL LIVE [LIE DOWN] IN SAFETY.
AND I WILL MAKE YOU MY PROMISED BRIDE [BETROTH YOU TO ME] FOREVER.
    I WILL BE GOOD AND FAIR [BETROTH YOU IN RIGHTEOUSNESS AND JUSTICE];
    I WILL SHOW YOU MY LOVE [LOYALTY; UNFAILING LOVE; LOVINGKINDNESS] AND MERCY.
I WILL BE TRUE TO YOU AS MY PROMISED BRIDE [BETROTH YOU IN FAITHFULNESS],
    AND YOU WILL KNOW [OR ACKNOWLEDGE ME AS] THE LORD.

"AT THAT TIME I WILL SPEAK TO YOU [ANSWER; RESPOND]," SAYS THE LORD.
    "I WILL SPEAK TO [ANSWER; RESPOND TO] THE SKIES [OR HEAVENS],
    AND THEY WILL GIVE RAIN TO [ANSWER; RESPOND TO] THE EARTH.
THE EARTH WILL PRODUCE [ANSWER/RESPOND WITH] GRAIN, NEW WINE, AND OIL;
    MUCH WILL GROW BECAUSE MY PEOPLE ARE CALLED [AND THEY WILL ANSWER/RESPOND TO] JEZREEL ["GOD PLANTS"; 1:4, 11].
I WILL PLANT MY PEOPLE [HER FOR MYSELF] IN THE LAND,
    AND I WILL SHOW PITY TO THE ONE I HAD CALLED 'NOT SHOWN PITY [LO-RUHAMAH; 1:6–7].'
I WILL SAY, 'YOU ARE MY PEOPLE'
    TO THOSE I HAD CALLED 'NOT MY PEOPLE [LO-AMMI; 1:9].'
AND THEY WILL SAY TO ME, 'YOU ARE OUR GOD.'" (Hosea 2:2-23)

THE LORD SAID TO ME AGAIN, "GO, SHOW YOUR LOVE TO A WOMAN [PROBABLY GOMER (1:3), WHO HAS SINCE DESERTED HIM] LOVED BY [OR WHO LOVES] SOMEONE ELSE, WHO HAS BEEN UNFAITHFUL TO YOU [IS COMMITTING ADULTERY]. IN THE SAME WAY THE LORD LOVES THE PEOPLE [SONS; CHILDREN] OF ISRAEL, EVEN THOUGH THEY WORSHIP [TURN TO] OTHER GODS AND LOVE TO EAT THE RAISIN CAKES [FOOD EATEN AT PAGAN TEMPLES]."

SO I BOUGHT HER FOR SIX OUNCES OF SILVER [SHEKELS] AND TEN BUSHELS [A HOMER AND A LETHEK; A HOMER WAS 5–6 BUSHELS; A LETHEK WAS ABOUT HALF THAT] OF BARLEY. THEN I TOLD HER, "YOU

MUST WAIT FOR [OR LIVE WITH] ME FOR MANY DAYS. YOU MUST NOT BE A PROSTITUTE, AND YOU MUST NOT HAVE SEXUAL RELATIONS WITH ANY OTHER MAN. I WILL ACT THE SAME WAY TOWARD YOU."

IN THE SAME WAY THE PEOPLE [SONS; CHILDREN] OF ISRAEL WILL LIVE MANY DAYS WITHOUT A KING OR LEADER [PRINCE], WITHOUT SACRIFICES OR HOLY STONE PILLARS [USED IN PAGAN WORSHIP; 2 KIN. 3:2; 10:26–28; 17:10], AND WITHOUT THE HOLY VEST [EPHOD; EX. 28:6–14; JUDG. 8:27] OR AN IDOL [HOUSEHOLD IDOLS; TERAPHIM; GEN. 31:19]. AFTER THIS, THE PEOPLE OF ISRAEL WILL RETURN AND FOLLOW [SEEK] THE LORD THEIR GOD AND THE KING FROM DAVID'S FAMILY [DAVID THEIR KING; AN HEIR FROM DAVID'S LINE]. IN THE LAST DAYS THEY WILL TURN IN FEAR [COME IN REVERENCE/AWE] TO THE LORD, AND HE WILL BLESS THEM. (Hosea 3:1-6)

Gomer proves that Eve is not the only Old Testament type of the church that fell into disrepair and needed redemption. Hosea stands as a type of Christ, the Redeemer, Who had to sacrifice and pursue His wife, who was lost in a state of sin and disarray. While some debate whether redemption is for women, the role of the woman in the stories of Hosea and the prophecy given to Eve prove that redemption is just as much for women as it is for men. This might seem like a secondary point, but it, in reality, is an important aspect of recognizing that salvation is for all, male and female alike, and that women are a part of that picture of redemption and the participation of church leadership, proven by no other fact than it is women themselves who are used as the illustration of salvation throughout the Old Testament.

> GOMER[6]
> - GOMER: A SON OF JAPHETH, ALSO HIS DESC., ALSO THE WIFE OF HOSEA
> - ORIGINAL WORD: גֹּמֶר
> - PART OF SPEECH: PROPER NAME; MASCULINE A.; FEMININE
> - TRANSLITERATION: GOMER
> - PHONETIC SPELLING: (GO'-MER)
> - SHORT DEFINITION: GOMER

The story of Hosea and Gomer has a personal air to it, one that we do not always find in Bible prophecies. While some seem to allude to distant facts or to situations we can't quite easily discern, Hosea and Gomer is up-close-and-personal, showing us the realities of redemption in a personal way. Hosea and Gomer were people, as were Adam and Eve, and instead of merely pointing to the redemption of Israel, God made sure that Hosea's prophecy was personal: personal to him and personal to Gomer. This personal touch also makes us very uncomfortable. By recognizing the personal nature of this prophecy, it should become personal to each one of us, as well. No, God is not saying that every married woman is a wayward prostitute. It's not meant to be personal in that specific manner, but in the manner of realizing how much God loves each of us, and how much God loves the women that are His own, and not just in an abstract sense.

The prophecies of Hosea all point to the nation of Israel, and the personal cry God made to Israel to return from spiritual idols unto Him. That personal cry was to Israel, as a type of the church, but there was more in God's words through the prophet. In promising to redeem Israel, and in the promise of the redemption of the church, God is also promising to restore the woman. No longer were women to be defined by a fallen nature (by the fall of Eve) but we were to be identified as restored, as fulfilling the promise of wholeness and completion. Those who forever see women because of fallen nature, no matter their spiritual status, are failing to see the work God made sure to specifically identify as belonging to and relating to women.

Embracing the promise

There are many women in the Bible who are beautiful examples of different things, and many of them are types, or shadows, of other things that were to come within Biblical and salvation history. The beauty that is present within them is present within all women, and we should be willing and excited to embrace these promises for ourselves. Within each and every woman lies the promise of the church, a type of the church, ready and prepared to move forward with the Gospel of life, unto a new day and a new hope. If we keep seeing ourselves as unredeemable, in one form or another, we will never live to see the church, alive and working, within each and every one of us. By continuing to look at different types, shadows, and yes, even realities present within our Christian spirituality, we, as women, can empower ourselves and others, and know that the church is not just a participation for us; it is us, as well.

Ruth swearing her allegiance to Naomi (Jan Victors)

CHAPTER THREE
A Female Perspective of God

THE books of Ruth and Esther are among the most controversial writings found in the Old Testament. It may seem hard to fathom, but the two books with central female characters have been despised, rejected, and questioned throughout history. While they are books we often conveniently overlook and ignore as lacking theological value, most still believe that, at minimum, Ruth and Esther have inspirational value. While they might not be books revered for great and powerful truths, most admire the courage of Ruth and Esther and the sentiments of their contents, and they show up from time to time, here and there, at women's and youth gatherings.

There is a reason we do not regard Ruth and Esther as highly as we ought in church, even unto the end of not respecting their contents and hearing the theology present in their works. This has led to an incomplete assessment of Ruth and Esther, as well as important truths about the church, about theological realities that were within the heart of God all long, even though they were not visible in that era; and the truth that we, as Christians, need to embrace the women in our lives in a different way, one that edifies and sees the type of the church alive and well in each of them.

The long story on the books of Ruth and Esther

The process of canonization, or what is determined to be

authentic and church-approved (canonical) versus those which are deemed uninspired or not approved, is not simple to describe. What we do need to understand, before anything else, is that canonization was (and remains) a political process. It is one debated and voted on by groups of clergies and is not as simple as a group reading a book and deciding that it is inspired (or uninspired). There are many different factors that determine a council's leanings on inspiration, and many of those factors are, well, less than spiritual. Politics, current trends, social implications, and aspirations all factor into whatever is classified as authoritative, and in the history of canonization, books have been included, then excluded at another council, then included, then excluded, then included or finally excluded. There are different accepted canons among different Christian groups, which may or may not include books included in the current canon you hold in your hands, bound and printed by an American company. Alternate canons typically include books that are not included in other canons, and those books may be considered totally uninspired by other groups.

The long and short of canonization is that there is no such thing as a universal canon. Different denominations acknowledge different collections of books. No one accepts the same exact combination of spiritual books as authoritative. The reason for this is simple: the different standards for canonization vary greatly. Whatever is trending, whatever marks of cultural importance, and whatever is front and center to a group – those are things central to determination of canonization. It's important to keep these concepts in mind when discussing Ruth and Esther, because the authenticity and inspiration of both books has been addressed repeatedly throughout history. If you do a search on these two books, the controversy continues to rage, as people question whether Ruth and Esther should be a part of the canon most embrace today.

Ruth has often had more canonical standing than Esther, for no other reason than it is an ancient book, one that has been accepted among Jewish canons for centuries. It still comes into question, however, because people are not sure how to interpret it, or what exactly its point is. The book of Ruth holds themes within its pages that are opposite of those found in other books of the Old Testament: interfaith marriage, a strong, central female character, and Gentile inclusion among the Jews. It seems foreign that such themes seem to present themselves problematic considering the Mosaic Law and the biases and tribal disagreements between Israel and its neighbors would create such an incredible book, an incredible story, that sounds like two women against the world, on the surface. Without proper understanding of Ruth, it can sound like nothing more than a story of distant faith, something that is uninteresting in a spiritual light, but makes us feel good to read it.

Esther's theological implications come into play as the name of God is found nowhere in the ten chapters of the book. An historical story very central to female characters (much as Ruth is, as well), the book details the courageous story of Esther, a Jewish orphan, who risks her life to save the Jewish people from annihilation. Despite the book of Esther's godly themes, many feel the book lacks something, and even Martin Luther himself felt it did not belong in the Bible canon.

Yet both Ruth and Esther have some very important realities to offer us: in character, in theology, and in general life perspective, and we, as students of the Scriptures, should be eager to hear them. There is much that God reveals in these two books about female spirituality as well as the church, herself, that we must fully embrace to understand the grace God extends to each and every one of us, here and now.

Seeing a feminine perspective of God

I believe one of the major reasons why Ruth and Esther have faced so much rejection throughout the years is because most people who attempt to teach on them don't understand the perspective they come from. Since most of history's Bible scholars, teachers, and professors have been male, their viewpoints trickle down to prospective students, both male and female, throughout the ages. If someone is reading something and does not properly understand it, they aren't going to properly teach it. The result has been a general consensus that Ruth and Esther aren't that important, they provide historical information more than spiritual food, and they don't offer a lot, if any, theological ideas. The people in them don't appear to be extremely devout, especially in the practice of their regular spiritual walk. They seem ordinarily human. When people discuss these books, their focus tends to be on secondary male characters, such as Boaz in Ruth and Xerxes, Haman, and Mordecai in Esther, because such characters are more comfortable and familiar to rely on for instruction and doctrine. There's nothing wrong with looking at these male characters but doing so continues to distract us from the central themes of the books. Instead of looking at our female characters and examining what we should observe therein, we are diverting attention to our traditions, to those things that make us most comfortable.

We don't understand Ruth and Esther properly because the narratives are not told from a male perspective. Their contents don't pretend to be about anything other than what they are. They are books about women, examining the struggles, difficulties, and decisions women faced in their day and age. This isn't where their purpose begins and ends, however. The realities of a female perspective of God show us theological realities we might not as easily have seen, nor been able to embrace, from a male perspective. This does not mean that the more spiritual contents of Ruth and Esther are easy for everyone to embrace. They require us to look at things abstractly, differently from how we typically examine the Bible, and to stretch our perspectives and grow as people.

The books of Ruth and Esther show us a uniquely feminine perspective on a relationship with God. They are not arguing the gender of God (as in being limited for male or female), but they show the way that many women approach their relationship with God and with others. There are a few things of note in it, which are characteristic of other female experiences in Scripture, as well:

- **God is not a patriarchal figure in the books**: While no one questions the fatherhood of God or His role as our Father, we don't see God as literally guiding or directing the women in either book, in any semblance, as a parental figure. God is present, and God is important in their lives, but there are no divine voices, angels, or other spiritual forms involved in the direction the women take. The tone of spiritual matters in Ruth and Esther is quieter, as the people involved follow instinct rather than signs, and do what they know is right to do, even in the face of obstacles and everything that speaks to the contrary.

- **There are no direct miracles**: In connection with a lack of patriarchal figures, there aren't any direct, heavenly miracles seen in either book. Famines still came, people still died, Vashti was still deposed, Esther had to still go through the normal processes to become queen and speak to the king, human intervention was still required to save the Jews from annihilation, Ruth still had to work hard, and Boaz still tried to avoid doing what he knew he was supposed to do. The people in Ruth and Esther have a uniquely human quality to them, one that mirrors everyday life and politics, and does so without any divine miracles or overtly divine direction.

- **The women seem to instinctively know what to do**: Someone might assume from Ruth and Esther that the two women aren't very spiritual, but to say such is incorrect. They are women who understand the value in praying without ceasing (1 Thessalonians 5:17), and they do so as they go about and do what they need to do in their lives. There is no conflict between the spiritual and the natural, as both are powerfully interwoven to transform the whole of their entire lives.

- **Spirituality is seen as a part of one's everyday life and decisions**: Ruth and Esther prove that the idea of going to church on Sunday doesn't save anyone. Spirituality must be a practical, applicable part of everyday life to be effective. It's not as much about looking devout from the outside looking in, but being devoted in internal places, those where we recognize God's leading in powerful ways. Both books prove that such spirituality applies to decision-making, choices, and impacts the ordinary aspects of life we often fail to think apply to God or to His nature.

- **We see the principle of "all things working together for good" at work in a powerful way**: None of the women in Ruth and Esther have easy lives. There are different reasons why they might have their difficulties (famine, grief, spousal mistreatment, alcoholism, being an orphan, compromising situations), but they all have difficulties in common. The reality of female lives is that historically speaking, women have had difficult lives. This honest, open reality proves God is aware of what we go through, experience and handle, and that God is there with us, every step of the way, to bring us to a place where all things work together for good (Romans 8:28).

- **Men are not always angels in the Bible**: One of the biggest gripes people have against women in ministry is that "all examples of women in the Bible are negative." They cite such as Jezebel, Delilah, Eve, and Sapphira as "proof" that Biblical women in power always do bad things. This is a gross exaggeration, of course, but the truth is that most of the male characters in Ruth and Esther don't come off looking perfect. The men in Ruth's family all died, leaving behind the women, and Boaz couldn't have been less interested in marrying Ruth. In the book of Esther, Xerxes has a particularly distasteful character early on, as do his men and those he positioned in power (and it is due to Esther's work that her people are saved). Men aren't perfect, and it is important to remember this when considering the work of women in the church. We serve a perfect Savior, who calls imperfect men – and women – into the church, to do His work. Neither gender is more qualified to serve than the other, and both must rise to the challenge and transform from glory to glory and faith to faith (2 Corinthians 3:18).

This feminine perspective of God shows a thorough counterbalance to the many forefathers of the faith who required divine direction or repeated proof to perform their tasks, such as Moses (Exodus 4:1-17) and Gideon (Judges 6:1-24). It shows faith in action; that faith is something to be lived, not something to muse over endlessly throughout one's days. In its most applicable form, faith must always have a practical, ordinary component. Life is full of different experiences, and relationship with God is not reserved for spiritual highs and religious ceremonies. When God motivates someone to move, they need to move. There is no hesitation among these women, and that challenges us (especially those of us who alike to think long and hard on things before doing them) to be doers, rather than just hearers, of God's Word to each of us. Even though the theology of Ruth and Esther may seem less forceful and more subtle than some books of the Bible, the powerful way that Esther and Ruth live their faith show us that women have the power to be doers, sometimes faster than men, sometimes ahead of male revelation, and sometimes without consulting or involving men in the process, at all, until they must become a part of the plan.

We need to see the feminine perspective of God because the world is full of women who experience God and follow God in the same, if not similar, ways that Ruth and Esther also followed God. It's no less important, nor valid, than the way a man might follow God. Ruth and Esther hold women up; validates their experience; and teaches us important things about God, His Church, and about Christ, just by being exactly who they were.

The church present in the book of Ruth

We've heard of Ruth and Naomi as great studies for friendship between women, relationships that should exist between in-laws, and even in some circles, a model for various relationships far more intimate than the text allows. There are some obvious things we tend to overlook in Ruth and Naomi, however. The most pressing thing we often overlook is that Ruth and Naomi are, by their very relationship, a type of the church. In terms of Jew and Gentile coming together to form a new body in Christ, it is the book of Ruth that first points to this type, thousands of years before Jesus was born.

Ruth, contrary to the way she is often painted in Christian circles, was not a Christian, nor was she a Jew. Ruth was a Moabite, from what is now known as a mountain-clad land located in modern-day Jordan, on the eastern shore of the Dead Sea. The Bible often depicts Israel at odds with Moab, thus making the story of Ruth that much more interesting. As a Moabite, Ruth would have most likely worshiped Chemosh, the national deity of Moab, in henotheistic fashion. This deity was associated with the goddess Ashteroth and was like Ba'al in nature. Some believe Moloch was the same god as Chemosh, just in a slightly different form. He was understood to be a destroyer or subduer and represented by a fish.[3]

Dr. Lee Ann B. Marino, Ph.D., D.Min., D.D.

RUTH

- *RUTH*: "FRIENDSHIP," A MOABITE ANCESTRESS OF DAVID
- ORIGINAL WORD: רוּת
- PART OF SPEECH: PROPER NAME FEMININE
- TRANSLITERATION: RUTH
- PHONETIC SPELLING: (ROOTH)
- SHORT DEFINITION: RUTH

NAOMI

- *NAOMI*: "PLEASANT;" MOTHER-IN-LAW OF RUTH
- ORIGINAL WORD: נָעֳמִי
- PART OF SPEECH: PROPER NAME FEMININE
- TRANSLITERATION: NOOMI
- PHONETIC SPELLING: (NO-OM-EE')
- SHORT DEFINITION: NAOMI

Chemosh was denounced as an idol by Biblical prophets, and was classified as the "abomination of Moab:"[4]

AS SOLOMON GREW OLD, HIS WIVES CAUSED HIM TO FOLLOW [LED HIM ASTRAY AFTER; TURNED HIS HEART AWAY AFTER] OTHER GODS. HE DID NOT FOLLOW THE LORD COMPLETELY [HIS HEART WAS NOT WHOLLY DEVOTED/FAITHFUL TO THE LORD HIS GOD] AS HIS FATHER DAVID HAD DONE [THE HEART OF HIS FATHER DAVID HAD BEEN]. SOLOMON WORSHIPED [FOLLOWED; WENT AFTER] ASHTORETH, THE GODDESS OF THE PEOPLE OF SIDON, AND MOLECH [MILCOM], THE HATED [DETESTABLE] GOD OF THE AMMONITES. SO SOLOMON DID WHAT THE LORD SAID WAS WRONG [EVIL IN THE EYES/SIGHT OF THE LORD] AND DID NOT [REFUSED TO] FOLLOW THE LORD COMPLETELY AS HIS FATHER DAVID HAD DONE.

ON A HILL EAST OF JERUSALEM [THE MOUNT OF OLIVES], SOLOMON BUILT TWO PLACES FOR WORSHIP [HIGH PLACES; 3:2]. ONE WAS A PLACE TO WORSHIP CHEMOSH, THE HATED [DETESTABLE] GOD OF THE MOABITES, AND THE OTHER WAS A PLACE TO WORSHIP MOLECH, THE HATED [DETESTABLE] GOD OF THE AMMONITES. (1 Kings 11:4-7)

The worship of Chemosh came into Hebrew culture through

King Solomon, when he turned to the worship of his pagan wives, and was later destroyed by King Josiah:

THEN THE KING SENT, AND ALL THE ELDERS OF JUDAH AND JERUSALEM WERE GATHERED TO HIM. AND THE KING WENT UP TO THE HOUSE OF THE LORD, AND WITH HIM ALL THE MEN OF JUDAH AND ALL THE INHABITANTS OF JERUSALEM AND THE PRIESTS AND THE PROPHETS, ALL THE PEOPLE, BOTH SMALL AND GREAT. AND HE READ IN THEIR HEARING ALL THE WORDS OF THE BOOK OF THE COVENANT THAT HAD BEEN FOUND IN THE HOUSE OF THE LORD. AND THE KING STOOD BY THE PILLAR AND MADE A COVENANT BEFORE THE LORD, TO WALK AFTER THE LORD AND TO KEEP HIS COMMANDMENTS AND HIS TESTIMONIES AND HIS STATUTES WITH ALL HIS HEART AND ALL HIS SOUL, TO PERFORM THE WORDS OF THIS COVENANT THAT WERE WRITTEN IN THIS BOOK. AND ALL THE PEOPLE JOINED IN THE COVENANT.

AND THE KING COMMANDED HILKIAH THE HIGH PRIEST AND THE PRIESTS OF THE SECOND ORDER AND THE KEEPERS OF THE THRESHOLD TO BRING OUT OF THE TEMPLE OF THE LORD ALL THE VESSELS MADE FOR BAAL, FOR ASHERAH, AND FOR ALL THE HOST OF HEAVEN. HE BURNED THEM OUTSIDE JERUSALEM IN THE FIELDS OF THE KIDRON AND CARRIED THEIR ASHES TO BETHEL. AND HE DEPOSED THE PRIESTS WHOM THE KINGS OF JUDAH HAD ORDAINED TO MAKE OFFERINGS IN THE HIGH PLACES AT THE CITIES OF JUDAH AND AROUND JERUSALEM; THOSE ALSO WHO BURNED INCENSE TO BAAL, TO THE SUN AND THE MOON AND THE CONSTELLATIONS AND ALL THE HOST OF THE HEAVENS. AND HE BROUGHT OUT THE ASHERAH FROM THE HOUSE OF THE LORD, OUTSIDE JERUSALEM, TO THE BROOK KIDRON, AND BURNED IT AT THE BROOK KIDRON AND BEAT IT TO DUST AND CAST THE DUST OF IT UPON THE GRAVES OF THE COMMON PEOPLE. AND HE BROKE DOWN THE HOUSES OF THE MALE CULT PROSTITUTES WHO WERE IN THE HOUSE OF THE LORD, WHERE THE WOMEN WOVE HANGINGS FOR THE ASHERAH. AND HE BROUGHT ALL THE PRIESTS OUT OF THE CITIES OF JUDAH, AND DEFILED THE HIGH PLACES WHERE THE PRIESTS HAD MADE OFFERINGS, FROM GEBA TO BEERSHEBA. AND HE BROKE DOWN THE HIGH PLACES OF THE GATES THAT WERE AT THE ENTRANCE OF THE GATE OF JOSHUA THE GOVERNOR OF THE CITY, WHICH WERE ON ONE'S LEFT AT THE GATE OF THE CITY. HOWEVER, THE PRIESTS OF THE HIGH PLACES DID NOT COME UP TO THE ALTAR OF THE LORD IN JERUSALEM, BUT THEY ATE UNLEAVENED BREAD AMONG

THEIR BROTHERS. AND HE DEFILED TOPHETH, WHICH IS IN THE VALLEY OF THE SON OF HINNOM, THAT NO ONE MIGHT BURN HIS SON OR HIS DAUGHTER AS AN OFFERING TO MOLECH. AND HE REMOVED THE HORSES THAT THE KINGS OF JUDAH HAD DEDICATED TO THE SUN, AT THE ENTRANCE TO THE HOUSE OF THE LORD, BY THE CHAMBER OF NATHAN-MELECH THE CHAMBERLAIN, WHICH WAS IN THE PRECINCTS. AND HE BURNED THE CHARIOTS OF THE SUN WITH FIRE. AND THE ALTARS ON THE ROOF OF THE UPPER CHAMBER OF AHAZ, WHICH THE KINGS OF JUDAH HAD MADE, AND THE ALTARS THAT MANASSEH HAD MADE IN THE TWO COURTS OF THE HOUSE OF THE LORD, HE PULLED DOWN AND BROKE IN PIECES AND CAST THE DUST OF THEM INTO THE BROOK KIDRON. AND THE KING DEFILED THE HIGH PLACES THAT WERE EAST OF JERUSALEM, TO THE SOUTH OF THE MOUNT OF CORRUPTION, WHICH SOLOMON THE KING OF ISRAEL HAD BUILT FOR ASHTORETH THE ABOMINATION OF THE SIDONIANS, AND FOR CHEMOSH THE ABOMINATION OF MOAB, AND FOR MILCOM THE ABOMINATION OF THE AMMONITES. AND HE BROKE IN PIECES THE PILLARS AND CUT DOWN THE ASHERIM AND FILLED THEIR PLACES WITH THE BONES OF MEN.

MOREOVER, THE ALTAR AT BETHEL, THE HIGH PLACE ERECTED BY JEROBOAM THE SON OF NEBAT, WHO MADE ISRAEL TO SIN, THAT ALTAR WITH THE HIGH PLACE HE PULLED DOWN AND BURNED, REDUCING IT TO DUST. HE ALSO BURNED THE ASHERAH. AND AS JOSIAH TURNED, HE SAW THE TOMBS THERE ON THE MOUNT. AND HE SENT AND TOOK THE BONES OUT OF THE TOMBS AND BURNED THEM ON THE ALTAR AND DEFILED IT, ACCORDING TO THE WORD OF THE LORD THAT THE MAN OF GOD PROCLAIMED, WHO HAD PREDICTED THESE THINGS. THEN HE SAID, "WHAT IS THAT MONUMENT THAT I SEE?" AND THE MEN OF THE CITY TOLD HIM, "IT IS THE TOMB OF THE MAN OF GOD WHO CAME FROM JUDAH AND PREDICTED THESE THINGS THAT YOU HAVE DONE AGAINST THE ALTAR AT BETHEL." AND HE SAID, "LET HIM BE; LET NO MAN MOVE HIS BONES." SO THEY LET HIS BONES ALONE, WITH THE BONES OF THE PROPHET WHO CAME OUT OF SAMARIA. AND JOSIAH REMOVED ALL THE SHRINES ALSO OF THE HIGH PLACES THAT WERE IN THE CITIES OF SAMARIA, WHICH KINGS OF ISRAEL HAD MADE, PROVOKING THE LORD TO ANGER. HE DID TO THEM ACCORDING TO ALL THAT HE HAD DONE AT BETHEL. AND HE SACRIFICED ALL THE PRIESTS OF THE HIGH PLACES WHO WERE THERE, ON THE ALTARS, AND BURNED HUMAN BONES ON THEM. THEN HE RETURNED TO JERUSALEM.

AND THE KING COMMANDED ALL THE PEOPLE, "KEEP THE PASSOVER TO THE LORD YOUR GOD, AS IT IS WRITTEN IN THIS BOOK OF THE COVENANT." FOR NO SUCH PASSOVER HAD BEEN KEPT SINCE THE DAYS OF THE JUDGES WHO JUDGED ISRAEL, OR DURING ALL THE DAYS OF THE KINGS OF ISRAEL OR OF THE KINGS OF JUDAH. BUT IN THE EIGHTEENTH YEAR OF KING JOSIAH THIS PASSOVER WAS KEPT TO THE LORD IN JERUSALEM.

MOREOVER, JOSIAH PUT AWAY THE MEDIUMS AND THE NECROMANCERS AND THE HOUSEHOLD GODS AND THE IDOLS AND ALL THE ABOMINATIONS THAT WERE SEEN IN THE LAND OF JUDAH AND IN JERUSALEM, THAT HE MIGHT ESTABLISH THE WORDS OF THE LAW THAT WERE WRITTEN IN THE BOOK THAT HILKIAH THE PRIEST FOUND IN THE HOUSE OF THE LORD. BEFORE HIM THERE WAS NO KING LIKE HIM, WHO TURNED TO THE LORD WITH ALL HIS HEART AND WITH ALL HIS SOUL AND WITH ALL HIS MIGHT, ACCORDING TO ALL THE LAW OF MOSES, NOR DID ANY LIKE HIM ARISE AFTER HIM.

STILL THE LORD DID NOT TURN FROM THE BURNING OF HIS GREAT WRATH, BY WHICH HIS ANGER WAS KINDLED AGAINST JUDAH, BECAUSE OF ALL THE PROVOCATIONS WITH WHICH MANASSEH HAD PROVOKED HIM. AND THE LORD SAID, "I WILL REMOVE JUDAH ALSO OUT OF MY SIGHT, AS I HAVE REMOVED ISRAEL, AND I WILL CAST OFF THIS CITY THAT I HAVE CHOSEN, JERUSALEM, AND THE HOUSE OF WHICH I SAID, MY NAME SHALL BE THERE."

NOW THE REST OF THE ACTS OF JOSIAH AND ALL THAT HE DID, ARE THEY NOT WRITTEN IN THE BOOK OF THE CHRONICLES OF THE KINGS OF JUDAH? IN HIS DAYS PHARAOH NECO KING OF EGYPT WENT UP TO THE KING OF ASSYRIA TO THE RIVER EUPHRATES. KING JOSIAH WENT TO MEET HIM, AND PHARAOH NECO KILLED HIM AT MEGIDDO, AS SOON AS HE SAW HIM. AND HIS SERVANTS CARRIED HIM DEAD IN A CHARIOT FROM MEGIDDO AND BROUGHT HIM TO JERUSALEM AND BURIED HIM IN HIS OWN TOMB. AND THE PEOPLE OF THE LAND TOOK JEHOAHAZ THE SON OF JOSIAH, AND ANOINTED HIM, AND MADE HIM KING IN HIS FATHER'S PLACE. (2 Kings 23:1-30, ESV)

The background for the book of Ruth is set years after a time of famine, when Jews relocated to find food. Elimelech, his wife, Naomi, and their two sons, relocated to Moab during the famine, as food was scarce. While there, the sons, both Jews, married two Moabite women – Orprah married Chilion and Ruth married Mahlon. Elimelech dies, leaving behind Naomi, and then Chilon and Mahlon also die, leaving behind Orprah and Ruth. Thus, we have a situation where three women are bound together by marriage and now loss – two who are pagan, living in their immediate land, and one who is a Jew – and decisions that must be made.

Right out of the gate, the book of Ruth addresses an initial issue that is perhaps rather uncomfortable for many, right within its opening passages: interfaith marriage. After many varied injunctions against interfaith marriage (Genesis 24:3-4, Exodus 34:12-16, Leviticus 17:7, Deuteronomy 7:3-4, Ezra 10:2, Nehemiah 13:25-27, Malachi 2:11), we have an entire book in the Old Testament that is all about that topic. It is of particular interest to note that this particular interfaith marriage doesn't seem to have contaminated, nor led to idolatry among the Jewish men who married these women, nor among the in-laws who lived in a nation of idolaters. The book doesn't provide a lot of information about their marriages because it isn't about that specific time in their lives, but nothing indicates they were married and lived with constant discord or problems. We have no evidence of divorce or marital regret. It appears from the text that Ruth and Orprah were both very concerned and caring toward their mother-in-law, Naomi, and that the three of them shared a powerful bond of loss, despite their differences in faith. This should speak to all of us as the powerful nature of human experience in evangelism and witness, in bad experience as well as good. The situations we go through, the things that bind us as people, all have the power to equate to evangelistic witness, if we will allow God to move in and through us, even in difficult times. Ruth picked up on enough about her in-laws' faith to move her to a profound sense of spiritual realization, to desire the knowledge of this God that she didn't know, but saw firsthand in her family life.

The book of Ruth has to feature an interfaith marriage, however, in order to create the stage for the spiritual type it contains. As with all things Scriptural, there is a purpose to the placement, and something we need to learn from it. Rather than create endless debates for and against interfaith marriage, the book of Ruth is present in the Bible to show us the unity, and the promise, of the church. For the church to even exist, we must see a most profound spiritual interfaith marriage: that of Jew and Gentile, not for one to become the other, but for both to become something else, something different, something greater and more than they are by themselves. Within the church, we become something new and different, a present unity that has never been done before, because of the work of our Redeemer, Christ.

CHRIST CAME AND PREACHED [PROCLAIMED THE GOOD NEWS OF] PEACE [IS. 52:7] TO YOU WHO WERE FAR AWAY FROM GOD [FAR AWAY/OFF], AND TO THOSE WHO WERE NEAR TO GOD [NEAR; IS. 57:19]. YES, IT IS [FOR; OR SO THAT] THROUGH CHRIST WE ALL HAVE THE RIGHT TO COME [FREE ACCESS] TO THE FATHER IN [BY] ONE SPIRIT.

NOW YOU GENTILES ARE NOT FOREIGNERS OR STRANGERS ANY LONGER, BUT ARE CITIZENS TOGETHER WITH GOD'S HOLY PEOPLE [THE SAINTS]. YOU BELONG TO GOD'S FAMILY [HOUSEHOLD]. YOU ARE LIKE A BUILDING THAT WAS BUILT [...HAVING BEEN BUILT] ON THE FOUNDATION OF THE APOSTLES AND PROPHETS. CHRIST JESUS HIMSELF IS THE MOST IMPORTANT STONE [CORNERSTONE; OR CAPSTONE; IS. 28:16; 1 COR. 3:11] IN THAT BUILDING, AND THAT WHOLE BUILDING IS JOINED TOGETHER IN CHRIST. HE MAKES IT GROW AND BECOME A HOLY TEMPLE IN THE LORD. AND IN CHRIST YOU, TOO, ARE BEING BUILT TOGETHER WITH THE JEWS [BUILT TOGETHER] INTO A PLACE WHERE GOD LIVES THROUGH THE SPIRIT. (Ephesians 2:17-22)

This reality, spoken of here in Ephesians, was shadowed years earlier in the relationship between Ruth and Naomi. Long before there were millions, there were two. A Jew and a Gentile bound by marriage, who forged a commitment, even after that marriage faded into non-existence due to spousal death. Ruth, a Gentile, makes a powerful pledge to her mother-in-law, a Jew, even though no such law, code, or expectation existed at this point in time. As Ruth made her commitment to Naomi, she heralded the heart of the church, the eternal unity that makes us one in Christ.

THE WOMEN CRIED TOGETHER OUT LOUD [RAISED THEIR VOICES AND WEPT] AGAIN. THEN ORPAH KISSED HER MOTHER-IN-LAW NAOMI GOOD-BYE, BUT RUTH HELD ON [CLUNG] TO HER TIGHTLY.

NAOMI SAID TO RUTH, "LOOK, YOUR SISTER-IN-LAW IS GOING BACK TO HER OWN PEOPLE AND HER OWN GODS [*OR* GOD; CHEMOSH WAS THE CHIEF GOD OF THE MOABITES; 1 KIN. 11:33]. GO BACK WITH HER."

BUT RUTH SAID, "DON'T BEG [URGE] ME TO LEAVE [ABANDON] YOU OR TO STOP FOLLOWING [TURN BACK FROM] YOU. WHERE YOU GO, I WILL GO. WHERE YOU LIVE, I WILL LIVE. YOUR PEOPLE WILL BE MY PEOPLE, AND YOUR GOD WILL BE MY GOD. AND WHERE YOU DIE, I WILL DIE, AND THERE I WILL BE BURIED. MAY THE LORD PUNISH ME TERRIBLY [DO TO ME AND EVEN MORE] IF I DO NOT KEEP THIS PROMISE: NOT EVEN [*OR* NOTHING BUT] DEATH WILL SEPARATE US." (Ruth 1:14-17)

Frequently cited at weddings, Ruth's pledge to Naomi is far more than an expression of human love and interaction. This passage contains the ultimate promise for the unity of the Jew and Gentile together, becoming one in Christ. There is nothing higher for us to aspire to: to remain together, for our people to become one, and for God to be our God. No matter what happens, we shall be together unto death, and even now, as believers, we know that we have the future of the resurrection to bind us together into eternity. This is the song of the church; a bond of love unbreakable, maintained through life beyond death, a unity and a power, one that cannot be overcome by any force present in this world.

Ruth literally lived her bond to Naomi, as she left her people, her place of dwelling, her nation, her identity, and her god to follow Naomi unto the place where they would find their personal redeemer. It was not simple; it required sacrifice; and proves that just because we are in Christ does not mean our lives will be easy. Ruth was the one who had to work hard, deal with an older and deeply grieved and unhappy, embittered woman, and confront the changes that were a part of her life. We, too, as believers, also experience these same issues. We must work hard, we must deal with older saints who are hardened and embittered by the difficulties of life and confront our own changes as we stay the course God has placed us on. There are many twists and turns that seem unfair and unjust, but the point of Ruth's work and commitment is that God has a way of working things out, bringing us to a place of redemption from what we experience as much as what we need spiritually, and often in places and ways we would never have considered.

The Kinsman-Redeemer

In ancient times, the warm, fuzzy feelings we expect to feel for our relatives (particularly relatives that were in-laws) were often not a part of everyday life. People aligned with their families and clans, they were quick to defend their family name and honor, but marriages were often tricky businesses brought about to create alliances and goodwill between families and tribal groups. It wasn't about love, romance, or establishing something new. Rather, married life was about connecting the old, creating lineages into perpetuity. The primary goal was to preserve land and property from generation to generation. This sounds simple enough, but it wasn't always so easily accomplished. Naomi encouraged Orprah and Ruth to return to their own families so they could be remarried, even though such wouldn't be an easy task. Bridal prices for virgins were significantly higher than for widowed women, even though Orprah and Ruth were still of childbearing age. Still, it was customary for Ruth and Orprah to return to their own families, because it was understood their family members would find new spouses for them among their own people to raise new families. Neither Ruth nor Orprah had any children, and there were no immediate living male relatives (brothers) to take Chilion and Mahlon's places, so the women were no longer bound to Naomi in a familial sense.

This makes Ruth's proclamation of commitment that much more extraordinary, and that much more spiritual in nature. Ruth knew that something more was connected to her life with Naomi, and she was to make that connection. Yet when Ruth proclaimed her commitment to Naomi, let's understand that she wasn't looking for a mate, or a spouse, or to get married again. She wasn't running around looking for Boaz. She was living her life, following the guidance of a God that she didn't know for herself, except through her interactions with her in-laws. Such was familiar and new, and required her to navigate her territory accordingly.

BOAZ[5]

- *BOAZ* "QUICKNESS," AN ANCESTOR OF DAVID, ALSO A
  PILLAR BEFORE THE TEMPLE
- ORIGINAL WORD: בֹּעַז
- PART OF SPEECH: PROPER NAME MASCULINE
- TRANSLITERATION: BOAZ
- PHONETIC SPELLING: (BO'-AZ)
- SHORT DEFINITION: BOAZ

Still, there would be someone who would enter the picture who would make Ruth and Naomi family again, in a literal sense. Where the church is, there we also find Christ, and while this book is about feminine spiritual expressions, we should examine the position of the Kinsman-Redeemer, because his work was parallel to that of Christ. It was Ruth's labor in the fields during the barley harvest that brought her to Boaz, who is Naomi's distant relative.

NOW NAOMI HAD A RICH [OR INFLUENTIAL; MAN OF GREAT WEALTH/STANDING] RELATIVE NAMED BOAZ, FROM ELIMELECH'S FAMILY [CLAN].

ONE DAY RUTH, THE MOABITE, SAID TO NAOMI, "[PLEASE] LET ME GO TO THE FIELDS. MAYBE SOMEONE WILL BE KIND ENOUGH TO [IN WHOSE EYES/SIGHT I FIND GRACE/FAVOR WILL] LET ME GATHER THE GRAIN HE LEAVES BEHIND [GLEAN AMONG THE SHEAVES/BUNDLES; DEUT. 24:21–22]."

NAOMI SAID, "GO, MY DAUGHTER."

SO RUTH WENT TO THE FIELDS AND GATHERED THE GRAIN THAT THE WORKERS CUTTING THE GRAIN HAD LEFT BEHIND [AND GLEANED IN THE FIELD BEHIND THE REAPERS/HARVESTERS]. IT JUST SO HAPPENED THAT THE FIELD BELONGED TO BOAZ, FROM ELIMELECH'S FAMILY [CLAN; A CHANCE EVENT FROM RUTH'S PERSPECTIVE, BUT PART OF GOD'S PLAN].

SOON [OR JUST THEN; AND LOOK/BEHOLD] BOAZ CAME FROM BETHLEHEM AND GREETED HIS WORKERS [REAPERS; HARVESTERS], "THE LORD BE WITH YOU!"

AND THE WORKERS ANSWERED, "MAY THE LORD BLESS YOU!"

THEN BOAZ ASKED HIS SERVANT [YOUNG MAN; FOREMAN] IN CHARGE OF THE WORKERS [REAPERS; HARVESTERS], "WHOSE GIRL IS THAT [TO WHOM DOES THAT YOUNG WOMAN BELONG; REFERRING, IN THIS PATRIARCHAL CULTURE, TO HER HUSBAND OR FATHER]?"

THE SERVANT [YOUNG MAN; FOREMAN] ANSWERED, "SHE IS THE YOUNG MOABITE WOMAN WHO CAME BACK WITH NAOMI FROM THE COUNTRY [LAND] OF MOAB. SHE SAID, 'PLEASE LET ME FOLLOW THE WORKERS CUTTING GRAIN [REAPERS; HARVESTERS] AND GATHER WHAT THEY LEAVE BEHIND [GLEAN AMONG THE SHEAVES/BUNDLES].' SHE CAME AND HAS REMAINED HERE, FROM MORNING UNTIL JUST NOW. SHE HAS STOPPED ONLY A FEW MOMENTS [OR JUST NOW STOPPED FOR A MOMENT] TO REST IN THE SHELTER [HUT; HOUSE]."

THEN BOAZ SAID TO RUTH, "LISTEN [HAVE YOU NOT HEARD...?], MY DAUGHTER. DON'T GO TO GATHER GRAIN FOR YOURSELF [GLEAN] IN ANOTHER FIELD. DON'T EVEN LEAVE THIS FIELD AT ALL, BUT CONTINUE FOLLOWING CLOSELY BEHIND [STAY CLOSE TO; CLING TO] MY WOMEN WORKERS [SERVANT GIRLS; YOUNG WOMEN]. WATCH TO SEE INTO WHICH FIELDS THEY [THE MEN REAPING; THE HEBREW PRONOUN IS MASCULINE] GO TO CUT GRAIN [REAP] AND FOLLOW THEM [THE WOMEN GATHERING; THE HEBREW PRONOUN IS FEMININE]. I HAVE WARNED [OR WILL WARN] THE YOUNG MEN NOT TO BOTHER [HARASS; TOUCH] YOU. WHEN YOU ARE THIRSTY, YOU MAY GO AND DRINK FROM THE WATER JUGS THAT THE YOUNG MEN HAVE FILLED [DRAWN (FROM THE WELL)]."

THEN RUTH BOWED LOW WITH HER FACE TO THE GROUND AND SAID TO HIM, "I AM NOT AN ISRAELITE [A FOREIGNER]. WHY HAVE YOU BEEN SO KIND TO NOTICE ME [I FOUND FAVOR/GRACE IN YOUR EYES]?"

BOAZ ANSWERED HER, "I KNOW [HAVE BEEN FULLY INFORMED] ABOUT ALL THE HELP YOU HAVE GIVEN [THAT YOU HAVE DONE FOR] YOUR MOTHER-IN-LAW AFTER YOUR HUSBAND DIED. YOU LEFT YOUR FATHER AND MOTHER AND YOUR OWN COUNTRY [NATIVE LAND] TO

COME TO A NATION [PEOPLE] WHERE YOU DID NOT KNOW ANYONE. MAY THE LORD REWARD YOU FOR ALL YOU HAVE DONE. MAY YOUR WAGES BE PAID IN FULL BY THE LORD, THE GOD OF ISRAEL, UNDER WHOSE WINGS YOU HAVE COME FOR SHELTER [LIKE A PROTECTIVE MOTHER BIRD]."

THEN RUTH SAID, "I HOPE I CAN CONTINUE TO PLEASE YOU [MAY I CONTINUE TO FIND GRACE/FAVOR IN YOUR EYES; OR I HAVE FOUND FAVOR/GRACE IN YOUR EYES], SIR [MY LORD]. [BECAUSE] YOU HAVE SAID KIND AND ENCOURAGING WORDS TO [COMFORTED AND SPOKEN TO THE HEART OF] ME, YOUR SERVANT, THOUGH I AM NOT ONE OF YOUR SERVANTS."

AT MEALTIME BOAZ TOLD RUTH, "COME HERE. EAT SOME OF OUR BREAD AND DIP IT IN OUR SAUCE [THE VINEGAR/WINE-VINEGAR]." SO RUTH SAT DOWN BESIDE THE WORKERS [REAPERS; HARVESTERS]. BOAZ HANDED [OFFERED; SERVED] HER SOME ROASTED GRAIN, AND SHE ATE UNTIL SHE WAS FULL [SATISFIED]; SHE EVEN HAD SOME FOOD LEFT OVER. WHEN RUTH ROSE AND WENT BACK TO WORK, BOAZ COMMANDED HIS WORKERS [YOUNG MEN], "LET HER GATHER [GLEAN] EVEN AROUND THE PILES OF CUT GRAIN [SHEAVES]. DON'T TELL HER TO GO AWAY [REPRIMAND/INSULT/HUMILIATE HER]. IN FACT, PULL OUT SOME FULL HEADS OF GRAIN FOR HER FROM THE BUNDLES AND LET HER GATHER THEM. DON'T TELL HER TO STOP [REBUKE/SCOLD HER]."

SO RUTH GATHERED GRAIN IN THE FIELD UNTIL EVENING. THEN SHE SEPARATED THE GRAIN FROM THE CHAFF [THRESHED/BEAT OUT WHAT SHE HAD GLEANED], AND THERE WAS ABOUT ONE-HALF BUSHEL [AN EPHAH; ABOUT 30 POUNDS] OF BARLEY. RUTH CARRIED THE GRAIN INTO TOWN, AND HER MOTHER-IN-LAW SAW HOW MUCH SHE HAD GATHERED [GLEANED]. RUTH ALSO TOOK OUT THE FOOD THAT WAS LEFT OVER FROM LUNCH [AFTER SHE WAS FULL/SATISFIED] AND GAVE IT TO NAOMI.

NAOMI [HER MOTHER-IN-LAW] ASKED HER, "WHERE DID YOU GATHER ALL THIS GRAIN [GLEAN] TODAY? WHERE DID YOU WORK? BLESSED BE WHOEVER NOTICED YOU!"

RUTH TOLD HER MOTHER-IN-LAW IN WHOSE FIELD SHE HAD WORKED. SHE SAID, "THE MAN I WORKED WITH TODAY IS NAMED BOAZ."

NAOMI TOLD HER DAUGHTER-IN-LAW, "THE LORD BLESS HIM! HE CONTINUES TO BE KIND TO US—BOTH [...WHO HAS NOT ABANDONED] THE LIVING AND THE DEAD!" THEN NAOMI TOLD RUTH, "BOAZ IS ONE OF OUR CLOSE RELATIVES, ONE WHO SHOULD TAKE CARE OF US [OF OUR GUARDIANS/KINSMEN-REDEEMERS; A RELATIVE WHO WOULD CARE FOR A BEREAVED FAMILY IN VARIOUS WAYS: LOOKING AFTER DESTITUTE MEMBERS (LEV. 25:35); AVENGING A MURDERED RELATIVE (NUM. 35:19); MARRYING A SISTER-IN-LAW TO RAISE UP CHILDREN FOR HER DECEASED HUSBAND (DEUT. 25:5–10; CALLED "LEVIRATE" MARRIAGE); BUYING BACK FAMILY LAND (LEV. 25:25) OR REDEEMING FAMILY MEMBERS WHO HAD BEEN SOLD AS SLAVES (LEV. 25:47–49)]." (Ruth 2:1-20)

We are not exactly sure how Boaz was related to Naomi, but we do know that in terms of familial redemption and restoration of the familial line, there was at least one other known person, closer to Ruth in age, in existence (Ruth 3:12-13). Boaz was close enough, however, to fulfill the requirements as kinsman-redeemer for them, required to care for them, marrying a relative to restore the line and raise up children in that line, and buying back family inherited land.

The kinsman-redeemer was specifically a male relative with the ability to act on behalf of another relative who was in need. The term literally relates to being or acting as a rescuer, redeemer, or vindicator. The traditional image, or role, of a kinsman-redeemer was very literal, as we can see within Ruth's story. His role was to redeem the inheritance lost due to familial male deaths with no living male heir.

We don't know very much about Boaz as a person, save a few Bible verses and some random traditions, none of which seem to agree with one another. The one universal facet we know about Boaz is that he was a pious and devout man, pious enough to become the kinsman-redeemer for Ruth and Naomi.

It's relevant that in examining the connection between Ruth and Naomi as church, Naomi's relative-in-law was the link, the bond, in the two coming together as lawful family. The promise of the spiritual Redeemer was to come through the tribe of Judah, and we all know that Ruth is mentioned in the lineage of Jesus Christ (Matthew 1:5). Through Naomi's side, we find the redeemer, Boaz. Through that lineage, the marriage of Boaz and Ruth, we find the spiritual Redeemer, Christ.

It is also important to note that Ruth was working for the kinsman-redeemer, in the fields, in the harvest, when she met him. We are called to work for the Redeemer when we herald the call, in the harvest of souls. It is a hard work, but in that place, that is where we find Him, the most, in our lives. Sometimes we seek to avoid the work He has called us to do, and go looking for Him in all sorts of places. No matter how tranquil we may find a space or how comfortable we might be, we cannot avoid the fact that God has called us to labor, to do hard things, and to do hard work, just as Ruth was called to do. If we desire to find what we seek, we must attune ourselves to the work of the harvest.

JESUS SAID TO HIS FOLLOWERS [DISCIPLES], "THERE ARE MANY PEOPLE TO HARVEST [THE HARVEST IS GREAT/LARGE] BUT THERE ARE ONLY A FEW WORKERS [THE WORKERS/LABORERS ARE FEW]. SO PRAY TO THE LORD WHO OWNS [WHO IS IN CHARGE OF; OF] THE HARVEST, THAT HE WILL SEND MORE WORKERS [LABORERS] TO GATHER [INTO] HIS HARVEST." (Matthew 9:37-38)
We do not have a church if we do not have a Redeemer, which is why Boaz emerges on scene in the story of Ruth and Naomi. His position was not one to create a fairy tale happy ending (which is how many take it), but to complete the picture of the Jew and Gentile coming together as one. The reality is that Boaz was a human being, a type of spiritual things, but that doesn't mean he ran into this deal head-first, thrilled and excited to do it. He was hesitant to take on this responsibility, most likely, for a number of reasons. Tradition cites Boaz as substantially older than Ruth (some place him around eighty years of age). We have no indication Boaz was looking to get married at whatever point of life he might have been at, and he wasn't interested in Ruth in a marital perspective. Getting married was not in Boaz's plan. If we look at the story, it was Naomi's persistence that directed Ruth in what she was to do with Boaz, and not at Boaz's persistence or desire. Often women pray for and desire a Boaz, when apparently, if we look at the story, they should ask God for a Naomi!

THEN NAOMI, RUTH'S MOTHER-IN-LAW, SAID TO HER, "MY DAUGHTER, I MUST [SHOULD I NOT...?] FIND A SUITABLE HOME [REST; A HUSBAND AND A HOME TO PROVIDE SECURITY] FOR YOU, ONE THAT WILL BE GOOD FOR YOU [OR SO YOU WILL BE SECURE; THAT IT WILL

GO/BE WELL FOR YOU]. NOW BOAZ, WHOSE YOUNG WOMEN [FEMALE SERVANTS] YOU WORKED WITH, IS OUR CLOSE RELATIVE [AND SO AN APPROPRIATE GUARDIAN/KINSMAN-REDEEMER TO MARRY RUTH; 2:20]. [LOOK; BEHOLD] TONIGHT HE WILL BE WORKING [WINNOWING BARLEY] AT THE THRESHING FLOOR. WASH YOURSELF, PUT ON PERFUME, CHANGE YOUR CLOTHES [OR GET DRESSED UP; OR PUT ON YOUR CLOAK], AND GO DOWN TO THE THRESHING FLOOR. BUT DON'T LET HIM KNOW YOU'RE THERE UNTIL HE HAS FINISHED HIS DINNER [EATING AND DRINKING]. WATCH HIM SO YOU WILL KNOW WHERE HE LIES DOWN TO SLEEP. WHEN HE LIES DOWN, GO AND LIFT THE COVER OFF [UNCOVER] HIS FEET [OR LEGS; EVIDENTLY AN APPEAL FOR MARRIAGE] AND LIE DOWN. HE WILL TELL YOU WHAT YOU SHOULD DO."

THEN RUTH ANSWERED, "I WILL DO EVERYTHING YOU SAY."

SO RUTH WENT DOWN TO THE THRESHING FLOOR AND DID ALL HER MOTHER-IN-LAW TOLD [INSTRUCTED; COMMANDED] HER TO DO. AFTER HIS EVENING MEAL [HE HAD EATEN AND DRUNK], BOAZ FELT GOOD [HIS HEART WAS GOOD/PLEASED] AND WENT TO SLEEP LYING BESIDE [AT THE END OF] THE PILE OF GRAIN. RUTH WENT TO HIM QUIETLY AND LIFTED THE COVER FROM HIS FEET AND LAY DOWN.

ABOUT MIDNIGHT BOAZ WAS STARTLED [OR SHUDDERED] AND ROLLED OVER. [AND LOOK/BEHOLD] THERE WAS A WOMAN LYING NEAR HIS FEET! BOAZ ASKED, "WHO ARE YOU?"

SHE SAID, "I AM RUTH, YOUR SERVANT GIRL. SPREAD YOUR COVER [OR THE CORNER OF YOUR GARMENT; OR YOUR WINGS; 2:12] OVER ME [A REQUEST FOR THE PROVISION AND PROTECTION OF MARRIAGE], BECAUSE YOU ARE A RELATIVE WHO IS SUPPOSED TO TAKE CARE OF ME [GUARDIAN; KINSMAN-REDEEMER; 2:20]."

THEN BOAZ SAID, "THE LORD BLESS YOU, MY DAUGHTER. THIS [SECOND; LAST] ACT OF KINDNESS IS GREATER THAN THE KINDNESS YOU SHOWED TO NAOMI IN THE BEGINNING [FIRST]. YOU DIDN'T LOOK FOR A YOUNG MAN TO MARRY, EITHER RICH OR POOR. NOW, MY DAUGHTER, DON'T BE AFRAID. I WILL DO EVERYTHING YOU ASK, BECAUSE ALL THE PEOPLE IN OUR TOWN KNOW YOU ARE A GOOD [WORTHY; NOBLE] WOMAN [PROV. 31:10]. IT IS TRUE THAT I AM A RELATIVE WHO IS TO TAKE CARE OF YOU [GUARDIAN; KINSMEN-

REDEEMER; 2:20], BUT YOU HAVE A CLOSER RELATIVE THAN I. STAY HERE TONIGHT, AND IN THE MORNING WE WILL SEE IF HE WILL TAKE CARE OF [BE A GUARDIAN FOR; REDEEM] YOU. IF HE DECIDES TO TAKE CARE OF [BE A GUARDIAN FOR; REDEEM] YOU, THAT IS FINE. BUT IF HE REFUSES, I WILL TAKE CARE OF [BE A GUARDIAN FOR; REDEEM] YOU MYSELF, AS SURELY AS THE LORD LIVES. SO STAY HERE [LIE DOWN] UNTIL MORNING."

SO RUTH STAYED NEAR HIS FEET UNTIL MORNING BUT GOT UP WHILE IT WAS STILL TOO DARK TO RECOGNIZE ANYONE. BOAZ THOUGHT, "PEOPLE IN TOWN MUST NOT KNOW THAT THE WOMAN CAME HERE TO THE THRESHING FLOOR." SO BOAZ SAID TO RUTH, "BRING ME YOUR SHAWL [CLOAK] AND HOLD IT OPEN."

SO RUTH HELD HER SHAWL [CLOAK] OPEN, AND BOAZ POURED SIX PORTIONS OF BARLEY INTO IT. BOAZ THEN PUT IT ON HER HEAD [*OR* HER BACK; HER] AND WENT BACK TO THE CITY.

WHEN RUTH WENT BACK TO HER MOTHER-IN-LAW, NAOMI ASKED, "HOW DID YOU DO [THINGS GO], MY DAUGHTER?"

RUTH TOLD NAOMI EVERYTHING THAT BOAZ [THE MAN] DID FOR HER. SHE SAID, "BOAZ GAVE ME THESE SIX PORTIONS OF BARLEY, SAYING, 'YOU MUST NOT GO HOME WITHOUT A GIFT FOR [EMPTY TO] YOUR MOTHER-IN-LAW.'"

NAOMI ANSWERED, "WAIT [STAY HERE; *OR* BE PATIENT], MY DAUGHTER, UNTIL YOU SEE WHAT HAPPENS. BOAZ [THE MAN] WILL NOT REST UNTIL HE HAS FINISHED DOING WHAT HE SHOULD DO TODAY." (RUTH 3:1-18)

The strategy and workable pursuit as pertain to Ruth's relationship with Boaz is an entire contrast to modern-day values and ideas about women. While many debate the legitimacy of a woman proposing to a man, that is exactly what happened in the book of Ruth. Had Ruth not followed Naomi's advice and literally thrown herself at Boaz to propose marriage, things would never have progressed, nor moved along, as hoped. It was Ruth's command to make the moves in the relationship, as is the case in some relationships even today, so that essential decisions can be made as relate to future possible relationship progress. Any time a woman chooses to propose to a man, she follows not only Ruth's footsteps, but the footsteps of church prophecy, and embodies that within her own life.

There is something else here, however, to which we need to pay careful attention, and yes, it relates to Ruth's type as a shadow of the church. Jeremiah's prophecy in chapter 31, verse 22 (as was mentioned earlier) cites a woman as a pursuer, wooer, and protector of a man. This was spoken of as being a "new thing," because it wasn't a common concept we have of women. Here in Ruth, we see her as compassing Boaz, as his pursuer. By so doing, Ruth took on a specific role that the church takes on for the Lord as part of our call and command in this "new thing." As Ruth desired to be with Boaz because she knew he was worth and worthy of her pursuit, so we should desire to be with our Lord, and we take on our role to protect His reputation, His work and His Gospel in this world. We must be willing to take the risk, because our Redeemer is worth our pursuit.

BOAZ WENT TO THE CITY GATE [THE HUB OF THE TOWN FOR JUDICIAL, BUSINESS, AND SOCIAL INTERACTION] AND SAT THERE UNTIL THE CLOSE RELATIVE [GUARDIAN; KINSMAN-REDEEMER; 2:20] HE HAD MENTIONED PASSED BY. BOAZ CALLED TO HIM, "COME HERE [TURN ASIDE], FRIEND [OR SO-AND-SO; THE MAN IS NOT NAMED, PERHAPS IRONICALLY BECAUSE HE REFUSED TO PRESERVE NAOMI'S FAMILY NAME], AND SIT DOWN." SO THE MAN CAME OVER [TURNED ASIDE] AND SAT DOWN. BOAZ GATHERED TEN OF THE ELDERS OF THE CITY AND TOLD THEM, "SIT DOWN HERE!" SO THEY SAT DOWN.

THEN BOAZ SAID TO THE CLOSE RELATIVE [GUARDIAN; KINSMAN-REDEEMER], "NAOMI, WHO HAS COME BACK FROM THE COUNTRY OF MOAB, WANTS TO SELL [IS SELLING] THE PIECE OF LAND THAT BELONGED TO OUR RELATIVE ELIMELECH [IT WAS IMPORTANT IN ISRAEL TO KEEP PROPERTY IN THE FAMILY]. SO I DECIDED [OR THOUGHT IT MY OBLIGATION] TO TELL YOU ABOUT IT: IF YOU WANT TO BUY BACK THE LAND [REDEEM IT], THEN BUY IT [REDEEM] IN FRONT OF THE PEOPLE WHO ARE SITTING HERE AND IN FRONT OF THE ELDERS OF MY PEOPLE. BUT IF YOU DON'T WANT TO BUY IT, TELL ME, BECAUSE YOU ARE THE ONLY ONE [OR FIRST IN LINE] WHO CAN BUY IT, AND I AM NEXT AFTER YOU."

THE CLOSE RELATIVE ANSWERED, "I WILL BUY BACK THE LAND [REDEEM IT]."

THEN BOAZ EXPLAINED, "WHEN YOU BUY [ACQUIRE] THE LAND FROM [THE HAND OF] NAOMI, YOU MUST ALSO MARRY [ACQUIRE] RUTH, THE MOABITE, THE DEAD MAN'S WIFE. THAT WAY, THE LAND WILL STAY IN THE DEAD MAN'S NAME [...TO RAISE UP A NAME FOR THE DEAD MAN UPON HIS INHERITANCE]."

THE CLOSE RELATIVE [GUARDIAN; KINSMAN-REDEEMER] ANSWERED, "I CAN'T BUY BACK THE LAND [REDEEM IT]. IF I DID, I MIGHT HARM [DESTROY; ENDANGER; PUT IN JEOPARDY] WHAT I CAN PASS ON TO MY OWN SONS [MY INHERITANCE]. I CANNOT BUY THE LAND BACK [REDEEM IT], SO BUY IT [REDEEM IT FOR] YOURSELF."

LONG AGO IN ISRAEL WHEN PEOPLE TRADED OR BOUGHT BACK [FOR THE REDEMPTION AND TRANSFER OF] SOMETHING, ONE PERSON TOOK OFF HIS SANDAL AND GAVE IT TO THE OTHER PERSON. THIS WAS THE PROOF OF OWNERSHIP [OR VALIDATION OF THE TRANSACTION] IN ISRAEL.

SO THE CLOSE RELATIVE [GUARDIAN; KINSMAN-REDEEMER] SAID TO BOAZ, "BUY THE LAND YOURSELF," AND HE TOOK OFF HIS SANDAL.

THEN BOAZ SAID TO THE ELDERS AND TO ALL THE PEOPLE, "YOU ARE WITNESSES TODAY. I AM BUYING [HAVE BOUGHT] FROM NAOMI EVERYTHING THAT BELONGED TO ELIMELECH AND KILION AND MAHLON. I AM ALSO TAKING [HAVE ALSO ACQUIRED] RUTH, THE MOABITE, WHO WAS THE WIFE OF MAHLON, AS MY WIFE. I AM DOING THIS SO HER DEAD HUSBAND'S PROPERTY WILL STAY IN HIS NAME AND HIS NAME WILL NOT BE SEPARATED [...SO THAT HIS NAME WILL NOT BE CUT OFF] FROM HIS FAMILY [BROTHERS] AND HIS HOMETOWN [THE GATE OF HIS PLACE]. YOU ARE WITNESSES TODAY."

SO ALL THE PEOPLE AND ELDERS WHO WERE AT THE CITY GATE SAID, "WE ARE WITNESSES. MAY THE LORD MAKE THIS WOMAN, WHO IS COMING INTO YOUR HOME, LIKE RACHEL AND LEAH, WHO TOGETHER BUILT UP THE PEOPLE [HOUSE] OF ISRAEL [THE TWELVE SONS OF ISRAEL WERE BORN TO LEAH, RACHEL AND THEIR SERVANT GIRLS; GEN. 29:31—30:24]. MAY YOU BECOME POWERFUL [OR WEALTHY; OR RENOWNED] IN THE DISTRICT OF EPHRATHAH AND FAMOUS

[RENOWNED] IN BETHLEHEM. AS TAMAR GAVE BIRTH TO JUDAH'S SON PEREZ [AN ANCESTOR OF BOAZ (V. 18) WHOSE BIRTH RESULTED FROM A LEVIRATE UNION (2:20; GEN. 38:27–30; DEUT. 25:5–10) AND SO WAS PARALLEL TO THIS SITUATION], MAY THE LORD GIVE YOU MANY CHILDREN THROUGH RUTH. MAY YOUR FAMILY BE GREAT LIKE HIS."

SO BOAZ TOOK RUTH HOME AS HIS WIFE AND HAD SEXUAL RELATIONS WITH [WENT IN TO] HER. THE LORD LET HER BECOME PREGNANT, AND SHE GAVE BIRTH TO A SON. THE WOMEN TOLD NAOMI, "PRAISE [BLESSED BE] THE LORD WHO GAVE YOU THIS GRANDSON [HAS NOT LEFT YOU TODAY WITHOUT A GUARDIAN/KINSMAN-REDEEMER]. MAY HE [HIS NAME] BECOME FAMOUS [RENOWNED] IN ISRAEL. HE WILL GIVE YOU NEW [RESTORE/RENEW YOUR] LIFE AND WILL TAKE CARE OF YOU IN YOUR OLD AGE BECAUSE OF YOUR DAUGHTER-IN-LAW WHO LOVES YOU. SHE IS BETTER FOR YOU THAN SEVEN SONS, BECAUSE SHE HAS GIVEN BIRTH TO YOUR GRANDSON [HIM]."

NAOMI TOOK THE BOY, HELD HIM IN HER ARMS [OR PUT HIM ON HER LAP; OR TOOK HIM TO HER BREAST], AND CARED FOR HIM [OR BECAME HIS NURSE/CAREGIVER]. THE NEIGHBORS GAVE THE BOY HIS NAME, SAYING, "THIS BOY WAS [A SON HAS BEEN] BORN FOR NAOMI." THEY NAMED HIM OBED ["SERVANT"]. OBED WAS THE FATHER OF JESSE, AND JESSE WAS THE FATHER OF DAVID [ISRAEL'S GREATEST KING, THROUGH WHOM THE MESSIAH WOULD COME; 2 SAM. 7:11–17; MATT. 1:1, 5–6; LUKE 3:32].

THIS IS THE FAMILY HISTORY OF PEREZ, THE FATHER OF HEZRON. HEZRON WAS THE FATHER OF RAM, WHO WAS THE FATHER OF AMMINADAB. AMMINADAB WAS THE FATHER OF NAHSHON, WHO WAS THE FATHER OF SALMON. SALMON WAS THE FATHER OF BOAZ, WHO WAS THE FATHER OF OBED. OBED WAS THE FATHER OF JESSE, AND JESSE WAS THE FATHER OF DAVID [MATT. 1:3–6; LUKE 3:31–33]. (Ruth 4:1-22)

The final chapter of Ruth provides the perspective of a happy ending, the family united thanks to the work of the kinsman-redeemer, existing and dwelling in peace. Everyone found their renewed purpose; everyone came to find the completeness they sought, as new life began. That is exactly what Christ does for us; He is the source of our completeness, of our new day, of the work of the church itself, and it is no accident that through this powerful lineage, created by the risk and love of two women, that King David's grandfather was born, and raised, by Ruth and Naomi.

Recognizing Christ within

As we've seen, the book of Ruth teaches us much about the nature of the church, and even the relationship between the church and Christ. In like fashion, the book of Esther teaches us about the nature of Christ, and the work of John the Baptist. It is not in an obvious or overstated way, but present in the book of Esther is one of the most powerful examples we have of the love of God and the way He often works among His people, unrecognized, and under-acknowledged. Within Esther, we see a place where the nature of Christ hides without consideration or fanfare, and for that reason, it benefits us to examine its purpose and placement, so we might understand it fully.

One of our greatest tasks as believers is to find Christ in our Scriptures, living and active, within and among the characters present in our Bible histories. The history of the Bible is not just for ancient times, but is relevant and alive now, and recognizing this should make every one of us aware of Christ's presence, within and among us, today. The Bible isn't just history, it is also now; and whether we consider it, we face the same predicaments and decisions that people did in Biblical times. The more we learn about Bible situations, characters, and individuals, the better we can see Christ with us, now, influencing and moving within us in the many different circumstances we face today.

The book of Esther is one such setting where Christ's presence is most relevant, even if it seems understated. The challenge of bigotry and annihilation of a specified group of people, potential genocide, injustice, mistreatment of women, and the question of our girls and their position in their relationships are all situations that we face today, as much as many of us would like to pretend to the contrary. Even though the Name of God is not spoken in Esther, God is still there, just as He is in all our situations and circumstances that are socially uncomfortable and challenging, whether noted by Name, or not. Sometimes God is present, just because we do the right thing, and there is nothing more to it than that.

I once heard a story about the founder of the ASPCA. The person who founded the organization looked around, in total horror, seeing cases of horrific animal cruelty and mistreatment. When he cried out to God, "Why don't you do something?" God said to him, "I did. I created you." This story, retold of countless people in history who rose to action in times of trouble or crisis reminds us that while we wait for God to do something, we overlook that God has created us to do something in response. We love the idea of people rising to the challenge, of doing what needs to be done when it needs to be done. We love this because so few people do it. Many look around and muse and question, but do not take the needed stand to effect change when it matters most. What we do not consider, however, is that God often works through people, and that it is His desire to work through each and every one of us, for His purpose and His glory, in this life.

Jesus was the One Who ultimately rose to the challenge, taking the consequences of sin and death upon Him, that we might have the opportunity to live through Him. Jesus empowers us to live this radical life, one based upon love and commitment to our faith and our fellow man. We may not always yield to the work we have been empowered to do, operate, and complete, but we have been equipped to do so, filled with the fire of the Holy Spirit at work within us.

Perhaps there is something in this command that connects us to Esther, and makes us uncomfortable, all at the same time. Esther is a social commentary on women; on sexism, racism and genocide; and on the way that God cares about each and every one of us, enough to push each and every one of us to do the right thing in hard situations, even when it would seem that doing such is impossible. It also examines spiritual positioning, or the concept that God places us in a certain place at a certain time, for a specific work or reason. God calls us to act, even if He does not manifest Himself to us in a great and mighty sign and realizing and knowing the right things to do within, rather than always looking for something outside of us. As much as people might try to defend finer points against the book of Esther, it doesn't change that Esther reveals to each and every one of us the power of the Kingdom of God within us (Luke 17:20-21).

A prefigure of John the Baptist

> *VASHTI*
> * *VASHTI*: QUEEN OF PERSIA
> * ORIGINAL WORD: וַשְׁתִּי
> * PART OF SPEECH: PROPER NAME FEMININE
> * TRANSLITERATION: VASHTI
> * PHONETIC SPELLING: (VASH-TEE')
> * SHORT DEFINITION: VASHTI

Vashti is on the list of controversial female Biblical figures for a few reasons. The first is that Vashti represents a certain independent identity and spirit that we do not tend to laud, nor encourage, in women. We often encourage women to embody a certain assimilation of identity into their families of origin, then their husbands, and then their nuclear families, all the while assuming and encouraging women to yield to male identity. Whenever we see evidence of a woman who lauds her own self-worth or personage above familial assimilation, society (and the church) are quick to condemn her for that.

Yet when a woman yields to male authority and it costs her something – whether it is virginity or sexual status, attire, or personal demoralization – we are quick to condemn women for yielding to that assimilation. We tell her she should have known better or done better, that somehow, she invited it on herself, and that somehow, some way, what happened to her was her fault. This is a practice known as victim shaming, and it is evident it isn't a new problem within greater society. When a woman is shamed no matter what she does, that tells us something about the greater regard for women (or shall I say, the lack thereof). We see this nowhere better than in the life of Vashti, who has received the public condemnation of preachers, scholars, and even women who see fit to judge her for her decisions, rather than to see her as an icon of independence and self-respect.

THIS IS WHAT HAPPENED DURING THE TIME [DAYS] OF KING XERXES [AHASUERUS; THE PERSIAN KING WHO REIGNED ABOUT 486–465 BC],

THE KING [AHASUERUS] WHO RULED THE ONE HUNDRED TWENTY-SEVEN STATES [PROVINCES] FROM INDIA TO CUSH [IN PRESENT-DAY SUDAN AND ETHIOPIA]. IN THOSE DAYS KING XERXES [AHASUERUS] RULED FROM HIS [SAT ON HIS ROYAL THRONE IN THE] CAPITAL CITY [OR FORTRESS; CITADEL; THE WINTER RESIDENCE OF PERSIAN KINGS, SEPARATE FROM THE CITY] OF SUSA. IN THE THIRD YEAR OF HIS RULE [REIGN; ABOUT 483 BC], HE GAVE A BANQUET FOR ALL HIS IMPORTANT MEN [NOBLES] AND ROYAL OFFICERS [MINISTERS; OFFICIALS]. THE ARMY [MILITARY] LEADERS FROM PERSIA AND MEDIA AND THE IMPORTANT MEN [NOBLES] FROM ALL XERXES' EMPIRE [HIS PROVINCES] WERE THERE.

THE BANQUET [CELEBRATION] LASTED ONE HUNDRED EIGHTY DAYS. ALL DURING THAT TIME KING XERXES [AHASUERUS] WAS SHOWING OFF [DISPLAYED] THE GREAT WEALTH OF HIS KINGDOM [RICHES OF HIS ROYAL GLORY] AND HIS OWN GREAT RICHES AND GLORY [SPLENDOR OF HIS GREAT MAJESTY]. WHEN THE ONE HUNDRED EIGHTY DAYS WERE OVER [COMPLETED], THE KING GAVE ANOTHER BANQUET [THESE CELEBRATIONS MAY HAVE BEEN IN PREPARATION FOR THE PERSIAN INVASION OF GREECE IN 480 BC]. IT WAS HELD IN THE COURTYARD OF THE PALACE GARDEN FOR SEVEN DAYS, AND IT WAS FOR EVERYBODY IN THE PALACE [CITADEL; FORTRESS] AT SUSA, FROM THE GREATEST TO THE LEAST. THE COURTYARD HAD FINE WHITE ·CURTAINS [LINEN HANGINGS] AND PURPLE [BLUE; VIOLET] DRAPES THAT WERE TIED TO SILVER RINGS ON MARBLE PILLARS BY WHITE AND PURPLE CORDS. AND THERE WERE GOLD AND SILVER COUCHES ON A FLOOR SET WITH TILES [MOSAICS] OF WHITE [PORPHYRY] MARBLE [ALABASTER], SHELLS [MOTHER-OF-PEARL], AND GEMS [PRECIOUS STONES]. WINE [DRINKS] WAS SERVED IN GOLD CUPS [GOBLETS] OF VARIOUS KINDS. AND THERE WAS PLENTY [AN ABUNDANCE] OF THE KING'S WINE, BECAUSE HE WAS VERY GENEROUS [IN KEEPING WITH HIS GENEROSITY/LIBERALITY]. THE KING COMMANDED THAT THE GUESTS BE PERMITTED TO DRINK AS MUCH AS THEY WISHED [THE DRINKING WAS ACCORDING TO LAW/EDICT WITHOUT COMPULSION]. HE TOLD THE WINE SERVERS [STAFF] TO SERVE EACH MAN WHAT HE WANTED.

QUEEN VASHTI ALSO GAVE A BANQUET FOR THE WOMEN IN THE ROYAL PALACE [HOUSE] OF KING XERXES [AHASUERUS].

ON THE SEVENTH DAY OF THE BANQUET, KING XERXES [AHASUERUS] WAS VERY HAPPY [IN HIGH SPIRITS], BECAUSE OF THE WINE. HE GAVE

A COMMAND TO THE SEVEN EUNUCHS WHO SERVED HIM—MEHUMAN, BIZTHA, HARBONA, BIGTHA, ABAGTHA, ZETHAR, AND CARCAS. HE COMMANDED THEM TO BRING HIM QUEEN VASHTI, WEARING HER ROYAL CROWN. SHE WAS TO COME TO SHOW [DISPLAY] HER BEAUTY TO THE PEOPLE AND IMPORTANT MEN [NOBLES] BECAUSE SHE WAS VERY BEAUTIFUL. THE EUNUCHS TOLD QUEEN VASHTI ABOUT THE KING'S COMMAND [WORD], BUT SHE REFUSED TO COME [POSSIBLY BECAUSE SHE FELT IT WOULD BE HUMILIATING; A DANGEROUS DECISION]. THEN THE KING BECAME VERY ANGRY; HIS ANGER WAS LIKE A BURNING FIRE [BURNED IN HIM; BECAUSE IT UNDERMINED HIS AUTHORITY].

IT WAS CUSTOMARY FOR THE KING TO ASK ADVICE FROM [CONFER WITH] EXPERTS [WISE MEN] ABOUT LAW AND ORDER [JUSTICE; CUSTOM; JUDGMENT]. SO KING XERXES [AHASUERUS] SPOKE WITH THE WISE MEN WHO WOULD KNOW THE RIGHT THING TO DO [THOSE WHO UNDERSTOOD THE TIMES]. THE WISE MEN THE KING USUALLY TALKED TO [CLOSEST TO THE KING] WERE CARSHENA, SHETHAR, ADMATHA, TARSHISH, MERES, MARSENA, AND MEMUCAN, SEVEN OF THE IMPORTANT MEN [NOBLES] OF PERSIA AND MEDIA. THESE SEVEN HAD SPECIAL PRIVILEGES TO SEE [ACCESS TO] THE KING AND HAD THE HIGHEST RANK [OFFICES] IN THE KINGDOM. THE KING ASKED THEM, "WHAT DOES THE LAW SAY MUST BE DONE TO QUEEN VASHTI? SHE HAS NOT OBEYED THE COMMAND OF KING XERXES [AHASUERUS], WHICH THE EUNUCHS TOOK TO HER."

THEN MEMUCAN SAID TO THE KING AND THE OTHER IMPORTANT MEN [NOBLES], "QUEEN VASHTI HAS NOT DONE WRONG TO THE KING ALONE. SHE HAS ALSO DONE WRONG TO ALL THE IMPORTANT MEN [NOBLES] AND ALL THE PEOPLE IN ALL THE EMPIRE [PROVINCES] OF KING XERXES [AHASUERUS]. ALL THE WIVES OF THE IMPORTANT MEN [NOBLES] OF PERSIA AND MEDIA WILL HEAR ABOUT THE QUEEN'S ACTIONS [CONDUCT]. THEN THEY WILL NO LONGER HONOR [BE CONTEMPTUOUS OF; DESPISE] THEIR HUSBANDS. THEY WILL SAY, 'KING XERXES [AHASUERUS] COMMANDED QUEEN VASHTI TO BE BROUGHT TO HIM, BUT SHE REFUSED TO COME.' TODAY THE WIVES [NOBLE LADIES] OF THE IMPORTANT MEN [NOBLES] OF PERSIA AND MEDIA HAVE HEARD ABOUT THE QUEEN'S ACTIONS. SO THEY WILL SPEAK IN THE SAME WAY TO THEIR HUSBANDS [THE KING'S NOBLES], AND THERE WILL BE NO END TO DISRESPECT [CONTEMPT] AND ANGER.

"SO, OUR KING, IF IT PLEASES YOU, GIVE A ROYAL ORDER [EDICT; DECREE], AND LET IT BE WRITTEN IN THE LAWS OF PERSIA AND MEDIA, WHICH CANNOT BE CHANGED [REPEALED; REVOKED; 8:8; DAN. 6:8, 12, 15]. THE LAW SHOULD SAY VASHTI [AT THIS POINT, THE TITLE "QUEEN" IS SYMBOLICALLY DROPPED FROM BEFORE HER NAME] IS NEVER AGAIN TO ENTER THE PRESENCE OF KING XERXES [AHASUERUS]. ALSO LET THE KING GIVE HER PLACE AS QUEEN TO SOMEONE WHO IS BETTER [MORE WORTHY/DESERVING] THAN SHE IS. AND LET THE KING'S ORDER [EDICT; DECREE] BE ANNOUNCED [SPREAD] EVERYWHERE IN HIS ENORMOUS [GREAT] KINGDOM. THEN ALL THE WOMEN WILL RESPECT [HONOR] THEIR HUSBANDS, FROM THE GREATEST TO THE LEAST."

THE KING AND HIS IMPORTANT MEN [NOBLES] WERE HAPPY [PLEASED] WITH THIS ADVICE, SO KING XERXES [AHASUERUS] DID AS MEMUCAN SUGGESTED [ADVISED; PROPOSED]. HE SENT LETTERS [DISPATCHES; SCROLLS] TO ALL THE STATES [PROVINCES] OF THE KINGDOM IN THE WRITING [SCRIPT] OF EACH STATE [PROVINCE] AND IN THE LANGUAGE OF EACH GROUP OF PEOPLE. THESE LETTERS [DISPATCHES; SCROLLS] ANNOUNCED THAT EACH MAN WAS TO BE THE RULER [MASTER] OF [OVER] HIS OWN FAMILY. (ESTHER 1:1-22)

The book of Esther begins with the details of Vashti to set the stage for why and how Esther found position in Xerxes' court, at all. Vashti was, according to the text, the wife of Xerxes, thus making her the queen of the Persian empire. It is a very detailed account of the situations leading up to Xerxes' dismissal of Vashti, and why it happened. What we find by looking at the chapter are great insights into both the character of Xerxes and Vashti, and if we look objectively, we walk away recognizing one of them was very much in the wrong, and one of them was in the right – but was victim shamed.

It is important for us to start off acknowledging that neither Xerxes, nor Vashti, were Jews. There is no way that someone can read the conduct and character of Xerxes and ever consider him to be a laudable spouse, let alone a type of Christ. They were pagan rulers of a pagan nation, and we have no evidence that either knew the true God. They were people, living their own lives, following their own customs, and doing their own thing – right up until the true God intervened with their traditions and customs to prepare for something bigger than both of them.

Xerxes was a Persian ruler, reigning from Susa. Due to their great political advances, Xerxes held a banquet, in his own honor. This wasn't just any party, however. This party ran for one hundred and eighty days, or about six months, celebrating the wonder that Xerxes felt he was. So, let's think on that for a moment. Six months of non-stop acclimation, praise, and displays of wealth for one man, throughout the entire province.

Talk about being in love with oneself.

According to custom, the women and men were separated in public, for separate feasting and parties. Vashti, as queen, would have been responsible for these festivities, and the text indicates she was faithful to her duties. In fact, nothing in the Scriptures attribute anything to Vashti but clear evidence that she was a good queen, following protocol, doing what was required of her. For the six months of the banquet, Vashti dealt with Xerxes' endless arrogance, conceit, hearing how wonderful he felt he was, the endless displays of wealth, party after party, and drunk and disorderly conduct.

The story on Vashti, from this point, is relatively simple: Xerxes called her to come out, wearing her crown, to dance before his men. The significance of this is clear: Xerxes wanted everyone to behold Vashti, scantily clad, wearing the crown, so they could look upon her, realize she was his property, and envy what he had. There are numerous reasons why this would be problematic, from the concept of treating Vashti as if she was common property, all the way up to something more serious, such as the question of rape or sexual assault. Vashti knew what awaited her after dealing with Xerxes and his men and parties for six months, and she knew that what she had but one option: not to go when she was called.

Just as Ruth and Esther followed spiritual instincts to make their decisions, so did Vashti. She might not have known God in the natural realm, but she knew her instincts, and enough to follow those. It wasn't a big encounter with an angel and a trumpet, but when Vashti knew it was time to stop playing along, that came from God. Vashti had to make a stand, not just on behalf of everyone, but on behalf of herself, to stop what was going on from causing further disruption. What she did was so radical, in fact, the laws of the nation were rewritten, to prevent women from making further stands, and Vashti was thrown out of the kingdom.

Vashti didn't start out as a rebel, but to maintain her own self-respect, dignity, and safety, she had to revolt and make a stand, on behalf of herself and all the women in the kingdom who were experiencing similar mistreatment on account of her husband's lead. She left the kingdom, into the wilderness, to make her mark as a type for another Biblical figure. Vashti is a type of John the Baptist, of one who goes before another, to make and prepare the way. Had Vashti not made her stand, there would have been no room for Esther to enter the picture, in order to save her people.

The stand that Vashti made was unconventional, unheard of for her time, and challenged the powers that be for her day. She was different, unique, and she knew instinctively what she had to do when she was called to do it. Vashti's wild nature, going out of the kingdom of the world and into the wilderness, as part of the plan to come deeper with the Kingdom of God, was all a part of God's plan, because a way had to be made for the one who was to come after her.

A female type of Christ

We pay great attention to male types of Christ, forgetting that if a type is a shadow, it does not have to be so literally bound by gender to be authentic. Types point to realities but are not those realities in and of themselves. If a type points to something else, then the gender of the type is irrelevant. Thus, if we can point out that Vashti was a type of John the Baptist, then Esther, the one who Vashti made way for, is a type of Jesus Christ.

LATER, WHEN KING XERXES [AHASUERUS] WAS NOT SO ANGRY, HE REMEMBERED VASHTI AND WHAT SHE HAD DONE AND HIS ORDER [DECREE; EDICT] ABOUT HER. THEN THE KING'S PERSONAL SERVANTS [ATTENDANTS] SUGGESTED, "LET A SEARCH BE MADE FOR BEAUTIFUL YOUNG GIRLS [YOUNG WOMEN, VIRGINS, GOOD OF FORM] FOR THE KING. LET THE KING CHOOSE SUPERVISORS [COMMISSIONERS] IN EVERY STATE [PROVINCE] OF HIS KINGDOM TO BRING BEAUTIFUL YOUNG GIRLS [YOUNG WOMEN, VIRGINS, GOOD OF FORM] TO THE PALACE [CITADEL; FORTRESS; 1:2] AT SUSA. THEY SHOULD BE TAKEN TO THE WOMEN'S QUARTERS [HAREM; HOUSE OF THE WOMEN] AND PUT UNDER THE CARE [CUSTODY; AUTHORITY] OF HEGAI, THE KING'S EUNUCH IN CHARGE OF THE WOMEN [HAREM]. AND LET BEAUTY

TREATMENTS [COSMETICS; OINTMENTS] BE GIVEN TO THEM. THEN LET
THE GIRL [YOUNG WOMAN] WHO MOST PLEASES [IS GOOD IN THE EYES
OF] THE KING BECOME QUEEN IN PLACE OF VASHTI." THE KING LIKED
[WAS PLEASED/DELIGHTED BY] THIS IDEA, SO HE DID AS THEY SAID.

NOW THERE WAS A JEW IN THE PALACE [CITADEL; FORTRESS; 1:2] OF
SUSA WHOSE NAME WAS MORDECAI SON OF JAIR. JAIR WAS THE SON
OF SHIMEI, THE SON OF KISH [THESE ARE RELATIVES OF SAUL,
SHOWING THAT MORDECAI WAS HIS DESCENDANT; 1 SAM. 9:1–3; 2
SAM. 16:5]. MORDECAI WAS FROM THE TRIBE OF BENJAMIN, WHICH
HAD BEEN TAKEN CAPTIVE [INTO EXILE] FROM JERUSALEM BY
NEBUCHADNEZZAR KING OF BABYLON. THEY WERE PART OF THE
GROUP TAKEN INTO CAPTIVITY [EXILE] WITH JEHOIACHIN KING OF
JUDAH [597 BC; 2 KIN. 24:8–17]. MORDECAI HAD A COUSIN NAMED
HADASSAH, WHO HAD NO FATHER OR MOTHER, SO MORDECAI TOOK
CARE OF HER [WAS HER GUARDIAN; BROUGHT HER UP]. HADASSAH
WAS ALSO CALLED ESTHER, AND SHE HAD A VERY PRETTY FIGURE AND
FACE [WAS BEAUTIFUL OF FORM]. MORDECAI HAD ADOPTED [RAISED;
TAKEN] HER AS HIS OWN DAUGHTER WHEN HER FATHER AND MOTHER
DIED.

WHEN THE KING'S COMMAND AND ORDER [DECREE; EDICT] HAD BEEN
HEARD [PROCLAIMED], MANY GIRLS [YOUNG WOMEN] HAD BEEN
BROUGHT TO THE PALACE [CITADEL; FORTRESS; 1:2] IN SUSA AND PUT
UNDER THE CARE [CUSTODY; AUTHORITY] OF HEGAI. ESTHER WAS
ALSO TAKEN TO THE KING'S PALACE [HOUSE] AND PUT UNDER THE
CARE [CUSTODY; AUTHORITY] OF HEGAI, WHO WAS IN CHARGE OF THE
WOMEN. ESTHER PLEASED [IMPRESSED; WAS GOOD IN HIS EYES]
HEGAI, AND HE LIKED HER [FOUND FAVOR WITH HIM]. SO HEGAI
QUICKLY BEGAN GIVING ESTHER HER BEAUTY TREATMENTS
[COSMETICS; OINTMENTS] AND SPECIAL FOOD. HE GAVE HER SEVEN
SERVANT GIRLS [MAIDS; ATTENDANTS] CHOSEN FROM THE KING'S
PALACE [HOUSE]. THEN HE MOVED [TRANSFERRED] HER AND HER
SEVEN SERVANT GIRLS [MAIDS; ATTENDANTS] TO THE BEST PART OF
THE WOMEN'S QUARTERS [HAREM; HOUSE OF THE WOMEN].

ESTHER DID NOT TELL ANYONE ABOUT HER FAMILY [PEOPLE;
NATIONALITY] OR WHO HER PEOPLE WERE [HER KINDRED/LINEAGE],
BECAUSE MORDECAI HAD TOLD [INSTRUCTED] HER NOT TO. EVERY
DAY MORDECAI WALKED BACK AND FORTH ·NEAR [IN FRONT OF] THE

COURTYARD WHERE THE KING'S WOMEN LIVED [OF THE HAREM] TO FIND OUT HOW ESTHER WAS AND WHAT WAS HAPPENING TO HER.

BEFORE A GIRL COULD TAKE HER TURN WITH [TO GO TO] KING XERXES [AHASUERUS], SHE HAD TO COMPLETE TWELVE MONTHS OF BEAUTY TREATMENTS THAT WERE ORDERED [PRESCRIBED; REQUIRED] FOR THE WOMEN. FOR SIX MONTHS SHE WAS TREATED WITH OIL AND [OR OF] MYRRH AND FOR SIX MONTHS WITH PERFUMES [SPICES] AND COSMETICS [OINTMENTS]. THEN SHE WAS READY TO GO [WOULD GO IN THIS WAY] TO THE KING. ANYTHING SHE ASKED FOR [DESIRED] WAS GIVEN TO HER TO TAKE WITH HER FROM THE WOMEN'S QUARTERS [HAREM; HOUSE OF THE WOMEN] TO THE KING'S PALACE [HOUSE]. IN THE EVENING SHE WOULD GO TO THE KING'S PALACE [HOUSE], AND IN THE MORNING SHE WOULD RETURN TO ANOTHER PART OF THE [OR TO A SECOND; OR AGAIN TO THE] WOMEN'S QUARTERS [HAREM; HOUSE OF THE WOMEN]. THERE SHE WOULD BE PLACED UNDER THE CARE [CUSTODY; AUTHORITY] OF SHAASHGAZ, THE KING'S EUNUCH IN CHARGE OF THE SLAVE WOMEN [CONCUBINES; SECONDARY WIVES]. THE GIRL WOULD NOT GO BACK TO THE KING AGAIN UNLESS HE WAS PLEASED WITH HER AND ASKED FOR [SUMMONED; REQUESTED] HER BY NAME.

THE TIME [TURN] CAME FOR ESTHER DAUGHTER OF ABIHAIL, MORDECAI'S UNCLE [ESTHER WAS MORDECAI'S YOUNGER COUSIN, V. 7], WHO HAD BEEN RAISED [TAKEN] BY MORDECAI AS HIS OWN DAUGHTER, TO GO TO THE KING. SHE ASKED FOR ONLY WHAT HEGAI SUGGESTED [ADVISED; RECOMMENDED] SHE SHOULD TAKE. (HEGAI WAS THE KING'S EUNUCH WHO WAS IN CHARGE OF [SUPERVISED] THE WOMEN.) EVERYONE WHO SAW ESTHER LIKED [FAVORED] HER. SO ESTHER WAS TAKEN TO KING XERXES [AHASUERUS] IN THE ROYAL PALACE [HOUSE] IN THE TENTH MONTH [EARLY WINTER], THE MONTH OF TEBETH, DURING XERXES' [AHASUERUS'S] SEVENTH YEAR AS KING [OF HIS REIGN].

AND THE KING WAS PLEASED WITH [LOVED] ESTHER MORE THAN WITH ANY OF THE OTHER VIRGINS [YOUNG WOMEN]. HE LIKED HER MORE THAN ANY OF THE OTHERS [OTHER VIRGINS], SO HE PUT A ROYAL CROWN ON HER HEAD AND MADE [PROCLAIMED; DECLARED] HER QUEEN IN PLACE OF VASHTI. THEN THE KING GAVE A GREAT BANQUET FOR ESTHER AND INVITED ALL HIS IMPORTANT MEN [NOBLES; OFFICIALS] AND ROYAL OFFICERS [MINISTERS; SERVANTS].

HE ANNOUNCED A HOLIDAY FOR ALL THE EMPIRE [PROVINCES] AND HAD THE GOVERNMENT GIVE AWAY GIFTS [GAVE GIFTS WITH ROYAL LIBERALITY/GENEROSITY]. (ESTHER 2:1-18)

There is a four-year gap between Esther chapters 1 and 2. Historians believe Xerxes spent extensive time in military battle during those four years. One can only hope his experiences served to mature him somewhat, recognizing realities of rulership and some personal humility. It does seem his interaction with Esther was different than that of Vashti, and somewhere in that four-year difference, Xerxes changed enough to be prepared and primed to handle the matters that would come before him, on behalf of Esther. It also appears that what Xerxes sought in a wife was a little bit different.

ESTHER[7]
- *HADASSAH:* "MYRTLE," ESTHER'S JEWISH NAME
- ORIGINAL WORD: הֲדַסָּה
- PART OF SPEECH: PROPER NAME FEMININE
- TRANSLITERATION: HADASSAH
- PHONETIC SPELLING: (HAD-AS-SAW')
- SHORT DEFINITION: HADASSAH

Unlike Vashti, Esther was a Jew. She was an orphan, raised by Mordecai (a close relative of hers) and was, at least somewhat, an adherent of her faith. We don't know how devout she was; the contents of the book don't suggest an overly pious religious devotion. More than anything, however, Jews faced racial discrimination, as a differing tribe, one frequently occupied and controlled by other nations that were larger and more powerful. To become queen, Esther had to keep some things to herself, including her familial lineage and her Jewish origin.

Kept to herself or not, Esther was who she was. As a woman of Jewish lineage, she assumed a royal position. In assuming that position, she also took the position over the enemy. Way back in Genesis, we can recall the promise of enmity between Satan and the woman, and by proxy, between Satan and all women. Here in Esther, and in the work of Vashti, as well, we see this visual enmity between Satan's work and these women who were appointed and positioned to take stands against the social evils of their day. That is why this work was handed over to women; it is why the book is called Esther, not Edward, or Earnest, or the name of some other male figure. Esther displayed a victory over the enemy, using skill and purpose, and being willing to make the ultimate sacrifice for her own people. The woman had the victory over the enemy; only as she was willing to be divinely led and crush his head.

AFTER THESE THINGS HAPPENED [EVENTS], KING XERXES [AHASUERUS] HONORED [PROMOTED; MADE GREAT] HAMAN SON OF HAMMEDATHA THE AGAGITE [A DESCENDANT OF KING AGAG OF THE AMALEKITES, THE HATED ENEMIES OF ISRAEL (WHICH SAUL FAILED TO ERADICATE; 1 SAM. 15); EX. 17:8–15; DEUT. 23:3–6]. HE GAVE HIM A NEW RANK THAT WAS [EXALTED/ELEVATED HIM] HIGHER THAN [ABOVE] ALL THE IMPORTANT MEN [NOBLES; OFFICIALS]. ALL THE ROYAL OFFICERS [KING'S MINISTERS; OFFICIALS] AT THE KING'S GATE WOULD BOW DOWN AND KNEEL BEFORE [PAY HOMAGE TO] HAMAN, AS THE KING HAD ORDERED [COMMANDED]. BUT MORDECAI WOULD NOT BOW DOWN OR SHOW HIM HONOR [PAY HIM HOMAGE; BECAUSE HE WAS A HATED AMALEKITE].

THEN THE ROYAL OFFICERS [MINISTERS; OFFICIALS] AT THE KING'S GATE ASKED MORDECAI, "WHY DON'T YOU OBEY THE KING'S COMMAND?" AND THEY SAID THIS TO HIM EVERY DAY. WHEN HE DID NOT LISTEN TO THEM, THEY TOLD HAMAN. THEY WANTED TO SEE IF HAMAN WOULD ACCEPT [TOLERATE; LET STAND] MORDECAI'S BEHAVIOR BECAUSE MORDECAI HAD TOLD THEM HE WAS A JEW.

WHEN HAMAN SAW THAT MORDECAI WOULD NOT BOW DOWN TO HIM OR HONOR [PAY HOMAGE TO] HIM, HE BECAME VERY ANGRY [ENRAGED]. HE THOUGHT OF HIMSELF AS TOO IMPORTANT [DISDAINED; THOUGHT IT BENEATH HIM] TO TRY TO KILL [LAY HANDS ON] ONLY MORDECAI. HE HAD BEEN TOLD WHO THE PEOPLE OF MORDECAI WERE, SO HE LOOKED FOR A WAY TO DESTROY ALL OF MORDECAI'S PEOPLE, THE JEWS, IN ALL OF XERXES' [AHASUERUS'S] KINGDOM [EMPIRE].

IT WAS IN THE FIRST MONTH [APRIL] OF THE TWELFTH YEAR [ABOUT 474 BC; APPROXIMATELY A YEAR LATER] OF KING XERXES'

[AHASUERUS'S] RULE [REIGN]—THE MONTH OF NISAN. PUR (THAT IS, THE LOT [DICE-LIKE OBJECTS]) WAS THROWN BEFORE HAMAN TO CHOOSE A DAY AND A MONTH. SO [...AND; ...UNTIL] THE TWELFTH MONTH, THE MONTH OF ADAR, WAS CHOSEN.

THEN HAMAN SAID TO KING XERXES [AHASUERUS], "THERE IS A CERTAIN GROUP OF [ONE] PEOPLE SCATTERED [DISPERSED AND SPREAD] AMONG THE OTHER PEOPLE [NATIONS; PEOPLES] IN ALL THE STATES [PROVINCES] OF YOUR KINGDOM [EMPIRE]. THEIR CUSTOMS [LAWS] ARE DIFFERENT FROM THOSE OF ALL THE OTHER PEOPLE [NATIONS; PEOPLES], AND THEY DO NOT OBEY [OBSERVE; KEEP] THE KING'S LAWS. IT IS NOT RIGHT FOR YOU [IN THE KING'S INTEREST] TO ALLOW THEM TO CONTINUE LIVING IN YOUR KINGDOM [REMAIN; CAUSE THEM TO REST]. IF IT PLEASES [IS GOOD TO] THE KING, LET AN ORDER BE GIVEN [IT BE DECREED] TO DESTROY THOSE PEOPLE. THEN I WILL PAY SEVEN HUNDRED FIFTY THOUSAND POUNDS [TEN THOUSAND TALENTS] OF SILVER TO THOSE WHO DO THE KING'S [THE OFFICIALS WHO CARRY OUT THIS] BUSINESS, AND THEY WILL PUT IT INTO THE ROYAL TREASURY."

SO THE KING TOOK HIS SIGNET RING OFF HIS HAND AND GAVE IT TO HAMAN SON OF HAMMEDATHA, THE AGAGITE, THE ENEMY [PERSECUTOR; OPPRESSOR] OF THE JEWS. THEN THE KING SAID TO HAMAN, "THE MONEY [SILVER] AND THE PEOPLE ARE YOURS [PERHAPS TELLING HAMAN TO KEEP HIS MONEY, OR THAT HE COULD HAVE THE JEWS' MONEY, OR THAT HE COULD SPEND HIS MONEY THIS WAY IF HE WISHED; SEE 4:7]. DO WITH THEM AS YOU PLEASE [IS GOOD IN YOUR EYES]."

ON THE THIRTEENTH DAY OF THE FIRST MONTH [APRIL 17], THE ROYAL SECRETARIES [SCRIBES] WERE CALLED, AND THEY WROTE OUT ALL OF HAMAN'S ORDERS [COMMANDS]. THEY WROTE TO THE KING'S GOVERNORS AND TO THE CAPTAINS OF THE SOLDIERS [HIGH OFFICIALS] IN EACH STATE [PROVINCE] AND TO THE IMPORTANT MEN [NOBLES] OF EACH GROUP OF PEOPLE [NATION]. THE ORDERS [EDICTS; DECREES] WERE WRITTEN IN THE WRITING [SCRIPT] OF EACH STATE [PROVINCE] AND IN THE LANGUAGE OF EACH PEOPLE. THEY WERE WRITTEN IN THE NAME OF KING XERXES [AHASUERUS] AND SEALED WITH HIS SIGNET RING. LETTERS [DISPATCHES; SCROLLS] WERE SENT BY MESSENGERS [COURIERS] TO ALL THE KING'S EMPIRE [PROVINCES] ORDERING THEM TO DESTROY, KILL, AND COMPLETELY WIPE OUT

[ANNIHILATE] ALL THE JEWS, YOUNG AND OLD, INCLUDING WOMEN AND LITTLE CHILDREN. IT WAS TO HAPPEN ON A SINGLE DAY—THE THIRTEENTH DAY OF THE TWELFTH MONTH [MARCH 7, ABOUT TWELVE MONTHS LATER], WHICH WAS ADAR. AND THEY COULD TAKE [PLUNDER; CONFISCATE] EVERYTHING THE JEWISH PEOPLE OWNED [THEIR POSSESSIONS]. A COPY OF THE ORDER [EDICT; DECREE] WAS GIVEN OUT AS A LAW IN EVERY STATE [PROVINCE] SO ALL THE PEOPLE [NATIONS; PEOPLES] WOULD BE READY FOR THAT DAY.

THE MESSENGERS [COURIERS] SET OUT, HURRIED [SPURRED ON; IMPELLED] BY THE KING'S COMMAND, AS SOON AS THE ·ORDER [EDICT; DECREE] WAS GIVEN IN THE PALACE [CITADEL; FORTRESS] AT SUSA. THE KING AND HAMAN SAT DOWN TO DRINK, BUT THE CITY OF SUSA WAS IN CONFUSION [BEWILDERED; IN AN UPROAR]. (Esther 3:1-15)

WHEN MORDECAI HEARD [LEARNED] ABOUT ALL THAT HAD BEEN DONE, HE TORE HIS CLOTHES, PUT ON ROUGH CLOTH [BURLAP; SACKCLOTH] AND ASHES [SIGNS OF GRIEF OR REPENTANCE], AND WENT OUT INTO THE CITY CRYING [WAILING] LOUDLY AND PAINFULLY [BITTERLY]. BUT MORDECAI WENT ONLY AS FAR AS THE KING'S GATE, BECAUSE NO ONE WAS ALLOWED TO ENTER THAT GATE DRESSED IN ROUGH CLOTH [BURLAP; SACKCLOTH]. AS THE KING'S ORDER [EDICT; DECREE] REACHED EVERY AREA, THERE WAS GREAT SADNESS AND LOUD CRYING [MOURNING] AMONG THE JEWS. THEY FASTED AND CRIED OUT LOUD [WEPT AND WAILED], AND MANY OF THEM LAY DOWN ON ROUGH CLOTH [BURLAP; SACKCLOTH] AND ASHES [SIGNS OF GRIEF OR REPENTANCE].

WHEN ESTHER'S SERVANT GIRLS [MAIDS; ATTENDANTS] AND EUNUCHS CAME TO HER AND TOLD HER ABOUT MORDECAI, SHE WAS VERY UPSET AND AFRAID [DEEPLY DISTRESSED; OVERCOME WITH ANGUISH]. SHE SENT CLOTHES FOR MORDECAI TO PUT ON INSTEAD OF THE ROUGH CLOTH [BURLAP; SACKCLOTH], BUT HE WOULD NOT WEAR [ACCEPT] THEM. THEN ESTHER CALLED FOR HATHACH, ONE OF THE KING'S EUNUCHS CHOSEN BY THE KING TO SERVE HER. ESTHER ORDERED HIM TO FIND OUT WHAT WAS BOTHERING MORDECAI AND WHY.

SO HATHACH WENT TO MORDECAI, WHO WAS IN THE CITY SQUARE IN FRONT OF THE KING'S GATE. MORDECAI TOLD HATHACH EVERYTHING THAT HAD HAPPENED TO HIM, AND HE TOLD HATHACH ABOUT THE

EXACT AMOUNT OF MONEY HAMAN HAD PROMISED TO PAY INTO THE KING'S TREASURY FOR THE KILLING [DESTRUCTION] OF THE JEWS. MORDECAI ALSO GAVE HIM A COPY OF THE ORDER [EDICT; DECREE] TO KILL [DESTROY] THE JEWS, WHICH HAD BEEN GIVEN [ISSUED] IN SUSA. HE WANTED HATHACH TO SHOW IT TO ESTHER AND TO TELL HER ABOUT [EXPLAIN] IT. AND MORDECAI TOLD HIM TO ORDER [DIRECT; INSTRUCT] ESTHER TO GO INTO THE KING'S PRESENCE TO BEG FOR MERCY AND TO PLEAD WITH [PETITION] HIM FOR HER PEOPLE.

HATHACH WENT BACK AND REPORTED TO ESTHER EVERYTHING MORDECAI HAD SAID [INSTRUCTED]. THEN ESTHER TOLD HATHACH TO TELL MORDECAI, "ALL THE ROYAL OFFICERS [MINISTERS; OFFICIALS] AND PEOPLE OF THE ROYAL [KING'S] STATES [PROVINCES] KNOW THAT NO MAN OR WOMAN MAY GO [COME] TO THE KING IN THE INNER COURTYARD WITHOUT BEING CALLED [UNINVITED]. THERE IS [HE HAS] ONLY ONE LAW ABOUT THIS: ANYONE WHO ENTERS MUST BE PUT TO DEATH UNLESS THE KING HOLDS OUT HIS GOLD SCEPTER. THEN THAT PERSON MAY LIVE. AND I HAVE NOT BEEN CALLED [SUMMONED; INVITED] TO GO TO THE KING FOR THIRTY DAYS."

ESTHER'S MESSAGE [WORDS] WAS GIVEN TO MORDECAI. THEN MORDECAI SENT BACK WORD [THIS ANSWER/REPLY] TO ESTHER: "JUST BECAUSE YOU LIVE IN [ARE PART OF] THE KING'S PALACE [HOUSE], DON'T THINK [IMAGINE] THAT OUT OF ALL THE JEWS YOU ALONE WILL ESCAPE. IF YOU KEEP QUIET [SILENT] AT THIS TIME, SOMEONE ELSE WILL HELP AND SAVE THE JEWS [LIBERATION/RELIEF AND PROTECTION/DELIVERANCE FOR THE JEWS WILL ARISE/APPEAR FROM ANOTHER PLACE], BUT YOU AND YOUR FATHER'S FAMILY [RELATIVES] WILL ALL DIE. AND WHO KNOWS, YOU MAY HAVE BEEN CHOSEN QUEEN [COME TO YOUR ROYAL POSITION; COME TO THE KINGDOM] FOR JUST SUCH A TIME AS THIS."

THEN ESTHER SENT THIS ANSWER TO MORDECAI: "GO AND GET [ASSEMBLE] ALL THE JEWS IN SUSA TOGETHER. FOR MY SAKE [ON MY BEHALF], FAST; DO NOT EAT OR DRINK FOR THREE DAYS, NIGHT AND [OR] DAY. I AND MY SERVANT GIRLS [MAIDS; ATTENDANTS] WILL ALSO FAST. THEN I WILL GO TO THE KING, EVEN THOUGH IT IS AGAINST THE LAW, AND IF I DIE, I DIE."

SO MORDECAI WENT AWAY AND DID EVERYTHING ESTHER HAD TOLD

[COMMANDED; INSTRUCTED] HIM TO DO. (ESTHER 4:1-17)

Esther was willing to make the ultimate sacrifice for her people, as Christ was willing to do for the salvation of mankind. A type of savior, Esther took on this role, willing to stand as the salvation of her people, who would be quickly exterminated without her willingness and intervention. It was not a little thing Esther was asked to do; she knew that she ran the risk of death to do what was right. Following Biblical principle, she showed her love for others, as we eloquently explained in the New Testament:

THIS IS MY COMMANDMENT, THAT YE LOVE ONE ANOTHER, AS I HAVE LOVED YOU. GREATER LOVE HATH NO MAN THAN THIS, THAT A MAN LAY DOWN HIS LIFE FOR HIS FRIENDS. (John 15:12-13, KJV)

We know life as a willing sacrifice is something we are called to live as Christians, but it seems difficult when we read it on its own. Reading Esther puts passages, as well as God's command to love others, into perspective. It is not so much about throwing ourselves on bombs or in front of flying bullets, as it is recognizing we are here for such a time as this, and if we are to live now, God has equipped us to operate and function in this day and age, as much for our neighbor, and doing the right thing, as we are to do for ourselves. Christ made this sacrifice; Esther was willing to take that risk to make it; and it is the least we can do in order to make a difference in this world. Soul winning, as many term evangelism, is a great idea, in concept. Esther and Christ both teach us that evangelizing and reaching out to others is far more than just a nice conversation about Jesus on a street corner. If we want to outwit the enemy, if we want to do more than meets the eye, if we want to reach others for the Lord, we have to do more than just talk.

THAT SAME DAY KING XERXES [AHASUERUS] GAVE QUEEN ESTHER EVERYTHING BELONGING TO [THE ESTATE OF; THE HOUSE OF] HAMAN, THE ENEMY OF THE JEWS. AND MORDECAI CAME IN TO SEE THE KING, BECAUSE ESTHER HAD TOLD [DISCLOSED/REVEALED TO] THE KING HOW HE WAS RELATED TO HER. THEN THE KING TOOK OFF HIS SIGNET RING THAT HE HAD TAKEN BACK FROM HAMAN, AND HE GAVE IT TO

MORDECAI. ESTHER PUT MORDECAI IN CHARGE OF EVERYTHING BELONGING TO [OVER THE HOUSE OF] HAMAN.

ONCE AGAIN ESTHER SPOKE TO THE KING. SHE FELL AT THE KING'S FEET AND CRIED [WEPT] AND BEGGED [IMPLORED] HIM TO STOP THE EVIL PLAN [PLOT] THAT HAMAN THE AGAGITE HAD PLANNED [DEVISED] AGAINST THE JEWS [ESTHER WISELY DID NOT IMPLICATE THE KING IN THE PLAN]. THE KING HELD OUT [EXTENDED] THE GOLD SCEPTER TO ESTHER. SO ESTHER GOT UP AND STOOD IN FRONT OF HIM.

SHE SAID, "MY KING, IF YOU ARE PLEASED WITH ME [I HAVE FOUND FAVOR IN THE KING'S SIGHT], AND IF IT PLEASES [SEEMS GOOD TO] YOU TO DO THIS, IF YOU THINK IT IS THE RIGHT THING TO DO, AND IF YOU ARE HAPPY WITH ME [I AM PLEASING/ATTRACTIVE TO YOU], LET AN ORDER [EDICT; DECREE] BE WRITTEN TO CANCEL [REVOKE; RESCIND] THE LETTERS [DISPATCHES; SCROLLS] HAMAN THE SON OF HAMMEDATHA THE AGAGITE WROTE [DEVISED] TO DESTROY THE JEWS IN ALL OF YOUR KINGDOM [PROVINCES]. I COULD NOT STAND [HOW COULD I ENDURE...?] TO SEE THAT TERRIBLE THING [CALAMITY; DISASTER] HAPPEN TO [FALL ON] MY PEOPLE. I COULD NOT STAND [HOW COULD I ENDURE...?] TO SEE MY FAMILY [RELATIVES; KINDRED] KILLED [DESTROYED]."

KING XERXES [AHASUERUS] ANSWERED QUEEN ESTHER AND MORDECAI THE JEW, "BECAUSE HAMAN WAS AGAINST THE JEWS, I HAVE GIVEN HIS THINGS [ESTATE; PROPERTY] TO ESTHER, AND MY SOLDIERS HAVE HANGED [IMPALED] HIM ON THE PLATFORM [GALLOWS; POLE]. NOW, IN THE KING'S NAME, WRITE ANOTHER ORDER [EDICT; DECREE] TO [CONCERNING] THE JEWS AS SEEMS BEST [APPROPRIATE] TO YOU. THEN SEAL THE ORDER [EDICT; DECREE] WITH THE KING'S SIGNET RING, BECAUSE NO LETTER [DISPATCH] WRITTEN IN THE KING'S NAME AND SEALED WITH HIS SIGNET RING CAN BE CANCELED [REVOKED; RESCINDED]."

AT THAT TIME THE KING'S SECRETARIES [SCRIBES] WERE CALLED. THIS WAS THE TWENTY-THIRD DAY OF THE THIRD MONTH [JUNE 25], WHICH IS SIVAN. THE SECRETARIES WROTE OUT ALL OF MORDECAI'S ORDERS [COMMANDS] TO [CONCERNING] THE JEWS, TO THE GOVERNORS, TO THE CAPTAINS OF THE SOLDIERS [HIGH OFFICIALS] IN EACH STATE [PROVINCE], AND TO THE IMPORTANT MEN [NOBLES] OF

THE ONE HUNDRED TWENTY-SEVEN STATES [PROVINCES] THAT REACHED FROM INDIA TO CUSH [1:1]. THEY WROTE IN THE WRITING [SCRIPT] OF EACH STATE [PROVINCE] AND IN THE LANGUAGE OF EACH PEOPLE. THEY ALSO WROTE TO THE JEWS IN THEIR OWN WRITING [SCRIPT] AND LANGUAGE. MORDECAI WROTE ORDERS [EDICTS; DECREES] IN THE NAME OF KING XERXES [AHASUERUS] AND SEALED THE LETTERS [DISPATCHES; SCROLLS] WITH THE KING'S SIGNET RING. THEN HE SENT THE KING'S ORDERS [EDICTS; DECREES] BY MESSENGERS [COURIERS] ON FAST HORSES, HORSES THAT WERE RAISED [BRED] JUST [ESPECIALLY] FOR THE KING.

THESE WERE THE KING'S ORDERS [EDICTS; DECREES]: THE JEWS IN EVERY CITY HAVE THE RIGHT TO GATHER TOGETHER [ASSEMBLE] TO PROTECT THEMSELVES [DEFEND THEIR LIVES]. THEY MAY DESTROY, KILL, AND COMPLETELY WIPE OUT [ANNIHILATE] THE ARMY OF ANY STATE [PROVINCE] OR PEOPLE [NATION] WHO ATTACK THEM [THE KING COULD NOT CANCEL HIS PREVIOUS UNALTERABLE DECREE, BUT HE COULD ALLOW THE JEWS TO DEFEND THEMSELVES AND ATTACK], INCLUDING THEIR WOMEN AND CHILDREN. THEY MAY ALSO TAKE BY FORCE [PLUNDER; CONFISCATE] THE PROPERTY OF THEIR ENEMIES. THE ONE DAY SET FOR THE JEWS TO DO THIS IN ALL THE EMPIRE [PROVINCES] OF KING XERXES [AHASUERUS] WAS THE THIRTEENTH DAY OF THE TWELFTH MONTH [MARCH 7, ABOUT TWELVE MONTHS AFTER HAMAN DEVISED HIS PLOT], THE MONTH OF ADAR. A COPY OF THE KING'S ORDER [EDICT; DECREE] WAS TO BE SENT OUT [ISSUED; PRESENTED] AS A LAW IN EVERY STATE [PROVINCE]. IT WAS TO BE MADE KNOWN TO THE PEOPLE OF EVERY NATION LIVING IN THE KINGDOM [ALL THE PEOPLES] SO THE JEWS WOULD BE READY ON THAT SET DAY TO STRIKE BACK AT [AVENGE THEMSELVES ON] THEIR ENEMIES.

THE MESSENGERS [COURIERS] HURRIED OUT, RIDING ON THE ROYAL HORSES, URGED ON BY THE KING'S COMMAND. AND THE ORDER [EDICT; DECREE] WAS ALSO GIVEN IN THE PALACE [CITADEL; FORTRESS; 1:2] AT SUSA. (Esther 8:1-14)

By Christ's sacrifice, He led us into freedom. Esther's risk paid off; it merited the salvation of her people, who were also free to worship and live among the Persian people. By taking and risking that sacrifice, she led her people to freedom. Both won the victory over Satan, doing what they were called to do, in that hour, at that appointed time.

We talk so often about winning the battle with Satan as if it can be wrought with spitting and shouting as we pretend to stomp on the devil's head. Esther proves winning the battle against the enemy comes down to one thing: do we do what is right when it is required of us? Are we catalysts, shadows, of a living epistle, being read of all, in our social conducts? Do we realize where we are needed and position ourselves there, accordingly? Are we willing to lay down our lives for the purpose of salvation?

Too many of us overlook Esther's duty because we don't want to adapt these things for ourselves. How many more people in our lives might both desire and follow the way of salvation if we were ready, willing, and able to do the right thing, even if it requires sacrifice? If we want people to find salvation, we must embody it for them. Esther was a master of this principle.

In my book *Feminine Perspectives of God: Becoming One New Woman in a Journey Through the Books of Ruth and Esther*(Righteous Pen Publications, 2023), I make the following observation about Esther's saving work:

The power of operating as a living letter, or a living type, being read (observed) of all people proves the work of the Spirit as alive, whereas the work of the Law kills. The difference is the purpose. The purpose of the Spirit is to give life; after all, the Spirit is, indeed, the life-giver. The purpose of the written law was to alert to death, to make us aware of the very need for the Savior in the first place, and to aware us that no matter our best efforts, we were never going to find life without divine intervention. The point of a type is to reveal that divine intervention, God's divine intention to the world, reminding others of God's true love and care for humanity. Now, as believers, we are called to stand as types ourselves, pointing to the realities that we know exist, but are not always visible, showing little bits and pieces of God's love to the entire world. As types, we become that encounter: something that points to something else, something greater, and lets them know that He is still there, and He still cares. It is being willing to take on that spiritual nature to reveal God to people who may not even realize they are missing Him in some way.[8]

In keeping with the principle of salvation, it is essential for us to embrace the idea of love as present in Esther. Christ's sacrifice was done of love, for the salvation of each and every one of us (Romans 5:8). The goal was salvation, but the motivation was love. Esther, too, did what she did out of a sense of love for others, not refraining and holding herself back out of selfish gain or conceit, but doing what she did because Esther genuinely cared about other people. Being so willing to make such a sacrifice proves Esther's love for others and enhances the evidence for her work as a type of that of Christ.

BUT THE JEWS IN SUSA MET [ASSEMBLED] ON THE THIRTEENTH AND FOURTEENTH DAYS OF THE MONTH OF ADAR [AND KILLED THEIR ENEMIES]. THEN THEY RESTED ON THE FIFTEENTH DAY AND MADE IT A DAY OF JOYFUL FEASTING [BANQUETING].

THIS IS WHY THE JEWS WHO LIVE IN THE COUNTRY AND SMALL VILLAGES CELEBRATE ON THE FOURTEENTH DAY OF THE MONTH OF ADAR [MARCH 8]. IT IS A DAY [HOLIDAY] OF JOYFUL FEASTING [BANQUETING] AND A DAY FOR EXCHANGING ·GIFTS [GIFTS OF FOOD].

MORDECAI WROTE DOWN [RECORDED] EVERYTHING THAT HAD HAPPENED. THEN HE SENT LETTERS [DISPATCHES; SCROLLS] TO ALL THE JEWS IN ALL THE EMPIRE [PROVINCES] OF KING XERXES [AHASUERUS], FAR AND NEAR. HE TOLD [CALLED ON] THEM TO CELEBRATE EVERY YEAR ON THE FOURTEENTH AND FIFTEENTH DAYS OF THE MONTH OF ADAR, BECAUSE THAT WAS WHEN THE JEWS GOT RID OF THEIR ENEMIES [A DESCENDANT OF SAUL (2:5–6) HAD OVERCOME AN AMALEKITE AND DESCENDANT OF KING AGAG (3:1), THUS COMPLETING GOD'S MANDATE (DEUT. 23:3–6) THAT SAUL FAILED TO ACCOMPLISH (1 SAM. 15)]. THEY WERE ALSO TO CELEBRATE IT AS THE MONTH THEIR SADNESS [SORROW] WAS TURNED TO JOY [GLADNESS] AND THEIR CRYING FOR THE DEAD [MOURNING] WAS TURNED INTO CELEBRATION [A HOLIDAY]. HE TOLD THEM TO CELEBRATE THOSE DAYS AS DAYS OF JOYFUL FEASTING [BANQUETING] AND AS A TIME FOR GIVING [PRESENTS OF] FOOD TO EACH OTHER AND PRESENTS [GIFTS] TO THE POOR [C PURIM THUS BECAME AN ANNUAL FESTIVAL STILL CELEBRATED BY THE JEWISH PEOPLE TODAY].

SO THE JEWS AGREED TO DO WHAT MORDECAI HAD WRITTEN TO THEM, AND THEY AGREED TO HOLD THE CELEBRATION EVERY YEAR [TO

CONTINUE WHAT THEY HAD BEGUN]. HAMAN SON OF HAMMEDATHA, THE AGAGITE, WAS THE ENEMY OF ALL THE JEWS. HE HAD MADE [DEVISED] AN EVIL PLAN [PLOT] AGAINST THE JEWS TO DESTROY THEM, AND HE HAD THROWN THE PUR (THAT IS, THE LOT [DICE-LIKE OBJECTS]) TO CHOOSE A DAY TO RUIN [CRUSH; AFFLICT] AND DESTROY THEM. BUT WHEN THE KING LEARNED OF THE EVIL PLAN [PLOT], HE SENT OUT WRITTEN ORDERS [EDICTS; DECREES] THAT THE EVIL PLANS [PLOT] HAMAN HAD MADE AGAINST THE JEWS WOULD BE USED AGAINST HIM [FALL/RETURN ON HIS OWN HEAD]. AND THOSE ORDERS [EDICTS; DECREES] SAID THAT HAMAN AND HIS SONS SHOULD BE HANGED [IMPALED] ON THE PLATFORM [GALLOWS; POLE]. SO THESE DAYS WERE CALLED PURIM, WHICH COMES FROM THE WORD "PUR" (THE LOT [DICE-LIKE OBJECTS]). BECAUSE OF EVERYTHING WRITTEN IN THIS LETTER [DISPATCH] AND WHAT THEY HAD SEEN AND WHAT HAPPENED TO THEM, THE JEWS SET UP THIS CUSTOM [TRADITION]. THEY AND THEIR DESCENDANTS AND ALL THOSE WHO JOIN THEM ARE ALWAYS [WITHOUT FAIL] TO CELEBRATE [OBSERVE; KEEP] THESE TWO DAYS EVERY YEAR. THEY SHOULD DO IT IN THE RIGHT WAY [AS IT IS WRITTEN] AND AT THE TIME MORDECAI HAD ORDERED [DECREED]. THESE TWO DAYS SHOULD BE REMEMBERED AND CELEBRATED [OBSERVED; KEPT] FROM NOW ON [THROUGH EVERY GENERATION] IN EVERY FAMILY, IN EVERY STATE [PROVINCE], AND IN EVERY CITY. THESE DAYS OF PURIM SHOULD ALWAYS [NOT FAIL TO] BE CELEBRATED [OBSERVED; KEPT] BY [AMONG] THE JEWS, AND THEIR MEMORY NEVER FADE AMONG THEIR DESCENDANTS.

SO QUEEN ESTHER DAUGHTER OF ABIHAIL, ALONG WITH MORDECAI THE JEW, WROTE WITH FULL AUTHORITY TO CONFIRM THIS SECOND LETTER [DISPATCH] ABOUT PURIM. AND MORDECAI SENT LETTERS [DISPATCHES; SCROLLS] TO ALL THE JEWS IN THE ONE HUNDRED TWENTY-SEVEN STATES [PROVINCES] OF THE KINGDOM OF XERXES [AHASUERUS], WRITING THEM A MESSAGE [WORDS] OF PEACE AND TRUTH [*OR* SECURITY; ASSURANCE]. HE WROTE TO SET UP [ESTABLISH] THESE DAYS OF PURIM AT THE CHOSEN [PROPER; APPOINTED] TIMES. MORDECAI THE JEW AND QUEEN ESTHER HAD SENT OUT THE ORDER [EDICT; DECREE] FOR THE JEWS, JUST AS THEY HAD SET UP [ESTABLISHED] FOR THEMSELVES AND THEIR DESCENDANTS INSTRUCTION CONCERNING FASTING AND LOUD WEEPING [LAMENTATIONS]. ESTHER'S LETTER [COMMAND] SET UP [ESTABLISHED] THE RULES FOR PURIM, AND THEY WERE WRITTEN DOWN IN THE RECORDS. (Esther 9:18-32)

The feast of Purim is a feast of overcoming. It celebrates the natural events found in the book of Esther as much as the spiritual principles we find therein. The Jews had the victory because of Esther, who was willing to do what was required of her. Of overcoming life versus death, Purim stands as a type of our overcoming in the resurrection, as well as a greater type of the Millennium period after Christ returns. On Purim, the enemy hung, for he received just judgment for his deeds. Those who were wicked faced judgment and ultimate death and were no more. Those who were victorious lived, empowered and recalling the greatest thing God could have given to any of them: life. The cycle of life held in the hands of a woman, the life-bearer, standing as a reminder in the feast of Purim.

Note that it was essential when and how Purim took place. If it is a celebration of life, of overcoming, then why not have Purim all the time, whenever the mood strikes? Through the life and work of Esther, God wanted to prove to people the essence of His timing and show that recognition of His timing is an essential thing in the spiritual lives of believers.

BUT WHEN THE FULNESS OF THE TIME WAS COME, GOD SENT FORTH HIS SON, MADE OF A WOMAN, MADE UNDER THE LAW, TO REDEEM THEM THAT WERE UNDER THE LAW, THAT WE MIGHT RECEIVE THE ADOPTION OF SONS. AND BECAUSE YE ARE SONS, GOD HATH SENT FORTH THE SPIRIT OF HIS SON INTO YOUR HEARTS, CRYING, ABBA, FATHER. WHEREFORE THOU ART NO MORE A SERVANT, BUT A SON; AND IF A SON, THEN AN HEIR OF GOD THROUGH CHRIST. (GALATIANS 4:4-7, KJV)

Just as the resurrection was an event that was for everyone who would believe, so, too was Purim. The festival of Purim was a requirement for men as well as women, and women were required to hear and read the word themselves for the festival, because the miracle of Purim was one that specifically involved women. It was a time of feasting, of coming forth from the place of mourning, fasting, and ashes over sin, and into the joy of new life, of the reality that we can overcome through God, through Christ. It was for everyone, male and female, because Esther's work, and victory, was also for everyone, just as Christ's redemption is also for everyone, and is a cause for us to celebrate.

The women of God, moving by the instinct God has placed within them, recognize the fullness of time as they participate in it. Knowing when to act, and doing so, is part of spiritual life. We don't always have time for divine signs, but when we act instinctually, we always know that we can be on time, because our leading isn't our feelings, isn't our thoughts, isn't emotional states, and certainly isn't hormonal – it is the work of God, guiding and directing to get things done that otherwise wouldn't come to pass.

Thoughts on feminine perspectives of God

The parallels present between the four women we've examined in this chapter and their experiences and encounters with God are not an accident. They reveal to us the way that women view spiritual things, and while women may deeply benefit from spiritual signs and wonders, they are not necessarily something they always seek out when making decisions. At times, we may not even recognize we are serving God or specifically doing something for God, but just that we are seeking out – and desiring – to do the right thing. This stems from our antithetical relationship with the enemy, prophesied and established in the garden, between Eve and the serpent.

Ultimately, these women prove to us that being a servant of Christ also means embodying a type of His nature, in everything we do, regardless of our gender. We do have the power to act in a godly manner, overcoming the work of the serpent in our lives, if we are only willing to do the right thing. The right thing doesn't just come in male packaging, nor does it always come in convenient packaging. Ruth and Esther prove, if nothing else, that doing the right thing is about an approach to life, an approach to viewing the things of this world through a spiritual lens and being sure to act accordingly as one views the world with different eyes.

There is nothing easy about serving God. It is wonderful to enjoy and benefit in the bounty of spiritual gifts and abilities given to us from above, but we don't have those things for our enjoyment; we have them to mobilize them and use them for God's glory. Ruth and Naomi, Esther and Vashti all display to us principles every person on the planet, male or female, should embrace in their spiritual relationship with God, as well as their spiritual outlook. They were women who were positioned, purposed, and established for things far greater than they even recognized in their own lifetimes, as they are with us today, reminding us of the truth of their positions, so we can see those purposes and positions within ourselves. Hard as it may be at times, we are here for a purpose, and we are here to live out that purpose, as we come to a greater understanding of what it means to be church by examining places where the church and Christ hide in the Scriptures, right in front of us, but out of plain sight, due to our pre-existing conditioning. If we are taught to overlook it, we will miss it, and such happens frequently when it comes to types of Christ that might not seem obvious in our line of view.

Huldah prophesies the destruction of Jerusalem (Caspar Luyken)

CHAPTER FOUR
The Prophetess

MOST [FIRST] OF ALL, YOU MUST UNDERSTAND THIS:
NO PROPHECY IN THE SCRIPTURES EVER COMES FROM
THE PROPHET'S OWN INTERPRETATION [OR IS A MATTER OF ONE'S OWN INTERPRETATION]. NO
PROPHECY EVER CAME FROM WHAT A PERSON WANTED TO SAY
[HUMAN WILL/INTENTION], BUT PEOPLE LED [CARRIED; MOVED]
BY THE HOLY SPIRIT SPOKE WORDS FROM GOD.
[TRUE PROPHECY ORIGINATES WITH GOD, NOT WITH THE PROPHET.]
(2 PETER 1:20-21)

THOSE who argue against female ordination and a female presence in ministry often do so with a great ignorance of the relevant role women played as leaders and spiritual forerunners in the Old Testament. With the change in understanding of the written law, it makes even less sense to exclude women from leadership if they were included under the written code. Recognizing the law does not exclude women from leadership within the faith community, hearing from God, and leading in any sense should make us wake up and pay attention. The God behind the written code is the same God Who is the Spirit leading and directing us today, and seeing this truth helps us to embrace the work that God wants to do through His women.

It is a mistake to think women never served in ministry prior to the 1800s within specific denominations. Given we often trace our histories back to the founding of what we know, we recognize, or what we see as plausible within our own experiences, many of us have done little to no research on women who served in other ways throughout history. It is even uncommon to see many Bible studies on women in leadership or authority, because much of teaching around women relates to defensive counterpoints formed against the arguments in favor of male-centered preaching, exclusively. In looking at matters from the mere perspective of he-says, she-says, we have ignored key figures in Bible history who disprove arguments against an all-male clergy force.

Properly understanding the role and female influence of clergy stems back to Biblical examples of the work, of women who filled positions traditionally viewed as male territory, and who did so to the best of their ability. While the work might not have always been perfect, we have numerous stories that attest to the success and empowerment of Israel through the leadership of these powerful and gracious leaders. There are even a few thrown in for good measure, that prove we must use proper discernment when it comes to following prophets, and not ever rely on gender as an indicator of spiritual veracity.

In this chapter, we will be looking at the work and role of female prophets, what they did and how they paved the way for women to serve in a greater capacity through the early church, and why these Biblical women, whom we often overlook and ignore, are so amazingly special.

Why prophetess?

> *PROPHETESS*
> - *NEBIAH:* A PROPHETESS
> - ORIGINAL WORD: נְבִיאָה
> - PART OF SPEECH: NOUN FEMININE
> - TRANSLITERATION: NEBIAH
> - PHONETIC SPELLING: (NEB-EE-YAW')
> - SHORT DEFINITION: PROPHETESS

I have been asked why the office of the prophet has been gender-assigned, while the rest of the Ephesians 4:11 offices have not. I believe in the New Covenant, we do not have any reason to specifically assign gender to prophetic title (Ephesians 4:11 does not indicate as such), but I am not opposed to it, either. I understand the different reasons why people desire to uphold the tradition (particularly the women who desire to emphasize their work in the office as women), but at the same time, I am not sure that the majority recognize, nor understand, where it comes from.

The Bible lists seven different women as prophetesses: five in the Old Testament, two in the New Testament. The first five are upheld as true, one is considered of debate, and one is clearly defined as false:

- Miriam
- Deborah
- Isaiah's wife
- Huldah
- Anna
- Noadiah
- Jezebel (of Revelation 2)

Jewish tradition also includes Sarah, Hannah, Abigail, and Esther as Biblical prophetesses. Because they are not specifically mentioned as such, we will not be examining them here. Still, there are obvious reasons why they would have been included as prophetic leaders among Old Testament women. Sarah heard from God and experienced divine encounters, Hannah prayed and recognized the power of God, Abigail knew David was to become a great king, and Esther's attire was believed to come from the clothing of the Spirit, rather than just exterior physical beauty. To recognize them in prophetic tradition raises them up in a way that many women in Biblical times did not come to experience, and this further expounds on why the work of the prophetess was important in Biblical times.

The Ephesians 4:11 ministry, as we understand it today, did not exist until after Christ's ascension into heaven. The Ephesians 4:11 ministry offices are also known as the ascension gifts, which mean they come, according to Scripture, because of Christ's ascent into heaven. The connection between the two relates to spiritual authority: as Christ assumed His position in heaven at His Father's right hand (the seat of authority), so Christ also established authority on earth, through the five-fold ministry leadership present in apostles, prophets, evangelists, pastors, and teachers.

EACH ONE OF US HAS BEEN GIVEN THE SPECIAL GIFT OF GRACE [GRACE; *OR* GIFT], SHOWING HOW GENEROUS CHRIST IS [*OR* IN PROPORTION TO CHRIST'S GIFT; ACCORDING TO THE MEASURE OF CHRIST'S GIFT]. THAT IS WHY IT SAYS IN THE SCRIPTURES,

"WHEN HE WENT UP [ASCENDED] TO THE HEIGHTS,
  HE LED A PARADE OF CAPTIVES [*OR* TOOK CAPTIVES INTO CAPTIVITY],
  AND HE GAVE GIFTS TO PEOPLE [PS. 68:18]."

WHEN IT SAYS, "HE WENT UP [ASCENDED]," WHAT DOES IT MEAN? IT MEANS [...EXCEPT] THAT HE FIRST CAME DOWN [DESCENDED] TO THE EARTH [*OR* LOWER REGIONS, NAMELY THE EARTH; *OR* THE DEPTHS OF THE EARTH; PROBABLY REFERS TO (1) THE INCARNATION, THOUGH POSSIBLY (2) CHRIST'S DESCENT TO HADES AFTER HIS DEATH (1 PET. 3:19–20), OR (3) CHRIST'S DESCENT THROUGH THE SPIRIT AT PENTECOST (ACTS 2)]. SO THE ONE WHO CAME DOWN [DESCENDED] IS THE SAME ONE WHO WENT UP [ASCENDED] ABOVE ALL THE HEAVENS. CHRIST DID THAT [...IN ORDER] TO FILL EVERYTHING WITH HIS PRESENCE [ALL THINGS]. AND CHRIST GAVE GIFTS TO PEOPLE— HE MADE SOME TO BE APOSTLES, SOME TO BE PROPHETS, SOME TO GO AND TELL THE GOOD NEWS, AND SOME TO HAVE THE WORK OF CARING FOR AND TEACHING GOD'S PEOPLE [HE HIMSELF GAVE APOSTLES, PROPHETS, EVANGELISTS, PASTORS/SHEPHERDS, AND TEACHERS]. CHRIST GAVE THOSE GIFTS TO PREPARE [...TO EQUIP] GOD'S HOLY PEOPLE FOR THE WORK OF SERVING, TO MAKE THE BODY OF CHRIST STRONGER. THIS WORK MUST CONTINUE UNTIL WE ARE ALL JOINED TOGETHER IN THE SAME FAITH [*OR* ALL REACH UNITY IN THE FAITH] AND IN THE SAME KNOWLEDGE OF THE SON OF GOD. WE MUST BECOME LIKE A MATURE PERSON [*OR* THE PERFECT MAN; CHRIST], GROWING UNTIL WE BECOME LIKE CHRIST AND HAVE HIS PERFECTION [TO THE MEASURE OF THE STATURE OF CHRIST'S FULLNESS]. (EPHESIANS 4:7-13)

The gender form of each term found in Ephesians 4 is masculine group form, which means the plural male form can include men and women (like when the Bible speaks of an entire church as "brothers"). Women were included in the Ephesians 4:11 ministry despite the language change (we will discuss this in a later chapter). Rather than gender identify the spiritual gifts, they were strictly considered as works of the Spirit. It was no longer as much about the vessel as identifying the gift that was present therein.

    The Ephesians 4:11 ministry represents a different understanding of spiritual offices than that which we see in the Old Testament. For one, the work of the prophet emerged over time in the Old Testament, to encompass the work of the School of the Prophets. This isn't the beginning and ending of the story, however. Not every school of the prophet was regarded as authentic, and there was notable conflict between prophets as to whether they were true, false, or from the northern or southern kingdoms. The prophetic work did not always reflect a balance of ideas or concepts, and many of the Old Testament prophets were very extreme in the measures they took to convey their spiritual messages.

We don't see limitations on prophetic assignment for women. Female prophets worked across the gender spectrum and served in diversified capacities. Thus, gender designations were just that – a way to distinguish different prophets by gender rather than gift or assignment. It didn't signify a different sphere of work (there wasn't female prophecy and male prophecy), just a different speaker. The gender identity of "prophetess" came into play as to identify female speakers and vessels of God's word, manifest through that individual. In Old Testament times, the only office of the Ephesians 4:11 ministry in existence was the prophet, and the ancient Hebrews had not yet come to the embodiment of their being neither male nor female in Christ (Galatians 3:28).

Is the identity of women as "prophetesses" – in a separate identity from their male counterparts – important? Actually, yes, very much so. The identity of female prophets is there for us today in spiritual clarity of the role and work of women in leadership. Biblical prophetesses prove leadership is not exclusively a man's game. Leadership is not a masculine quality, but a spiritual purpose, a spiritual gift and ability. They remind every female leader that she should be proud to serve as she has been called, and that being called is all right. They also dispel many notions about female inequality within spiritual settings. It is still largely understood that if a woman is in a situation with a man, she should defer to the man, even if she is of a higher spiritual office than the man might be. In elevating the work of the prophetess, we celebrate that spiritual gifts are given across the gender spectrum, and it is genuinely not about gender; it never has been. God qualifies those He calls, and gifts are given without repentance.

Even though the Ephesians 4:11 ministry did not exist in pre-church times, we can see types of the female Ephesians 4;11

ministry in the prophetic work of female prophets. These women teach and guide us into important things for ourselves, both those who are leaders and those who follow leadership. Looking at their positives and negatives helps to lift the leadership of women, particularly in the Ephesians 4:11 ministry (and specifically the prophetic).

Miriam[2, 3]

MIRIAM[4]
- *MIRYAM:* A SISTER OF AARON, ALSO A MAN OF JUDAH
- ORIGINAL WORD: מִרְיָם
- PART OF SPEECH: PROPER NAME FEMININE
- TRANSLITERATION: MIRYAM
- PHONETIC SPELLING: (MEER-YAWM')
- SHORT DEFINITION: MIRIAM

Miriam is one of the best-known Bible prophetesses, alongside Deborah. She has the unique position of being the first one mentioned, and from what we can see in the Torah, Miriam's role among the Israelite community was huge. She wasn't just the latch-key sister of Moses and Aaron; she had the ability to stand on her own, working in her own right, as a representative of the word of God and the leadership of the community.

Miriam was the daughter of Amram and Jacobed and was the older sister of both Moses and Aaron. Jewish tradition cites Miriam was prophetically gifted from the time she was a child, and that it was Miriam who prophesied Moses' role as liberator of the Hebrew people. There are some additional traditions that also cite her as a child midwife and was involved in the rescue of Moses from Pharaoh's genocide. From the Biblical accounts of Moses' early life, we can see she was involved in monitoring the rescue of the infant Moses from the Nile River.

NOW A MAN FROM THE FAMILY [HOUSE] OF LEVI MARRIED A WOMAN WHO WAS ALSO FROM THE FAMILY [TOOK A DAUGHTER] OF LEVI. SHE BECAME PREGNANT [CONCEIVED] AND GAVE BIRTH TO A SON. WHEN SHE SAW HOW WONDERFUL THE BABY [GOOD/HANDSOME/HEALTHY HE] WAS, SHE HID HIM FOR THREE MONTHS. BUT AFTER THREE

MONTHS SHE WAS NOT ABLE TO HIDE THE BABY ANY LONGER, SO SHE GOT A BASKET [ARK] MADE OF REEDS [PAPYRUS] AND COVERED IT WITH TAR SO THAT IT WOULD FLOAT [BITUMEN AND PITCH]. SHE PUT THE BABY IN THE BASKET. THEN SHE PUT THE BASKET AMONG THE TALL STALKS OF GRASS [REEDS] AT THE EDGE OF THE NILE RIVER [RIVER]. THE BABY'S SISTER STOOD A SHORT DISTANCE AWAY [AFAR OFF] TO SEE WHAT WOULD HAPPEN TO HIM. (EXODUS 2:1-4)

Moses' ministry was an incredible testimony to the wonders of God and the power of God to liberate those who follow Him, even from the most horrible of situations and conditions. Moses did not do this work alone, however. The leadership of Israel was due to three individuals: Moses, Aaron, and Miriam. It has been said that the three great divine gifts that led the Israelites (manna, glory clouds, and water from the rock) were the merit of the three leaders. The water from the rock, which rolled from place to place with the Israelites and provided fresh water, was traditionally known as "Miriam's Well," and such shows the nature of Miriam's wisdom, insight, and sustainability to the community. Through the water from the rock, life came forth, much as a river of living water offers life to all who receive it.

THE WHOLE ISRAELITE COMMUNITY [CONGREGATION/ASSEMBLY OF THE SONS/CHILDREN OF ISRAEL] LEFT THE DESERT [WILDERNESS] OF SIN AND TRAVELED FROM PLACE TO PLACE [JOURNEYED BY STAGES], AS THE LORD COMMANDED. THEY CAMPED AT REPHIDIM, BUT THERE WAS NO WATER THERE FOR THE PEOPLE TO DRINK. SO THE PEOPLE QUARRELED WITH [ACCUSED; MADE A CASE AGAINST] MOSES AND SAID, "GIVE US WATER TO DRINK."

MOSES SAID TO THEM, "WHY DO YOU QUARREL WITH [ACCUSE; MAKE A CASE AGAINST] ME? WHY ARE YOU TESTING [PUTTING ON TRIAL] THE LORD?"

BUT THE PEOPLE WERE VERY THIRSTY FOR WATER, SO THEY GRUMBLED [COMPLAINED] AGAINST MOSES. THEY SAID, "WHY DID YOU BRING US OUT OF EGYPT? WAS IT TO KILL US, OUR CHILDREN, AND OUR FARM ANIMALS WITH THIRST?"

SO MOSES CRIED TO THE LORD, "WHAT CAN I DO WITH THESE PEOPLE? THEY ARE ALMOST READY TO STONE ME TO DEATH."

THE LORD SAID TO MOSES, "GO AHEAD OF THE PEOPLE, AND TAKE SOME OF THE ELDERS OF ISRAEL WITH YOU. CARRY WITH YOU THE WALKING STICK [STAFF] THAT YOU USED TO STRIKE THE NILE RIVER [14:21]. NOW GO! I WILL STAND IN FRONT OF YOU ON A ROCK AT MOUNT SINAI [HOREB; ANOTHER NAME FOR SINAI; 3:1]. HIT [STRIKE] THAT ROCK WITH THE STICK [STAFF], AND WATER WILL COME OUT OF IT SO THAT THE PEOPLE CAN DRINK." MOSES DID THESE THINGS AS THE ELDERS OF ISRAEL WATCHED. HE NAMED THAT PLACE MASSAH [HEBREW FOR "TEST"], BECAUSE THE ISRAELITES TESTED THE LORD WHEN THEY ASKED, "IS THE LORD WITH US OR NOT?" HE ALSO NAMED IT MERIBAH [HEBREW FOR "QUARREL"], BECAUSE THEY QUARRELED [ACCUSED; MADE A CASE]. (Exodus 17:1-7)

THE HORSES, CHARIOT DRIVERS, AND CHARIOTS OF THE KING OF EGYPT [PHARAOH] WENT INTO THE SEA, AND THE LORD COVERED THEM WITH [RETURNED ON THEM THE] WATER FROM THE SEA. BUT THE ISRAELITES WALKED THROUGH THE SEA ON DRY LAND. THEN AARON'S SISTER MIRIAM, A PROPHETESS, TOOK A TAMBOURINE IN HER HAND. ALL THE WOMEN FOLLOWED HER, PLAYING TAMBOURINES AND DANCING. MIRIAM TOLD THEM:

"SING TO THE LORD,
BECAUSE HE IS WORTHY OF GREAT HONOR [IS HIGHLY EXALTED; *OR* HAS TRIUMPHED GLORIOUSLY];
HE HAS THROWN THE HORSE AND ITS RIDER
INTO THE SEA." (Exodus 15:29-21)

We only have limited accounts of Miriam in the Bible, but those accounts show us the wealth of purpose she had as a female prophet, one who was a literal prophet of her day, and also a type of New Covenant prophet, as well:

- **Song, Praise, and Worship**: The realm of the prophetic is the realm of spiritual artistic expression. Through the inspiration of the Spirit, those who operate in the prophetic often exercise the balance of spiritual arts, including sacred music and writing, sacred poetry, creation of physical works of art (design, painting, etc.), spiritual dance, and spiritual performing arts. Miriam was not just a singer, but one who led the community of Israel in spiritual song and worship, much as a worship

47

THE DIVINE FEMININE

leader does so today (Exodus 15:20). Through musical leads, Miriam knew how to lift the ultimate song to God, the song that echoed a knowledge of the God through experience.

- **Leadership of other women**: Tradition states Miriam not only led the women out of Egypt, but it was also her responsibility to teach them the Torah. Perhaps one of the greatest defenses of female leadership in the ancient world was the way most societies were segregated by gender. Women were required to teach the women, especially on matters unsuitable for mixed company. While some Jewish communities and many Christian ones debate the role of women as instructors of theological matters and some do not believe women should even learn about spirituality, Miriam's role as a front-and-center instructor on essential spiritual matters proves otherwise.

- **Equality**: Miriam was considered on par with Aaron and Moses in her leadership position. While her function was different from that of Moses and Aaron, all were considered leaders, and of value among the people. Miriam wasn't the same as Moses, but she was certainly as important to Israel and Israel's history.

- **Prophetic word**: It is obvious that Miriam spoke the word of God, and her words were considered authoritative, life-giving, and official.

- **Relationship with God**: Miriam's challenge to Moses over Zipporah (which had nothing to do with race) was more about Moses' separation from his wife to handle prophetic matters. It didn't have anything to do with her. She challenged Moses because her relationship with God did not compel her to leave her spouse in prophetic pursuit, as she was able to balance the two. Moses had more responsibility than she did, and it wasn't her place to cast such judgement over him or his marriage. Regardless, her objections do prove she had a

129

relationship with God, one that was her own, and one that enabled her to hear from God directly, for herself.

MIRIAM AND AARON SPOKE AGAINST MOSES BECAUSE OF THE CUSHITE WOMAN WHOM HE HAD MARRIED, FOR HE HAD MARRIED A CUSHITE WOMAN. AND THEY SAID, "HAS THE LORD INDEED SPOKEN ONLY THROUGH MOSES? HAS HE NOT SPOKEN THROUGH US ALSO?" AND THE LORD HEARD IT. NOW THE MAN MOSES WAS VERY MEEK, MORE THAN ALL PEOPLE WHO WERE ON THE FACE OF THE EARTH. AND SUDDENLY THE LORD SAID TO MOSES AND TO AARON AND MIRIAM, "COME OUT, YOU THREE, TO THE TENT OF MEETING." AND THE THREE OF THEM CAME OUT. AND THE LORD CAME DOWN IN A PILLAR OF CLOUD AND STOOD AT THE ENTRANCE OF THE TENT AND CALLED AARON AND MIRIAM, AND THEY BOTH CAME FORWARD. AND HE SAID, "HEAR MY WORDS: IF THERE IS A PROPHET AMONG YOU, I THE LORD MAKE MYSELF KNOWN TO HIM IN A VISION; I SPEAK WITH HIM IN A DREAM. NOT SO WITH MY SERVANT MOSES. HE IS FAITHFUL IN ALL MY HOUSE. WITH HIM I SPEAK MOUTH TO MOUTH, CLEARLY, AND NOT IN RIDDLES, AND HE BEHOLDS THE FORM OF THE LORD. WHY THEN WERE YOU NOT AFRAID TO SPEAK AGAINST MY SERVANT MOSES?" AND THE ANGER OF THE LORD WAS KINDLED AGAINST THEM, AND HE DEPARTED.

WHEN THE CLOUD REMOVED FROM OVER THE TENT, BEHOLD, MIRIAM WAS LEPROUS, LIKE SNOW. AND AARON TURNED TOWARD MIRIAM, AND BEHOLD, SHE WAS LEPROUS. AND AARON SAID TO MOSES, "OH, MY LORD, DO NOT PUNISH US BECAUSE WE HAVE DONE FOOLISHLY AND HAVE SINNED. LET HER NOT BE AS ONE DEAD, WHOSE FLESH IS HALF EATEN AWAY WHEN HE COMES OUT OF HIS MOTHER'S WOMB." AND MOSES CRIED TO THE LORD, "O GOD, PLEASE HEAL HER—PLEASE." BUT THE LORD SAID TO MOSES, "IF HER FATHER HAD BUT SPIT IN HER FACE, SHOULD SHE NOT BE SHAMED SEVEN DAYS? LET HER BE SHUT OUTSIDE THE CAMP SEVEN DAYS, AND AFTER THAT SHE MAY BE BROUGHT IN AGAIN." SO MIRIAM WAS SHUT OUTSIDE THE CAMP SEVEN DAYS, AND THE PEOPLE DID NOT SET OUT ON THE MARCH TILL MIRIAM WAS BROUGHT IN AGAIN. AFTER THAT THE PEOPLE SET OUT FROM HAZEROTH, AND CAMPED IN THE WILDERNESS OF PARAN. (Numbers 12:1-16, ESV)

Miriam was not perfect, not in any sense of the word, and seeing her imperfections is to prove to us that the excellency of her work was God's, and not hers personally. She dealt with her own issues as a woman, as a sister of two very powerful brothers in the history of her own people and her own nation, personal rivalries between the siblings, and her own struggles, those which we know nothing about. Yet despite Miriam's flaws, some of which are put on display through Scripture, we gain a true sense from her of spiritual purpose and empowerment. She was chosen by God, not because of her gender, but because she had the power to convey and embolden His word. Her gender put her in a unique position to work with and empower the Hebrew women, and at such a point in Israeli history, such was needed. The Hebrews had spent several generations in slavery, the women as well as the men, and the women needed a greater sense of themselves as spiritual beings with the ability to overcome. They needed to hear the word of God from a woman, and Miriam was the woman for the job.

Deborah

At every turning point of salvation history, there has always been a woman central to the rebuilding of God's people. This is, perhaps, the most convincing argument in favor of women's ordination and the work of women in ministry: whenever something new had to happen, God always made sure a woman was there. This is a part of the fulfillment of the "new thing" in the earth, that which involves not just the woman, but the spiritual embodiment of female leadership and the church herself. Women are essential in the rebuilding phase, in that time when people have been lost and disorganized, forgotten and distant from God, and now the time has come for them to be brought near, once again, through true spiritual relationship and principle. There is no greater example of a woman in this role than Deborah, who served as judge and prophet over Israel during a rebuilding phase of Israel's history. When Deborah entered the scene, there were no roads, no government, and an inefficient nation, one that was turning to the right, and the left, and everything in between. Because Deborah was so front-and-center with her leadership, she is a favorite of most who embody – and defend – the work of female ministry, especially that of the apostle, of which Deborah was a type.

> ## DEBORAH
> - *DEBORAH*: A BEE
> - ORIGINAL WORD: דְּבוֹרִים
> - PART OF SPEECH: NOUN FEMININE
> - TRANSLITERATION: DEBORAH
> - PHONETIC SPELLING: (DEB-O-RAW')
> - SHORT DEFINITION: BEES

Have we ever stopped to consider just why women are sent in when things have reached a point that seems to be of no return? Surely, God could have sent in anyone He desired, but it was His choice to send in a woman, one who could lead with the skill and instruction to bring the people back to wherever it was they needed to be. When Israel acted like a bunch of spoiled children, they needed a mother to set them straight. It was Deborah's position, as a prophet and a judge, to instruct and guide, to do more than just hand down verdict, but also to teach, instruct, and lead the people of God back with the guidance and perspective only a woman could provide.

AFTER EHUD DIED, THE ISRAELITES [SONS/CHILDREN OF ISRAEL] AGAIN DID WHAT THE LORD SAID WAS WRONG [EVIL IN THE EYES/SIGHT OF THE LORD]. SO HE LET THEM BE DEFEATED BY [SOLD THEM INTO THE HANDS OF] JABIN, A KING OF CANAAN WHO RULED IN THE CITY OF HAZOR. SISERA, WHO LIVED IN HAROSHETH HAGGOYIM, WAS THE COMMANDER OF JABIN'S ARMY. BECAUSE HE HAD NINE HUNDRED IRON [IRON-CLAD; IRON-FITTED; 1:19] CHARIOTS AND WAS VERY CRUEL TO [HARSHLY OPPRESSED] THE PEOPLE [SONS; CHILDREN] OF ISRAEL FOR TWENTY YEARS, THEY CRIED TO THE LORD FOR HELP.

A PROPHETESS NAMED DEBORAH, THE WIFE OF LAPPIDOTH, WAS JUDGING [LEADING; 2:16] ISRAEL AT THAT TIME. DEBORAH WOULD SIT UNDER THE PALM TREE OF DEBORAH, WHICH WAS BETWEEN THE CITIES OF RAMAH AND BETHEL, IN THE MOUNTAINS [HILL COUNTRY] OF EPHRAIM. AND THE PEOPLE [SONS; CHILDREN] OF ISRAEL WOULD COME TO HER TO SETTLE THEIR ARGUMENTS [FOR JUDGMENT]. (JUDGES 4:1-5)

Deborah was the fourth judge of Israel. After the death of the second judge (named Ehud), the people of Israel started to move wayward, doing whatever they desired and following idols. God delivered them to Canaan, and Sisera, the general of Canaan's army, oppressed Israel for twenty years. Deborah enters the picture at this time in history. She was from Ephraim, between Raman and Beth-El. She was faithful to God's precepts and assumed her position as both a prophet and leader of the nation, addressing the different situations people brought before her. She was the wife of Lappidoth, who we know nothing about, except that he appears to have been a supportive husband, and true to encourage her in her governance of Israel. They had to figure out their own limits and boundaries and come to the conclusions as to what was best for them, rather than an abstract concept of relationships that came through someone else's advice.

Deborah was a prophetess, but that was not the beginning and ending of her position over Israel. She was also a judge, which indicates she had a governmental position. She addressed disputes, handled matters between individuals, and was the one to consult about property, legalities, and other issues of a governing nature. Her spiritual position as a prophetess gave her the insight to lead wisely and should bespeak to all of us as to the spiritual nature of our work, and how hearing from God (as we can all do that) can help all of us as we do the work of the Lord.

So, it should have been a surprise to no one that Deborah was front and center at a point of obedience in the governance of Israel, and one who was sought out for guidance and leadership at an essential point in time. Deborah stepped up as a military leader in Israel's history in the midst of her governance, when the time came to overthrow Sisera's reign of terror. This is perhaps her greatest legacy and provides us with the most insight into her work, and her courage. When she was called, she went, and when she was needed, she rose to the challenge.

DEBORAH SENT A MESSAGE TO [OR SENT FOR; SUMMONED] BARAK SON OF ABINOAM. BARAK LIVED IN THE CITY OF KEDESH, WHICH IS IN THE AREA OF NAPHTALI [KEDESH-NAPHTALI]. DEBORAH SAID TO BARAK, "THE LORD, THE GOD OF ISRAEL, COMMANDS YOU: 'GO AND GATHER TEN THOUSAND MEN [SONS] OF NAPHTALI AND ZEBULUN [TWO TRIBES COVERING MOST OF ISRAEL'S AREA NORTH OF THE

JEZREEL VALLEY] AND LEAD THEM TO MOUNT TABOR [A CONE-
SHAPED MOUNTAIN IN JEZREEL VALLEY SOUTHWEST OF LAKE
GALILEE]. I WILL MAKE [DRAW/PULL OUT] SISERA, THE COMMANDER
OF JABIN'S ARMY, AND HIS CHARIOTS, AND HIS ARMY MEET YOU AT
THE KISHON RIVER. I WILL HAND SISERA OVER TO YOU [GIVE HIM
INTO YOUR HAND].'" (Judges 4:6-7)

The book of Judges reveals to us that God gave Deborah the
command to activate the military and overcome Sisera. They
were to take back their nation from their captors, for one simple
reason: Israel handed itself over to them through idolatry, and
now, they needed to position themselves to take their nation
back. The word could have come through anyone, but it came
through Deborah, proving her position within the nation.

THEN BARAK SAID TO DEBORAH, "I WILL GO IF YOU WILL GO WITH ME,
BUT IF YOU WON'T GO WITH ME, I WON'T GO."

"OF COURSE [CERTAINLY; GOING] I WILL GO WITH YOU," DEBORAH
ANSWERED, "BUT YOU WILL NOT GET CREDIT [HONOR; GLORY; FAME]
FOR THE VICTORY [IN THE ROAD/WAY/VENTURE YOU ARE TAKING].
THE LORD WILL LET A WOMAN DEFEAT SISERA [SELL SISERA INTO THE
HAND OF A WOMAN]." SO DEBORAH [AROSE AND] WENT WITH BARAK
TO KEDESH. AT KEDESH, BARAK CALLED [SUMMONED] THE PEOPLE
OF ZEBULUN AND NAPHTALI TOGETHER. FROM THEM, HE GATHERED
TEN THOUSAND MEN TO FOLLOW HIM [TEN THOUSAND MEN WENT UP
AT HIS FEET], AND DEBORAH WENT WITH HIM ALSO.

NOW HEBER THE KENITE HAD LEFT [SEPARATED/MOVED AWAY
FROM] THE OTHER KENITES, THE DESCENDANTS OF HOBAB, MOSES'
BROTHER-IN-LAW [OR FATHER-IN-LAW]. HEBER HAD PUT UP HIS TENT
BY THE GREAT TREE IN ZAANANNIM, NEAR KEDESH [THIS VERSE
INTRODUCES THE FAMILY OF JAEL, THE WOMAN ALLUDED TO BY
DEBORAH IN V. 9; SEE V. 17].

WHEN SISERA WAS TOLD THAT BARAK SON OF ABINOAM HAD GONE TO
MOUNT TABOR, SISERA GATHERED HIS NINE HUNDRED IRON [IRON-
CLAD; IRON-FITTED; V. 3] CHARIOTS AND ALL THE MEN WITH HIM,
FROM HAROSHETH HAGGOYIM TO THE KISHON RIVER.

THEN DEBORAH SAID TO BARAK, "GET UP! TODAY IS THE DAY THE LORD WILL HAND OVER SISERA [HAS GIVEN SISERA INTO YOUR HAND]. THE LORD HAS ALREADY CLEARED THE WAY FOR [GONE OUT BEFORE] YOU." SO BARAK LED TEN THOUSAND MEN DOWN MOUNT TABOR. AS BARAK APPROACHED, THE LORD CONFUSED [CAUSED TO PANIC; OR ROUTED] SISERA AND HIS ARMY AND CHARIOTS. THE LORD DEFEATED THEM WITH THE [EDGE OF THE] SWORD, BUT SISERA LEFT [JUMPED OUT OF] HIS CHARIOT AND RAN AWAY ON FOOT. BARAK AND HIS MEN CHASED SISERA'S CHARIOTS AND ARMY TO HAROSHETH HAGGOYIM. WITH THEIR SWORDS [BY THE EDGE OF THE SWORD] THEY KILLED ALL OF SISERA'S MEN; NOT ONE OF THEM WAS LEFT ALIVE.

BUT SISERA HIMSELF RAN AWAY TO THE TENT WHERE JAEL LIVED. SHE WAS THE WIFE OF HEBER, ONE OF THE KENITE FAMILY GROUPS [V. 11]. HEBER'S FAMILY [THE HOUSE OF HEBER] WAS AT PEACE [OR HAD AN ALLIANCE] WITH JABIN KING OF HAZOR. JAEL WENT OUT TO MEET SISERA AND SAID TO HIM, "COME INTO MY TENT [TURN ASIDE], MASTER! COME IN. DON'T BE AFRAID." SO SISERA WENT INTO JAEL'S TENT, AND SHE COVERED HIM WITH A RUG [OR BLANKET].

SISERA SAID TO JAEL, "I AM THIRSTY. PLEASE GIVE ME SOME WATER TO DRINK." SO SHE OPENED A LEATHER BAG [GOATSKIN] OF MILK AND GAVE HIM A DRINK. THEN SHE COVERED HIM UP.

HE SAID TO HER, "GO STAND AT THE ENTRANCE TO THE TENT. IF ANYONE COMES AND ASKS YOU, 'IS ANYONE HERE?' SAY, 'NO.'"

BUT JAEL, THE WIFE OF HEBER, TOOK A TENT PEG AND A HAMMER AND QUIETLY [SECRETLY] WENT TO SISERA. SINCE HE WAS VERY TIRED, HE WAS IN A DEEP SLEEP. SHE HAMMERED THE TENT PEG THROUGH THE SIDE OF SISERA'S HEAD [TEMPLE; OR MOUTH] AND INTO THE GROUND. AND SO SISERA DIED.

AT THAT VERY MOMENT [AND BEHOLD] BARAK CAME BY JAEL'S TENT, CHASING SISERA. JAEL WENT OUT TO MEET HIM AND SAID, "COME. I WILL SHOW YOU THE MAN YOU ARE LOOKING FOR." SO BARAK ENTERED HER TENT, AND THERE SISERA LAY DEAD, WITH THE TENT PEG IN HIS HEAD [TEMPLE; OR MOUTH].

ON THAT DAY GOD DEFEATED [SUBDUED; HUMILIATED] JABIN KING OF CANAAN IN THE SIGHT OF [BEFORE THE SONS/CHILDREN OF] ISRAEL.

ISRAEL BECAME STRONGER AND STRONGER [THE HAND OF SONS/CHILDREN OF ISRAEL PRESSED HARDER AND HARDER] AGAINST JABIN KING OF CANAAN UNTIL FINALLY THEY DESTROYED HIM. (JUDGES 4:8-24)

Let me say upfront that there are many who paint a particularly unflattering picture of Barak, who was military general over the nation of Israel during Deborah's reign. They say he was afraid, or he was weak, and that's why the prophecy was made that the victory would go to the woman. The text doesn't indicate this, and there is no tradition that supports it, either. Barak came forth to his leader, the prophet and judge of his nation, wanting her to come and guide on their military journey. It was very common for prophets to serve not just as spiritual leaders, but military guides in Biblical times. He went to his leader and sought her insight, and we judge him as weak or insecure for that. Ten thousand men followed the command of Deborah (which should quell any arguments against women in the military), and Barak recognized order. He knew the importance of this victory. In his obedience, he received the ultimate test: the battle would go to a woman, which tells us God had something divine to prove in this battle victory. It wouldn't be typical, nor would it follow the course most battles did. Because of his obedience, he could accept that God's plan for the battle involved a woman. Whether or not the victory went to a man, there were still many men involved in the process, and they had to position themselves properly to bring the battle to the place it needed to stand for the victory to come about. Yes, the one who brought down Sisera was a woman, but she did it with the help of everyone who was a part of the process – Deborah, Barak, and the entire army – showing we can do far more if we are only willing to work together. Teamwork matters.

Still, it is most relevant the hand of victory went to a woman. The world in which Deborah led, and Jael lived was not one of pure victory for women, and I haven't a single doubt that Deborah dealt with discrimination in her position as judge of Israel. There was someone who thought a female positioned for leadership over the nation indicated weakness, and that is part of the reason the victory had to lay in the hands of a woman. Deborah's position in Israel proved something about the leadership of women, and Jael's victory proved something about the skill and abilities of women. In this one story, we see every stereotype of women dispelled, all because God dared to call women to do jobs that no one felt either could do. The victory was not just for Israel, but for all women who are challenged to move outside the comfortable boundaries of societal placement. Jael herself wasn't a woman who would be selected as a warrior, or one with great prestige, but God proves that no matter what we might think of a woman on the outside, she can move with the skill and precision of a true warrior.

One of the reasons we don't hear about Deborah (or Jael, for that matter) as often as we should is because it seems, on the surface, that Deborah and Jael represent a violent nature, contrary to femininity. When we start talking about spiritual warfare, we don't think of women in that context, or in the context of aggression. It's never a topic for a women's conference and it is never something we consider when we start hearing about victory over the enemy. Women who are warlike or fierce in battle are considered "vengeful," and such behavior is often regarded as wrong.

The underlying message that women can't be warriors, whether natural or spiritual, is just as sexist as it is to say that women should always stay at home and have no lives or purpose outside of their homes. We can't be strong in the Spirit, but passive as people, and this is especially true when it comes to the realm of the prophetic and apostolic.

I TELL YOU THE TRUTH, JOHN THE BAPTIST IS GREATER THAN ANY OTHER PERSON EVER BORN [BORN TO WOMEN], BUT EVEN THE LEAST IMPORTANT PERSON IN THE KINGDOM OF HEAVEN IS GREATER THAN JOHN [BECAUSE JOHN PREPARES FOR, BUT DOES NOT FULLY PARTICIPATE IN THE BLESSINGS OF THE KINGDOM]. SINCE THE TIME [FROM THE DAYS] JOHN THE BAPTIST CAME UNTIL NOW, THE KINGDOM OF HEAVEN HAS BEEN GOING FORWARD IN STRENGTH [ADVANCING FORCEFULLY; OR SUBJECT TO VIOLENCE; SUFFERING VIOLENT ATTACKS], AND FORCEFUL [OR VIOLENT] PEOPLE HAVE BEEN TRYING TO TAKE IT BY FORCE [LAY HOLD OF IT; OR ATTACK IT]. ALL THE PROPHETS AND THE LAW OF MOSES TOLD ABOUT WHAT WOULD

HAPPEN [PROPHESIED] UNTIL THE TIME JOHN CAME [JOHN]. AND IF YOU WILL BELIEVE WHAT THEY SAID, YOU WILL BELIEVE THAT JOHN IS ELIJAH [ARE WILLING TO ACCEPT IT, HE IS ELIJAH], WHOM THEY SAID WOULD COME. LET THOSE WITH EARS USE THEM AND LISTEN [THE ONE WHO HAS EARS TO HEAR, LET HIM HEAR]! (Matthew 11:11-15)

From what we can see of Deborah in these powerful passages, we learn the following about her as a type of apostle:

- **Being sent**: When we talk about the work of the apostle in terms of "being sent," we often think of wherever it is that an apostle goes. There's nothing wrong with this, and when it comes to missions, the apostle is the one who does, indeed, go into a nation first (or should), to help establish the needed structure and foundation to build up not just a church, but the church, in that area. Being sent is not just about going somewhere, however. Anyone can go anywhere for any reason and say they have been "sent." Being sent is also about positioning, about being in a specific reason for a specific time and about fulfilling a specific purpose. Nobody embodied this quite like Deborah, who was in a place that was ready to disintegrate and destroy itself, until she rose up. Apostles are not just sent to go somewhere – they are sent for a purpose.

- **Going first**: I've often described the apostolic office as one where we "go first." This means the apostle delves into places and territories the church has often never gone before. This is not just about physical location, but about ideas and concepts, new approaches, and new ways that we make the Gospel relevant in each generation.

- **Breaking stereotypes**: Deborah did not fit into a stereotypical female role. For a true apostle to do the work of the apostle, he or she cannot fit into a stereotypical box of comfort and societal acceptance. Those who are apostles are outside of the box, outside of the boundaries of what's conventional, and what is convenient. The whole concept of going first means pushing limits, and doing what no one thinks you can do within custom.

- **The ability to lead**: Leadership is spoken of in the Scriptures as a spiritual gift (Proverbs 11:14, Romans 12:8, 1 Corinthians 12:28, 1 Timothy 5:22). That means we can take as many leadership classes as we like, on as many diverse topics as we like, but if we aren't gifted for leadership, we will never be leaders. Deborah wasn't selected because there were no qualified leaders. She was selected because she was gifted for leadership, and God knew she had the ability to lead in the unique situation she would find as leader over Israel.

Deborah is a stellar example of the competency of women as leaders, actively hearing from God, able to take His leading, and in turn, leading others. It may sound like a simplistic explanation of leadership to describe it as the ability to follow God so others in turn are able to follow Him too, but that's exactly what is required for excellent spiritual leadership. We see so many examples of military battle in Scripture because they are examples of following direction and instruction, and Deborah's position as the female leader of the military is no exception to this rule. She was able to lead because she knew how to follow God. Whether male or female, if we want to stand as leaders, we must be able to follow divine leadership. Leadership quality is not predicated on gender (what we are down here), but on Who we are willing to follow into eternity.

Huldah

> *HULDAH*
> - *CHULDAH:* AN ISRAELITE PROPHETESS; "WEASEL" OR "MOLE"
> - ORIGINAL WORD: חֻלְדָּה
> - PART OF SPEECH: PROPER NAME FEMININE
> - TRANSLITERATION: CHULDAH
> - PHONETIC SPELLING: (KHOOL-DAW')
> - SHORT DEFINITION: HULDAH

Huldah is one of those Bible women that we don't know about because we have never heard about her. Her story, much like that of Isaiah's wife, is moderately obscure in Scripture. It's not a passage we pick out and examine for preaching or content, although it is actually a very relevant – and important – passage within the history of Scripture and canon. While part of this is, most likely, because the authority in the passage does belong to a woman, it is also probably because we do not always respect traditions of scholarship and inspiration within our own circles. When stories in the Bible feel like they are over our heads, our inclination is to disregard and overlook them in favor of passages that seem easier to understand.

Huldah, identified as a prophetess, was the wife of Shallum, who worked as the keeper of the wardrobe (cared for royal clothing) during King Josiah's reign. It was during Josiah's reign that Huldah discovered her prophetic calling and started her prophetic work. There is no question Huldah fulfilled a prophetic office, and it is believed that she was over a School of the Prophets or perhaps an instructor in one. The School of the Prophets were centers of prophetic training, typically where older, seasoned prophets trained newer prophets in the delivery of God's word. This set her in a position of authority, one where she could be consulted about matters, as well as teach on them. This is exactly what happened in our accounts of Huldah and proves how vital she was among the people of her day.

We find Huldah's story in 2 Kings 22:13-20 and 2 Chronicles 34:14-33:

"GO AND ASK [INQUIRE OF] THE LORD ABOUT THE WORDS IN THE BOOK [SCROLL] THAT WAS FOUND. ASK FOR ME, FOR ALL THE PEOPLE, AND FOR ALL JUDAH. THE LORD'S ANGER IS BURNING GREATLY [FIERCELY] AGAINST US, BECAUSE OUR ANCESTORS [FATHERS] DID NOT OBEY [LISTEN TO] THE WORDS OF THIS BOOK [SCROLL]; THEY DID NOT DO ALL THE THINGS WRITTEN FOR US TO DO [CONCERNING US]."

SO HILKIAH THE PRIEST, AHIKAM, ACBOR, SHAPHAN, AND ASAIAH WENT TO TALK TO HULDAH THE PROPHETESS. SHE WAS THE WIFE OF SHALLUM SON OF TIKVAH, THE SON OF HARHAS, WHO TOOK CARE OF THE KING'S CLOTHES [WARDROBE]. HULDAH LIVED IN JERUSALEM, IN THE NEW AREA [NEW QUARTER] OF THE CITY.

SHE SAID TO THEM, "THIS IS WHAT THE LORD, THE GOD OF ISRAEL, SAYS [THUS SAYS THE LORD, THE GOD OF ISRAEL]: TELL THE MAN WHO SENT YOU TO ME, 'THIS IS WHAT THE LORD SAYS: I WILL BRING TROUBLE TO [DISASTER/EVIL ON] THIS PLACE AND TO THE PEOPLE LIVING HERE, AS IT IS WRITTEN [IN ACCORDANCE WITH THE WORDS] IN THE BOOK [SCROLL] WHICH THE KING OF JUDAH HAS READ. THE PEOPLE OF JUDAH HAVE LEFT [ABANDONED; FORSAKEN] ME AND HAVE BURNED INCENSE TO OTHER GODS. THEY HAVE MADE ME ANGRY [AROUSED/PROVOKED ME TO ANGER] BY ALL THAT THEY HAVE DONE. MY ANGER BURNS AGAINST THIS PLACE, AND IT WILL NOT BE PUT OUT [QUENCHED].' TELL THE KING OF JUDAH, WHO SENT YOU TO ASK [SEEK; INQUIRE OF] THE LORD, 'THIS IS WHAT THE LORD, THE GOD OF ISRAEL, SAYS ABOUT THE WORDS YOU HEARD: WHEN YOU HEARD MY WORDS [WHAT I SPOKE] AGAINST THIS PLACE AND ITS PEOPLE, YOU BECAME SORRY FOR WHAT YOU HAD DONE [YOUR HEART WAS TOUCHED/RESPONSIVE/PENITENT/TENDER] AND HUMBLED YOURSELF BEFORE ME. I SAID THEY WOULD BE CURSED AND WOULD BE DESTROYED [DESOLATED]. YOU TORE YOUR CLOTHES [A SIGN OF MOURNING OR DISTRESS], AND YOU CRIED IN MY PRESENCE [WEPT BEFORE ME]. THIS IS WHY I HAVE HEARD YOU, SAYS THE LORD. SO I WILL LET YOU DIE [GATHER YOU TO YOUR FATHERS/ANCESTORS], AND YOU WILL BE BURIED [GATHERED TO YOUR GRAVE] IN PEACE. YOU WON'T SEE ALL THE TROUBLE [DISASTER; EVIL] I WILL BRING TO THIS PLACE.'"

SO THEY TOOK HER MESSAGE BACK TO THE KING. (2 KINGS 22:13-20)

THE LEVITES BROUGHT OUT THE MONEY THAT WAS IN THE TEMPLE [HOUSE] OF THE LORD. AS THEY WERE DOING THIS, HILKIAH THE PRIEST FOUND THE BOOK [SCROLL] OF THE LORD'S TEACHINGS [INSTRUCTIONS; LAWS] THAT HAD BEEN GIVEN THROUGH MOSES. HILKIAH SAID TO SHAPHAN THE ROYAL SECRETARY [SCRIBE], "I'VE FOUND THE BOOK [SCROLL] OF THE TEACHINGS [INSTRUCTIONS; LAWS] IN THE TEMPLE [HOUSE] OF THE LORD!" THEN HE GAVE IT TO SHAPHAN.

SHAPHAN TOOK THE BOOK [SCROLL] TO THE KING AND REPORTED TO JOSIAH, "YOUR OFFICERS [OFFICIALS] ARE DOING EVERYTHING YOU TOLD [ASSIGNED; ENTRUSTED] THEM TO DO. THEY HAVE PAID OUT THE MONEY [SILVER] THAT WAS IN THE TEMPLE [HOUSE] OF THE

LORD AND HAVE GIVEN [DELIVERED; ENTRUSTED] IT TO THE SUPERVISORS [OVERSEERS] AND THE WORKERS."

THEN SHAPHAN THE ROYAL SECRETARY [SCRIBE] TOLD THE KING, "HILKIAH THE PRIEST HAS GIVEN ME A BOOK [SCROLL]." AND SHAPHAN READ FROM THE BOOK [SCROLL] TO THE KING.

WHEN THE KING HEARD THE WORDS OF THE TEACHINGS [INSTRUCTIONS; LAWS], HE TORE HIS CLOTHES [A SIGN OF MOURNING OR DISTRESS]. HE GAVE ORDERS TO HILKIAH, AHIKAM SON OF SHAPHAN, ACBOR SON OF MICAIAH, SHAPHAN THE ROYAL SECRETARY [SCRIBE], AND ASAIAH, THE KING'S SERVANT. THESE WERE THE ORDERS: "GO AND ASK [INQUIRE OF] THE LORD ABOUT THE WORDS IN THE BOOK [SCROLL] THAT WAS FOUND. ASK FOR ME AND FOR THE PEOPLE WHO ARE LEFT ALIVE IN [REMNANT OF] ISRAEL AND JUDAH. THE LORD IS VERY ANGRY WITH [POURING OUT/IGNITING HIS WRATH ON] US, BECAUSE OUR ANCESTORS [FATHERS] DID NOT OBEY [SEEK] THE LORD'S WORD; THEY DID NOT DO [ACT IN ACCORDANCE WITH] EVERYTHING THIS BOOK [SCROLL] SAYS TO DO."

SO HILKIAH AND THOSE THE KING SENT WITH HIM WENT TO TALK TO HULDAH THE PROPHETESS. SHE WAS THE WIFE OF SHALLUM SON OF TIKVAH, THE SON OF HARHAS, WHO TOOK CARE OF THE KING'S CLOTHES [KEEPER OF THE WARDROBE]. HULDAH LIVED IN JERUSALEM, IN THE NEW AREA OF THE CITY [SECOND QUARTER].

SHE SAID TO THEM, "THIS IS WHAT THE LORD, THE GOD OF ISRAEL, SAYS [THUS SAYS THE LORD, THE GOD OF ISRAEL]: TELL THE MAN WHO SENT YOU TO ME, 'THIS IS WHAT THE LORD SAYS: I WILL BRING TROUBLE TO [DISASTER/EVIL ON] THIS PLACE AND TO [ON] THE PEOPLE LIVING HERE. I WILL BRING ALL THE CURSES THAT ARE WRITTEN IN THE BOOK [SCROLL] THAT WAS READ TO THE KING OF JUDAH [DEUT. 27–28]. THE PEOPLE OF JUDAH HAVE LEFT [ABANDONED; FORSAKEN] ME AND HAVE BURNED INCENSE TO OTHER GODS. THEY HAVE MADE ME ANGRY [PROVOKED/AROUSED ME TO ANGER] BY ALL THE EVIL THINGS [IDOLS] THEY HAVE MADE. SO I WILL PUNISH THEM IN MY ANGER [MY WRATH WILL BE POURED OUT ON THIS PLACE], WHICH WILL NOT BE PUT OUT [QUENCHED; EXTINGUISHED].' TELL THE KING OF JUDAH, WHO SENT YOU TO ASK [INQUIRE OF] THE LORD, 'THIS IS WHAT THE LORD, THE GOD OF ISRAEL, SAYS ABOUT THE WORDS [MESSAGE] YOU HEARD: WHEN YOU HEARD MY WORDS

AGAINST THIS PLACE AND ITS PEOPLE, YOU BECAME SORRY FOR WHAT YOU HAD DONE [YOUR HEART WAS TENDER/RESPONSIVE/SENSITIVE] AND YOU HUMBLED YOURSELF BEFORE ME. YOU TORE YOUR CLOTHES [A SIGN OF MOURNING OR DISTRESS], AND YOU CRIED IN MY PRESENCE. THIS IS WHY I HAVE HEARD YOU, SAYS THE LORD. SO I WILL LET YOU DIE AND BE BURIED [GATHER YOU TO YOUR ANCESTORS/FATHERS AND TO YOUR GRAVE/TOMB] IN PEACE. YOU WON'T SEE ALL THE TROUBLE [DISASTER; EVIL] I WILL BRING TO THIS PLACE AND THE PEOPLE LIVING HERE.'"

SO THEY TOOK HER MESSAGE [RESPONSE; ANSWER] BACK TO THE KING.

THEN THE KING GATHERED [SUMMONED] ALL THE ELDERS OF JUDAH AND JERUSALEM TOGETHER. HE WENT UP TO THE TEMPLE [HOUSE] OF THE LORD, AND ALL THE PEOPLE FROM JUDAH AND FROM JERUSALEM WENT WITH HIM. THE PRIESTS, THE LEVITES, AND ALL THE PEOPLE—FROM THE MOST IMPORTANT TO THE LEAST IMPORTANT [BOTH GREAT AND SMALL; *OR* FROM THE OLDEST TO THE YOUNGEST]— WENT WITH HIM. HE READ TO THEM ALL THE WORDS IN THE BOOK [SCROLL] OF THE AGREEMENT [COVENANT; TREATY] THAT WAS FOUND IN THE TEMPLE [HOUSE] OF THE LORD. THE KING STOOD BY HIS PILLAR [A PLACE OF AUTHORITY] AND MADE AN AGREEMENT [COVENANT; TREATY] IN THE PRESENCE OF [BEFORE] THE LORD TO FOLLOW THE LORD AND OBEY [KEEP] HIS COMMANDS, RULES, AND LAWS WITH HIS WHOLE BEING [ALL HIS HEART] AND TO OBEY THE WORDS OF THE AGREEMENT [COVENANT; TREATY] WRITTEN IN THIS BOOK [SCROLL]. THEN JOSIAH MADE [REQUIRED] ALL THE PEOPLE IN JERUSALEM AND BENJAMIN PROMISE TO ACCEPT [STAND WITH HIM REGARDING] THE AGREEMENT [COVENANT; TREATY]. SO THE PEOPLE OF JERUSALEM OBEYED [ACTED IN ACCORDANCE WITH] THE AGREEMENT [COVENANT; TREATY] OF GOD, THE GOD OF THEIR ANCESTORS [FATHERS].

AND JOSIAH THREW OUT THE [DETESTABLE; ABOMINABLE] IDOLS FROM ALL THE LAND THAT BELONGED TO THE ISRAELITES. HE LED [FORCED; CAUSED] EVERYONE IN ISRAEL TO SERVE THE LORD THEIR GOD. WHILE JOSIAH LIVED, THE PEOPLE OBEYED [DID NOT TURN FROM] THE LORD, THE GOD OF THEIR ANCESTORS [FATHERS]. (2 CHRONICLES 34:14-33)

The basics of what might sound like a complicated encounter are as follows: A book of the law was discovered and there was a question as to the authenticity of its contents. Part of the concern was the prophetic insights contained within the writing (all of which would come to pass later in time). King Josiah commanded Hilkiah the priest, Ahikam, Achbor, Shapan the scribe, and Asiah (Josiah's servant) to find someone who could interpret and discern its contents. This sounds like natural work for a prophet, and it was most natural that when the men sought someone to identify it, they would go to the School of the Prophets, where prophets were present to seek out and instruct on such matters. There they found Huldah, who was serving in her position as prophetess, and she was on duty, ready to do what was necessary.

As much as Deborah held a national position, Huldah had a spiritual one recognized beyond a local gathering or city of believers. She was nationally recognized, recommended by the government in place in her time, as a legitimate, authorized spiritual leader. This speaks much to the confidence that others had within her but also speaks to a greater reality: her ministry gifts were noted, and obvious, by others. Sometimes we jump up and down about non-acceptance when what we need to do is let our gifts become so notable. There is no denying them. Of course, we advocate for our work and our gender in our work, but we should never get so busy standing as advocates that we forget about the work of the Spirit, and its ability to transform everything we touch. Huldah received her position because of her abilities, and her abilities outshined everything anyone might have wanted to say to the contrary, including negative words about her gender.

The concerns about the scroll Huldah was to interpret are of most relevance to the time in which Huldah lived, as the law was not properly followed, nor obeyed, by their ancestors. Its contents were deemed authentic, and if the people did not follow it (from the simplest peasant to the king himself), destruction would come upon them. King Josiah, however, was assured the destruction to come would not be in his lifetime, because he had been faithful to God, and to his service.

Huldah was the first person ever, in the history of Scripture, to declare any part of Scripture as authentic and inspired. She also clearly saw the connection between prophecy and Scripture, and the way the two relate to one another. It might seem like a simple concept, but the reality is understanding the nature between the two is often misunderstood. Sometimes prophecy is over-emphasized and given authority over Scripture, and sometimes Scripture is used to devalue prophecy. The two should work together, and Huldah exemplifies the balance needed when handling the prophetic work of God and assessing things properly and rightly.

Huldah was a type of the New Covenant apostle. The evidence for such is as follows:

- **Not easily intimidated**: Huldah referred to the King of Judah, Josiah, as "the man that sent you to me." Now if most of us got a recommend from a national leader, we probably wouldn't call him, "that man who sent you here," but that's just what Huldah did. She did not regard him as any more special than anyone else, and saw him from a spiritual perspective, rather than a person in "high places." Huldah wasn't easily impressed with people and their earthly positions, and this proves a higher calling, one that enabled her to work with people across many different platforms and boundaries.

- **Governance**: All offices of the Ephesians 4:11 ministry have some level of governance. The rule of deciding written authority and inspiration is a governance of the apostle, as it relates to spiritual administration. Huldah's entire work was administrative: it declared a rule of authority and law for the entire nation of Israel and established the rule of divine consequence if such was not followed. Never to be abused, the role of governance must consider all involved, and the spiritual role a leader is to play in such a situation.

- **Renown**: There is considerable debate about the work of the apostle in the church today, including its relevance and the boundaries of such authority. Apostles (and prophets, as well) represent universal authority, one that extends beyond the borders of a local church. Huldah was of such note, even the government knew about her. While we might not have the same system today and our government leaders might not be as warm to embrace or identify with a religious figure, what apostles do should be known beyond the boundaries of a local or immediate church or building.

- **Interpretation of Scripture**: The Scriptures themselves teach that Scripture is inspired (2 Timothy 3:16-17), and that in many instances, we must interpret what the Scriptures say in order to understand just how they apply for our day and age. Huldah was involved in the interpretation of Scripture, as well as the way that it would apply in days to come.

- **Operation of institution**: The church today often backs away from institutionalization, feeling that such is a step toward denominationalism or some sort of cultic control. The reality is, however, that having institutions, whether they are colleges, schools, ministries, seminaries, or other works that relate to ministerial education, rather than just church services, are an essential part of the apostolic as we understand it, and the training of ministers of all types.

Huldah's work was extremely authoritative, beyond that which much of the church is often comfortable embracing for women. Yet I believe that is part of Huldah's role as establishing canon, reiterating inspiration, and standing as an ensign that women in such positions does not have to be such an obscure, rare thing. While there are only a few women who may rise to such a role, the reality is there are only a few men who rise to such position, as well. They aren't works that are for everyone, but that doesn't exclude women from staking a spiritual place at the table of apostolic purpose.

Isaiah's Wife

If you never realized Isaiah's wife held the prophetic office yourself (or maybe even that Isaiah had a wife), you are not alone. Reference to her as such is in an obscure part of Scripture that is seldom studied and often overlooked. Because the passage isn't in a part of Isaiah that is easy to preach about, nor is it easy to muse on for public preaching, we don't walk away with a sense of Isaiah's wife as a prophetess for our own selves and personal musings.

The book of Isaiah is home to some very complicated prophecy and theology, much of which isn't the easiest to understand. It speaks of events, both immediate and distant. Some prophecies overlap, containing words for both Isaiah's day and the future glory to come. Understanding the book of Isaiah requires a pretty hefty understanding of Israel's history in the time of the prophecy. What Isaiah spoke about and related was spoken through the realities and impending realities of Israel in his lifetime, and what he saw futuristically related to what he saw in real-time. When delivering the words of promise, Isaiah knew the relevance of such intense spiritual gifts. This means he didn't identify people as having or not having them lightly and took prophetic responsibility seriously.

Isaiah wasn't the only one in his household who heard from God, however. In this prophetically complex book, we find the following words on a woman whose name we don't even have. There is no tradition of a name for Isaiah's wife, neither in Christianity, nor Judaism. She is simply referred to, by her own husband, as "the prophetess:"

THE LORD TOLD ME, "TAKE A LARGE SCROLL [OR TABLET] AND WRITE ON IT WITH AN ORDINARY PEN [OR ORDINARY LETTERS/SCRIPT; THE STYLUS OF A MAN]: 'MAHER-SHALAL-HASH-BAZ ["QUICK TO THE PLUNDER; SWIFT TO THE SPOIL"].' I WILL CALL [OR SO I CALLED; OR CALL...!] SOME MEN TO BE RELIABLE WITNESSES: URIAH THE PRIEST AND ZECHARIAH SON OF JEBEREKIAH."

THEN I WENT TO [EUPHEMISM FOR SEXUAL RELATIONS] THE PROPHETESS, AND SHE BECAME PREGNANT [CONCEIVED] AND HAD A SON. THE LORD TOLD ME, "NAME THE BOY MAHER-SHALAL-HASH-BAZ [V. 1], BECAUSE THE KING OF ASSYRIA WILL TAKE AWAY [CARRY OFF] THE WEALTH OF DAMASCUS AND THE POSSESSIONS [SPOIL; PLUNDER] OF SAMARIA BEFORE THE BOY LEARNS TO SAY 'MY FATHER' OR 'MY MOTHER' [ABOUT AGE TWO; THE FIRST STAGE OF THE DESTRUCTION, WHICH CULMINATED IN 722 BC; SEE 7:15–16]."

AGAIN THE LORD SPOKE TO ME, SAYING,

"[BECAUSE] THESE PEOPLE REFUSE TO ACCEPT
   THE SLOW-MOVING [GENTLY FLOWING] WATERS OF THE POOL OF
SHILOAH [PROBABLY THE STREAM FLOWING FROM THE GIHON SPRING
TO THE POOL OF SILOAM (JOHN 9:7); GOD'S GENTLE INFLUENCE IS
CONTRASTED WITH THE "FLOOD" OF THE ASSYRIAN INVASION; V. 7]
AND ARE TERRIFIED OF [*OR* REJOICE OVER] REZIN
   AND THE SON OF REMALIAH [PEKAH; 7:1, 4–5].
SO I, THE LORD, [LOOK/BEHOLD, THE LORD] WILL BRING AGAINST
THEM
   A POWERFUL FLOOD OF WATER FROM THE EUPHRATES RIVER
[RIVER]—
   THE KING OF ASSYRIA AND ALL HIS POWER [GLORY].
THE ASSYRIANS WILL BE LIKE WATER RISING [IT WILL RISE] OVER THE
BANKS OF THE RIVER [ITS CHANNELS],
   FLOWING OVER THE LAND [ITS BANKS].
THAT WATER WILL FLOW [SWEEP] INTO JUDAH AND PASS THROUGH IT,
   RISING TO JUDAH'S THROAT [THE NECK].
THIS ARMY [IT] WILL SPREAD ITS WINGS LIKE A BIRD
   UNTIL IT COVERS YOUR WHOLE COUNTRY [THE BREADTH OF OUR
LAND], IMMANUEL [*OR* GOD IS WITH US]."

BE BROKEN [*OR* YOU WILL BE BROKEN], ALL YOU NATIONS,
   AND [YOU WILL] BE SMASHED TO PIECES [SHATTERED].
LISTEN, ALL YOU FARAWAY COUNTRIES [LANDS].
   PREPARE FOR BATTLE [GIRD YOURSELVES] AND [YOU WILL] BE
SMASHED TO PIECES [SHATTERED]!
   PREPARE FOR BATTLE [GIRD YOURSELVES] AND [YOU WILL] BE
SMASHED TO PIECES [SHATTERED]!
MAKE YOUR PLANS FOR THE FIGHT [DEVISE YOUR STRATEGY],
   BUT THEY WILL BE DEFEATED [IT WILL BE THWARTED].
GIVE ORDERS TO YOUR ARMIES [SPEAK A COMMAND/WORD],
   BUT THEY WILL BE USELESS [IT WILL NOT STAND],
BECAUSE GOD IS WITH US [IMMANUEL].

[FOR] THE LORD SPOKE TO ME WITH HIS GREAT POWER [STRONG
HAND] AND WARNED ME NOT TO FOLLOW THE LEAD [WALK IN THE
WAY] OF THE REST OF THE [THIS] PEOPLE. HE SAID,
"PEOPLE ARE SAYING THAT OTHERS MAKE PLANS AGAINST THEM,
   BUT YOU SHOULD NOT BELIEVE THEM [DON'T CALL 'CONSPIRACY'
EVERYTHING THIS PEOPLE CALLS 'CONSPIRACY'].
DON'T BE AFRAID OF WHAT THEY FEAR;

DO NOT DREAD THOSE THINGS.
BUT REMEMBER THAT THE LORD ALL-POWERFUL [ALMIGHTY; OF HEAVEN'S ARMIES; OF HOSTS] IS HOLY.

HE IS THE ONE YOU SHOULD [YOUR] FEAR;
HE IS THE ONE YOU SHOULD [YOUR] DREAD.
THEN HE WILL BE A PLACE OF SAFETY FOR YOU [SANCTUARY; HOLY PLACE; OR SNARE].

BUT [OR AND] FOR THE TWO FAMILIES [HOUSES] OF ISRAEL [ISRAEL AND JUDAH],
HE WILL BE LIKE A STONE THAT CAUSES PEOPLE TO STUMBLE,
LIKE A ROCK THAT MAKES THEM FALL [ROM. 9:33; 1 PET. 2:6–8].
HE WILL BE LIKE A TRAP FOR THE PEOPLE [INHABITANTS] OF JERUSALEM,
AND HE WILL CATCH THEM IN HIS TRAP [SNARE].
MANY PEOPLE WILL FALL OVER THIS ROCK [STUMBLE OVER THEM].
THEY WILL FALL AND BE BROKEN;
THEY WILL BE TRAPPED [SNARED] AND CAUGHT."
MAKE AN AGREEMENT [OR PRESERVE THIS PROPHECY; BIND UP THIS TESTIMONY].

SEAL UP THE TEACHING WHILE MY FOLLOWERS ARE WATCHING [OR AND ENTRUST IT TO MY FOLLOWERS/DISCIPLES; AMONG MY FOLLOWERS/DISCIPLES].
I WILL WAIT FOR [PATIENTLY TRUST] THE LORD [FOR HIS HELP],
THE LORD WHO IS ASHAMED OF [HIDING HIS FACE FROM] THE FAMILY OF ISRAEL [HOUSE OF JACOB].
I WILL WAIT FOR [HOPE IN; TRUST IN] HIM.

I AM HERE, AND WITH ME ARE [LOOK/BEHOLD, I AND] THE CHILDREN THE LORD HAS GIVEN ME. WE ARE SIGNS AND PROOFS [SYMBOLS; WARNINGS; OMENS] FOR THE PEOPLE OF ISRAEL FROM THE LORD ALL-POWERFUL [ALMIGHTY; OF HEAVEN'S ARMIES; OF HOSTS], WHO LIVES [DWELLS] ON MOUNT ZION.

SOME PEOPLE SAY, "ASK THE MEDIUMS AND FORTUNE-TELLERS [NECROMANCERS; SPIRITISTS], WHO WHISPER [OR CHIRP] AND MUTTER [USING INCANTATIONS TO CALL UP SPIRITS; 1 SAM. 28:8–11], WHAT TO DO." BUT I TELL YOU THAT PEOPLE SHOULD ASK THEIR GOD FOR HELP. WHY SHOULD PEOPLE WHO ARE STILL ALIVE ASK SOMETHING FROM THE DEAD? [OR "SHOULD NOT A NATION CONSULT THEIR GODS, ASKING THE DEAD ON BEHALF OF THE LIVING?"; IN THIS INTERPRETATION THE QUOTATION CONTINUES TO THE END OF THE

VERSE]. YOU SHOULD FOLLOW THE TEACHINGS AND THE AGREEMENT WITH THE LORD [(LOOK) TO THE LAW/INSTRUCTION AND TO THE TESTIMONY]. THE MEDIUMS AND FORTUNE-TELLERS DO NOT [THOSE WHO DO NOT; *OR* IF THEY DO NOT] SPEAK THE WORD OF THE LORD [ACCORDING TO THIS WORD], SO THEIR WORDS ARE WORTH NOTHING [*OR* THEY ARE SPIRITUALLY BLINDED; THEY HAVE NO DAWN].

PEOPLE WILL WANDER THROUGH THE LAND [THEY WILL PASS THROUGH] TROUBLED [*OR* DESTITUTE] AND HUNGRY. WHEN THEY BECOME HUNGRY, THEY WILL BECOME ANGRY AND WILL LOOK UP AND CURSE THEIR KING AND THEIR GOD. THEY WILL LOOK AROUND THEM AT THEIR LAND AND SEE ONLY TROUBLE [DISTRESS], DARKNESS, AND AWFUL GLOOM. AND THEY WILL BE FORCED INTO THE DARKNESS. (ISAIAH 8:1-22)

There is some debate as to whether Isaiah's wife was a genuine prophetess or just the wife of one. Given our other Old Testament examples of women who were identified as such all indicate having certain gifts, I think it's safe to say that Isaiah's wife was called prophetess because of her own spiritual abilities, not those of her husband. If she was identified as a female prophet, she met the prophetic tests to be such and had the ability to speak the words she heard from God, all by herself. The passage indicates she was the mother of Isaiah's children, specifically Maher-shalal-hash-baz ("Destruction is Imminent"), and also Sherajashub ("A Remnant Shall Return"), as well. Part of her prophetic ministry was bearing these two sons, both of whom were named in connection with prophetic realities coming to befall upon Israel, and the types that were found in her pregnancy, naming, and raising of these children.

From the limited information we have about Isaiah's wife, I would classify her as a type of a New Covenant prophet, but in a very different sense than that we have of Miriam. Isaiah's wife literally lived the spoken prophecy, from conception, to pregnancy, to the raising of her children. As a result, her ministry appears, at least from the outside looking in, to fulfill a more stereotypically traditional role for women. This view, however, didn't stop her from standing in the prophetic gap, living the word from a literal perspective.

Isaiah's prophecies to Israel were educational and general, but for Isaiah's wife, prophecy was personal. It was more than just a word or a musing to others; it was literal. This literal embodiment of the word of God is something that some prophets experience and gives an experiential-based aspect to the spiritual life. Not everything we go through with God is textual; some of it is lived, some of it felt, and much of it perceived and figured out as we discern it through textual experience. Some of the examples of her prophetic type are:

- **Bearing the prophetic word**: Isaiah's wife literally bore the prophetic word of Isaiah through her children, whose names were connected to the prophecy. Their purpose was to point to the Word itself, and live out its symbolism in their lives, which relates to the prophetic call of a New Covenant prophet: carry the word and live out its meaning.

- **Delivering the prophetic word**: When we think of Isaiah's prophecy, we think of it as a word that he delivered. In reality, his wife also delivered it, by giving birth to their children.

- **Guarding the word**: As a mother to their children, Isaiah's wife guarded the symbolic prophecy within them as she raised them up and nurtured the word that was within their lives.

- **Living the word**: For Isaiah's wife, the prophetic word was personal. It was her life, it was in her body, it was in her children. The words that Isaiah spoke, and she spoke were her very life. For a true prophet, the prophetic word isn't just a nice musing or idea, it's not something that is just a passing phase, and it is not something that just comes and goes. It is their lives, and impacts all areas of their lives, as we can see it encompassing the way of life for Isaiah's wife.

One important note about Isaiah's wife that is important and relevant to her calling: we meet many women who are quickly overshadowed by their spouses' spiritual gifts. Those abilities might seem larger than life, or it may be nothing more than those women are diminished within church communities on account of their gender. Either way, there are lots of women who have their own spiritual abilities, but those gifts go unacknowledged and underdeveloped because people don't take the time to note, or care, about them. Isaiah's wife was of no lesser relevance because she was Isaiah's wife, and because she lived the prophecy that was made, rather than standing front-and-center over Israel. No matter how Isaiah's wife executed her spiritual gifts (be it just as living out the word in their family or as speaking over Israel herself, or perhaps even contributing to Isaiah's prophecy in some other way), her work as prophetess stands, whether she stood over much, or over a specific assignment.

Anna

> ANNA[6]
> * HANNA: ANNA, A PROPHETESS, "FAVORED"
> * ORIGINAL WORD: ΆΝΝΑ, ΑΣ, ἡ
> * PART OF SPEECH: NOUN, FEMININE
> * TRANSLITERATION: HANNA
> * PHONETIC SPELLING: (AN'-NAH)
> * SHORT DEFINITION: ANNA
> * DEFINITION: ANNA, A PROPHETESS, WHO VISITED THE INFANT JESUS.

Most believers know about the Prophetess Anna. Unlike a few of the other women we have examined, she isn't an obscure figure, buried in the pages of the Bible in between stories people seldom, if ever, study. She is front and center at the presentation of the child Jesus, spending years in preparation for His arrival. We don't ignore her as having a role in salvation history.

We just severely downplay it.

Anna is identified as a prophetess, the first mentioned by office in the New Testament. She was the daughter of Phanuel, of the tribe of Asher. We don't have any other information about her life, and there are no Christian traditions to supplement what the Scriptures don't tell us. From what we do know, she was somewhere between 84 years old and 105 years old. She was a widow, her husband dying after a seven-year marriage. For the remaining part of her life, she remained in the temple, day and night, fasting and praying, instead of remarrying.

This fact by itself is important. Under regulations found around the time of Christ's birth, women weren't allowed in the temple proper. Anna was allowed in the temple courts, or the outdoor portion of the temple...not the interior. This means for all those years, she was outside. Praying, fasting, seeking God, and awaiting the coming Messiah, all while battling the elements. She experienced the cold of night and the hot, dry days. She was dedicated, because she knew what was coming.

THERE WAS A PROPHETESS, ANNA, [HANNAH] FROM THE FAMILY [THE DAUGHTER] OF PHANUEL IN [WHO WAS FROM] THE TRIBE OF ASHER. SHE WAS VERY OLD AND HAD ONCE BEEN MARRIED FOR SEVEN YEARS. THEN HER HUSBAND DIED, AND SHE WAS A WIDOW FOR [OR TO THE AGE OF] EIGHTY-FOUR YEARS. SHE NEVER LEFT THE TEMPLE BUT WORSHIPED GOD, GOING WITHOUT FOOD [FASTING] AND PRAYING DAY AND NIGHT. STANDING THERE [OR COMING UP TO THEM] AT THAT TIME, SHE THANKED [PRAISED; BLESSED] GOD AND SPOKE ABOUT JESUS [HIM] TO ALL WHO WERE WAITING FOR GOD TO FREE [THE REDEMPTION/DELIVERANCE OF] JERUSALEM. (Luke 2:36-38)

Anna made the prophetic her entire life. She embodied it, lived it, felt it, and anticipated what was to come. It was so much of her life, she knew to anticipate the coming of the Word made flesh, the redemption of Jerusalem, that she fully believed – and knew – she would see in her lifetime.

When Anna saw Jesus presented in the temple, she immediately knew Who He was, and went boldly over to Jesus and His parents, thanking God for His presence in this world. She didn't stay there, however. For the first time in a long time, Anna left where she was and went and told people about the child Jesus, as they were looking forward to the coming Redeemer.

Many of the "firsts" we attribute to Bible men are incorrect. Due to conditioning, we are quick to assume the obvious first man to do things was, indeed, the first. This is untrue, as we can see in the case of Anna. The first person to ever tell others about Christ and spread the Gospel that He was in the world, and was, in fact, the Redeemer, was the Prophetess Anna. This makes Anna a type of the evangelist, one whose very heart and center of their ministry and message remains the salvation and redemption we find through Christ. Examples of this include:

- **The central heart of redemption**: The evangelist is the "Christ-bearer," one who, in their message and preaching, carries the literal word of redemption and life through Christ. The message of the evangelist is not embitterment or "holiness or hell," as some would have us believe. It is bearing Christ, bringing Christ to others, and announcing the promise that we can find in none but Him – salvation is here.

- **Bearing Christ**: Anna bore Christ in a unique way: she anticipated Him, knew He was coming, she awaited His arrival, and then she carried news of Him, everywhere she went. This is analogous to the way the evangelist "bears Christ:" they discover Him, anticipate His release in others' lives, and they carry news of Him, recognizing that "His arrival" in the lives of others comes in the form of manifestation of His presence.

- **Recognizing Christ**: There is nothing in the text to suggest anyone told Anna Who Christ was. She saw Him and recognized Him for herself and knew His manifestation. The evangelist, too, should recognize Christ for himself or herself, so that awareness can be heralded to others.

Anna proves to all of us that we are never too old, nor too young, to recognize Christ in our lives. She might not have had the prestige of Deborah or Huldah, but her recognition, and awareness, is just as important. Her dedication speaks volumes, as an inspiration for all of us, even today. There is nothing wrong with exercise of different spiritual gifts, and of watching and waiting for the appointed time to come, so that the fullness of what has been anticipated can be transformed, and made real, to those who receive the benefit of the promise.

Noadiah[7,8]

The last two prophetesses in our study have what we could call a spurious history. One is definitely a false prophetess, identified clearly as such, and one has a divided reputation as false and not false, just a little misguided. It is the latter which we shall study first: a woman who opposed the prophetic word of another Biblical figure, and has paid the price for that stance, ever since.

NOADIAH[10]
- *NOADYAH:* "MEETING WITH YAH," A LEVITE, ALSO A PROPHETESS
- ORIGINAL WORD: נוֹעַדְיָה
- PART OF SPEECH: PROPER NAME; MASCULINE; FEMININE
- TRANSLITERATION: NOADYAH
- PHONETIC SPELLING: (NO-AD-YAW')
- SHORT DEFINITION: NOADIAH

Noadiah is found in the book of Nehemiah. There are some questions as to her gender. The Septuagint identifies Noadiah as masculine. In Ezra chapter 8, there is a Levite named Noadiah, leading some to believe Noadiah was male rather than female. The Hebrew text, however, identifies Noadiah as a prophetess, and it is unfortunate that we don't have more to draw on from Noadiah's ministry. All we have as pertains to her is her opposition to the rebuilding of the wall, but we really don't know why. This means we really don't understand the entire story behind the conflict of Nehemiah and Noadiah.

ONE DAY [THEN] I WENT TO THE HOUSE OF SHEMAIAH SON OF DELAIAH, THE SON OF MEHETABEL. SHEMAIAH HAD TO STAY AT [WAS CONFINED TO HIS; PERHAPS RELATED TO A VOW OR TO RITUAL UNCLEANNESS] HOME. HE SAID, "NEHEMIAH, LET'S MEET IN THE TEMPLE [HOUSE] OF GOD. LET'S GO INSIDE THE TEMPLE AND CLOSE [BAR] THE DOORS, BECAUSE MEN ARE COMING AT NIGHT TO KILL YOU."

BUT I SAID, "SHOULD A MAN LIKE ME [IN HIS POSITION] RUN AWAY? SHOULD I RUN FOR [TO SAVE] MY LIFE INTO THE TEMPLE [TO SEEK ASYLUM; EX. 21:13–14; 1 KIN. 1:50–53; 2:28–34; 2 CHR. 26:16–20; 27:2]? I WILL NOT GO." I KNEW [REALIZED; PERCEIVED; RECOGNIZED] THAT GOD HAD NOT SENT HIM BUT THAT TOBIAH AND SANBALLAT HAD

PAID [HIRED] HIM TO PROPHESY AGAINST ME. THEY PAID [HIRED] HIM TO FRIGHTEN [INTIMIDATE; TERRORIZE] ME SO I WOULD DO THIS AND SIN. THEN THEY COULD GIVE ME A BAD NAME TO SHAME [ACCUSE AND DISCREDIT/BLAME] ME.

I PRAYED, "MY GOD, REMEMBER TOBIAH AND SANBALLAT AND WHAT THEY HAVE DONE. ALSO REMEMBER THE PROPHETESS NOADIAH AND THE OTHER PROPHETS WHO HAVE BEEN TRYING TO FRIGHTEN [INTIMIDATE; TERRORIZE] ME." (NEHEMIAH 6:10-14)

Noadiah lived during Nehemiah's lifetime. It appears her ministry was relevant during the time of rebuilding the wall of Jerusalem. She does not appear to have been married, but we don't know if that was because she was single and never married, or because she was a widow. Perhaps the first thing we need to recognize is Noadiah is acknowledged as a prophet by Nehemiah himself. There are no words in the passage that hint at Noadiah speaking false words, lies, or false prophecies, just that she opposed the work Nehemiah was doing. Nothing suggests he considered her a false prophet (when he did make the earlier accusation that Shemaiah was lying), so we should not be so hasty to identify her as such. What it does say is that she, along with the rest of the prophets (whoever they are) were opposed to the building of the wall in one form or another and stated their objections.

It is probably safe to say that Noadiah was of certain status and renown in her day, simply because she is mentioned by name, whereas the "other prophets" are mentioned as a group. She may have formalized action against the rebuilding of the wall, or held some sort of influence against its rebuilding, encouraging others to take a similar position. This is, most likely, why Noadiah was mentioned by name, and why Nehemiah took such issue with her opposition.

However, none of this means Noadiah was a false prophet. It simply means that, whatever her reason, she took issue with the building of the wall. Just as we know Miriam also opposed Moses (Numbers 12:1-16), she never lost her standing as a valid prophet. The same is true for Noadiah; she did not lose her status for objecting to the wall. The question still remains, however: why did she oppose the wall?

The prophetic word to rebuild the wall went to Nehemiah,

and not the general community of prophets in his day and age. This means there was conflict over the rebuilding of the wall, because it wasn't a vision that most prophets received. There were probably several reasons for this, such as cultural fear, concerns for divisions and dividing families (which we shall talk about more shortly), jealousy, or political questions. It might have also been nothing more than a group of prophets misunderstanding the reasoning behind a project or seeing other sides to it that we don't always consider.

When we read about Nehemiah's decision to rebuild the wall, especially in light of the opposition he received, we cheer that spirit on as a part of American independence and the idea that any one person can do whatever they feel called to do, all by themselves. This is fine and nice, but the counterpoint of such reality is that whenever someone ventures to do things without the consensus or agreement of the larger group, conflict arises. It is very possible the prophets opposed the wall because they were not consulted, the reasons for rebuilding the wall were not clear to them, or because they saw the issues differently.

What it sounds like happened among Noadiah and Nehemiah is classic of what we see among prophets today. We often assume that for a prophet to be valid, their word or vision must align with every other prophet's word or vision. Sometimes we forget that God can provide different assignments, and there may be reasons why prophets don't receive the same instructions for a specific project. We are quick to associate sameness with unity, and uniformity with ideal purpose. When we don't see the results of identical word, we automatically assume someone isn't hearing from God instead of examining the contents of the message and considering different aspects of different works.

It also sounds like Nehemiah expected the rest of the prophetic community to line up and support the vision to rebuild the wall, and he was bereft when they did not. There were probably many reasons why this wall didn't seem advantageous to others, and given we don't have the information about their prophetic insights, it's hard to determine true or false prophecy unless such is clearly identified as false. In his state of upset, he easily exaggerated what was said or attributed their conflicts to the rebuilding of the wall itself. Sometimes when we know we have heard from God and others raise points we haven't considered, we attribute their understanding (or limited understanding, as the case might be), to be outright opposition.

So why did Noadiah oppose the wall? The answer to this question is, we don't know. There are speculations that Noadiah had concern for dividing families of mixed marriages (because the building of the wall would have done such), or because the wall would have meant further alienation and separation for pagan women whose husbands divorced them considering spiritual renewal. It is reasonable to suggest that Noadiah would have understood the political reasons for the wall, including the safety of Jerusalem's inhabitants, but to know for sure, we can't identify just what their conflicts were. It is safe to say, however, that the issues between Noadiah and Nehemiah were disagreements, and the spiritual veracity of Noadiah's word was never in question.

Perhaps the situation with Noadiah and Nehemiah could have been resolved with a prophetic meeting of the minds, so to speak. This is an example where a School of the Prophets might have come in handy, offering the two the opportunity to speak on what was revealed to each. Maybe they could have found a way to work together, or at the very least, figured out some way to better understand each other's views. Regardless, this didn't happen, and such led to intense, unresolved conflict between the two. Nehemiah's wall was built, but we also learn the people of Israel didn't maintain their spiritual integrity for very long. I wonder if Noadiah's work might have been more relevant considering such, rather than the two arguing amongst themselves.

Examining Noadiah in this light isn't to say false prophets don't exist. This is not to say there is no false word, or that people don't come against the people of God when a work is to be done. It is just to point out that sometimes what we perceive as opposition is simply someone else's issue or burden at hand. We can feel like the entire world is against us when, in actuality, it is nothing more than a different perspective or a misunderstanding. This is why discernment is key in ministry, and why it is essential we take note of different gifts and callings, rather than instantly deciding someone who is different from us is always false.

Jezebel

JEZEBEL[11]

- *IEZABEL*: JEZEBEL, THE SYMBOLIC NAME OF A FALSE PROPHETESS, "BA'AL EXALTS, IS HUSBAND TO"
- ORIGINAL WORD: Ἰεζάβελ, ή
- PART OF SPEECH: PROPER NOUN, INDECLINABLE
- TRANSLITERATION: IEZABEL
- PHONETIC SPELLING: (EE-ED-ZAB-ALE')
- SHORT DEFINITION: JEZEBEL
- DEFINITION: JEZEBEL, NAME GIVEN TO A FALSE PROPHETESS OF THYATIRA, POSSIBLY BORROWED FROM THE NAME OF AHAB'S WIFE, QUEEN OF ISRAEL.

The last woman identified as prophetess in the Bible is clearly identified as a false prophet. She is identified only as Jezebel in Revelation 2:20. The passage itself is an address to the church in Thyatira, and the various praises and condemnations merited for their conduct:

"WRITE THIS TO THE ANGEL [MESSENGER; SEE 1:20] OF THE CHURCH IN THYATIRA [A SMALL CITY IN WESTERN ASIA MINOR]:

"THE SON OF GOD, WHO HAS EYES THAT BLAZE LIKE FIRE [1:14] AND FEET LIKE SHINING BRONZE [1:15; THE RESURRECTED JESUS], SAYS THIS [THESE THINGS]: I KNOW WHAT YOU DO [YOUR WORKS]. I KNOW ABOUT YOUR LOVE, YOUR FAITH, YOUR SERVICE, AND YOUR PATIENCE [ENDURANCE; PERSEVERANCE]. I KNOW THAT YOU ARE DOING MORE NOW THAN YOU DID AT FIRST [YOUR LAST WORKS ARE GREATER THAN THE FIRST].

"BUT I HAVE THIS AGAINST YOU: YOU LET THAT WOMAN JEZEBEL SPREAD FALSE TEACHINGS [TOLERATE THE WOMAN JEZEBEL; PROBABLY THE LEADER OF THE NICOLAITANS, HERE GIVEN THE NAME OF THE NOTORIOUS BAAL-WORSHIPING QUEEN; 1 KIN. 16:31–34; 21:25–26; 2 KIN. 9:22]. SHE SAYS SHE IS [CALLS HERSELF] A PROPHETESS, BUT BY HER TEACHING SHE LEADS [TEACHES AND MISLEADS/DECEIVES] MY PEOPLE [SERVANTS] TO TAKE PART IN SEXUAL SINS AND TO EAT FOOD THAT IS OFFERED TO IDOLS. I HAVE GIVEN HER TIME TO CHANGE HER HEART AND TURN AWAY FROM HER

SIN [REPENT OF HER SEXUAL IMMORALITY], BUT SHE DOES NOT WANT TO CHANGE [REPENT]. SO [LOOK!] I WILL THROW HER ON A BED OF SUFFERING [OR A SICKBED; THE BED USED FOR SEXUAL SIN IS NOW A BED OF SUFFERING]. AND ALL THOSE WHO TAKE PART IN ADULTERY WITH HER WILL SUFFER GREATLY IF THEY DO NOT TURN AWAY FROM THE WRONGS SHE DOES [REPENT OF HER WORKS/DEEDS]. I WILL ALSO KILL HER FOLLOWERS [CHILDREN]. THEN ALL THE CHURCHES WILL KNOW I AM THE ONE WHO SEARCHES HEARTS AND MINDS, AND I WILL REPAY EACH OF YOU FOR WHAT YOU HAVE DONE [YOUR WORKS/DEEDS].

"BUT OTHERS [THE REST] OF YOU IN THYATIRA HAVE NOT FOLLOWED HER TEACHING AND HAVE NOT LEARNED WHAT SOME CALL SATAN'S DEEP SECRETS. I SAY TO YOU THAT I WILL NOT PUT ANY OTHER LOAD [BURDEN] ON YOU. ONLY CONTINUE IN YOUR LOYALTY [HOLD FAST TO WHAT YOU HAVE] UNTIL I COME.

"I WILL GIVE POWER [AUTHORITY] OVER THE NATIONS TO EVERYONE WHO WINS THE VICTORY [OVERCOMES; CONQUERS] AND CONTINUES TO BE OBEDIENT TO ME [OR KEEPS WORKING FOR ME; KEEPS/OBEYS MY WORKS] UNTIL THE END.

'YOU [HE; THE ONE WHO OVERCOMES] WILL RULE OVER [SHEPHERD] THEM WITH AN IRON ROD [OR SCEPTER],
    AS WHEN POTTERY IS BROKEN INTO PIECES [OR AND WILL BREAK THEM INTO PIECES LIKE POTTERY; PS. 2:9].'

THIS IS THE SAME POWER [AUTHORITY] I RECEIVED FROM MY FATHER. I WILL ALSO GIVE HIM THE MORNING STAR [USUALLY THE PLANET VENUS AS SEEN BEFORE SUNRISE, BUT HERE SYMBOLICALLY CHRIST AT HIS RETURN; 22:16; NUM. 24:17; 2 PET. 1:19]. EVERYONE WHO HAS EARS SHOULD LISTEN TO [HEAR; OBEY] WHAT THE SPIRIT SAYS TO THE CHURCHES. (REVELATION 2:18-29)

Thyatira was a wealthy Lydian community near the ancient country of Mysia. It was known for its artisan trade guilds. Every participating artisan had to belong to one of those applicable guilds. They included fabric dying (and their signature purple-red color), buildings, altars, and fixed items. Everything intertwined with everything else in those days, and the guilds often intersected with the pagan culture of the city, including the different temples to honor their pagan deities. The most famous deities of Thyatir were Tyrimnos, the sun god, Boreatene, a goddess associated with the sun god, and Sambethe, a Persian-inspired sibyl.

This was the scene for Jezebel, the false prophet, to arrive on the scene and deceive the church at Thyatira. There were already extensive pressures for artisans and other workers of the city to honor pagan gods, and to maintain the wealth and comforts to which they were accustom, Christians there were often compromised in their spirituality. There was concern that they were compromising their faith for wealth and profit. While they did do good deeds, they had fallen into the tempting hands of Jezebel, the prophetess.

We don't know anything about Jezebel, including whether this was her real name. It might have been her name, or an illusion to Queen Jezebel of the Old Testamen. If this is the case (which is likely), it is a reference to describe the pagan woman of Revelation as an idolater sought out by the people and brought into the church. There is nothing to indicate she had a mysterious "spirit of Jezebel," nor does it indicate that such can be transferred to other people (and such would not fit, as Jezebel was not a valid prophetess or a pagan priestess in her own belief system). It's assumed she was probably a female oracle who sat in the temple of Sambethe and spoke words on behalf of the sibyl to the people. Along with her role as an oracle, she encouraged practices common to the paganism of the day: eat food sacrificed to the idols in connection with the pagan rites performed and participate in pagan sexual and fertility rites.

Jezebel was leading Christian believers in pagan worship...all within their local community! It looked and sounded good, but she wasn't doing the right thing from a spiritual perspective. Much like Jezebel of old positioned herself against true prophecy, this Jezebel led Christians through false prophecy.

There is no question what Jezebel was doing was against Christian value and belief, but this letter of Revelation isn't addressed to her; it is addressed to the church at Thyatira. For this reason, what she does relates to the community, and not with her, by herself. She does prove, however, that a woman can be a false prophet, just as a man can be, and the relevance and importance of discerning spirits, rather than following charismatic people who have great followings. Such can easily lead us astray, far from where we are supposed to be.

Jezebel also teaches us the lesson that bad leadership is bad leadership, regardless of gender. This prophetess wasn't condemned because she was female, nor was she given a free pass because of such. Being led astray is a real thing, and it's not right to lead others astray, whether a female leader, or not.

The lessons of the prophetesses

The true and false prophetesses we see presented in the Scriptures have a wealth of realities to offer us. We are not called to follow a gender or something else that relates to this world, but after the Spirit, which works and lives through a person who is rightly called of God. As was stated earlier, leadership is not a quality predicated on gender. God calls, and moves through whoever He desires, and that includes women, as well as men. As most of the Biblical examples of prophetesses are found pre-New Covenant, that should speak to us: if in the shadow of the covenant we see women operating and functioning in spiritual purpose, the reality to come would be women operating in the Spirit more frequently and profoundly, becoming the reality of each and every type we see in operation in the Old Covenant. True or false, we do not assign false prophecy to all men on account of their gender. We have true male prophets and false ones, which attune us to the need for discernment and readiness to the Spirit. The same is true of women. We cannot label every single female prophet as false, because there have been false female prophets, or because we are speaking of a woman. We must attune to the Spirit to discern true from false.

The gift of discernment calls us to draw ourselves out of natural barriers and regulations (such as those of gender) and attune to the Spirit in a deeper way. This is essential, as a general principle, when assessing any prophetic message, regardless of who might deliver it to us. From the beginning of salvation history, women have always been part of the process to deliver spiritual word in due season. We can also see they've done so while serving in many different capacities, recognizing women's roles to extend far beyond the comfortable borders established by modern society.

In eternity, our gender is not of consequence, but our work

of the Spirit most definitely is. Instead of judging someone as qualified by gender, we must look at the purpose and fruitage of the Spirit and become people who assess by things that are more than merely surface deep.

The woman Wisdom holding the Ecclesia (church) (Hildegard of Bingen)

CHAPTER FIVE
Female Expressions and Values

So [THEREFORE] LET US GO ON TO GROWN-UP TEACHING
[MOVE FORWARD TO MATURITY/COMPLETENESS].
LET US NOT GO BACK OVER [LEAVE BEHIND] THE BEGINNING [RUDIMENTARY; ELEMENTARY]
LESSONS [TEACHING; WORD] WE LEARNED ABOUT CHRIST [OR THE MESSIAH; 5:5].
WE SHOULD NOT AGAIN START TEACHING [LAY A FOUNDATION]
ABOUT TURNING AWAY [REPENTANCE] FROM THOSE ACTS THAT LEAD TO DEATH
[OR USELESS WORKS; DEAD WORKS] AND ABOUT FAITH IN GOD.
WE SHOULD NOT RETURN TO THE TEACHING ABOUT BAPTISMS
[EITHER CHRISTIAN BAPTISM OR JEWISH CEREMONIAL WASHINGS],
ABOUT LAYING ON OF HANDS [A RITUAL OF BLESSING AND/OR CONFERRING OF AUTHORITY],
ABOUT THE RAISING OF THE DEAD AND ETERNAL JUDGMENT
[THESE MAY BE JEWISH PRACTICES OR FOUNDATIONAL CHRISTIAN TEACHING].
AND WE WILL GO ON TO GROWN-UP TEACHING [DO THIS] IF GOD ALLOWS.
(HEBREWS 6:1-3)

WE already examined the way that words are identified as masculine and feminine in many foreign languages, and such is a large premise of the concept behind this book. In terms of our faith, there are many words, terms, and identities that are feminine, even though we aren't aware of it. The question in the minds of those who study then naturally becomes, why are they feminine, and does it matter? If a word is identified in some way as masculine, we would always believe such matters – and the same is true if terminology is feminine. God is teaching us things through each and every word that is a part of the Scriptures reminds us – or brings to recall – some spiritual principle we can embrace in our lives.

Some Biblical references seem easier to understand than others, and some require more digging and study. Here we will examine both those that we get right away and those we don't, to come to a better understanding of just what God has to say to us. Embracing the Scriptures is about more than just reading them, but also, seeing God's heart present to us, in them. This happens when we tackle challenges, and find God present in them. From the term El-Shaddai to the concept of life as female, we see God present in a different way, one that might cause us to question everything we have always learned, but to learn about God in a way that transcends the comfortable boundaries that we often hold dear. In every believer's life, we have the call to go beyond what we think we have always felt about God and discover God for ourselves.

In this chapter, this is exactly what we will be doing. We will be learning about aspects of the divine nature and spiritual things in a context most of us have never considered. Without jumping to the alternate extremes of alternative religion or pagan spirituality, we will see what is within the confines of our faith, but has been overlooked, for centuries.

The original Jewish Mother

> *I AM (YHVH)*
> - YHVH: THE PROPER NAME OF THE GOD OF ISRAEL, "TO BECOME, GET"
> - ORIGINAL WORD: יְהֹוָה
> - PART OF SPEECH: PROPER NAME
> - TRANSLITERATION: YHVH
> - PHONETIC SPELLING: (YEH-HO-VAW')
> - SHORT DEFINITION: LORD

When it comes to the Names of God, we find a mixed bag of gender identity. Yahweh or "I AM THAT I AM," is technically gender neutral. Among traditional Jewish understanding, masculine gender was used in identity of God, but they did not identify God as having the concept of sex, just gender. This varied among the Jewish mystics, but for the most part, the concept of God and gender often fit what we would classify as gender non-binary. This means they would identify God as male, but that did not mean God was a literal man, or that God fit the literal standard identity of a male as we recognize on earth. Maybe what God was trying to convey through this sort of concept is that God transcends our understanding of gender, and is embraceable by both male and female, as well as those who might identify outside of the binary understandings of male and female. God didn't just want to be relatable to men or to males, or understood in a stereotypical sense, thus making some uncomfortable or feeling lost; and to enable a solid human connection, our God Himself has literally, and in all possible ways, made Himself all things to all people.

This is further confirmed – and complicated – by study of God reflected in the Old Testament, study of the Names of God, and of the roles that God often takes on throughout Old Covenant theological relationship. Attempting to understand God in a limited concept of gender just doesn't work and makes it nearly impossible to see God fully if we only understand God through one, singular, gender-specific lens. To better understand the different aspects of divine gender identity in the Old Testament, we must also understand more of the way that ancient pagan ideas influenced Biblical people.

It's unrealistic to assume that Bible people were devoid of their pagan neighbors, even in light of the law and the extensive regulations created to discipline the ancient Hebrews into obedience. Their neighbors surrounded them, each with their host of pagan gods and goddesses, and the concepts of such influenced Israel, time and time again, away from the worship of the true God. The monotheism of the Hebrews was unique, especially for where they lived, and understanding one God meant that God had to embody the multi-faceted best characteristics of every other god and goddess that was around them. This led to some interesting identifiers to the one God: some masculine, some feminine, some gender neutral, but all seen as an essential part of the one God, their God, Who was unique among all gods.

This means some of the characteristics and descriptions of God lie in the realm of the feminine, attributing a feminine characteristic to God. This can be interpreted to mean more than one thing. Some say that it means God is a woman, but that would apply sex, beyond gender, to the divine, which is theologically incorrect. If we shouldn't do it in male identity, we should not do such with female identity, either. Some say it challenges male identity or what it means to be a man, which is a little bit more believable, but it is still limiting concepts of gender. What it is safer to assume is that God's characteristics aren't limited to male or female concepts, but are explained in gender-specific language in order to help those who read it better understand it. It reaches to men and women alike, giving them visual and relatable clues to the nature of God.

Perhaps most relevant, the concept of female expression and value in the very identity of God makes God less exclusionary. In ancient societies, the different gods and goddesses were known for one thing or a limited number of things, rather than for everything. Seeing God as more than just a man or a woman, but with the ability to do more than we can ever imagine (including crossing gender roles and barriers) makes God approachable, in every culture, throughout the world. It is God's desire that we can know Him, and we cannot do this if God fails to be multidimensional.

The Old Testament provides ten different verses where the nature of God is given a female imagery, or female perspective.[2]

- **Image of God is spoken to be both male and female:**
  SO GOD CREATED [1:1] HUMAN BEINGS [MAN; THE HEBREW *ADAM* CAN MEAN HUMAN BEINGS, HUMANKIND, PERSON, MAN, OR THE PROPER NAME ADAM] IN HIS IMAGE [REFLECTING GOD'S NATURE/CHARACTER AND REPRESENTING HIM IN THE WORLD]. IN THE IMAGE OF GOD HE CREATED THEM. HE CREATED THEM MALE AND FEMALE. (Genesis 1:27)

- **God is spoken of as a mother eagle:**
  LIKE AN EAGLE
    THAT STIRS UP ITS NEST
      AND HOVERS OVER ITS YOUNG,
  THAT SPREADS ITS WINGS TO CATCH THEM
      AND CARRIES THEM ALOFT.
  THE LORD ALONE LED HIM;
      NO FOREIGN GOD WAS WITH HIM. (Deuteronomy 32:11-12, NIV)

- **God is spoken of as giving birth:**
  YOU LEFT GOD
  WHO IS THE ROCK, YOUR FATHER [WHO BORE YOU; *OR* WHO BEGOT YOU],
      AND YOU FORGOT THE GOD WHO GAVE YOU BIRTH.
  (Deuteronomy 32:18)

- **God is compared to a woman**:
  BEHOLD, AS THE EYES OF SERVANTS LOOK TO THE HAND OF THEIR MASTER, AND AS THE EYES OF A MAID TO THE HAND OF HER MISTRESS, SO OUR EYES LOOK TO THE LORD OUR GOD, UNTIL HE HAS MERCY *AND* LOVING-KINDNESS FOR US. HAVE MERCY ON US, O LORD, HAVE MERCY ON *AND* LOVING-KINDNESS FOR US, FOR WE ARE EXCEEDINGLY SATIATED WITH CONTEMPT. (Psalm 123:2-3, AMPC)

- **God is spoken of as a mother**:
  BUT I AM CALM AND QUIET
  [HAVE STILLED AND QUIETED MY SOUL]
  LIKE A BABY [WEANED CHILD] WITH ITS MOTHER,
  LIKE A BABY [WEANED CHILD] WITH ITS MOTHER [A RELATIONSHIP WITH GOD IS LIKE THAT OF A MOTHER WITH HER WEANED CHILD RESTING COMFORTABLY IN HER ARMS].
  (Psalm 131:2)

- **God is compared to a woman in labor and a nursing mother:**
  THE LORD SAYS, "FOR A LONG TIME I HAVE SAID NOTHING [KEPT SILENT/STILL];
  I HAVE BEEN QUIET [STILL] AND HELD MYSELF BACK.
  BUT NOW I WILL CRY OUT
  AND STRAIN [PANT AND GASP] LIKE A WOMAN GIVING BIRTH TO A CHILD.
  I WILL DESTROY [LEVEL; LAY WASTE] THE HILLS AND MOUNTAINS
  AND DRY UP ALL THEIR PLANTS.
  I WILL MAKE THE RIVERS BECOME DRY LAND [ISLANDS; *OR* COASTLANDS]
  AND DRY UP THE POOLS OF WATER. (Isaiah 42:14-15)

- **God is spoken of as a comforting mother:**
  I WILL COMFORT YOU
  AS A MOTHER COMFORTS HER CHILD.
  YOU WILL BE COMFORTED IN JERUSALEM. (Isaiah 66:13)

- **God is spoken of as a mother raising her children:**
  IT WAS I WHO TAUGHT ISRAEL [EPHRAIM; 4:17] TO WALK,

AND I TOOK THEM BY THE ARMS,
BUT THEY DID NOT UNDERSTAND [OR ACKNOWLEDGE]
   THAT I HAD HEALED THEM.
I LED THEM WITH CORDS OF HUMAN KINDNESS [HUMANITY; OR
LEATHER],
   WITH ROPES OF LOVE.
I LIFTED THE YOKE FROM THEIR NECK [OR THEM LIKE A LITTLE
CHILD TO MY CHEEK]
   AND BENT DOWN AND FED THEM. (Hosea 11:3-4)

- ## God is described as a mother bear:
   I WILL ATTACK [MEET THEM] LIKE A BEAR ROBBED OF HER
CUBS,
    RIPPING THEIR BODIES [CHEST] OPEN.
I WILL DEVOUR THEM LIKE A LION
   AND TEAR THEM APART LIKE A WILD ANIMAL. (Hosea 13:8)

These counters to specifically male imagery were seen as feminine attributes because they were associated with motherhood or the characteristics of mothers: life-giving, protection, nurturing, comforting, and guiding. Attributed to God, they gave God a feminine-like characteristic, one that reflected behaviors and feelings associated with women. Using such analogy gave the hearers (and later readers) a proper understanding of essential natures of God that lead us to trust and hope in Him.

In modern society that sometimes takes on an anti-father or anti-male characteristic due to patristic abandonment or abuse, the world of all-male genderisms: father, he, him, worker, creator, provider, and beyond, can cause some intimidation in approaching their heavenly Father, not recognizing the difference. Yet in God's provision, thousands of years earlier God provided a way to educate those who might feel leery of male identity in the divine with an alternative. Our God truly is the God for everyone, whether they acknowledge Him as such, or not. Providing so many different perspectives of our one God does not threaten our faith; it enhances it, making way for anyone who wants to learn more to find their place, therein.

El-Shaddai

The Bible lists several interpersonal titular identities for God. Many of them are so personal, so related to His nature and character, we often classify them as "names" of God, because they are a part of the revelation of just Who God is, and several even include the proper Name of God itself. These names are:

- **Adonai**: My Lord
- **Adonai Elohim**: The Lord God
- **Adonai Elohim Tz'va'ot**: Lord, our God of armies (hosts) (2 Kings 6:16-17)
- **Adonai Elohim Elohei-Tzva'ot**: The Lord God, God of Hosts
- **Jehovah Jireh**: The Lord will provide (Genesis 22:13-14)
- **Jehovah Rapha**: The Lord that heals me (Exodus 15:26)
- **Jehovah Nissi**: The Lord, our banner (Exodus 17:8-15)
- **Jehovah Shalom**: The Lord, our peace (Judges 6:24)
- **Jehovah Ra'ah**: The Lord my Shepherd (Psalm 23:1)
- **Jehovah Tzidikenu**: The Lord our Righteousness (Jeremiah 23:6)
- **Jehovah Shammah**: The Lord is present (Ezekiel 48:35)
- **Ehyeh Asher Ehyeh**: I AM THAT I AM (Exodus 3:14, John 8:58)
- **El**: God
- **El Bethel**: God of Bethel, God of the house of God (Genesis 31:13)
- **El Echad**: One God (Malachi 2:10)
- **El Elyon**: God Most High (Genesis 14:20)
- **El Gibbor**: Mighty God (Isaiah 10:21)
- **El Olam**: Eternal God, Everlasting God
- **El Roi**: God who sees (Genesis 16:13)
- **El Shaddai**: Almighty God (Genesis 17:1, Exodus 6:2-3)
- **El Tzur**: God, our rock (2 Samuel 22:47)
- **Elah Yisrael**: God of Israel (Ezra 5:1)
- **Elah Yerushelem**: God of Jerusalem (Ezra 7:19)
- **Elah Shemaya**: God of heaven (Ezra 7:23)

- **Elah avahati**: God of my fathers (Daniel 2:23)
- **Elah Elahin**: God of gods (Daniel 2:47)
- **Eloah**: God
- **Elohim**: Lord Almighty (Deuteronomy 10:17, Jeremiah 32:27)
- **Elyon**: Supreme
- **HaShem**: The Name (Leviticus 24:11, Deuteronomy 28:58)

Of this list, most of the names are either neuter in tense (such as those which appear with the divine name proper) or are masculine in form. There is one divine name that has a spurious history, and one of the different theories about its origin gives a uniquely female twist to God's identity.

The name El Shaddai is the divine the Name by which Abraham, Isaac, and Jacob knew God, prior to the revelation as "I AM." Frequently translated into English as "God Almighty" or "Almighty Lord," it appears in the Bible seven different times: five in Genesis, once in Exodus, and once in Ezekiel. The term "Shaddai" appears forty-eight different times, all of which drive home the same point: a reference to God, almighty and powerful, having the quality of the God Who is above other gods, and is more powerful than anyone or anything else.

EL SHADDAI[3,4]
- *EL*: GOD, IN PL. GODS
- ORIGINAL WORD: אֵל
- PART OF SPEECH: NOUN MASCULINE
- TRANSLITERATION: EL
- PHONETIC SPELLING: (ALE)
- SHORT DEFINITION: GOD

- *SHADDAY*: ALMIGHTY
- ORIGINAL WORD: שַׁדַּי
- PART OF SPEECH: NOUN MASCULINE
- TRANSLITERATION: SHADDAY
- PHONETIC SPELLING: (SHAD-DAH'-EE)
- SHORT DEFINITION: ALMIGHTY

The first time we see the name "El Shaddai" is in Genesis 17:1:

WHEN ABRAM WAS NINETY-NINE YEARS OLD, THE LORD APPEARED TO HIM AND SAID, "I AM GOD ALMIGHTY [EL SHADDAI]. OBEY [WALK BEFORE] ME AND DO WHAT IS RIGHT [BE INNOCENT/BLAMELESS; JOB 1:1].

Later, in Genesis 35:11, we find:

GOD SAID TO HIM, "I AM GOD ALMIGHTY [EL SHADDAI]. HAVE MANY CHILDREN [BE FRUITFUL] AND GROW IN NUMBER [MULTIPLY; 1:22] AS A NATION. YOU WILL BE THE ANCESTOR OF MANY NATIONS [A COMPANY/ASSEMBLY OF NATIONS WILL COME FROM YOU] AND KINGS [WILL SPRING FROM YOUR LOINS]."

Exodus 6:2-3 reveals just how important the name is:

THEN GOD SAID TO MOSES, "I AM THE LORD. I APPEARED TO ABRAHAM, ISAAC, AND JACOB BY THE NAME GOD ALMIGHTY [EL SHADDAI], BUT THEY DID NOT KNOW ME BY MY NAME, THE LORD [YAHWEH].

Among a number of ancient tribes with different gods, it was most appropriate for God to reveal Himself as God Almighty, because He was revealing Himself to be the supreme spiritual answer for this lineage that was about to begin. No matter what one might think of the Hebrew term El Shaddai, there is no question of its relevance in the life of the ancient Hebrews. Such a revelation made it clear the God they were to worship, and how important monotheism would become, as they rose above their pagan roots to become something more than they ever imagined they could be.

This is where agreement about just what "El Shaddai" means ends. While we know "El" was a common word for God or a god in Canaanite culture, the word "Shaddai" is of far more debate. We don't know for certain what it meant, but there are a few different theories, a few of which point to the reality of another feminine identity for God.[5]

- **Means "God of the wilderness"**: Not the most widely embraced theory, but one nonetheless that raises the identity of God as the leader of a people known for hunting, in the sense of lacking cultivation or civilization.

- **<u>Means "God of the mountains"</u>**: Believing the word may reference ancient Mesopotamian religion or an ancient Mesopotamian tribal god, such theorizes that it is a reference to the Mesopotamian divine mountain, or a reference to Mt. Sinai, where the Israelites received the Ten Commandments. This echoes henotheistic religious practice, establishing that El Shaddai became Abram's tribal god, selected among other Mesopotamian gods, although there doesn't seem to be much evidence to support such a theory.

- **<u>Means "The Destroyer"</u>**: The root word of Shaddai is *shadad*, and means "to plunder, overpower, or make desolate." This would reflect a specific nature of God, representing divine strength and ability to overcome or take whatever is needed. This could also stand for a new beginning in a spiritual sense, as God destroys those false idols, and begins a new day for those who follow Him.

- **<u>Means "Many breasted one" or "dual breasted one"</u>**: This echoes a completely different concept from "the destroyer." To be the "dual breasted one" gives a uniquely female imagery to God, one as life-giver, sustainer, and nurturer.

It is this last one that reflects the feminine imagery we see of God throughout the Scriptures. The concept of God as El Shaddai provides a beautiful picture of God as our life-giver, of the source from Whom all life, all sustainability, all nurturing comes. The concept of being Almighty God, of being all-powerful, is associated with the foundations of life, of being foundationally connected to the creation by which all was created, and of sustaining that life. Being all-powerful isn't about conquering as much as it is about creating and keeping, having the ability to maintain the complexities of life on this planet instead of destroying it.

We often associate the concept of being Almighty and all-powerful with a dictator, but God comes in with El-Shaddai, as

His first revelation to humanity, as the complete opposite. This teaches us about leadership as much as it teaches us about feminine imagery, and the total contradiction to the concept that women are weak or incapable of leadership. The ability to produce and sustain life is the very thing that gives life to this planet, and whenever a woman nurses or feeds a child or life is born, we reflect this nature of God. To be almighty is to be over life, rather than death; and God does this both in the natural, and the spiritual. Such qualifies our God to stand as El Shaddai, over all life, over all truth, over all other beings, as He cares and tends to us in every possible way.

The glorious presence of God

In the Old Testament, the different words translated as "glory" are both masculine and feminine. This adds to their intrigue, as well as the nature of how those different glorious presences manifested.

Then there is a powerful word, one that echoes beyond the work of "glory" the very presence of God, often translated as "glory." That word is *shekinah*.

The word *shekinah*, as we hear it commonly spoken today, is not a word found in the Old Testament. It is a term from Jewish literature and mystical tradition, used to refer to the presence of God (not unlike the concept of the *Logos*, although the way *logos* is expressed is different). Sometimes interpreted as the glory of God or God's dwelling, settling, or "placement" of God, the word is feminine in form. This has led many Jewish scholars and mystics to refer to it as the feminine aspect of God, better known as the "divine presence." Because it is commonly used today and is even found in parts of certain Messianic and Hebrew Roots translations of the Bible, it is an important concept for us to embrace and see for ourselves, as something spiritual to understand.[14]

As an abstract embodiment in the New Testament, *shekinah* is often alluded to light and radiance, and there are instances where it is spoken as the "glory of the Lord." There are over twenty different references to it in the New Testament, including common passages:

IN THE COUNTRYSIDE NEARBY WERE SOME SHEPHERDS SPENDING THE

GLORY:

- *ADDERETH:* GLORY, A CLOAK, "MAJESTIC"[6]
- ORIGINAL WORD: אַדֶּרֶת
- PART OF SPEECH: NOUN FEMININE
- TRANSLITERATION: ADDERETH
- PHONETIC SPELLING: (AD-DEH'-RETH)
- SHORT DEFINITION: MANTLE

- *TIPHARAH:* BEAUTY, GLORY[7]
- ORIGINAL WORD: תִּפְאָרָה
- PART OF SPEECH: NOUN FEMININE
- TRANSLITERATION: TIPHARAH
- PHONETIC SPELLING: (TIF-AW-RAW')
- SHORT DEFINITION: GLORY

- *PAAR:* TO BEAUTIFY, GLORIFY[8]
- ORIGINAL WORD: פָּאַר
- PART OF SPEECH: VERB
- TRANSLITERATION: PAAR
- PHONETIC SPELLING: (PAW-AR')
- SHORT DEFINITION: GLORIFIED

- *KABOWD:* GLORIOUS[9]
- ORIGINAL WORD: כָּבוֹד
- PART OF SPEECH: NOUN MASCULINE
- TRANSLITERATION: KABOWD
- PHONETIC SPELLING: (KAW-BODE')
- SHORT DEFINITION: GLORIOUS
- RARELY, KABOD: ABUNDANCE, HONOR, GLORY; TO BE HEAVY, WEIGHTED, OR BURDENSOME
- TRANSLITERATION: KABOD
- SHORT DEFINITION: GLORY

- *YOKEBED.* "THE LORD IS GLORY," MOTHER OF MOSES[10]
- ORIGINAL WORD: יוֹכֶבֶד
- PART OF SPEECH: PROPER NAME FEMININE
- TRANSLITERATION: YOKEBED
- PHONETIC SPELLING: (YO-KEH'-BED)
- SHORT DEFINITION: JOCHEBED

- *HADARAH.* ADORNMENT, GLORY[11]
- TRANSLITERATION: HADARAH
  SHORT DEFINITION: ARRAY

- *EDER*: GLORY, MAGNIFICENCE, A MANTLE, CLOAK[12]
- ORIGINAL WORD: אֶדֶר
- PART OF SPEECH: NOUN
- TRANSLITERATION: EDER
- PHONETIC SPELLING: (EH'-DER)
- SHORT DEFINITION: MAGNIFICENT

- *YEQAR*: HONOR[13]
- ORIGINAL WORD: יְקָר
- PART OF SPEECH: NOUN MASCULINE
- TRANSLITERATION: YEQAR
- PHONETIC SPELLING: (YEK-AWR')
- SHORT DEFINITION: GLORY

NIGHT IN THE FIELDS, GUARDING THEIR FLOCKS, WHEN AN ANGEL OF *ADONAI* APPEARED TO THEM, AND THE *SH'KHINAH* OF *ADONAI* SHONE AROUND THEM. THEY WERE TERRIFIED; BUT THE ANGEL SAID TO THEM, "DON'T BE AFRAID, BECAUSE I AM HERE ANNOUNCING TO YOU GOOD NEWS THAT WILL BRING GREAT JOY TO ALL THE PEOPLE. (Luke 2:8-10, CJB)

THE WORD BECAME A HUMAN BEING AND LIVED WITH US, AND WE SAW HIS *SH'KHINAH*, THE *SH'KHINAH* OF THE FATHER'S ONLY SON, FULL OF GRACE AND TRUTH. (John 1:14, CJB)

I HEARD A LOUD VOICE FROM THE THRONE SAY, "SEE! GOD'S

SH'KHINAH IS WITH MANKIND, AND HE WILL LIVE WITH THEM. THEY
WILL BE HIS PEOPLE, AND HE HIMSELF, GOD-WITH-THEM, WILL BE
THEIR GOD. (Revelation 21:3, CJB)

GLORY[15,16]
- *SHEKHINAH (SHEKINAH, SHEKINA, SHECHINAH, SCHECHINA, SHECHINAH, SHECHINA):* DWELLING OR SETTLING, AS IN THE DWELLING OR SACRED PRESENCE OF THE DIVINE GOD, THE DIVINE PRESENCE, GLORY.
- ORIGINAL WORD: שכינה
- PART OF SPEECH: NOUN FEMININE
- PHONETIC SPELLING: (SHE-KIN-AH)
- SHORT DEFINITION: GLORY OR PRESENCE OF GOD

No one is exactly sure where the term "*shekinah*" originated, but as the concept is found in the New Testament, it is obvious that it was a concept that emerged pre-New Testament times, one that echoed a certain concept about the presence of God as an emerging, undeniable light that transcended time and space. While we often think of God as dwelling in heaven, the *shekinah* manifests when we see the presence of God on earth, making His presence known, even down here, to mere mortals. The concept that God dwells in humans, as we are His temple, is an expressed concept of the *shekinah* glory, making sure that we are attuned to and visually seeing God in each and every situation, inhabiting us as we are the light of the world.[17]

ALL OF GOD LIVES FULLY IN CHRIST [FOR IN HIM ALL THE FULLNESS OF DEITY DWELLS] IN A HUMAN BODY [BODILY; EMBODIED]. (Colossians 2:9)

WHAT AGREEMENT [UNION] CAN THE TEMPLE OF GOD HAVE WITH IDOLS? FOR WE ARE THE TEMPLE OF THE LIVING GOD [1 COR. 3:16]. AS GOD SAID: "I WILL LIVE WITH THEM AND WALK WITH THEM. AND I WILL BE THEIR GOD, AND THEY WILL BE MY PEOPLE [LEV. 26:11–12; JER. 32:38; EZEK. 37:27]." (2 Corinthians 6:16)

YESHUA ANSWERED HIM, "IF SOMEONE LOVES ME, HE WILL KEEP MY WORD; AND MY FATHER WILL LOVE HIM, AND WE WILL COME TO HIM

AND MAKE OUR HOME WITH HIM. (John 14:23, CJB)

This incredible majestic side of God's glorious presence, in particular of feminine form, was a principal aspect of the spiritual understanding in the early church. It was a concept that had the ability to transcend from Jewish culture to the Gentile cultures that became a part of the church, and the result was an imagery that was easy to understand. The *shekinah* glory is universally understandable, relatable, and embraceable, and for that reason, it is something anyone who came into Christianity, from anywhere, could adopt for themselves.

Why exactly is the *shekinah* so universal? Many have speculated (and some have even come to dismiss) the aspects of the divine that are sterner and boundary oriented. As with all things in God, we see a balance of natures, all of which complete the entire picture of divine love. We are free to choose, but not free from consequence; we are free to walk away from God, but there are realities that go along with that; we are free to disobey God, but that means we will live outside of His favor; and we are free, as always, to turn around and repent, to find our place of solace in His loving embrace. It can seem contradictory to have a spiritual parent who both disciplines and loves, but as we know (or should know), all good parents find that balance with their children. Sometimes what God may do doesn't always make sense to us, but that calls us to rise to the occasion, all the more, and understand it better.

Most of the behaviors we associate with spiritual sternness are characteristics commonly associated with men and male nature. We think in terms of men as disciplinarians, violent, aggressive, and hostile, and that means when people adopt the idea of God as being a "man," they tend to consider God unapproachable, unreachable, and unrelenting. The imagery of the big, bad God in the sky Who is going to get you for the smallest thing is, indeed, a male-dominated image. Yet this is the very reason why we see the feminine characteristics present in the divine, and it is an extremely important reason why the *shekinah* glory has such a universal appeal. It is human nature to avoid rejection, and we instinctively turn away from those we think will reject us.

Many reject God because the image we have of God is out-of-balance and too harsh to embrace. Yet we expect people to want to accept God as being male, in a literal sense, without considering the way such turns many off. The *shekinah* glory, the presence of God, regarded as feminine, sees a "softer side," a balance, to the spiritual realm. It draws one in, intrigues, causes questions, and makes people want to know more. Rather than a state of aversion, the *shekinah* brings people to intrigue and interest.

The image of *shekinah* most likely emerged because the people of God needed to see a "softer side" to the divine. For decades, through occupation and the hand of oppression, the Jews recognized the disciplinary side of God. They had come to see and experience Him through their hardship, and now they needed to see something beyond that, to experience something new with Him. It was time to recognize the compassionate love of God and find within themselves a greater sense of His love and mercy, despite all of their wrongdoing.

The *shekinah* is also associated with grandeur and glory, with a sense of grace that comes in and envelops wherever it resides, just by being present. The *shekinah* glory is a presence of God that does not necessarily have to speak, nor does it have to introduce itself. Its radiant splendor is beautiful and notable, without having to intrude. The way in which *shekinah* operates is quieter than thunder, but just as recognizable. It is a quiet, yet overwhelming, manner of God, one that we embrace, that invites us, welcomes us, and ultimately, changes us, as well.

This is how the ancients often thought of royal women, and how many regard women, even now. Grace and poise are considered feminine attributes, and the ability to radiate beauty without a word was done by dignitaries and "proper" women throughout the ages. Without having to speak a word, most of us know the comfort in running to a graceful and quiet woman in our lives, one who seemed to be beautiful without uttering a word. Whether it was mom, grandma, auntie, or someone else, their presence drew them in, just as the *shekinah* glory does for us. It reminds us of their authority but does it in such a way that we remember their comfort and care, as well.

The *shekinah* glory is also a prefigure of the Holy Spirit as feminine, because it brings with it a sense of life, of majesty, and comfort, reminding us of who we are, and Who God is, all at the same time. (We will speak more on this, later.) It was the first awakening of the people of God to manifestations of God within us, working, that were not distant, nor abstract, and that were life-changing. To witness the *shekinah* glory was to witness God Himself, in a comforting and relevant way, so the glory could touch us, and we could be forever changed.

Wisdom comforts her children

WISDOM:

- *CHOKMAH.* WISDOM[18]
- ORIGINAL WORD: חָכְמָה
- PART OF SPEECH: NOUN FEMININE
- TRANSLITERATION: CHOKMAH
- PHONETIC SPELLING: (KHOK-MAW')
- SHORT DEFINITION: WISDOM

- *CHOKMOTH.* WISDOM, EVERY WISE WOMAN[19]
- ORIGINAL WORD: חָכְמוֹת
- PART OF SPEECH: NOUN FEMININE
- TRANSLITERATION: CHOKMOTH
- PHONETIC SPELLING: (KHOK-MOTH')
- SHORT DEFINITION: WISDOM

- *TUSHIYYAH.* SOUND, EFFICIENT WISDOM, ABIDING SUCCESS[20]
- ORIGINAL WORD: תּוּשִׁיָּה
- PART OF SPEECH: NOUN FEMININE
- TRANSLITERATION: TUSHIYYAH
- PHONETIC SPELLING: (TOO-SHEE-YAW')
- SHORT DEFINITION: WISDOM

- *GNÓSIS.* A KNOWING, KNOWLEDGE[21]
- ORIGINAL WORD: ΓΝῶΣΙΣ, ΕΩΣ, ἡ
- PART OF SPEECH: NOUN, FEMININE
- TRANSLITERATION: GNOSIS
- PHONETIC SPELLING: (GNO'-SIS)
- SHORT DEFINITION: KNOWLEDGE, DOCTRINE, WISDOM
- DEFINITION: KNOWLEDGE, DOCTRINE, WISDOM.

- *SOPHIA*: SKILL, WISDOM[22]
- ORIGINAL WORD: ΣΟΦΊΑ, ΑΣ, ἡ
- PART OF SPEECH: NOUN, FEMININE
- TRANSLITERATION: SOPHIA
- PHONETIC SPELLING: (SOF-EE'-AH)\
- SHORT DEFINITION: WISDOM
- DEFINITION: WISDOM, INSIGHT, SKILL (HUMAN OR DIVINE), INTELLIGENCE.

- *PHILOSOPHIA*: THE LOVE OR PURSUIT OF WISDOM[23]
- ORIGINAL WORD: ΦΙΛΟΣΟΦΊΑ, ΑΣ, ἡ
- PART OF SPEECH: NOUN, FEMININE
- TRANSLITERATION: PHILOSOPHIA
- PHONETIC SPELLING: (FIL-OS-OF-EE'-AH)
- SHORT DEFINITION: LOVE OF WISDOM, PHILOSOPHY
- DEFINITION: LOVE OF WISDOM, PHILOSOPHY, IN THE NT OF TRADITIONAL JEWISH THEOLOGY.

- *PHRONÉSIS*: UNDERSTANDING, PRACTICAL WISDOM[24]
- ORIGINAL WORD: ΦΡΌΝΗΣΙΣ, ΕΩΣ, ἡ
- PART OF SPEECH: NOUN, FEMININE
- TRANSLITERATION: PHRONESIS
- PHONETIC SPELLING: (FRON'-AY-SIS)
- SHORT DEFINITION: UNDERSTANDING
- DEFINITION: UNDERSTANDING (WHICH LEADS TO RIGHT ACTION), PRACTICAL WISDOM, PRUDENCE.

The idea that wisdom is feminine in language – both in Hebrew and Greek – was my first brush with curiosity as to why certain words were feminine. The work of wisdom isn't one often thought to have a specific gender, so the concept that wisdom is a feminine word, identifying it as a feminine characteristic, is of intrigue. Why would a concept that is so often associated with thinkers and teachers, most often male in nature, be considered a feminine characteristic, identified in female overtones? Why is it that in wisdom literature, women are also seen in personified form – some as wise, and some as unwise?

Not surprising, the answers are often in front of our faces, without much thought to them.

GOD'S WISDOM IS DEEP [HE IS WISE OF HEART], AND HIS POWER IS
GREAT;
    NO ONE CAN FIGHT [PRESS] HIM WITHOUT GETTING HURT [AND
COME OUT WHOLE/UNSCATHED].
HE MOVES MOUNTAINS [AN EARTHQUAKE] WITHOUT ANYONE
KNOWING IT
    AND TURNS THEM OVER WHEN HE IS ANGRY.
HE SHAKES THE EARTH OUT OF ITS PLACE
    AND MAKES ITS FOUNDATIONS [PILLARS] TREMBLE [SHUDDER].
HE COMMANDS THE SUN NOT TO [SPEAKS TO THE SUN AND IT DOES
NOT] SHINE
    AND SHUTS OFF THE LIGHT OF [SEALS UP] THE STARS.
HE ALONE STRETCHES OUT THE SKIES [HEAVENS]
    AND WALKS [TREADS] ON THE WAVES [HIGH PLACES] OF THE SEA.
IT IS GOD WHO MADE THE BEAR, ORION, AND THE PLEIADES [WELL-
KNOWN CONSTELLATIONS]
    AND THE GROUPS OF STARS IN THE SOUTHERN SKY [CHAMBERS OF
THE SOUTH].
HE DOES WONDERS [GREAT THINGS] THAT CANNOT BE UNDERSTOOD;
    HE DOES SO MANY MIRACLES [*OR* MARVELOUS THINGS] THEY
CANNOT BE COUNTED.
WHEN [*OR* IF] HE PASSES ME, I CANNOT SEE HIM;
    WHEN [*OR* IF] HE GOES BY ME, I DO NOT RECOGNIZE [PERCEIVE]
HIM.
IF HE SNATCHES SOMETHING [*OR* SOMEONE] AWAY, NO ONE CAN STOP
HIM [*OR* BRING THEM BACK]
    OR SAY TO HIM, 'WHAT ARE YOU DOING?'
GOD WILL NOT HOLD BACK [RELENT FROM] HIS ANGER.
    EVEN THE HELPERS [ALLIES] OF THE MONSTER RAHAB [A SEA
MONSTER; PS. 89:10] LIE AT HIS FEET IN FEAR [COWER UNDER HIM].
SO HOW CAN I ARGUE WITH [ANSWER] GOD,
    OR EVEN FIND WORDS TO ARGUE [CHOOSE WORDS] WITH HIM?
EVEN IF I WERE RIGHT [RIGHTEOUS], I COULD NOT ANSWER HIM;
    I COULD ONLY BEG GOD [PLEAD], MY JUDGE, FOR MERCY. (JOB 9:4-
15)

"BUT WHERE SHALL WISDOM BE FOUND?
    AND WHERE IS THE PLACE OF UNDERSTANDING?
MAN DOES NOT KNOW ITS WORTH,

AND IT IS NOT FOUND IN THE LAND OF THE LIVING.
THE DEEP SAYS, 'IT IS NOT IN ME,'
  AND THE SEA SAYS, 'IT IS NOT WITH ME.'
IT CANNOT BE BOUGHT FOR GOLD,
  AND SILVER CANNOT BE WEIGHED AS ITS PRICE.
IT CANNOT BE VALUED IN THE GOLD OF OPHIR,
  IN PRECIOUS ONYX OR SAPPHIRE.
GOLD AND GLASS CANNOT EQUAL IT,
  NOR CAN IT BE EXCHANGED FOR JEWELS OF FINE GOLD.
NO MENTION SHALL BE MADE OF CORAL OR OF CRYSTAL;
  THE PRICE OF WISDOM IS ABOVE PEARLS.
THE TOPAZ OF ETHIOPIA CANNOT EQUAL IT,
  NOR CAN IT BE VALUED IN PURE GOLD.

"FROM WHERE, THEN, DOES WISDOM COME?
  AND WHERE IS THE PLACE OF UNDERSTANDING?
IT IS HIDDEN FROM THE EYES OF ALL LIVING
  AND CONCEALED FROM THE BIRDS OF THE AIR.
ABADDON AND DEATH SAY,
  'WE HAVE HEARD A RUMOR OF IT WITH OUR EARS.'

"GOD UNDERSTANDS THE WAY TO IT,
  AND HE KNOWS ITS PLACE.
FOR HE LOOKS TO THE ENDS OF THE EARTH
  AND SEES EVERYTHING UNDER THE HEAVENS.
WHEN HE GAVE TO THE WIND ITS WEIGHT
  AND APPORTIONED THE WATERS BY MEASURE,
WHEN HE MADE A DECREE FOR THE RAIN
  AND A WAY FOR THE LIGHTNING OF THE THUNDER,
THEN HE SAW IT AND DECLARED IT;
  HE ESTABLISHED IT, AND SEARCHED IT OUT.
AND HE SAID TO MAN,
'BEHOLD, THE FEAR OF THE LORD, THAT IS WISDOM,
  AND TO TURN AWAY FROM EVIL IS UNDERSTANDING.'" (Job 28:12-28, ESV)

WISDOM [THE PERSONIFICATION OF GOD'S WISDOM; 8:1–36; 9:1–6]
IS LIKE A WOMAN SHOUTING [SHOUTS] IN THE STREET;
  SHE RAISES HER VOICE [YELLS OUT] IN THE CITY SQUARES [THE HUB
FOR BUSINESS, GOVERNMENT, AND SOCIAL INTERACTION].
SHE CRIES OUT IN THE NOISY STREET [AT THE TOP OF THE NOISY

THRONG]
    AND SHOUTS AT THE [ENTRANCES OF] CITY GATES:
"YOU FOOLS [SIMPLETONS; IMMATURE ONES], HOW LONG WILL YOU BE
FOOLISH [IMMATURE]?
    HOW LONG WILL YOU MAKE FUN OF WISDOM [MOCKING SO DEAR TO
YOU]
    AND HATE KNOWLEDGE?
IF ONLY YOU HAD LISTENED [RESPONDED] WHEN I CORRECTED YOU,
    I WOULD HAVE TOLD YOU WHAT'S IN MY HEART [POURED FORTH MY
SPIRIT TO YOU];
    I WOULD HAVE TOLD YOU WHAT I AM THINKING [REVEALED MY
WORDS TO YOU].
I CALLED, BUT YOU REFUSED TO LISTEN [REJECTED ME];
    I HELD OUT MY HAND, BUT YOU PAID NO ATTENTION.
YOU DID NOT FOLLOW [IGNORED] MY ADVICE
    AND DID NOT LISTEN WHEN I CORRECTED [WANT ME TO CORRECT]
YOU.
SO I WILL LAUGH WHEN YOU ARE IN TROUBLE [AT YOUR CALAMITY].
    I WILL MAKE FUN [RIDICULE YOU] WHEN DISASTER STRIKES YOU,
WHEN DISASTER [DREAD] COMES OVER YOU LIKE A STORM [TEMPEST],
    WHEN TROUBLE STRIKES YOU LIKE A WHIRLWIND,
WHEN PAIN [DISTRESS] AND TROUBLE [OPPRESSION] OVERWHELM
YOU.

"THEN YOU WILL CALL TO ME,
    BUT I WILL NOT ANSWER.
YOU WILL LOOK FOR [SEEK] ME,
    BUT YOU WILL NOT FIND ME.
IT IS BECAUSE YOU REJECTED [HATED] KNOWLEDGE
    AND DID NOT CHOOSE TO RESPECT [FEAR; HOLD IN AWE] THE LORD.
YOU DID NOT ACCEPT [WANT] MY ADVICE,
    AND YOU REJECTED MY CORRECTION.
SO YOU WILL GET WHAT YOU DESERVE [EAT FROM THE FRUIT OF YOUR
PATH];
    YOU WILL GET WHAT YOU PLANNED FOR OTHERS [OR BE SATISFIED
WITH YOUR OWN COUNSEL].
FOOLS [THE SIMPLE/IMMATURE] WILL DIE BECAUSE THEY REFUSE TO
LISTEN [TURN AWAY];
    THEY [FOOLS] WILL BE DESTROYED BECAUSE THEY DO NOT CARE [OF
COMPLACENCY].
BUT THOSE WHO LISTEN TO [OBEY] ME WILL LIVE IN SAFETY

AND BE AT PEACE, WITHOUT FEAR OF INJURY [UNTROUBLED BY THE DREAD OF HARM]." (PROVERBS 1:20-33)

IT [WISDOM] WILL SAVE YOU FROM THE UNFAITHFUL WIFE [STRANGE WOMAN]
　WHO TRIES TO LEAD YOU INTO ADULTERY [FROM THE FOREIGN WOMAN] WITH PLEASING WORDS [FLATTERY; COMPLIMENTS].
SHE LEAVES THE HUSBAND SHE MARRIED WHEN SHE WAS YOUNG [THE INTIMATE RELATIONSHIP OF HER YOUTH].
　SHE IGNORES [FORGETS] THE PROMISE SHE MADE BEFORE [HER COVENANT WITH] GOD.
HER HOUSE IS ON THE WAY [SINKS DOWN] TO DEATH;
　THOSE WHO TOOK THAT PATH ARE NOW ALL DEAD [*OR* HER PATHS COME DOWN TO HER DEAD ANCESTORS].

NO ONE WHO GOES TO HER COMES BACK
　OR WALKS THE PATH OF LIFE AGAIN.
BUT WISDOM WILL HELP YOU BE GOOD [*OR* STAY ON THE PATH OF GOOD PEOPLE]
　AND DO WHAT IS RIGHT [GUARD THE ROAD OF THE RIGHTEOUS].
THOSE WHO ARE HONEST [HAVE INTEGRITY/VIRTUE] WILL LIVE IN THE LAND,
　AND THOSE WHO ARE INNOCENT [BLAMELESS] WILL REMAIN IN IT.
BUT THE WICKED WILL BE REMOVED [CUT OFF] FROM THE LAND,
　AND THE UNFAITHFUL WILL BE THROWN OUT OF [UPROOTED FROM] IT. (Proverbs 2:16-22)

HAPPY [BLESSED] IS THE PERSON WHO FINDS WISDOM,
　THE ONE WHO GETS [GAINS] UNDERSTANDING.
WISDOM [HER PROFIT] IS WORTH MORE THAN SILVER;
　IT BRINGS MORE PROFIT [HER YIELD MORE] THAN GOLD.
WISDOM IS MORE PRECIOUS THAN RUBIES [*OR* PEARLS];
　NOTHING YOU COULD WANT IS EQUAL TO IT.
WITH [IN] HER RIGHT HAND WISDOM OFFERS YOU A LONG LIFE [ARE LENGTH OF DAYS],
　AND WITH [IN] HER LEFT HAND SHE GIVES YOU [ARE] RICHES AND HONOR.
WISDOM WILL MAKE YOUR LIFE [HER PATHS ARE] PLEASANT
　AND WILL BRING YOU [HER TRAILS ARE] PEACE.
AS A TREE PRODUCES FRUIT, WISDOM GIVES LIFE TO THOSE WHO USE IT,

AND EVERYONE WHO USES IT WILL BE HAPPY. (Proverbs 3:13-18)

HOLD ON TO WISDOM [DON'T ABANDON HER; WISDOM IS HERE PERSONIFIED AS A WOMAN; 1:20–33; 8:1—9:6], AND IT [OR SHE] WILL TAKE CARE OF [GUARD] YOU.
  LOVE IT [OR HER], AND IT [OR SHE] WILL KEEP YOU SAFE [PROTECT YOU].
WISDOM IS THE MOST IMPORTANT THING; SO GET WISDOM [THE BEGINNING OF WISDOM IS: GET/ACQUIRE WISDOM].
  IF IT COSTS EVERYTHING YOU HAVE [ABOVE ALL YOUR ACQUISITIONS], GET [ACQUIRE] UNDERSTANDING.
TREASURE WISDOM [HIGHLY ESTEEM HER], AND IT [OR SHE] WILL MAKE YOU GREAT [EXALT YOU];
  HOLD ON TO IT [OR EMBRACE HER], AND IT [OR SHE] WILL BRING YOU HONOR.
IT WILL BE LIKE FLOWERS IN YOUR HAIR [SHE WILL PLACE ON YOUR HEAD A GRACEFUL GARLAND;]
  AND LIKE A BEAUTIFUL CROWN ON YOUR HEAD [SHE WILL BESTOW ON YOU A CROWN OF GLORY]." (Proverbs 4:6-9)

TREAT WISDOM AS A SISTER [SAY TO WISDOM, "YOU ARE MY SISTER"; 1:20–33; 8:1—9:6],
  AND MAKE UNDERSTANDING YOUR CLOSEST FRIEND [CALL UNDERSTANDING "FRIEND"].
WISDOM AND UNDERSTANDING [SHE] WILL KEEP YOU AWAY [GUARD YOU] FROM ADULTERY [THE STRANGE WOMAN],
  AWAY FROM THE UNFAITHFUL WIFE [FOREIGN WOMAN] AND HER PLEASING [FLATTERING] WORDS. (Proverbs 7:4-5)

WISDOM CALLS TO YOU LIKE SOMEONE SHOUTING [DOES NOT WISDOM CALL OUT?];
  UNDERSTANDING RAISES [DOES NOT UNDERSTANDING RAISE...?] HER VOICE.
ON THE HILLTOPS [TOP OF THE HIGH PLACES] ALONG THE ROAD
  AND AT THE CROSSROADS, SHE STANDS CALLING [TAKES HER STAND].
BESIDE THE CITY GATES,
  AT THE ENTRANCES INTO THE CITY, SHE CALLS OUT:
"LISTEN, EVERYONE [MEN], I'M CALLING OUT TO YOU;
  I AM SHOUTING [MY VOICE GOES OUT] TO ALL PEOPLE [THE SONS OF HUMANITY].

YOU WHO ARE UNEDUCATED [SIMPLEMINDED; IMMATURE; NAIVE],
SEEK WISDOM [UNDERSTAND PRUDENCE].
YOU WHO ARE FOOLISH, GET UNDERSTANDING [TAKE THIS TO
HEART].
LISTEN, BECAUSE I HAVE IMPORTANT [NOBLE] THINGS TO SAY,
AND WHAT I TELL YOU IS RIGHT [VIRTUOUS].
WHAT I SAY IS TRUE [MY MOUTH UTTERS THE TRUTH],
I REFUSE TO SPEAK EVIL [MY LIPS DESPISE WICKEDNESS].
EVERYTHING I SAY IS HONEST [ALL THE SPEECHES OF MY MOUTH ARE
RIGHTEOUS];
NOTHING I SAY IS CROOKED [TWISTED] OR FALSE [PERVERSE].
PEOPLE WITH GOOD SENSE [WHO UNDERSTAND] KNOW WHAT I SAY IS
TRUE [STRAIGHTFORWARD];
AND THOSE WITH [WHO SEEK] KNOWLEDGE KNOW MY WORDS ARE
RIGHT [VIRTUOUS]. (Proverbs 8:1-9)

BECAUSE WISDOM WILL NOT ENTER A DECEITFUL SOUL,
OR DWELL IN A BODY ENSLAVED TO SIN.
FOR A HOLY AND DISCIPLINED SPIRIT WILL FLEE FROM DECEIT,
AND WILL LEAVE FOOLISH THOUGHTS BEHIND,
AND WILL BE ASHAMED AT THE APPROACH OF UNRIGHTEOUSNESS.
(Wisdom of Solomon 1:4-5, NRSV)

WISDOM IS RADIANT AND UNFADING,
AND SHE IS EASILY DISCERNED BY THOSE WHO LOVE HER,
AND IS FOUND BY THOSE WHO SEEK HER.
SHE HASTENS TO MAKE HERSELF KNOWN TO THOSE WHO DESIRE HER.
ONE WHO RISES EARLY TO SEEK HER WILL HAVE NO DIFFICULTY,
FOR SHE WILL BE FOUND SITTING AT THE GATE.
TO FIX ONE'S THOUGHT ON HER IS PERFECT UNDERSTANDING,
AND ONE WHO IS VIGILANT ON HER ACCOUNT WILL SOON BE FREE
FROM CARE...
I WILL TELL YOU WHAT WISDOM IS AND HOW SHE CAME TO BE,
AND I WILL HIDE NO SECRETS FROM YOU,
BUT I WILL TRACE HER COURSE FROM THE BEGINNING OF CREATION,
AND MAKE KNOWLEDGE OF HER CLEAR,
AND I WILL NOT PASS BY THE TRUTH;
NOR WILL I TRAVEL IN THE COMPANY OF SICKLY ENVY,
FOR ENVY DOES NOT ASSOCIATE WITH WISDOM.
THE MULTITUDE OF THE WISE IS THE SALVATION OF THE WORLD,
AND A SENSIBLE KING IS THE STABILITY OF ANY PEOPLE.

THEREFORE BE INSTRUCTED BY MY WORDS, AND YOU WILL PROFIT. (Wisdom of Solomon 6:12-15, 22-25, NRSV)

FOR WISDOM, THE FASHIONER OF ALL THINGS, TAUGHT ME.

THERE IS IN HER A SPIRIT THAT IS INTELLIGENT, HOLY,
UNIQUE, MANIFOLD, SUBTLE,
MOBILE, CLEAR, UNPOLLUTED,
DISTINCT, INVULNERABLE, LOVING THE GOOD, KEEN,
IRRESISTIBLE, BENEFICENT, HUMANE,
STEADFAST, SURE, FREE FROM ANXIETY,
ALL-POWERFUL, OVERSEEING ALL,
AND PENETRATING THROUGH ALL SPIRITS
THAT ARE INTELLIGENT, PURE, AND ALTOGETHER SUBTLE.
FOR WISDOM IS MORE MOBILE THAN ANY MOTION;
BECAUSE OF HER PURENESS SHE PERVADES AND PENETRATES ALL
THINGS.
FOR SHE IS A BREATH OF THE POWER OF GOD,
AND A PURE EMANATION OF THE GLORY OF THE ALMIGHTY;
THEREFORE NOTHING DEFILED GAINS ENTRANCE INTO HER.
FOR SHE IS A REFLECTION OF ETERNAL LIGHT,
A SPOTLESS MIRROR OF THE WORKING OF GOD,
AND AN IMAGE OF HIS GOODNESS.
ALTHOUGH SHE IS BUT ONE, SHE CAN DO ALL THINGS,
AND WHILE REMAINING IN HERSELF, SHE RENEWS ALL THINGS;
IN EVERY GENERATION SHE PASSES INTO HOLY SOULS
AND MAKES THEM FRIENDS OF GOD, AND PROPHETS;
FOR GOD LOVES NOTHING SO MUCH AS THE PERSON WHO LIVES WITH
WISDOM.
SHE IS MORE BEAUTIFUL THAN THE SUN,
AND EXCELS EVERY CONSTELLATION OF THE STARS.
COMPARED WITH THE LIGHT SHE IS FOUND TO BE SUPERIOR,
FOR IT IS SUCCEEDED BY THE NIGHT,
BUT AGAINST WISDOM EVIL DOES NOT PREVAIL. (Wisdom of Solomon 7:22-30, NRSV)

I LOVED HER AND SOUGHT HER FROM MY YOUTH;
I DESIRED TO TAKE HER FOR MY BRIDE,
AND BECAME ENAMORED OF HER BEAUTY.
SHE GLORIFIES HER NOBLE BIRTH BY LIVING WITH GOD,
AND THE LORD OF ALL LOVES HER.

FOR SHE IS AN INITIATE IN THE KNOWLEDGE OF GOD,
AND AN ASSOCIATE IN HIS WORKS.
IF RICHES ARE A DESIRABLE POSSESSION IN LIFE,
WHAT IS RICHER THAN WISDOM, THE ACTIVE CAUSE OF ALL THINGS?
(Wisdom of Solomon 8:2-5, NRSV)

TO FEAR THE LORD IS THE BEGINNING OF WISDOM;
    SHE IS CREATED WITH THE FAITHFUL IN THE WOMB.
SHE MADE AMONG HUMAN BEINGS AN ETERNAL FOUNDATION,
    AND AMONG THEIR DESCENDANTS SHE WILL ABIDE FAITHFULLY.
TO FEAR THE LORD IS FULLNESS OF WISDOM;
    SHE INEBRIATES MORTALS WITH HER FRUITS;
SHE FILLS THEIR WHOLE HOUSE WITH DESIRABLE GOODS,
    AND THEIR STOREHOUSES WITH HER PRODUCE.
THE FEAR OF THE LORD IS THE CROWN OF WISDOM,
    MAKING PEACE AND PERFECT HEALTH TO FLOURISH.
SHE RAINED DOWN KNOWLEDGE AND DISCERNING COMPREHENSION,
    AND SHE HEIGHTENED THE GLORY OF THOSE WHO HELD HER FAST.
TO FEAR THE LORD IS THE ROOT OF WISDOM,
    AND HER BRANCHES ARE LONG LIFE. (Sirach 1:14-21, NRSV)
MY CHILD, FROM YOUR YOUTH CHOOSE DISCIPLINE,
    AND WHEN YOU HAVE GRAY HAIR YOU WILL STILL FIND WISDOM.
COME TO HER LIKE ONE WHO PLOWS AND SOWS,
    AND WAIT FOR HER GOOD HARVEST.
FOR WHEN YOU CULTIVATE HER YOU WILL TOIL BUT LITTLE,
    AND SOON YOU WILL EAT OF HER PRODUCE.
SHE SEEMS VERY HARSH TO THE UNDISCIPLINED;
    FOOLS CANNOT REMAIN WITH HER.
SHE WILL BE LIKE A HEAVY STONE TO TEST THEM,
    AND THEY WILL NOT DELAY IN CASTING HER ASIDE.
FOR WISDOM IS LIKE HER NAME;
    SHE IS NOT READILY PERCEIVED BY MANY. (Sirach 6:18-22, NRSV)

WHILE I WAS STILL YOUNG, BEFORE I WENT ON MY TRAVELS,
    I SOUGHT WISDOM OPENLY IN MY PRAYER.
BEFORE THE TEMPLE I ASKED FOR HER,
    AND I WILL SEARCH FOR HER UNTIL THE END.

FROM THE FIRST BLOSSOM TO THE RIPENING GRAPE
    MY HEART DELIGHTED IN HER;

MY FOOT WALKED ON THE STRAIGHT PATH;
    FROM MY YOUTH I FOLLOWED HER STEPS.

I INCLINED MY EAR A LITTLE AND RECEIVED HER,
    AND I FOUND FOR MYSELF MUCH INSTRUCTION.
I MADE PROGRESS IN HER;
    TO HIM WHO GIVES WISDOM I WILL GIVE GLORY.

FOR I RESOLVED TO LIVE ACCORDING TO WISDOM,
    AND I WAS ZEALOUS FOR THE GOOD,
    AND I SHALL NEVER BE DISAPPOINTED.
MY SOUL GRAPPLED WITH WISDOM,
    AND IN MY CONDUCT I WAS STRICT;

I SPREAD OUT MY HANDS TO THE HEAVENS,
    AND LAMENTED MY IGNORANCE OF HER.
I DIRECTED MY SOUL TO HER,
    AND IN PURITY I FOUND HER.

WITH HER I GAINED UNDERSTANDING FROM THE FIRST;
    THEREFORE I WILL NEVER BE FORSAKEN.
MY HEART WAS STIRRED TO SEEK HER;
    THEREFORE I HAVE GAINED A PRIZE POSSESSION.
THE LORD GAVE ME MY TONGUE AS A REWARD,
    AND I WILL PRAISE HIM WITH IT.

DRAW NEAR TO ME, YOU WHO ARE UNEDUCATED,
    AND LODGE IN THE HOUSE OF INSTRUCTION.
WHY DO YOU SAY YOU ARE LACKING IN THESE THINGS,
    AND WHY DO YOU ENDURE SUCH GREAT THIRST?
I OPENED MY MOUTH AND SAID,
    ACQUIRE WISDOM FOR YOURSELVES WITHOUT MONEY.

PUT YOUR NECK UNDER HER YOKE,
    AND LET YOUR SOULS RECEIVE INSTRUCTION;
    IT IS TO BE FOUND CLOSE BY. (Sirach 51:13-26, NRSV)

The classification of "wisdom literature" in the Bible extends to the books of Job, Proverbs, Ecclesiastes, and the Song of Songs. In traditions that embrace the Deuterocanonical books, it also includes the Wisdom of Solomon (sometimes called Wisdom),

Wisdom of Sirach (often called Sirach), Baruch, and Ecclesiasticus. The identity of these books as records of wisdom has to do with their style of writing: they exemplify Near-East styles of sayings, proverbs, and wise thoughts that have been compiled and quoted, often through the years, to help people acquire mental, emotional, and spiritual footing to make decisions in their lives. They weren't selected to be particularly philosophical or start debate, nor do they stand to be the solution to every problem a person has. Rather, the wisdom literature of the Scriptures seeks to give insight to help people develop wisdom and do so with a spiritual footing that extends beyond worship patterns or religious observances.

The identity of wisdom as feminine is very deliberately chosen, especially when we consider much of the contents assigned encouraging wisdom and the pursuit of wisdom were written by men. Wisdom is associated with maturity, solid behavioral choices, making good decisions, and teaching and education that come from life decisions. They were things that seemed foreign and hard-to-come by, and no matter how much they might have called out to them or desired them, wisdom often seemed just out of reach and difficult to obtain. Wisdom was the ideal attainment, something that would guide and enhance one's decision making throughout life. No matter where one went, wisdom would be there.

In other words, the men who wrote wisdom literature associated and compared wisdom to a woman. They understood a good woman to be the catalyst of everything associated with wisdom: maturity, behaving consistently, making good decision, teaching and educating (especially to children), hard-to-come-by, and often out of reach and difficult to obtain. As we can see in their pursuits throughout wisdom literature, women of a negative influence were easily found, but a good woman, she was hard to find.

ONCE WHILE I WAS AT THE WINDOW OF MY HOUSE
  I LOOKED OUT THROUGH THE SHUTTERS [LATTICE; CURTAINS]
AND SAW SOME FOOLISH [SIMPLEMINDED; IMMATURE; NAÏVE], YOUNG MEN.
  I NOTICED ONE OF THEM HAD NO WISDOM [HAD NO SENSE; LACKED HEART].
HE WAS WALKING DOWN [CROSSING] THE STREET NEAR THE CORNER

ON THE ROAD LEADING TO HER HOUSE.
IT WAS THE TWILIGHT OF THE EVENING;
    THE DARKNESS OF THE NIGHT WAS JUST BEGINNING.
THEN THE WOMAN APPROACHED [OR PROPOSITIONED] HIM,
    DRESSED LIKE A PROSTITUTE
    AND PLANNING TO TRICK HIM [WITH A GUARDED HEART].
SHE WAS LOUD [BOISTEROUS; NOISY] AND STUBBORN [DEFIANT]
    AND NEVER STAYED AT [HER FEET DO NOT REST IN HER OWN] HOME.
SHE WAS ALWAYS OUT [A FOOT] IN THE STREETS OR IN [A FOOT IN]
THE CITY SQUARES,
    WAITING AROUND [LURKING] ON THE CORNERS OF THE STREETS.
SHE GRABBED HIM AND KISSED HIM.
    WITHOUT SHAME [HER FACE WAS BRAZEN AS] SHE SAID TO HIM,
"I MADE MY FELLOWSHIP OFFERING [LEV. 3; 7:11–21; THE OFFERER
ATE THE MEAT OF THE OFFERING].
    TODAY I HAVE KEPT [PAID BACK] MY SPECIAL PROMISES [VOWS].
SO I HAVE COME OUT TO MEET YOU;
    I HAVE BEEN LOOKING FOR YOU [SEEKING YOUR FACE] AND HAVE
FOUND YOU.
I HAVE COVERED [ORNAMENTED] MY BED
    WITH COLORED SHEETS FROM EGYPT.
I HAVE MADE MY BED SMELL SWEET [SPRINKLED MY BED]
    WITH MYRRH, ALOES, AND CINNAMON.
COME, LET'S MAKE [BE INTOXICATED WITH] LOVE UNTIL MORNING.
    LET'S ENJOY EACH OTHER'S [REJOICE IN] LOVE.
MY HUSBAND IS NOT HOME;
    HE HAS GONE ON A LONG [FARAWAY] TRIP.
HE TOOK A LOT OF MONEY WITH HIM [POUCH OF MONEY IN HIS HAND]
    AND WON'T BE HOME FOR WEEKS [UNTIL THE NEW MOON]."
BY HER CLEVER WORDS SHE MADE HIM GIVE IN [SEDUCES HIM];
    BY HER PLEASING WORDS [THE FLATTERY OF HER LIPS] SHE LED HIM
INTO DOING WRONG [PERSUADES/COMPELS HIM].
ALL AT ONCE HE FOLLOWED HER,
    LIKE AN OX LED TO THE BUTCHER [SLAUGHTER],
LIKE A DEER CAUGHT IN A TRAP [OR FOOL TO THE STOCKS]
    AND SHOT THROUGH THE LIVER WITH AN ARROW [UNTIL AN ARROW
PIERCES HIS LIVER].
LIKE A BIRD CAUGHT IN [HURRYING TO] A TRAP,
HE DIDN'T KNOW WHAT HE DID WOULD KILL HIM [IT WOULD COST HIM
HIS LIFE].

NOW, MY SONS, LISTEN TO ME;
    PAY ATTENTION TO WHAT I SAY [THE SPEECH OF MY MOUTH].
DON'T LET YOURSELF BE TRICKED BY SUCH A WOMAN [TURN YOUR
HEART TO HER PATHS];
    DON'T GO WHERE SHE LEADS YOU [WANDER ONTO HER PATHS].
SHE HAS RUINED MANY GOOD MEN [CAUSED MANY CORPSES TO FALL],
    AND MANY HAVE DIED BECAUSE OF HER [ARE THOSE SHE HAS
KILLED].
HER HOUSE IS ON THE ROAD [PATH] TO DEATH [SHEOL; THE GRAVE OR
THE UNDERWORLD],
    THE ROAD THAT LEADS DOWN TO THE GRAVE [GOING DOWN TO THE
CHAMBERS OF DEATH]. (Proverbs 7:6-27)

IT IS HARD TO [WHO CAN...?] FIND A GOOD [NOBLE; VIRTUOUS] WIFE
[RUTH 3:11],
    BECAUSE SHE IS WORTH MORE THAN RUBIES [*OR* PEARLS].
HER HUSBAND TRUSTS HER COMPLETELY [ENTRUSTS HIS HEART TO
HER].
    WITH HER, HE HAS EVERYTHING HE NEEDS [LACKS NO PLUNDER; A
MILITARY IMAGE].
SHE DOES [BRINGS] HIM GOOD AND NOT HARM [TROUBLE; EVIL]
    FOR AS LONG AS SHE LIVES [ALL THE DAYS OF HER LIFE].
SHE LOOKS FOR [GOES OUT TO FIND] WOOL AND FLAX
    AND LIKES TO WORK WITH HER HANDS.
SHE IS LIKE A TRADER'S [MERCHANT] SHIP,
    BRINGING FOOD FROM FAR AWAY.
SHE GETS UP WHILE IT IS STILL DARK [NIGHT]
    AND PREPARES FOOD FOR [GIVES PREY TO] HER FAMILY
    AND FEEDS [A PORTION TO] HER SERVANT GIRLS.
SHE INSPECTS [SURVEYS] A FIELD AND BUYS IT [TAKES IT OVER].
    WITH MONEY SHE EARNED [THE FRUITS OF HER HANDS], SHE
PLANTS A VINEYARD.
SHE DOES HER WORK WITH ENERGY [HER LOINS ARE GIRDED WITH
STRENGTH],
    AND HER ARMS ARE STRONG.
SHE KNOWS THAT WHAT SHE MAKES IS GOOD [*OR* HER TRADING IS
SUCCESSFUL].
    HER LAMP BURNS LATE INTO THE [SHE DOES NOT EXTINGUISH AT]
NIGHT.
SHE MAKES THREAD WITH HER HANDS [SENDS HER HANDS TO THE
DISTAFF]

AND WEAVES HER OWN CLOTH [HER PALMS HOLD THE SPINDLE TIGHTLY].
SHE WELCOMES [STRETCHES HER PALM TO] THE POOR
  AND HELPS [SENDS HER HANDS TO] THE NEEDY.
SHE DOES NOT WORRY ABOUT [IS NOT AFRAID FOR] HER FAMILY WHEN IT SNOWS,
  BECAUSE THEY ALL HAVE FINE CLOTHES TO KEEP THEM WARM.
SHE MAKES BED COVERINGS FOR HERSELF;
  HER CLOTHES ARE MADE OF LINEN [FROM EGYPT] AND OTHER EXPENSIVE MATERIAL [PURPLE].
HER HUSBAND IS KNOWN AT THE CITY MEETINGS [GATES; THE PLACE WHERE CITY LEADERS MEET],
  WHERE HE MAKES DECISIONS AS ONE OF [SITS WITH] THE LEADERS [ELDERS] OF THE LAND.
SHE MAKES LINEN CLOTHES [GARMENTS] AND SELLS THEM
  AND PROVIDES [SUPPLIES] BELTS [SASHES] TO THE MERCHANTS.
SHE IS STRONG AND IS RESPECTED BY THE PEOPLE [STRENGTH AND DIGNITY/HONOR ARE HER CLOTHING].
  SHE LOOKS FORWARD TO THE FUTURE WITH JOY [LAUGHS AT THE FUTURE; SHE IS NOT ANXIOUS].
SHE SPEAKS WISE WORDS [OPENS HER MOUTH WITH WISDOM]
  AND TEACHES OTHERS TO BE KIND [LOVING INSTRUCTION IS ON HER TONGUE].
SHE WATCHES OVER HER FAMILY [IS A LOOKOUT POINT FOR THE DOINGS OF HER HOUSEHOLD]
  AND NEVER WASTES HER TIME [DOES NOT EAT THE BREAD/FOOD OF LAZINESS].
HER CHILDREN SPEAK WELL OF [RISE UP AND BLESS] HER.
  HER HUSBAND ALSO PRAISES HER,
SAYING, "THERE ARE MANY FINE WOMEN [MANY DAUGHTERS ACT NOBLY],
  BUT YOU ARE BETTER THAN [SURPASS] ALL OF THEM."
CHARM CAN FOOL YOU [IS DECEPTIVE], AND BEAUTY CAN TRICK YOU [IS MEANINGLESS; OR FLEETING],
  BUT A WOMAN WHO RESPECTS [FEARS] THE LORD [1:7] SHOULD BE PRAISED.
GIVE HER THE REWARD SHE HAS EARNED [FRUIT OF HER HANDS];
  SHE SHOULD BE PRAISED IN PUBLIC [THE GATES; 31:23] FOR WHAT SHE HAS DONE. (Proverbs 31:10-31)

It's not an accident that while problematic women are found in wisdom literature, the ultimate victory was to find one who was good, noble, the embodiment of characteristics unique in wisdom. These writers understood a good woman had to be sought, pursued, desired, and was ultimately a complete and total blessing. These are all realities of wisdom, and if wisdom is a choice, it starts when we make the right decisions and pursue the right virtues in our lives. This is why wisdom is personified as female; because just as pursuing the right kind of woman is a choice, so is pursuing wisdom. Anyone can pursue a wrong relationship, but it takes special discipline to pursue one that is genuinely, truly wise. It doesn't just fall in our laps because we are cute and we hope that it will find its way there; we must have a relationship with it. To find the best woman, one must make the effort. One will go through much to find her, but in the end, doing so is worth the effort and trials that come along with finding her. To find the greatest wisdom, you must also, throughout life, make the same effort.

The power of life over death

It's an interesting fact to note that the Biblical words for "life" are always feminine (with one exception, as relates strictly to biology), while the Biblical words for "death" are both masculine and feminine. This may seem backward, in a sense, because while natural life comes through a woman, spiritual life comes through Christ. It is not as off-putting as it may seem, however. The reality is that death comes to both men and women alike, and that would make sense that it would have a presence among both. In endings are beginnings, and in life itself, we find the manifestation of death. While it might seem strange that life comes through Christ and it is identified as a female value, this is exactly a part of God's bigger spiritual plan, and it teaches us much in the process.

We learn in the Scriptures that the power of death came through one man, Adam, and thus spread to all human beings.

[THEREFORE, JUST AS] SIN CAME INTO THE WORLD BECAUSE OF WHAT ONE MAN DID [THROUGH ONE MAN], AND WITH SIN CAME DEATH. THIS IS WHY [...AND SO; *OR* AND IN THIS WAY] EVERYONE MUST DIE [DEATH SPREAD/PASSED TO ALL PEOPLE]—BECAUSE EVERYONE SINNED. SIN WAS IN THE WORLD BEFORE THE LAW OF MOSES [THE LAW], BUT SIN IS

NOT COUNTED AGAINST US AS BREAKING A COMMAND [CHARGED TO ONE'S ACCOUNT; RECORDED AS SIN] WHEN THERE IS NO LAW [4:15]. BUT FROM THE TIME OF ADAM TO THE TIME OF MOSES, EVERYONE HAD TO DIE [DEATH REIGNED/RULED], EVEN THOSE WHO HAD NOT SINNED BY BREAKING A COMMAND, AS ADAM HAD [IN THE LIKENESS OF ADAM'S DISOBEDIENCE/TRANSGRESSION].

ADAM WAS LIKE [A TYPE/PATTERN/PREFIGUREMENT OF] THE ONE WHO WAS COMING IN THE FUTURE. BUT GOD'S FREE GIFT [THE GIFT] IS NOT LIKE ADAM'S SIN [VIOLATION; TRANSGRESSION]. [FOR IF] MANY PEOPLE DIED BECAUSE OF THE SIN [VIOLATION; TRANSGRESSION] OF THAT ONE

LIFE

- *CHAVVAH:* "LIFE," THE FIRST WOMAN[25]
- ORIGINAL WORD: חַוָּה
- PART OF SPEECH: PROPER NAME FEMININE
- TRANSLITERATION: CHAVVAH
- PHONETIC SPELLING: (KHAV-VAW')
- SHORT DEFINITION: EVE

- *ZÓÉ:* LIFE[26]
- ORIGINAL WORD: ΖΩΉ, ῆΣ, ἡ
- PART OF SPEECH: NOUN, FEMININE
- TRANSLITERATION: ZÓÉ
- PHONETIC SPELLING: (DZO-AY')
- SHORT DEFINITION: LIFE
- DEFINITION: LIFE, BOTH OF PHYSICAL (PRESENT) AND OF SPIRITUAL (PARTICULARLY FUTURE) EXISTENCE.

DEATH

- *MAVETH:* DEATH[27]
- ORIGINAL WORD: מָוֶת
- PART OF SPEECH: NOUN MASCULINE
- TRANSLITERATION: MAVETH
- PHONETIC SPELLING: (MAW'-VETH)
- SHORT DEFINITION: DEATH

- *TIMUTHAH:* DEATH[28]
- ORIGINAL WORD: תְּמוּתָה
- PART OF SPEECH: NOUN FEMININE
- TRANSLITERATION: TIMUTHAH
- PHONETIC SPELLING: (TEM-OO-THAW')
- SHORT DEFINITION: DEATH

- *THANATOS:* DEATH[29]
- ORIGINAL WORD: ΘΆΝΑΤΟΣ, ΟΥ, ὁ
- PART OF SPEECH: NOUN, MASCULINE
- TRANSLITERATION: THANATOS
- PHONETIC SPELLING: (THAN'-AT-OS)
- SHORT DEFINITION: DEATH
- DEFINITION: DEATH, PHYSICAL OR SPIRITUAL.

- *OLETHROS:* DESTRUCTION, DEATH[30]
- ORIGINAL WORD: ὄλΕΘΡΟΣ, ΟΥ, ὁ
- PART OF SPEECH: NOUN, MASCULINE
- TRANSLITERATION: OLETHROS
- PHONETIC SPELLING: (OL'-ETH-ROS)
- SHORT DEFINITION: RUIN, DOOM, DESTRUCTION
- DEFINITION: RUIN, DOOM, DESTRUCTION, DEATH.

- *TELEUTÉ:* A FINISHING, END, I.E. DEATH[31]
- ORIGINAL WORD: ΤΕΛΕΥΤΉ, ῆΣ, ἡ
- PART OF SPEECH: NOUN, FEMININE
- TRANSLITERATION: TELEUTÉ
- PHONETIC SPELLING: (TEL-YOO-TAY')
- SHORT DEFINITION: END OF LIFE, DEATH
- DEFINITION: END OF LIFE, DEATH.

MAN. BUT THE GRACE FROM GOD WAS MUCH GREATER, SINCE MANY PEOPLE RECEIVED GOD'S GIFT OF LIFE [...HOW MUCH MORE DID GOD'S GRACE AND GIFT ABOUND/MULTIPLY TO THE MANY] BY THE GRACE OF

THE ONE MAN, JESUS CHRIST [THE DEATH OF THE "ONE" SAVED THE "MANY"; SEE V. 19; IS. 53:11]. BUT THE GIFT OF GOD IS DIFFERENT FROM ADAM'S [THE ONE MAN'S] SIN. AFTER ADAM SINNED ONCE, HE WAS JUDGED GUILTY [HIS JUDGMENT BROUGHT CONDEMNATION]. [BUT] GOD'S FREE GIFT CAME AFTER MANY SINS [VIOLATIONS; TRANSGRESSIONS], AND IT MAKES PEOPLE RIGHT WITH GOD [BROUGHT JUSTIFICATION]. [FOR IF] ONE MAN'S SIN [VIOLATION; TRANSGRESSION] CAUSED DEATH TO RULE OVER ALL PEOPLE [REIGN; RULE] BECAUSE OF THAT ONE MAN. HOW MUCH MORE, THEN, WILL THOSE PEOPLE WHO ACCEPT [RECEIVE] GOD'S FULL GRACE [THE ABUNDANCE OF GRACE] AND THE GREAT GIFT OF BEING MADE RIGHT WITH HIM [RIGHTEOUSNESS] HAVE TRUE LIFE AND RULE [OR RULE IN THE FUTURE LIFE; REIGN/RULE IN LIFE] THROUGH THE ONE MAN, JESUS CHRIST. [JUST AS DEATH "RULED" IN ADAM, SO BELIEVERS "RULE" OVER DEATH THROUGH CHRIST.]

SO AS ONE SIN OF ADAM [VIOLATION; TRANGRESSION] BROUGHT THE PUNISHMENT OF DEATH [CONDEMNATION] TO ALL PEOPLE, SO TOO ONE GOOD ACT THAT CHRIST DID [RIGHTEOUS ACT/DEED] MAKES ALL PEOPLE RIGHT WITH GOD, BRINGING THEM TRUE LIFE [BRINGS JUSTIFICATION OF LIFE TO ALL PEOPLE]. [FOR JUST AS...] ONE MAN DISOBEYED GOD, AND MANY BECAME SINNERS. IN THE SAME WAY, [...SO ALSO] ONE MAN OBEYED GOD, AND MANY WILL BE MADE RIGHT [RIGHTEOUS]. THE LAW CAME TO MAKE SIN WORSE [OR TO REVEAL THE TRUE EXTENT OF SIN; TO INCREASE THE VIOLATION/TRANSGRESSION]. BUT WHEN SIN GREW WORSE [INCREASED; MULTIPLIED], GOD'S GRACE INCREASED [MULTIPLIED/ABOUNDED ALL THE MORE]. SIN ONCE USED DEATH TO RULE US [JUST AS SIN REIGNED IN DEATH...], BUT GOD GAVE PEOPLE MORE OF HIS GRACE SO THAT GRACE COULD RULE [...SO GRACE WILL REIGN] BY MAKING PEOPLE RIGHT WITH HIM [THROUGH JUSTIFICATION/RIGHTEOUSNESS]. AND THIS BRINGS LIFE FOREVER [ETERNAL LIFE] THROUGH JESUS CHRIST OUR LORD. (Romans 5:12-21)

On the inverse, we learn that life first entered the world through a woman, and such was heralded – and proclaimed – even after the fall.

THE MAN NAMED HIS WIFE EVE [THE NAME DERIVES FROM AN EARLY FORM OF THE VERB "TO LIVE"], BECAUSE SHE WAS THE MOTHER OF ALL THE LIVING. (Genesis 3:20)

Since women were associated with bringing life into the world, it only made sense to the ancients that life was, indeed, by virtue of its identity, feminine. Women carried life, bore life, maintained and took care of life, and were associated with every aspect of life, in many ways, from birth until death. Women, within their very selves, carried and were bearers of life.

Now, through the church, we see the feminine church – the female spiritual work present in this world. Life comes through Christ, but it is the church that bears and carries that work throughout this world, as a part of the commission to proclaim the Gospel to the entire world. Endowed with life, with the good news of salvation and the promise of life and hope, the church goes forth, to act as agents of life in this world. Death will forever be associated with mortal man, with sin and with the things of this world that are temporal and passing away. Life will forever remind us of the spiritual life of the church, and the contrast of where we are going versus where we have been.

THE SPIRIT OF GOD CREATED [HAS MADE] ME, AND THE BREATH OF THE ALMIGHTY [SHADDAI] GAVE ME LIFE. (Job 33:4)

We also see the promise of life manifesting as a result of death, spiritual death, as we die to this world, and live eternally, unto the Lord.

JESUS SAID TO [ANSWERED; REPLIED TO] THEM, "THE TIME [HOUR] HAS COME FOR THE SON OF MAN [A TITLE FOR THE MESSIAH; DAN. 7:13–14] TO RECEIVE HIS GLORY [BE GLORIFIED; THROUGH HIS DEATH, RESURRECTION, AND ASCENSION]. I TELL YOU THE TRUTH [TRULY, TRULY I SAY TO YOU], A GRAIN OF WHEAT MUST FALL TO THE GROUND AND DIE TO MAKE MANY SEEDS [MUCH FRUIT]. BUT IF IT NEVER DIES, IT REMAINS ONLY A SINGLE SEED [GRAIN]. THOSE WHO [THE ONE WHO...] LOVE THEIR LIVES WILL LOSE THEM, BUT THOSE WHO HATE THEIR LIVES IN THIS WORLD WILL KEEP [GUARD; PRESERVE] TRUE LIFE FOREVER [IT FOR ETERNAL LIFE]. WHOEVER SERVES ME MUST FOLLOW ME. THEN MY SERVANT WILL BE WITH ME EVERYWHERE I AM. MY FATHER WILL HONOR ANYONE WHO SERVES ME. (John 12:23-26)

It all ties us back to El Shaddai, and the principle of returning to that from which we came. El Shaddai was the first official named revelation of God to mankind, and it is of the Almighty, of the all-powerful, of the One Who gives life, and the One Who gives it alone. It's not an accident the identity of such is indeed female, because it is associated with life. As we return through our lives to the One Who created us, we see a transformation, from death to life, from mortality to eternity, that comes as we accept and fully receive a spiritual revelation identified from stem to stern as female.

Embracing the feminine aspects of our faith

In a spiritual atmosphere that is decidedly and almost always appears to be patriarchal, it can be easy for us to forget that there is a softer side to our spiritual world, to our spiritual understandings, that is frequently lost. If we adapt a perspective that is out of balance (as many have), then our theology will embody a certain coldness and harshness to it that will distance us from the love of God, and of others. If we see God as unapproachable, operating almost a business-like sense of spiritual matters, we will lack the essential virtues of our faith that come from seeing a spiritual revelation in the realm of the divine feminine. By observing the spiritual balances, we find in God through non-binary gender identities, we learn that we do truly serve a God that is for everyone, and there for everyone, available to everyone, and that male, female, or somewhere in between, the virtues of our faith are for is all, waiting and ready to be fully embraced.

Mary and Elizabeth (Carl Bloch)

CHAPTER SIX
All Generations Will Call Them Blessed

I WILL MAKE YOU A GREAT NATION,
AND I WILL BLESS YOU.
I WILL MAKE YOU FAMOUS [YOUR NAME GREAT],
AND [OR SO THAT] YOU WILL BE A BLESSING TO OTHERS.
I WILL BLESS THOSE WHO BLESS YOU,
AND I WILL PLACE A CURSE ON THOSE WHO HARM [OR CURSE] YOU.
AND ALL THE PEOPLE [FAMILIES; CLANS] ON EARTH
WILL BE BLESSED THROUGH YOU [THE PROMISES OF THE ABRAHAMIC COVENANT]."
(GENESIS 12:2-3)

THE problematic passages of Scripture often fail to be understood because we do not examine them in the light of other passages that offer the illumination we seek. In a culture that strives for literalism in each passage, hoping such can be achieved on its own, we fail to realize that just as no person is an island, no passage is an island either. To understand one problematic verse, we need to look at other verses that are easier to understand and see that in some verses we take quickly at face value, there is an entire deeper meaning behind them. One of the things I hope to accomplish through is book is an open door to looking at the Scriptures in a new way, one that opens them up more fully and completely for all of you who read it and love the word.

Mary, mother of Jesus, and Elizabeth, mother of John the Baptist, are hardly obscure Bible figures. We hear about both at Christmastime, and we recognize them to be important women in the lives of the forerunner of Christ and Christ Himself. From this point onward, however, we tend to overshadow the role of Mary and Elizabeth (not to mention that of other women) in salvation history. We are so busy trying to prove that we do not desire to idolize Mary and Elizabeth, we have started to push them out of the picture all together, rather than learning from them and even coming to a place where we are able to identify with their stories to see ourselves in them.

Mary and Elizabeth are also not without their theological contributions, showing us pieces of God's nature through their stories and their experiences, and an echo of praise that we should all reflect, and embrace, as we hear the herald that all generations will call them blessed, not just those who surrounded them. The theology present in their experiences may be more subtle than some Bible stories, but it still remains, if for no other reason, than to remind us of the important women that are a part of salvation history.

The experience that changed the world

> MARY*
> - *MARIA* OR *MARIAM*: MARY, THE NAME OF SEVERAL CHRISTIAN WOMEN
> - ORIGINAL WORD: ΜΑΡΊΑ, ΑΣ, ή
> - PART OF SPEECH: NOUN, FEMININE; PROPER NOUN, INDECLINABLE
> - TRANSLITERATION: MARIA OR MARIAM
> - PHONETIC SPELLING: (MAR-EE'-AH)
> - SHORT DEFINITION: MARY, MIRIAM
> - DEFINITION: MARY, MIRIAM, (A) THE MOTHER OF JESUS, (B) OF MAGDALA, (C) SISTER OF MARTHA AND LAZARUS, (D) WIFE OF CLEOPAS, (E) MOTHER OF JOHN MARK, (F) A CHRISTIAN WOMAN IN ROME.

Much like we spoke of earlier, marriage was considered a conduit for family, particularly and especially male offspring. By the time of Mary and Elizabeth, it was very much understood that this wasn't just a purpose of a woman, but the only purpose of women. Brides were young, marriages were arranged, and girls were regarded as a huge burden on their families. They would not be eligible to inherit family property, and a woman and her entire life and identity would assimilate into her husband's world. There was an intense push to marry women off as soon as the option was feasible, with no consideration to just what she would marry into, or who she would marry.

THIS IS HOW THE BIRTH OF JESUS CHRIST [THE MESSIAH] CAME ABOUT. HIS MOTHER MARY WAS ENGAGED [PLEDGED; BETROTHED; A FORMAL AGREEMENT BETWEEN FAMILIES THAT REQUIRED A "DIVORCE" TO ANNUL] TO MARRY JOSEPH, BUT BEFORE THEY MARRIED [CAME TO LIVE TOGETHER], SHE LEARNED SHE WAS [OR WAS FOUND/DISCOVERED TO BE] PREGNANT [WITH CHILD] BY THE POWER OF [THROUGH] THE HOLY SPIRIT. BECAUSE MARY'S HUSBAND, JOSEPH, WAS A GOOD [RIGHTEOUS] MAN, HE DID NOT WANT TO DISGRACE HER IN PUBLIC, SO HE PLANNED TO DIVORCE HER [END THE ENGAGEMENT] SECRETLY [PRIVATELY; QUIETLY].

WHILE JOSEPH THOUGHT ABOUT [CONSIDERED; DECIDED; RESOLVED TO DO] THESE THINGS, [LOOK; BEHOLD] AN ANGEL OF THE LORD CAME [APPEARED] TO HIM IN A DREAM. THE ANGEL SAID, "JOSEPH, DESCENDANT [SON] OF DAVID, DON'T BE AFRAID TO TAKE MARY AS YOUR WIFE, BECAUSE THE BABY [WHAT IS CONCEIVED] IN HER IS FROM THE HOLY SPIRIT. SHE WILL GIVE BIRTH TO A SON, AND YOU WILL NAME HIM JESUS, BECAUSE HE WILL SAVE HIS PEOPLE FROM THEIR SINS [THE NAME JESUS MEANS "THE LORD SAVES"]."

ALL THIS HAPPENED TO BRING ABOUT [FULFILL] WHAT THE LORD HAD SAID [SPOKEN] THROUGH THE PROPHET: [LOOK; BEHOLD] THE VIRGIN WILL BE PREGNANT [CONCEIVE IN HER WOMB; IS. 7:14]. SHE WILL HAVE [GIVE BIRTH TO] A SON, AND THEY WILL NAME HIM IMMANUEL," WHICH [IN HEBREW] MEANS "GOD IS WITH US."

WHEN JOSEPH WOKE UP, HE DID WHAT THE LORD'S ANGEL HAD TOLD [COMMANDED] HIM TO DO. JOSEPH TOOK MARY AS HIS WIFE, BUT HE DID NOT HAVE SEXUAL RELATIONS WITH HER UNTIL SHE GAVE BIRTH TO A SON. AND JOSEPH [HE] NAMED HIM JESUS. (MATTHEW 1:18-25)

When the Bible opens with Mary's experience, we learn she was "betrothed" to Joseph. Betrothal is somewhat analogous to engagement, with a few exceptions. When a couple was betrothed, they had already gone through the exchange of dowry items and were awaiting the formal marriage ceremony and relationship to officially begin. Had Joseph died, Mary would have been considered a widow; had Mary died, Joseph would have been free to marry again. That was Mary's life, the old double standard, in a world that was unfair and unkind to women. There was nothing to suggest it was in any way out of the ordinary, at least up until this point.

Even though women in Jesus' time didn't have access to learn the Torah or the Scriptures, every Jewish girl would pray to God, hoping they would be selected to become the mother of the Messiah. This was, most likely, more of a social understanding than a theological one. The Jews of Jesus' day were occupied by the Roman government, and it was their hope and expectation that the great and mighty prophesied Messiah would come into their lives, overthrow the Romans, and lead the Jews into the prophesied time of peace and perfect rule.

There was an important theology in that prayer, however, that most of the women in that time would not have properly understood. They were recognizing that for the Messiah to come into this world, God would have to call, and appoint, a woman for that task. No one might have thought about it, but the Messiah's incarnation was intimately tied to the work of a woman. The line of salvation is not exclusive to men, or even to one man, but to the work of God through men and women alike, all throughout history. But when it came to birthing the Messiah, that was something unique to a woman – something done between God and a woman – that could not ever be duplicated, nor done, ever again.

DURING ELIZABETH'S SIXTH MONTH OF PREGNANCY, GOD SENT THE ANGEL GABRIEL [1:19] TO NAZARETH, A TOWN IN GALILEE, TO A VIRGIN. SHE WAS ENGAGED TO MARRY [PLEDGED TO; ENGAGEMENT WAS A BINDING CONTRACT BETWEEN TWO FAMILIES AND COULD ONLY BE BROKEN BY DIVORCE] A MAN NAMED JOSEPH FROM THE FAMILY [A DESCENDENT; FROM THE HOUSE] OF DAVID. HER [THE VIRGIN'S] NAME WAS MARY. THE ANGEL CAME TO HER AND SAID, "GREETINGS [HELLO; REJOICE; A COMMON GREETING]! THE LORD HAS BLESSED YOU AND IS WITH YOU [OR ...FAVORED ONE, THE LORD IS WITH YOU]."

BUT MARY WAS VERY STARTLED [DISTURBED; PERPLEXED; TROUBLED] BY WHAT THE ANGEL SAID AND WONDERED WHAT THIS GREETING MIGHT MEAN [SORT OF GREETING THIS WAS].

THE ANGEL SAID TO HER, "DON'T BE AFRAID, MARY; [FOR; BECAUSE] GOD HAS SHOWN YOU HIS GRACE [YOU HAVE FOUND FAVOR/GRACE WITH GOD]. LISTEN [LOOK; BEHOLD]! YOU WILL BECOME PREGNANT [CONCEIVE IN YOUR WOMB] AND GIVE BIRTH TO A SON, AND YOU WILL

NAME HIM JESUS [IS. 7:14]. HE WILL BE GREAT AND WILL BE CALLED THE SON OF THE MOST HIGH. THE LORD GOD WILL GIVE HIM THE THRONE OF KING DAVID, HIS ANCESTOR [HIS FATHER DAVID]. HE WILL RULE [REIGN] OVER THE PEOPLE [HOUSE] OF JACOB FOREVER, AND HIS KINGDOM WILL NEVER END [2 SAM. 7:13, 16; DAN. 7:14, 27]."

MARY SAID TO THE ANGEL, "HOW WILL [CAN] THIS HAPPEN SINCE I AM A VIRGIN [I HAVE NOT KNOWN A MAN (SEXUALLY)]?"

THE ANGEL SAID TO MARY, "THE HOLY SPIRIT WILL COME UPON [OVER] YOU, AND THE POWER OF THE MOST HIGH WILL COVER [OVERSHADOW] YOU. FOR THIS REASON THE BABY WILL BE HOLY AND [HOLY ONE TO BE BORN] WILL BE CALLED THE SON OF GOD. NOW [AND LOOK/BEHOLD] ELIZABETH, YOUR RELATIVE, IS ALSO PREGNANT WITH [HAS ALSO CONCEIVED] A SON THOUGH SHE IS VERY OLD [IN HER OLD AGE]. EVERYONE THOUGHT SHE COULD NOT HAVE A BABY, BUT SHE HAS BEEN PREGNANT FOR SIX MONTHS. [AND THIS IS THE SIXTH MONTH FOR THE WOMAN THEY CALLED BARREN!] GOD CAN DO ANYTHING [...BECAUSE NOTHING IS IMPOSSIBLE WITH GOD; OR ...BECAUSE NO WORD/MESSAGE FROM GOD WILL EVER FAIL; GEN. 18:14; JER. 32:17]!"

MARY SAID, "[LOOK; BEHOLD] I AM THE SERVANT [BONDSERVANT; HANDMAID] OF THE LORD. LET THIS HAPPEN TO ME AS YOU SAY [ACCORDING TO YOUR WORD]!" THEN THE ANGEL WENT AWAY [LEFT HER]. (Luke 1:26-38)

The Gospel accounts don't get into great detail of the ins and outs of Mary and Joseph's experience, but we can understand that it would have been nearly impossible for it to not change things between them. Mary's acceptance of her position in the theological order of salvation wasn't something Joseph would have been excited to embrace, and whether or not Joseph is viewed as upstanding for keeping his long-term commitment to Mary, the Scriptures do tell us that he was ready to pack it in and divorce her, although he was willing to do it quietly (like that made things a lot better for her in the long run). Every sweet, sincere picture of the Holy Family glowing around the baby Jesus doesn't bespeak reality, and it doesn't bespeak the intense theology that could change the very life and course of Mary's life.

By accepting God's call, she was well acknowledging that she was doing something with God that could not, and would not, be done again in her life, with anyone else.

That is in essence the message we should all receive regarding our spiritual lives: what we do with God is something that we cannot do with anyone else. We might cheer and celebrate this when we are at church, but seldom do we hear of the way that such a change might impact on the relationships we have with others. We will run into complications if we expect that everything will remain the same, even though we have accepted the call to receive what God has done, and thus become a part of salvation history, ourselves. Not everyone understands it; it is not the same for everyone when they are going through it; and the perception of it to others is not the same as it is for us, either. We cannot expect that God will do great things through any of us and such will not change our lives.

The concept of Mary's conception is of some debate, particularly as the years go by and different groups attempt to try and define it within a doctrinal perspective. The woman who literally carried the Gospel before anyone else had to receive the Word, in some form, for the Word to be made flesh within her. The reality is that I don't think we can know exactly how it happened, but the Scriptures tell us that the power of the Most High was to overshadow her, and she would receive the Holy Spirit, so what would be born of her would be the Son of God. The point of this wasn't to debate on artificial insemination or surmise about sex with the gods (which yes, is an extreme some have gone). This wasn't a political statement; it was a spiritual one, celebrating the incarnation of the Word into this world. The points we should, and must, drive home from this are:

- The conception of Christ fulfills prophecy.
- The conception of Christ did not involve a man.
- The conception of Christ could not have been accomplished with any sort of human intervention.
- The conception of Christ was a miracle: supernatural, spiritual, and beyond anything we can imagine within our minds.
- The conception of Christ was the work of God and a woman.

In Mary's conception of Christ, we discover how God births within us spiritually. The spiritual realm does not operate by the laws present in natural order, and for God to bring something forth within us, it does not have to operate by a natural means or understanding. Whatever God wants to do within someone – not exclusive to women, but especially through women – He does through His own overshadowing, and His own Holy Spirit. It does not have to make sense, it does not take a natural route, but it does have to be one with a theological grounding. This means it is done via God, through us, and that the credit goes to divine attribution, rather than something humans can concoct, this side of heaven.

Mary was one whose firsthand experience of living theology was not easy, in more than one way. Mary literally carried the Gospel and was the first one to do so. She carried the Word in her literal body, with the literal difficulties of that call. Carrying the Word was joyful, because the Messiah was coming into the world, but it was also laborious, because the Word brought change. In Mary, we see a literal picture of what we experience from a spiritual perspective; we rejoice, for the blessing of the Word, but we also deal with the pangs and pains of the difficulty of having the Word in a world that does not easily understand it.

Mary was the first to learn that the Messiah would come into the world, in her lifetime. The first to hear the Gospel in her day and age, that prayer that Mary said a million times, like every other girl in her day and age, was to come true – through her. For this, she was most blessed among all women. It was not a question that she would be blessed among some women, or over just the Jewish women, or even the women of her family. Mary was most blessed among all women, because she was also the fulfillment of the prophecy, made to Eve, back in the garden. Through Mary, the Redeemer would come, who would crush the head of the serpent, and proclaim a victory over the enemy for all of humankind.

This requires Mary to also be found in Old Testament types. We find shadows of Mary present in Hannah, mother of Samuel:

THERE WAS A CERTAIN MAN FROM RAMATHAIM, A ZUPHITE FROM THE HILL COUNTRY OF EPHRAIM, WHOSE NAME WAS ELKANAH SON OF JEROHAM, THE SON OF ELIHU, THE SON OF TOHU, THE SON OF ZUPH, AN EPHRAIMITE. HE HAD TWO WIVES; ONE WAS CALLED HANNAH AND

THE OTHER PENINNAH. PENINNAH HAD CHILDREN, BUT HANNAH HAD
NONE.

YEAR AFTER YEAR THIS MAN WENT UP FROM HIS TOWN TO WORSHIP
AND SACRIFICE TO THE LORD ALMIGHTY AT SHILOH, WHERE HOPHNI
AND PHINEHAS, THE TWO SONS OF ELI, WERE PRIESTS OF THE LORD.
WHENEVER THE DAY CAME FOR ELKANAH TO SACRIFICE, HE WOULD
GIVE PORTIONS OF THE MEAT TO HIS WIFE PENINNAH AND TO ALL HER
SONS AND DAUGHTERS. BUT TO HANNAH HE GAVE A DOUBLE PORTION
BECAUSE HE LOVED HER, AND THE LORD HAD CLOSED HER WOMB.
BECAUSE THE LORD HAD CLOSED HANNAH'S WOMB, HER RIVAL KEPT
PROVOKING HER IN ORDER TO IRRITATE HER. THIS WENT ON YEAR
AFTER YEAR. WHENEVER HANNAH WENT UP TO THE HOUSE OF THE
LORD, HER RIVAL PROVOKED HER TILL SHE WEPT AND WOULD NOT
EAT. HER HUSBAND ELKANAH WOULD SAY TO HER, "HANNAH, WHY
ARE YOU WEEPING? WHY DON'T YOU EAT? WHY ARE YOU
DOWNHEARTED? DON'T I MEAN MORE TO YOU THAN TEN SONS?"

ONCE WHEN THEY HAD FINISHED EATING AND DRINKING IN SHILOH,
HANNAH STOOD UP. NOW ELI THE PRIEST WAS SITTING ON HIS CHAIR
BY THE DOORPOST OF THE LORD'S HOUSE. IN HER DEEP ANGUISH
HANNAH PRAYED TO THE LORD, WEEPING BITTERLY. AND SHE MADE A
VOW, SAYING, "LORD ALMIGHTY, IF YOU WILL ONLY LOOK ON YOUR
SERVANT'S MISERY AND REMEMBER ME, AND NOT FORGET YOUR
SERVANT BUT GIVE HER A SON, THEN I WILL GIVE HIM TO THE LORD
FOR ALL THE DAYS OF HIS LIFE, AND NO RAZOR WILL EVER BE USED ON
HIS HEAD."

AS SHE KEPT ON PRAYING TO THE LORD, ELI OBSERVED HER MOUTH.
HANNAH WAS PRAYING IN HER HEART, AND HER LIPS WERE MOVING
BUT HER VOICE WAS NOT HEARD. ELI THOUGHT SHE WAS DRUNK AND
SAID TO HER, "HOW LONG ARE YOU GOING TO STAY DRUNK? PUT AWAY
YOUR WINE."

"NOT SO, MY LORD," HANNAH REPLIED, "I AM A WOMAN WHO IS
DEEPLY TROUBLED. I HAVE NOT BEEN DRINKING WINE OR BEER; I WAS
POURING OUT MY SOUL TO THE LORD. DO NOT TAKE YOUR SERVANT
FOR A WICKED WOMAN; I HAVE BEEN PRAYING HERE OUT OF MY GREAT
ANGUISH AND GRIEF."

ELI ANSWERED, "GO IN PEACE, AND MAY THE GOD OF ISRAEL GRANT YOU WHAT YOU HAVE ASKED OF HIM."

SHE SAID, "MAY YOUR SERVANT FIND FAVOR IN YOUR EYES." THEN SHE WENT HER WAY AND ATE SOMETHING, AND HER FACE WAS NO LONGER DOWNCAST.

EARLY THE NEXT MORNING THEY AROSE AND WORSHIPED BEFORE THE LORD AND THEN WENT BACK TO THEIR HOME AT RAMAH. ELKANAH MADE LOVE TO HIS WIFE HANNAH, AND THE LORD REMEMBERED HER. SO IN THE COURSE OF TIME HANNAH BECAME PREGNANT AND GAVE BIRTH TO A SON. SHE NAMED HIM SAMUEL, SAYING, "BECAUSE I ASKED THE LORD FOR HIM."

WHEN HER HUSBAND ELKANAH WENT UP WITH ALL HIS FAMILY TO OFFER THE ANNUAL SACRIFICE TO THE LORD AND TO FULFILL HIS VOW, HANNAH DID NOT GO. SHE SAID TO HER HUSBAND, "AFTER THE BOY IS WEANED, I WILL TAKE HIM AND PRESENT HIM BEFORE THE LORD, AND HE WILL LIVE THERE ALWAYS."

"DO WHAT SEEMS BEST TO YOU," HER HUSBAND ELKANAH TOLD HER. "STAY HERE UNTIL YOU HAVE WEANED HIM; ONLY MAY THE LORD MAKE GOOD HIS WORD." SO THE WOMAN STAYED AT HOME AND NURSED HER SON UNTIL SHE HAD WEANED HIM.

AFTER HE WAS WEANED, SHE TOOK THE BOY WITH HER, YOUNG AS HE WAS, ALONG WITH A THREE-YEAR-OLD BULL, AN EPHAH OF FLOUR AND A SKIN OF WINE, AND BROUGHT HIM TO THE HOUSE OF THE LORD AT SHILOH. WHEN THE BULL HAD BEEN SACRIFICED, THEY BROUGHT THE BOY TO ELI, AND SHE SAID TO HIM, "PARDON ME, MY LORD. AS SURELY AS YOU LIVE, I AM THE WOMAN WHO STOOD HERE BESIDE YOU PRAYING TO THE LORD. I PRAYED FOR THIS CHILD, AND THE LORD HAS GRANTED ME WHAT I ASKED OF HIM. SO NOW I GIVE HIM TO THE LORD. FOR HIS WHOLE LIFE HE WILL BE GIVEN OVER TO THE LORD." AND HE WORSHIPED THE LORD THERE.

THEN HANNAH PRAYED AND SAID:

"MY HEART REJOICES IN THE LORD;
  IN THE LORD MY HORN IS LIFTED HIGH.

MY MOUTH BOASTS OVER MY ENEMIES,
　　FOR I DELIGHT IN YOUR DELIVERANCE.

"THERE IS NO ONE HOLY LIKE THE LORD;
　　THERE IS NO ONE BESIDES YOU;
　　THERE IS NO ROCK LIKE OUR GOD.

"DO NOT KEEP TALKING SO PROUDLY
　　OR LET YOUR MOUTH SPEAK SUCH ARROGANCE,
FOR THE LORD IS A GOD WHO KNOWS,
　　AND BY HIM DEEDS ARE WEIGHED.

"THE BOWS OF THE WARRIORS ARE BROKEN,
　　BUT THOSE WHO STUMBLED ARE ARMED WITH STRENGTH.
THOSE WHO WERE FULL HIRE THEMSELVES OUT FOR FOOD,
　　BUT THOSE WHO WERE HUNGRY ARE HUNGRY NO MORE.
SHE WHO WAS BARREN HAS BORNE SEVEN CHILDREN,
　　BUT SHE WHO HAS HAD MANY SONS PINES AWAY.

"THE LORD BRINGS DEATH AND MAKES ALIVE;
　　HE BRINGS DOWN TO THE GRAVE AND RAISES UP.
THE LORD SENDS POVERTY AND WEALTH;
　　HE HUMBLES AND HE EXALTS.
HE RAISES THE POOR FROM THE DUST
　　AND LIFTS THE NEEDY FROM THE ASH HEAP;
HE SEATS THEM WITH PRINCES
　　AND HAS THEM INHERIT A THRONE OF HONOR.

"FOR THE FOUNDATIONS OF THE EARTH ARE THE LORD'S;
　　ON THEM HE HAS SET THE WORLD.
HE WILL GUARD THE FEET OF HIS FAITHFUL SERVANTS,
　　BUT THE WICKED WILL BE SILENCED IN THE PLACE OF DARKNESS.

"IT IS NOT BY STRENGTH THAT ONE PREVAILS;
　　THOSE WHO OPPOSE THE LORD WILL BE BROKEN.
THE MOST HIGH WILL THUNDER FROM HEAVEN;
　　THE LORD WILL JUDGE THE ENDS OF THE EARTH.

"HE WILL GIVE STRENGTH TO HIS KING
　　AND EXALT THE HORN OF HIS ANOINTED."

AND THE BOY SAMUEL CONTINUED TO GROW IN STATURE AND IN FAVOR WITH THE LORD AND WITH PEOPLE. (1 Samuel 1:1-2:10, 26, NIV)

- Both were, for their own reasons, unable to conceive in the natural.
- Both had boys as their firstborn children.
- Both had spiritual encounters surrounding the conception of their firstborn sons.
- Both had children who were set apart for God, from their birth, for service in the Kingdom.
- Both had to surrender their children back to God.
- Both women made powerful prophetic utterances that praised God and predicted a future shifting between the powers of this age and the promise of divine intervention in world affairs.
- Both women's sons grew in stature and gained favor with God and with people.

In a more untraditional fashion, we also see shadows of Mary present in Hagar:

BUT ABRAM SAID TO SARAI, "YOU ARE HAGAR'S MISTRESS [YOUR SLAVE GIRL IS IN YOUR HAND/POWER]. DO ANYTHING YOU WANT [WHAT IS GOOD IN YOUR EYES] TO HER." THEN SARAI WAS HARD ON [AFFLICTED; ABUSED] HAGAR, AND HAGAR RAN AWAY [FLED FROM HER PRESENCE].

THE ANGEL [MESSENGER] OF THE LORD [THE ANGEL OF THE LORD WAS EITHER A REPRESENTATIVE OF THE LORD OR THE LORD HIMSELF; V. 13; JUDG. 6:11, 14] FOUND HAGAR BESIDE A SPRING OF WATER IN THE DESERT [WILDERNESS], BY THE ROAD TO SHUR [LIKELY A LOCATION IN SOUTHERN CANAAN; 20:1; 25:18; EX. 15:22; 1 SAM. 15:7]. THE ANGEL [HE] SAID, "HAGAR, SARAI'S SLAVE GIRL, WHERE HAVE YOU COME FROM? WHERE ARE YOU GOING?"

HAGAR ANSWERED, "I AM RUNNING AWAY [FLEEING] FROM MY MISTRESS SARAI."

THE ANGEL [MESSENGER] OF THE LORD [16:7] SAID TO HER, "GO HOME TO YOUR MISTRESS AND OBEY [SUBMIT TO] HER." THE ANGEL OF

THE LORD ALSO SAID, "I WILL GIVE YOU SO MANY DESCENDANTS [GREATLY MULTIPLY YOUR SEED SO THAT] THEY CANNOT BE COUNTED."

THE ANGEL [MESSENGER] ADDED,
"YOU ARE NOW PREGNANT [HAVE CONCEIVED],
    AND YOU WILL HAVE [GIVE BIRTH TO] A SON.
YOU WILL NAME HIM ISHMAEL [SOUNDS LIKE THE VERB "TO HEAR"],
    BECAUSE THE LORD HAS HEARD YOUR CRIES [OF YOUR AFFLICTION].
ISHMAEL WILL BE LIKE A WILD DONKEY [A WILD DONKEY/ASS OF A MAN].
    HE [HIS HAND] WILL BE AGAINST EVERYONE,
    AND EVERYONE [EVERYONE'S HAND] WILL BE AGAINST HIM.
HE WILL ATTACK [DWELL AGAINST] ALL HIS BROTHERS."

THE SLAVE GIRL GAVE A NAME TO THE LORD WHO SPOKE TO HER: "YOU ARE 'GOD WHO SEES ME [OR GOD OF SEEING; HEBREW *EL-ROI*]'" BECAUSE SHE SAID TO HERSELF, "HAVE I REALLY SEEN GOD WHO SEES ME?" SO THE WELL THERE, BETWEEN KADESH [ALSO KNOWN AS KADESH BARNEA IN NORTHEAST SINAI] AND BERED [LOCATION UNKNOWN], WAS CALLED BEER LAHAI ROI [THE WELL OF THE LIVING ONE WHO SEES ME].

HAGAR GAVE BIRTH TO A SON FOR ABRAM, AND ABRAM NAMED HIM [HIS SON WHICH HAGAR BORE HIM] ISHMAEL. ABRAM WAS EIGHTY-SIX YEARS OLD WHEN HAGAR GAVE BIRTH TO ISHMAEL. (Genesis 16:6-16)

- Both had a divine encounter with an angel.
- Both became pregnant outside of the bounds of traditional marriage (one a virgin, one a concubine).
- Both had to fear societal perceptions of their pregnancies.
- Both were told they were carrying a child who would impact multitudes.
- Both left their homes while pregnant.
- Both gave birth to a child of covenant promise.

Unique prophecies that relate to Mary:

- The virgin would conceive a child, and shall name Him Immanuel (Isaiah 7:1-17).

- She shall travail in labor and give birth while in Bethlehem (Micah 5:2-3).

These words prove to us that Mary was a part of God's plan, and an important part, at that. The responsibility to first carry the Gospel was not to go to just anyone, but to a woman who would be able to handle her own theology, up close and personal. This makes Mary a type of the church, as well; one who lived the literal type experience of the church, as she literally carried the Word within her. Mary understood the church from her experience, because it was her, and was one who celebrated and lived that promise, from long before the Pentecost experience.

A prophetic visit

We don't know much about Elizabeth, neither in the Scriptures, nor in the apocrypha or various traditions that emerged later. What we do know is Elizabeth was a Levite, of Aaron's descendants, and was married to Zechariah, a Levite. They were of advanced age, devout, Law-observing, and childless, when the angel Gabriel came to deliver Zechariah a message:

ELIZABETH[2]
- ELISABET: ELIZABETH, AN ISRAELITESS "GOD IS AN OATH"
- ORIGINAL WORD: Ἐλισάβετ, ἡ
- PART OF SPEECH: PROPER NOUN, INDECLINABLE
- TRANSLITERATION: ELISABET
- PHONETIC SPELLING: (EL-EE-SAB'-ET)
- SHORT DEFINITION: ELISABETH
- DEFINITION: ELIZABETH, MOTHER OF JOHN THE BAPTIZER.

BUT THE ANGEL SAID TO HIM, "ZECHARIAH, DON'T BE AFRAID. GOD HAS HEARD YOUR PRAYER [PETITION]. YOUR WIFE, ELIZABETH, WILL GIVE BIRTH TO [BEAR FOR YOU] A SON, AND YOU WILL NAME HIM JOHN. HE WILL BRING YOU JOY AND GLADNESS [DELIGHT], AND MANY PEOPLE WILL BE HAPPY [REJOICE] BECAUSE OF HIS BIRTH. [FOR;

BECAUSE] JOHN WILL BE A GREAT MAN FOR [IN THE EYES OF; BEFORE] THE LORD. HE WILL NEVER DRINK WINE OR BEER [INDICATING HE WILL BE SET APART TO GOD FOR SPECIAL SERVICE; NUM. 6:3], AND EVEN FROM BIRTH [*OR* IN HIS MOTHER'S WOMB; 1:41, 44], HE WILL BE FILLED WITH THE HOLY SPIRIT. HE WILL HELP MANY PEOPLE [OF THE CHILDREN] OF ISRAEL RETURN TO THE LORD THEIR GOD [1 KIN. 18:37]. HE WILL GO BEFORE THE LORD [HIM] IN [THE] SPIRIT AND POWER LIKE [OF] ELIJAH. HE WILL MAKE PEACE BETWEEN PARENTS AND [TURN THE HEARTS OF PARENTS/FATHERS BACK TO] THEIR CHILDREN AND WILL BRING THOSE WHO ARE NOT OBEYING GOD BACK TO THE RIGHT WAY OF THINKING [*OR* WISDOM OF THE RIGHTEOUS], TO MAKE A PEOPLE READY [TO PREPARE A PEOPLE WHO ARE FIT/READY] FOR THE COMING OF THE LORD [LORD; MAL. 4:5–6]."

ZECHARIAH SAID TO THE ANGEL, "HOW CAN I KNOW THAT WHAT YOU SAY IS TRUE [THIS]? [FOR] I AM AN OLD MAN, AND MY WIFE IS OLD, TOO [GEN. 17:17]."

THE ANGEL ANSWERED HIM, "I AM GABRIEL [ONE OF TWO NAMED ANGELS IN SCRIPTURE (THE OTHER IS MICHAEL); DAN. 8:16; 9:21; 10:10–14]. I STAND BEFORE GOD, WHO SENT ME TO TALK TO YOU AND TO TELL YOU THIS GOOD NEWS. NOW, LISTEN [LOOK; BEHOLD]! YOU WILL [BE SILENT AND] NOT BE ABLE TO SPEAK UNTIL THE DAY THESE THINGS HAPPEN, BECAUSE YOU DID NOT BELIEVE WHAT I TOLD YOU [MY WORDS]. BUT THEY WILL REALLY HAPPEN [...WHICH WILL BE FULFILLED AT THEIR APPOINTED TIME]."

OUTSIDE, THE PEOPLE WERE STILL WAITING FOR ZECHARIAH AND WERE SURPRISED THAT [WONDERING WHY] HE WAS STAYING SO LONG [DELAYED] IN THE TEMPLE. WHEN ZECHARIAH CAME OUTSIDE, HE COULD NOT SPEAK TO THEM, AND THEY KNEW HE HAD SEEN A VISION IN THE TEMPLE. HE COULD ONLY MAKE SIGNS [MOTION; GESTURE] TO THEM AND REMAINED UNABLE TO SPEAK. WHEN HIS TIME [PERIOD; DAYS] OF SERVICE AT THE TEMPLE WAS FINISHED, HE WENT HOME.

LATER [AFTER THESE DAYS], ZECHARIAH'S WIFE, ELIZABETH, BECAME PREGNANT AND DID NOT GO OUT OF HER HOUSE [WENT INTO SECLUSION; HID HERSELF; THE REASON IS UNKNOWN, PERHAPS FOR QUIET WORSHIP OR TO AVOID GAWKING NEIGHBORS] FOR FIVE MONTHS. ELIZABETH SAID, "LOOK WHAT [THIS IS WHAT; THUS] THE LORD HAS DONE FOR ME! HE HAS [WATCHED OVER ME AND] TAKEN

AWAY MY DISGRACE AMONG THE PEOPLE [THE JEWISH PEOPLE THOUGHT IT WAS A DISGRACE FOR A WOMAN NOT TO HAVE CHILDREN; GEN. 30:23]." (Luke 1:13-25)

We don't have a specified reason for Elizabeth's seclusion during her pregnancy, although we can draw conclusions. Being of advanced age and pregnant might have required careful precautions to avoid miscarriage or stillbirth. It also may have been nothing more than Elizabeth's need to handle and process the situation for herself, and such required her to distance herself. What we do know is that somewhere, in that process, Mary visited Elizabeth for a most remarkable meeting. Much like Elizabeth's seclusion, we don't know the exact reason why Mary visited Elizabeth, and for such an extended period of time. The most obvious reason seems to have been to get away from her hometown, to preserve her life, and avoid accusation and gossip during such a sensitive time, particularly in her cultural period of history. Regardless of why Mary visited Elizabeth, the meeting of these two cousins, one of whom was much older than the other, but both pregnant at the same time, reveals much to us about the female role of life and spiritual life, present at this most prophetic time in history.

AT THAT TIME MARY GOT READY AND HURRIED TO A TOWN IN THE HILL COUNTRY OF JUDEA, WHERE SHE ENTERED ZECHARIAH'S HOME AND GREETED ELIZABETH. WHEN ELIZABETH HEARD MARY'S GREETING, THE BABY LEAPED IN HER WOMB, AND ELIZABETH WAS FILLED WITH THE HOLY SPIRIT. IN A LOUD VOICE SHE EXCLAIMED: "BLESSED ARE YOU AMONG WOMEN, AND BLESSED IS THE CHILD YOU WILL BEAR! BUT WHY AM I SO FAVORED, THAT THE MOTHER OF MY LORD SHOULD COME TO ME? AS SOON AS THE SOUND OF YOUR GREETING REACHED MY EARS, THE BABY IN MY WOMB LEAPED FOR JOY. BLESSED IS SHE WHO HAS BELIEVED THAT THE LORD WOULD FULFILL HIS PROMISES TO HER!"

AND MARY SAID:

"MY SOUL GLORIFIES THE LORD
    AND MY SPIRIT REJOICES IN GOD MY SAVIOR,
FOR HE HAS BEEN MINDFUL
    OF THE HUMBLE STATE OF HIS SERVANT.

FROM NOW ON ALL GENERATIONS WILL CALL ME BLESSED,
    FOR THE MIGHTY ONE HAS DONE GREAT THINGS FOR ME—
HOLY IS HIS NAME.
HIS MERCY EXTENDS TO THOSE WHO FEAR HIM,
    FROM GENERATION TO GENERATION.
HE HAS PERFORMED MIGHTY DEEDS WITH HIS ARM;
    HE HAS SCATTERED THOSE WHO ARE PROUD IN THEIR INMOST
THOUGHTS.
HE HAS BROUGHT DOWN RULERS FROM THEIR THRONES
    BUT HAS LIFTED UP THE HUMBLE.
HE HAS FILLED THE HUNGRY WITH GOOD THINGS
    BUT HAS SENT THE RICH AWAY EMPTY.
HE HAS HELPED HIS SERVANT ISRAEL,
    REMEMBERING TO BE MERCIFUL
TO ABRAHAM AND HIS DESCENDANTS FOREVER,
    JUST AS HE PROMISED OUR ANCESTORS."

MARY STAYED WITH ELIZABETH FOR ABOUT THREE MONTHS AND
THEN RETURNED HOME. (Luke 1:39-56, NIV)

The first two people in the New Testament to be filled with the
Holy spirit were Mary (in conception of Christ) and Elizabeth (in
proclamation of the coming Savior, the Word, into the world).
Filled with the Spirit, Elizabeth spoke out a word of knowledge,
proclaiming what was already true, and heralding Mary as most
blessed among all women. Even though Jesus was not yet born,
the promise was already present, and the prophecy was in place.
Because Mary dared to live out theology, Mary's blessing was to
be most blessed among all women. She was blessed for her
confession of faith; she was blessed for her trust in God; and she
was blessed for being the mother of Christ, Who would bless all
generations. She was blessed by the child she would bear, Who
would bring salvation, and because she was the one who was
chosen to bring Him into this world.

Mary's song, also called "the Magnificat," are the words of
utmost praise spoken by Mary in the moments after Elizabeth's
proclamation. They bespeak not just the words of a happy
woman, but the prophecies of the result of spiritual shift. This
song is not just Mary's song, however. By proxy, it is the song of
every woman to come before, and after, Mary. It is Elizabeth's
song, because without John the Baptist, her son, we would not

have had the Messiah. They were prophecy; future and living; and now in them, this song is ours, our praise, our promise, our future. Thanks to these two women, all generations call us blessed, because the Mighty One has done great things for us, and holy is His Name.

Saved through childbearing

SAVED[3]

- *SŌZŌ*. TO SAVE
- ORIGINAL WORD: Σῴζω
- PART OF SPEECH: VERB
- TRANSLITERATION: SŌZŌ
- PHONETIC SPELLING: (SODE'-ZO)
- SHORT DEFINITION: I SAVE, HEAL
- DEFINITION: I SAVE, HEAL, PRESERVE, RESCUE.

CHILDBEARING[4]

- *TEKNOGONIA*: CHILDBEARING
- ORIGINAL WORD: ΤΕΚΝΟΓΟΝΊΑ, ΑΣ, ἡ
- PART OF SPEECH: NOUN, FEMININE
- TRANSLITERATION: TEKNOGONIA
- PHONETIC SPELLING: (TEK-NOG-ON-EE'-AH)
- SHORT DEFINITION: CHILD BEARING
- DEFINITION: CHILD BEARING, THE REARING OF A FAMILY.

One of the most complicated and misinterpreted verses of Scripture relates to Mary, but not in an obvious way. The seeming nature of ambiguity in the passage causes confusion, and has led to all sorts of aberrant interpretations, some of which have been downright problematic for women throughout church history.

ALSO [I DESIRE] THAT WOMEN SHOULD ADORN THEMSELVES MODESTLY *AND* APPROPRIATELY AND SENSIBLY IN SEEMLY APPAREL,

NOT WITH [ELABORATE] HAIR ARRANGEMENT OR GOLD OR PEARLS OR EXPENSIVE CLOTHING, BUT BY DOING GOOD DEEDS (DEEDS IN THEMSELVES GOOD AND FOR THE GOOD AND ADVANTAGE OF THOSE CONTACTED BY THEM), AS BEFITS WOMEN WHO PROFESS REVERENTIAL FEAR FOR *AND* DEVOTION TO GOD.

LET A WOMAN LEARN IN QUIETNESS, IN ENTIRE SUBMISSIVENESS. I ALLOW NO WOMAN TO TEACH OR TO HAVE AUTHORITY OVER MEN; SHE IS TO REMAIN IN QUIETNESS *AND* KEEP SILENCE [IN RELIGIOUS ASSEMBLIES]. FOR ADAM WAS FIRST FORMED, THEN EVE; AND IT WAS NOT ADAM WHO WAS DECEIVED, BUT [THE] WOMAN WHO WAS DECEIVED *AND* DELUDED AND FELL INTO TRANSGRESSION.

NEVERTHELESS [THE SENTENCE PUT UPON WOMEN OF PAIN IN MOTHERHOOD DOES NOT HINDER THEIR SOULS' SALVATION, AND] THEY WILL BE SAVED [ETERNALLY] IF THEY CONTINUE IN FAITH AND LOVE AND HOLINESS WITH SELF-CONTROL, [SAVED INDEED] THROUGH THE CHILDBEARING *OR* BY THE BIRTH OF THE DIVINE CHILD. (1 Timothy 2:9-15, AMPC)

The last section of Timothy 2 seems confusing. The entire first part of the chapter is about worship, about the unity of the people that pleases God in worship, and on the proper focus of Christ in worship. The Apostle Paul then goes on to advise men to worship properly, lifting their hands, without fighting and quarreling with one another. From there, the shift moves to women's attire, and then an entire discourse on matters as relate to women that don't seem so much about worship anymore, but rather, designed to pick on women. Or so it is used to do, and often makes many women feel.

The difficulty in understanding this passage relates to the way that we often cut it off from the rest of the chapter, as if the Apostle Paul has moved into an entirely different course of thought from the first half. The entire chapter is about worship and avoiding the divisions that were present in churches during worship. This goes for the commentary on the women as much as the men, but instead of addressing arguing and grumbling, the matters at hand were those that affected the women present at that time.

Nobody reads the first eight verses of 1 Timothy 2 and believes they cannot apply to women as well as the men addressed. We take for granted that women are included in that passage, but we never assume that the passages specific to women can apply to men, as well. This is because of teaching and indoctrination throughout the centuries and is part of patriarchal notion that what is for men might somehow include women as an afterthought, but what is exclusive to women is only for women. This has led to offense and hurt, and a general feeling that women are less important than men in the eyes of God.

Sometimes we are overly sensitive to Biblical rebukes toward women because we have heard them as offensive, used to hurt or offend women, one too many times. We never hear anyone preach on the topics for everyone, in a way that everyone can understand, and that leads women to feel as if they are being singled out for all of eternity. 1 Timothy 2:9-15 is one of the most common passages used as a weapon to try and keep women in a certain place or state, when that is not what it was ever intended to do. As women, however, we must accept that we do not do everything right all the time, and neither have women throughout history. Reading these passages in a different light helps connect us back to our ancestry and helps us to realize that some things – such as dressing for the right reason and reminding ourselves of the importance in proper focus for worship – is timeless.

This is exactly how the passage connects us back to Mary and Elizabeth, even though it might not seem obvious. 1 Timothy 2 clarifies one thing: women were, and always have been, allowed to worship God. Just like Mary and Elizabeth, however, our focus in worship must genuinely be on God, not on trying to make ourselves the center of attention or draw attention away from God, unto ourselves. As living out their theology in full, their theology that was beyond anything they'd ever been taught or imagined in their lives, those women echoed a praise that was not worried about what anyone else thought, how they looked at that moment, or about trying to produce something within their own flesh. It was all about God, and throughout all time, our worship should be, and must be, about God to be authentic.

The issue of women's attire comes up in a few places in the New Testament (1 Corinthians 11:5-10, 1 Timothy 2:9-10, 1 Peter 3:3), and they all seem to have certain things in common. In modern society, we take issue with the commentaries, as if it is somehow saying there is something shameful about or with women. That was not the point, as the passages are about modesty, but not in the context of sex or gender identity. The issue of Biblical modesty, in each and every passage, is about money, and refraining from flaunting one's wealth or social status in church. Understandably so, dressing with the goal to impress distracts in worship, and makes those moments about us instead of about God. This was of particular issue in New Testament times, and that's why it kept coming up, over and over again. The issue wasn't so much about the specifics, such as jewelry, pearls, or hairstyles, but about why one wore those, and why they insisted on bringing such a custom into the church, out of vanity and wrong motive.

Instead of the internal motive of vanity, the Apostle Paul encouraged the women to focus on things that bring about inner beauty, that prepare and encourage women for eternity. They should focus on proper learning, education, and good deeds, rather than chasing after the vanities of the world that create competition, offense, and hatred between women. It is better that we lay down the things of the world and worship like Elizabeth and Mary, rather than bringing the world into our spiritual lives.

The values and issues addressed in this passage can also extend to men, just as much as to women. The women were targeted because in that day and age, it was their issue, but the passage is not indicating men are never immodest or vain, just like it is not saying women can't fight and argue with others during worship. The Apostle was doing his work as a leader and trying to handle issues that were specific to the churches he was addressing. Instead of hearing them apply for everyone, now we are busy trying to uphold a culture that has long died, and in some ways, should never have invaded church in the way it has.

Verses 11-14 are often equally troubling, if not more so for women, as we have heard much of our lives that these passages prohibit women from ever speaking or teaching in church on account of the way they read. If we remember the spiritual worship and prophecy of Elizabeth and Mary, we know that such cannot be the way we should interpret this passage.

In New Testament times, women were segregated from the men in the synagogues. This is the way it is in many Orthodox Jewish assemblies to this day, as well. Men and women were segregated for numerous reasons, but the main one was to avoid distraction. It was believed that intersex activity in the synagogue or temple would distract the men and women from prayer, and over time, men and women grew more and more distant in their spiritual positioning for worship and other activities. This led to a general ignorance on the part of women, who were not educated in any semblance in the law or the Scriptures. Enter Christianity, where women are permitted to learn about matters for the first time, and are included in spiritual assemblies. You also had pagan women present, who knew nothing about salvation history, and nothing about the Scriptures.

With women and men still separated, questions arising, and women uncertain as to proper protocol in a worship assembly, you can see where chaos might quickly erupt when the women were uncertain as to what to think, believe, or do in any given situation. From what we know of history, certain married women were yelling at their husbands to provide information and guidance during the Apostle Paul's lectures, following by their husbands' replies, followed by the women's replies, and so on, and so forth. This does represent improper behavior, and the context of the passage is that of married women but doesn't have to be so exclusive to women in a modern understanding. We can recognize the passage to remind anyone who has issues with how to behave in church as to how one should properly conduct themselves, and that any and all disruptive behavior should cease, because it is not proper, nor respectful, for an atmosphere of worship. If a man doesn't have the right information, he shouldn't be trying to talk over the speaker or preacher. If a child is disruptive, they should be removed from the sanctuary until they can calm down. The passage itself identifies who it is speaking about – disruptive wives – and that means rather than understanding it for all women, we look at it and examine it as being for disruptive people.

Because the passage specifically identifies disruptive wives as the culprit, it does not apply to women who were unmarried, or women who were not disruptive at church. It also, likewise, does not apply to women who had been properly taught and were qualified to speak in church, praying, prophesying, and teaching, as we find in other passages of Scripture:

APOLLOS BEGAN TO SPEAK VERY BOLDLY [CONFIDENTLY; FEARLESSLY] IN THE SYNAGOGUE, AND WHEN PRISCILLA AND AQUILA HEARD HIM, THEY TOOK HIM TO THEIR HOME [OR TOOK HIM ASIDE; RECEIVED/TOOK HIM] AND HELPED HIM BETTER UNDERSTAND [EXPLAINED MORE ACCURATELY/PRECISELY] THE WAY [OR WAY; 9:2] OF GOD. (Acts 18:26)

I PRAISE YOU BECAUSE YOU REMEMBER ME IN EVERYTHING [ARE ALWAYS THINKING OF ME], AND YOU FOLLOW CLOSELY THE TEACHINGS [TRADITIONS] JUST AS I GAVE THEM [PASSED THEM ON] TO YOU. BUT I WANT YOU TO UNDERSTAND THIS: THE HEAD OF EVERY MAN IS CHRIST, THE HEAD OF A WOMAN IS THE MAN [OR HER HUSBAND], AND THE HEAD OF CHRIST IS GOD. EVERY MAN WHO PRAYS OR PROPHESIES WITH HIS HEAD COVERED [OR WITH LONG HAIR; HAVING DOWN THE HEAD; MOST SCHOLARS THINK THE PASSAGE CONCERNS HEAD COVERINGS; OTHERS LONG OR SHORT HAIR (SEE V. 14)] BRINGS SHAME TO HIS HEAD [MEANING SHAME TO CHRIST, WHO IS THE HEAD OF THE MAN; V. 3]. BUT EVERY WOMAN WHO PRAYS OR PROPHESIES WITH HER HEAD UNCOVERED [OR NO COVERING (OF HAIR); V. 4] BRINGS SHAME TO HER HEAD. SHE IS THE SAME AS A WOMAN WHO HAS HER HEAD SHAVED. IF A WOMAN DOES NOT COVER HER HEAD, SHE SHOULD HAVE HER HAIR CUT OFF. BUT SINCE IT IS SHAMEFUL FOR A WOMAN TO CUT OFF HER HAIR OR TO SHAVE HER HEAD, SHE SHOULD COVER HER HEAD. BUT A MAN SHOULD NOT COVER HIS HEAD, BECAUSE HE IS THE LIKENESS AND GLORY OF GOD. BUT WOMAN IS MAN'S GLORY [GOD'S GLORY SHOULD BE UNVEILED (REVEALED), WHILE HUMAN GLORY SHOULD BE VEILED]. [FOR] MAN DID NOT COME FROM WOMAN, BUT WOMAN CAME FROM MAN. AND MAN WAS NOT MADE FOR WOMAN, BUT WOMAN WAS MADE FOR MAN [GEN. 2:18]. SO THAT IS WHY A WOMAN SHOULD HAVE A SYMBOL OF AUTHORITY ON [OR AUTHORITY OVER] HER HEAD, BECAUSE OF THE ANGELS [THE SIGNIFICANCE OF THE ANGELS IS UNCLEAR; PERHAPS THEIR PRESENCE AT WORSHIP CALLS FOR REVERENCE AND PROPRIETY].

BUT IN THE LORD WOMEN ARE NOT INDEPENDENT OF MEN, AND MEN ARE NOT INDEPENDENT OF WOMEN. THIS IS TRUE BECAUSE WOMAN CAME FROM MAN, BUT ALSO MAN IS BORN FROM WOMAN. BUT EVERYTHING COMES FROM GOD. DECIDE [JUDGE] THIS FOR YOURSELVES: IS IT RIGHT [FITTING; PROPER] FOR A WOMAN TO PRAY TO GOD WITH HER HEAD UNCOVERED? EVEN [DOES NOT...?] NATURE [OR CUSTOM; CULTURE] ITSELF TEACHES YOU THAT WEARING LONG

HAIR IS SHAMEFUL FOR A MAN [GRECO-ROMAN MEN NORMALLY WORE THEIR HAIR SHORT]. BUT LONG HAIR IS A WOMAN'S GLORY. LONG HAIR IS GIVEN TO HER AS A COVERING. SOME PEOPLE [IF ANYONE] MAY STILL WANT TO ARGUE ABOUT THIS, BUT I WOULD ADD THAT NEITHER WE NOR THE CHURCHES OF GOD HAVE ANY OTHER PRACTICE [CUSTOM]. (1 Corinthians 11:2-16)

IN THE SAME WAY, TEACH OLDER WOMEN TO BE HOLY [REVERENT] IN THEIR BEHAVIOR, NOT SPEAKING AGAINST [SLANDERING; GOSSIPING ABOUT] OTHERS OR ENSLAVED TO TOO MUCH WINE [EXCESSIVE DRINKING], BUT TEACHING WHAT IS GOOD. THEN THEY CAN TEACH [TRAIN] THE YOUNG WOMEN TO LOVE THEIR HUSBANDS, TO LOVE THEIR CHILDREN, TO BE WISE [SENSIBLE; SELF-CONTROLLED] AND PURE, TO BE GOOD WORKERS AT HOME [DEVOTED TO HOME LIFE], TO BE KIND, AND TO YIELD [SUBMIT] TO THEIR HUSBANDS. THEN NO ONE WILL BE ABLE TO CRITICIZE [DISCREDIT; MALIGN; BLASPHEME] THE TEACHING GOD GAVE US [ORD OF GOD]. (Titus 2:3-4)

An additional point is one of authority, where the Apostle Paul mentions prohibition on women teaching or assuming authority over a man. This is not to bespeak a woman who is genuinely called, or genuinely positioned for what she does by God, but the question of someone coming along and assuming they have authority somewhere when they do not. This issue addressed pagan women, who were used to standing as priestesses and holding a certain status within their community of origins, who were now a part of the church. Just because someone held status in a different religious system does not mean they automatically have it in church, and problems of power and control are apparently not new to the church community. If the Apostle Paul recognized authority as given by God (which he did), we don't have the right (whether male or female) to try and usurp control of any situation we may find ourselves in. This is an example that, once again, the issue addressed here relates to women because that's who dealt with this issue in that day, but it doesn't mean that it only applies to women. Men were taught first in Judaism because Adam was first, and right or wrong, this was the way they approached education in that era of history. Women were uneducated; men, at least, had some knowledge of the Scriptures and salvation, and so they learned first. It's not to say this is how it always should be, but how it was.

1 Timothy 2:15 shifts the game, however, yet again. Note the shift from "women" to "she."

BUT SHE SHALL BE SAVED THROUGH HER CHILD-BEARING, IF THEY CONTINUE IN FAITH AND LOVE AND SANCTIFICATION WITH SOBRIETY. (ASV)

YET SHE WILL BE SAVED THROUGH CHILDBEARING, PROVIDED THEY CONTINUE IN FAITH AND LOVE AND HOLINESS, WITH MODESTY. (NRSV)

NEVERTHELESS, THE WOMAN WILL BE DELIVERED THROUGH CHILDBEARING, PROVIDED THAT SHE CONTINUES TRUSTING, LOVING AND LIVING A HOLY LIFE WITH MODESTY. (CJB)

NEVERTHELESS [THE SENTENCE PUT UPON WOMEN OF PAIN IN MOTHERHOOD DOES NOT HINDER THEIR SOULS' SALVATION, AND] THEY WILL BE SAVED [ETERNALLY] IF THEY CONTINUE IN FAITH AND LOVE AND HOLINESS WITH SELF-CONTROL, [SAVED INDEED] THROUGH THE CHILDBEARING *OR* BY THE BIRTH OF THE DIVINE CHILD. (AMPC)

NOTWITHSTANDING SHE SHALL BE SAVED IN CHILDBEARING, IF THEY CONTINUE IN FAITH AND CHARITY AND HOLINESS WITH SOBRIETY. (KJV)

BUT WOMEN (GREEK SHE) WILL BE SAVED THROUGH CHILDBEARING— IF THEY CONTINUE IN FAITH, LOVE AND HOLINESS WITH PROPRIETY. (NIV)

This passage appears, on the surface, to encourage a salvation by works: women are saved not through Christ, but through their own childbearing. Interpreters have used this passage to justify women having children until she died, to say childless or unmarried women can't be saved, and some even questioning whether or not salvation is for women. This is not what it is saying, at all, in the least.

The word "women" in verse 15 can also be translated as "she," which becomes a play on words as to the salvation of women, and of all the women the Apostle Paul speaks of in the chapter. Yes, they had their issues, but they were still saved and still could be saved if they were still in a discernment period. The woman was saved through childbearing – Eve's redemption came through the one who was born of a woman – and Mary herself, also, saved through childbearing – because she gave birth to the Redeemer. Women were saved because of the intervention of a woman in the salvation process, who literally gave birth to the Word. With thanks and worship, women are free to continue in their faith, without the competition of the world, and without hatred of other women. Women can come together, as Mary and Elizabeth did, and speak forth the Word, worship in the Word, and rejoice in love, because what was done for men was also done for them.

The praise of a woman

If Mary's song is, by virtue, every woman's song, then we can do no more than prophesy, sing, and praise our way through this world as we pursue the true heart of worship. Instead of seeing passages about women as oppressive or intimidating, we must take our cue from Mary and Elizabeth, who both lived in oppressive and intimidating times. They were women who changed the very course of history, not just for themselves, but for all women. Even though there will forever be those who refuse to hear the beautiful song of Mary down through the ages, we know it is there, echoing and resonating every time women worship. We were not created to be subordinate or secondary, nor are we prohibited from placement and leadership within the church, but we have been created for something amazing: discipleship. If we are willing to accept our place in history, we too can recognize that all generations will call us blessed, alongside Mary and Elizabeth.

Dove of the Holy Spirit (Gian Lorenzo Bernini)

CHAPTER SEVEN
The Comforter Comes

NOW WE DID NOT RECEIVE THE SPIRIT OF THE WORLD,
BUT WE RECEIVED THE SPIRIT THAT IS FROM GOD SO THAT WE CAN KNOW
ALL THAT GOD HAS [FREELY] GIVEN US. AND WE SPEAK ABOUT THESE THINGS,
NOT WITH WORDS TAUGHT US BY HUMAN WISDOM BUT WITH WORDS TAUGHT US
BY THE SPIRIT. AND SO WE EXPLAIN SPIRITUAL TRUTHS TO SPIRITUAL PEOPLE
[*OR* TO THOSE WHO HAVE THE SPIRIT; *OR* WITH THE SPIRIT'S WORDS].
(1 CORINTHIANS 2:12-13)

THE early church did not always feel, nor regard things, in the same way that we do today. Our understanding of our faith is as the result of over 2,000 years' worth of discussion, debate, and often heated argument over just what is right, accurate, true, or the way it should be. Whether good, bad, or indifferent, the realities of how we see God and how we see what we believe has been shaped by other people who brought and carried with them their own opinions about certain matters, down to the present day. Whether or not our ancestors in the faith always anticipated being quoted and reiterated for thousands of years is not an issue, because they are here, still teaching and educating us, and bringing us to greater insights of spiritual matters, down to you and me.

The catch with what I have just pointed out is simple: the majority of individuals who dictated faith, laid it out, set it up, and explained and established it have been, throughout the years, overwhelmingly male. Whether intended or not, our perceptions of God come through their eyes, and often always reflect imagery and ideals of God that are associated with masculine concepts and ideas as to just what it means to be male, imposed upon our theological concepts. Looking at past chapters where we see different aspects of God in a more feminine light show a more universal sense of spiritual belief, and a drawing that will hold a more balanced and universal appeal than only acknowledging God as a singular gender, within our limitations of understanding such.

Even though the ancients didn't have the same exact view of God and gender as many do today, we have come to a view of God that is often literally male, overwhelming, intimidating, and scary. As New Covenant believers, it should be easier for us to find a softer side of the divine, but unfortunately, that is often not the case. As times change and we hold even harder and faster to spiritual imagery that reflects what is seen as embracing changing times and cultures, we get further and further away from images and reflections of God that may not fall into our more traditional understandings.

Discussing any aspect of God as feminine typically ruffles a few feathers. Yet if we explore the early church, it made perfect sense to them that a specific aspect of the Godhead had a feminine identity. This concept was readily embraced by groups that were considered schismatic, and then the concept of a feminine aspect in the Godhead later became grounds for heresy, rather than seeing how it tied back to the earliest of believers within Christianity. Looking at this belief, however, should make all of us think, and consider the precept of spiritual continuity that it creates. Instead of allowing us to create God in our own image, God has always made sure that He stands alone, independent of what He has created, with an image and reception that is embraceable by all who will come, willing to receive it.

Spiritual continuity

One of the common mistakes we make when viewing the New Testament is thinking it poses an entirely new revelation, unheard of before and unfathomable by those under the Old Testament law. It is true to say that the revelation of God present in the New Testament was not embraced by everyone under the Old Covenant, but it is inappropriate for us to think the identity of God present in the New Testament evolved out of a vacuum. It is a mistake to believe that God ceased speaking in the 400-year period between the end of the prophecy of Malachi and the beginning of the Gospel of Matthew, and what happened in those years is most relevant to bridge eras and periods for us, in terms of theological revelation and understanding. It is, most likely, during this period that the concept of *shekinah* began to emerge. The heaviness of the law combined with the heaviness of occupation made them seek refuge, comfort, and love from their heavenly Originator. It wasn't that they discovered a whole new aspect to God that never existed prior, but instead, that they discovered attributes of God that they had never explored. If we understand God to be the One Who does not change, that means discovery of His different natures and attributes come about as we change.

FOR I AM THE LORD, I CHANGE NOT; THEREFORE YE SONS OF JACOB ARE NOT CONSUMED. (Malachi 3:6, KJV)

JESUS CHRIST IS THE SAME YESTERDAY, TODAY, AND FOREVER. (Hebrews 13:8)

Between 500 B.C. and around 7 A.D. (as our calendar is a few years off), the following happened:[1,2,3]

- The Jews were dispersed after Nebuchadnezzar sacked Jerusalem and destroyed the temple
- The Persian Empire arose, the temple was, once again rebuilt (to be destroyed again around 70 A.D.)
- The Roman Empire started to rise up
- The Torah first appeared in its final form.
- Nehemiah rebuilt the walls in Jerusalem
- Greece rises to the top of world powers.
- Rome conquers Greece.

In this 500-year period, the Jews found themselves far away from their origins. They now lived in diverse countries, away from their ancestors and the traditions they'd established throughout the years, and were forced to accept occupations, new ways of living, and new approaches to life. They needed a touch of God that connected them to home, that was familiar and comforting, and it is no accident that their image of God had that feminine appeal, one that was softer in contrast to their harsh way of living.

The world that Christ entered was rift with strife, angst, war, occupation, and division. Through Christ, the love of God was clearly seen and manifest in early believers, because God's work was sacrificial, rather than requiring something else of humanity. It was a free gift; something irreplaceable; something that had a cost beyond anything anyone could imagine. The work of Christ on the cross is the most powerful example of the love of God, but it is not the only example we see of God's love in the New Testament. Examination of Christ's genealogy displays a pervasive love for the ages, even through a people who constantly turned away from God at every chance they got. We see God's love present in Christ's teaching, even before His death. We see God's love present in the works of the early church, and in the conversion of the Apostle Paul. God's love is everywhere, seen in the pursuit of humanity, as a lived experience with the Most High.

Even in the New Testament, we find references to God in female personification, seeking out humanity, doing His work, looking for people who would become a part of His kingdom. These images continue the idea of a feminine presence within the divine, begun and seen in Old Testament times. The imagery of God in the New Testament is less intense than in the Old, thanks to the identity and forethought of a compassionate, loving God Who recognizes what we go through and is there for us. There are three direct passages where God is referred to in feminine terms in the Gospels:[4]

- **God as a mother hen:**
  "JERUSALEM, JERUSALEM! YOU KILL THE PROPHETS AND STONE TO DEATH THOSE WHO ARE SENT TO YOU. MANY TIMES [HOW OFTEN] I WANTED TO GATHER YOUR PEOPLE [CHILDREN] AS A HEN GATHERS HER CHICKS UNDER HER WINGS, BUT YOU DID NOT LET ME [REFUSED]." (Matthew 23:37)

  "JERUSALEM, JERUSALEM! YOU KILL THE PROPHETS AND STONE TO DEATH THOSE WHO ARE SENT TO YOU. MANY TIMES [HOW OFTEN] I WANTED TO GATHER YOUR PEOPLE [CHILDREN] AS A HEN GATHERS HER CHICKS UNDER HER WINGS, BUT YOU WOULD NOT LET ME [MATT. 23:37–39]." (Luke 13:34)

- **God as a woman looking for a lost coin:**
  "[OR] SUPPOSE A WOMAN HAS TEN SILVER COINS [GREEK: *DRACHMAS*; EACH EQUAL TO ABOUT A DAY'S WAGE], BUT LOSES ONE. SHE WILL [WON'T SHE...?] LIGHT A LAMP, SWEEP THE

HOUSE, AND LOOK [SEARCH] CAREFULLY FOR THE COIN UNTIL SHE FINDS IT. AND WHEN SHE FINDS IT, SHE WILL CALL HER FRIENDS AND NEIGHBORS AND SAY, 'BE HAPPY [REJOICE] WITH ME BECAUSE I HAVE FOUND THE COIN [DRACHMA] THAT I LOST.' IN THE SAME WAY, [I TELL YOU] THERE IS JOY IN THE PRESENCE OF THE ANGELS OF GOD WHEN ONE SINNER CHANGES HIS HEART AND LIFE [REPENTS]." (Luke 15:8-10)

These different expressions addressed the concerns of the people in New Testament times. Feeling scattered, feeling abandoned, feeling isolated, and feeling a sense of loss, not just of their own homeland but their own spiritual understanding led them to desire a sense of wholeness, completeness, and returning. Feminine language was perfect to describe this concept and role of God as a gatherer, taking care of the scattered people as a mother hen guards and gathers her chicks. They sought protection and identity, and in the female view of God, they received just what they were seeking.

The image of God as a woman, looking for a lost coin, also brings a certain sense of hope and comfort to the one who first heard this parable live, and to the reader today, as well. We've all lost something, and the determination to find it brings in a characteristic of readiness, of interest, of pursuit in the thing that we have lost. Seeing God as a pursuant woman, looking for the very thing that she lost, is not a common image that we have of women, and is certainly not embracing gender stereotypes. Pursuing something (or someone) is almost always seen as a male game in stereotypical male/female relationships, but this makes this imagery all the more interesting, and fascinating, from the concept of feminine images as pertain to the divine. If a woman was seeking out God's people, it was understood such was to care, to love them, to protect and guide them, much as the imagery with the mother hen. In essence, God was seeing His people as children, as beings in need of making the active fight to discover and find and bring back to Him. This related to their being as much as their salvation, which was of expressed concern to God. It is for this reason Christ enters the picture, to facilitate the seeking and saving of those who were lost.

The love of God that pursues, finds, keeps, and carries us through is a gift of immeasurable worth and value. While it is obvious that such a concept brings comfort to those who know

He has pursued them with this love, there is the other end of it, and that is the clear nature of God that is revealed in such pursuit. But God didn't just stop here in His pursuit and love for us. There is another gift God provided to us, expressively feminine in form, although we don't often speak of it in that light. It is there to carry us, guide us, lead us, and work within us, in all situations. That gift to each and every one of us who believes is the work of the Holy Spirit.

The promised One

One of Jesus' greatest promises was the One Who was to come, Who He would send in His Name. Growing up with traditional doctrine, we often assume the Holy Spirit to be male, just as we assume God is male, and as we know Jesus to be male. The truth about the gender identity of the Holy Spirit is not quite as simple as we learned it to be in the language of Trinitarian theology, however. Understanding how the Holy Spirit became identified as male, rather than female, requires a little background understanding, as well as a little bit of practical understanding as to how the Holy Spirit has often taken a less central role in church belief than should be.

It is unfortunate that so much of the church has unplugged when it comes to the work and nature of the Holy Spirit. Too many denominations claim to believe in the Holy Spirit but almost treat the work of the Spirit as if it went into retirement at some point in time. They do not recognize the beautiful work, activity, and passionate pursuit, the spiritual work of God, present in the ministry of the Holy Spirit. I can't help but feel part of this retraction of the Spirit's relevance and power comes from a lack of proper understanding on the Spirit, the Spirit's nature, and the Spirit's work. If we don't see the Holy Spirit through the eyes of those who first encountered Her, we are going to forever misunderstand just what the Spirit does and the unique purpose it has in our lives.

The work of the Spirit has long been a controversial topic within Christian circles, as the questions continues to arise: Just how does the Spirit work within us? How do we know and recognize the Spirit at work in the church? The answer to these questions lies in how we perceive the Spirit to work, and in the way we come to know the Spirit, intimately, as she works within us. We either have the Spirit, do not have the Spirit, or do not properly recognize the Spirit, and it is frequently the latter that creates confusion. Because we treat the Spirit as if it did not exist prior to Christ's coming, we don't see how it has worked in and through God's people through centuries, and we are deeply out of touch with the way it breathes life and transforms the church, today.

That is the basic nature of the Spirit: to breathe and give life, both natural life and spiritual life. It is the work of the Spirit that keeps the church alive and relevant, from generation to generation. The Spirit leads and guides us into what is true, much like a parent leads and guides their children into adulthood. By providing essential gifts, it is the Spirit that helps the church to function, giving each person a purpose. It's a work, an identity, and a power, rolled into one, as the Spirit of God, the power of God, and the way we experience God, in this era, this side of heaven. A most beautiful and lasting gift, it is the Holy Spirit that connects to God.

If we understand the Spirit like this, it becomes more understandable for the identity of the Holy Spirit to come through as feminine for believers and readers in the early centuries of Christianity. Rather than being seen as solely a force to be reckoned with, the Holy Spirit displays different facets of intensity: the gentleness of the dove, the fire of purification, water, and the wind. This reflects flexibility; strength; ability; and the innate adaptability that is truly the Spirit.

In the Old Testament, the identity of the Holy Spirit is constantly and consistently female, as one of those little secrets we often overlook, or ignore, in study. In fact, the word "spirit" in connection with God is always identified as female.

There are approximately 22 different references to the Holy Spirit in the Old Testament, identified as: the Spirit of God, the Spirit, the Spirit of the Lord, a Spirit of the holy gods, and as Holy Spirit. By the power of this Spirit, we see everything from creation, to fashioning, to prophecy, and speaking. Every single one of these references identify the Spirit of God as being feminine in form.

There are a few reasons why this probably is, the first, and most obvious, is because the Spirit of God is identified first in the Old Testament, in connection with creation.

The language of the Spirit

HOLY SPIRIT

- *QADOSH:* SACRED, HOLY[5]
- ORIGINAL WORD: קָדוֹשׁ
- PART OF SPEECH: ADJECTIVE
- TRANSLITERATION: QADOSH
- PHONETIC SPELLING: (KAW-DOSHE')
- SHORT DEFINITION: HOLY

- *RUACH:* WIND, SPIRIT[6]
- ORIGINAL WORD: רוּחַ
- PART OF SPEECH: NOUN FEMININE
- TRANSLITERATION: RUACH
- PHONETIC SPELLING: (ROO'-AKH)
- SHORT DEFINITION: SPIRIT

- *HAGIOS:* SACRED, HOLY[7]
- ORIGINAL WORD: ἅγιος, ΊΑ, ΟΝ
- PART OF SPEECH: ADJECTIVE
- TRANSLITERATION: HAGIOS
- PHONETIC SPELLING: (HAG'-EE-OS)
- SHORT DEFINITION: SET APART, HOLY, SACRED
- DEFINITION: SET APART BY (OR FOR) GOD, HOLY, SACRED

- *PNEUMA:* WIND, SPIRIT[8]
- ORIGINAL WORD: πνεῦμα, ΑΤΟΣ, ΤΌ
- PART OF SPEECH: NOUN, NEUTER
- TRANSLITERATION: PNEUMA
- PHONETIC SPELLING: (PNYOO'-MAH)
- SHORT DEFINITION: WIND, BREATH, SPIRIT
- DEFINITION: WIND, BREATH, SPIRIT

THE [OR...THE] EARTH HAD NO FORM AND WAS EMPTY [OR WAS A FORMLESS VOID]. DARKNESS COVERED THE OCEAN [DEEP], AND GOD'S SPIRIT [OR A MIGHTY WIND] WAS MOVING [HOVERING] OVER THE

WATER. (Genesis 1:2)

HE BREATHES, AND THE SKY CLEARS [HE MAKES THE HEAVENS
BEAUTIFUL].
  HIS HAND STABS [SLAYS] THE FLEEING SNAKE [SERPENT;
LEVIATHAN, ANOTHER SEA MONSTER REPRESENTING CHAOS; 3:8; IS.
27:1]. (Job 26:13)

THE SKY WAS [HEAVENS WERE] MADE AT THE LORD'S COMMAND
[WORD; GEN. 1:8].
  BY THE BREATH FROM HIS MOUTH, HE MADE ALL THE STARS [ITS
HOSTS; GEN. 1:16].
HE GATHERED THE WATER OF THE SEA INTO A HEAP [OR JARS;
BOTTLES].
  HE MADE THE GREAT OCEAN STAY IN ITS PLACE [PLACED THE DEEPS
IN A STOREHOUSE; JOB 38:8–11]. (Psalm 33:6-7)

WHEN YOU BREATHE [SEND YOUR BREATH/OR SPIRIT] ON THEM,
  THEY ARE CREATED [GEN. 2:7],
AND YOU MAKE THE LAND NEW AGAIN. (Psalm 104:30)

THIS WILL CONTINUE UNTIL GOD POURS HIS SPIRIT [THE SPIRIT IS
POURED] FROM ABOVE [HEAVEN; ON HIGH] UPON US.
  THEN THE DESERT WILL BE LIKE RICH FARMLAND [A
FERTILE/FRUITFUL FIELD]
  AND THE RICH FARMLAND [FERTILE/FRUITFUL FIELD] LIKE A
FOREST [29:17; 35:1, 2]. (Isaiah 32:15)

It's important to see the work of the feminine spirit in creation, because it associates life with female virtue and power before the creation or fall of Eve. It's not uncommon to hear of life spoken of as some sort of punishment, lining up creation with such a notion, because Eve fell into temptation back in the garden.

It is, likewise, compared with the ability to create elsewhere in the New Testament:

JESUS ANSWERED, "I TELL YOU THE TRUTH [TRULY, TRULY I SAY TO
YOU], UNLESS YOU ARE BORN AGAIN [OR FROM ABOVE; THIS MAY BE A
PLAY ON WORDS, MEANING BOTH "AGAIN" AND "FROM ABOVE"], YOU
CANNOT BE IN [EXPERIENCE; SEE] GOD'S KINGDOM."

NICODEMUS SAID TO HIM, "BUT IF A PERSON IS ALREADY OLD, HOW CAN HE BE BORN AGAIN [OR FROM ABOVE; 3:3]? HE CANNOT ENTER HIS MOTHER'S WOMB AGAIN. SO HOW CAN A PERSON BE BORN A SECOND TIME [CAN HE ENTER HIS MOTHER'S WOMB A SECOND TIME AND BE BORN]?"

BUT JESUS ANSWERED, "I TELL YOU THE TRUTH [TRULY, TRULY I SAY TO YOU], UNLESS YOU ARE BORN FROM WATER AND THE SPIRIT [EQUIVALENT TO BEING BORN AGAIN (3:3); WATER COULD SYMBOLIZE PHYSICAL BIRTH, BUT MORE LIKELY SYMBOLIZES SPIRITUAL CLEANSING WHICH BRINGS RENEWAL; EZEK. 36:25–27], YOU CANNOT ENTER GOD'S KINGDOM. HUMAN LIFE COMES FROM HUMAN PARENTS [THAT WHICH IS BORN OF THE FLESH IS FLESH; FLESH HERE MEANS HUMAN NATURE], BUT SPIRITUAL LIFE COMES FROM THE SPIRIT [THAT WHICH IS BORN OF THE SPIRIT IS SPIRIT]. DON'T BE SURPRISED [AMAZED; ASTONISHED] WHEN I TELL YOU, 'YOU [PLURAL, REFERRING TO THE JEWS OR THE JEWISH LEADERS] MUST BE BORN AGAIN [OR FROM ABOVE; 3:3].' THE WIND [ONE WORD MEANS BOTH "WIND" AND "SPIRIT" IN GREEK] BLOWS WHERE IT WANTS TO AND YOU HEAR THE SOUND OF IT, BUT YOU DON'T KNOW WHERE THE WIND COMES FROM OR WHERE IT IS GOING. IT IS THE SAME WITH EVERY PERSON WHO IS BORN FROM THE SPIRIT." [WE CANNOT COMPREHEND OR CONTROL THE SPIRIT, BUT WE EXPERIENCE HIS EFFECT.] (John 3:3-8)

The New Testament Greek as pertains to the Holy Spirit is neuter in tense, but with an overt undertone of femininity, even in the neuter identity. The Greek word *pneuma* was used throughout the Greek Septuagint for the Holy Spirit. The term itself is neuter, but is often implied with feminine characteristics, and there is no passage that specifically links *pneuma* to a masculine identity or general energy. There is nothing in its language to suggest that those in the first century ever considered the Holy Spirit to be masculine: not speakers, and certainly not Christ, or those of the first-century church. They would have continued to acknowledge the Aramaic and Hebrew traditions of the Spirit as feminine in entity, and nobody would have ever thought that the shift from Hebrew to Greek would render a change in spiritual identity. The Spirit was about life, and connecting life to women was a huge identifying point in ancient culture.

The only masculine word used to refer to the Holy Spirit is

that of "comforter," or "Paraclete," in John 14:26 and 16:13-14:

BUT THE HELPER [COUNSELOR; ADVOCATE; SEE 14:15] WILL TEACH YOU EVERYTHING [ALL THINGS] AND WILL CAUSE YOU TO REMEMBER [REMIND YOU OF] ALL THAT I TOLD YOU. THIS HELPER IS THE HOLY SPIRIT WHOM THE FATHER WILL SEND IN MY NAME. (John 14:26)

BUT WHEN THE SPIRIT OF TRUTH [THE HELPER; SEE 16:7] COMES, HE WILL LEAD [GUIDE] YOU INTO ALL TRUTH. HE WILL NOT SPEAK HIS OWN WORDS [FROM HIS OWN AUTHORITY; FROM HIMSELF], BUT HE WILL SPEAK ONLY WHAT HE HEARS [FROM THE FATHER], AND HE WILL TELL [ANNOUNCE/DECLARE TO] YOU WHAT IS TO COME. THE SPIRIT OF TRUTH WILL BRING GLORY TO [GLORIFY; HONOR] ME, BECAUSE HE WILL TAKE WHAT I HAVE TO SAY [IS MINE] AND TELL [ANNOUNCE; DECLARE] IT TO YOU. (John 16:13-14)

COMFORTER[9]

- *PARAKLÉTOS*: CALLED TO ONE'S AID
- ORIGINAL WORD: ΠΑΡΆΚΛΗΤΟΣ, ΟΥ, ὁ
- PART OF SPEECH: NOUN, MASCULINE
- TRANSLITERATION: PARAKLÉTOS
- PHONETIC SPELLING: (PAR-AK'-LAY-TOS)
- SHORT DEFINITION: AN ADVOCATE, COMFORTER, HELPER, PARACLETE
- DEFINITION: AN ADVOCATE, INTERCESSOR, A CONSOLER, COMFORTER, HELPER, PARACLETE.

This does not mean the Spirit was thought of as a man, but that the work of the Spirit was associated with that of advocacy, specifically paralleling the work of a legal advocate, or what we might understand today as a lawyer. That was a profession understood to be held by men in ancient times and describing it as such not only gives a certain sense of empowerment, but also prominence, to the work of the Holy Spirit. Just as *shekinah*, El Shaddai, and other terms prove a certain gender non-conformity when speaking of things related to God, so the same is done for the Holy Spirit. Feminine or not, the Spirit of God has the ability to advocate on our behalf, to help us out with any conviction, and with anything that might arise, through this life, that will require divine help.

Connecting to life

Recognizing the connection between women and life was obvious to the ancients, so it was most obvious to recognize the creativity of the Spirit as feminine. A second reason why the Spirit is identified as female probably relates to the feminine identifying connection with El Shaddai, a female identity, recognizing the power of the Almighty, relating to life and death. The Spirit of God was seen as having power, as a manifestation of God with persona and identity, and as such, it was seen as a feminine component to the divine's makeup. It is no accident that *dunamis* and *exousia* power, both spoken of in the New Testament, as coming from the Spirit Herself, is also feminine in identity.

"BUT I WILL PROVE TO YOU [SO THAT YOU MAY KNOW] THAT THE SON OF MAN [A TITLE FOR THE MESSIAH; DAN. 7:13–14] HAS AUTHORITY [POWER] ON EARTH TO FORGIVE SINS." THEN JESUS SAID TO THE PARALYZED MAN, "STAND UP, TAKE [PICK UP] YOUR MAT [COT; BED], AND GO HOME." (Matthew 9:6)

JESUS CALLED HIS TWELVE FOLLOWERS [DISCIPLES] TOGETHER AND GAVE THEM AUTHORITY [POWER] TO DRIVE [FORCE; CAST] OUT EVIL [DEFILING; UNCLEAN] SPIRITS AND TO HEAL EVERY KIND OF DISEASE AND SICKNESS. (Matthew 10:1)

JESUS SAID, "I SAW SATAN FALL LIKE LIGHTNING FROM HEAVEN [SYMBOLICALLY IN THE EXORCISMS; IS. 14:12; REV. 12:13]. LISTEN [LOOK; BEHOLD], I HAVE GIVEN YOU POWER [AUTHORITY] TO WALK ON [TRAMPLE] SNAKES AND SCORPIONS, POWER THAT IS GREATER THAN THE ENEMY HAS [...AND AUTHORITY OVER ALL THE POWER OF THE ENEMY]. SO NOTHING WILL HURT YOU. (Luke 10:18-19)

The very force and virtue of life, both spiritual and natural, was seen as connected to female identity and purpose. It takes a certain level of strength and power to bring forth natural life, and we all know the same is true when we are co-creating with God in the spiritual realm. That power, that concept of spiritual force that had the power to change life, was, therefore, also seen

---

POWER

- *DUNAMIS.* (MIRACULOUS) POWER, MIGHT, STRENGTH[10]
- ORIGINAL WORD: ΔΎΝΑΜΙΣ, ΕΩΣ, ἡ
- PART OF SPEECH: NOUN, FEMININE
- TRANSLITERATION: DUNAMIS
- PHONETIC SPELLING: (DOO'-NAM-IS)
- SHORT DEFINITION: MIGHT, POWER, MARVELOUS WORKS
- DEFINITION: PHYSICAL POWER, FORCE, MIGHT, ABILITY, EFFICACY, ENERGY, MEANING PLUR: POWERFUL DEEDS, DEEDS SHOWING (PHYSICAL) POWER, MARVELOUS WORKS.

- *EXOUSIA:* POWER TO ACT, AUTHORITY[11]
- ORIGINAL WORD: ἐΞΟΥΣΊΑ, ΑΣ, ἡ
- PART OF SPEECH: NOUN, FEMININE
- TRANSLITERATION: EXOUSIA
- PHONETIC SPELLING: (EX-OO-SEE'-AH)
- SHORT DEFINITION: POWER, AUTHORITY, WEIGHT
- DEFINITION: POWER, AUTHORITY, WEIGHT, ESPECIALLY: MORAL AUTHORITY, INFLUENCE, IN A QUASI-PERSONAL SENSE, DERIVED FROM LATER JUDAISM, OF A SPIRITUAL POWER, AND HENCE OF AN EARTHLY POWER.

---

as feminine. Through spiritual power, one had the power to create spiritual life, and change the immediate realities of life and creation, unto aligning them more efficiently with spiritual vision.

Beyond the immediate connection to creation, the Spirit often operated by a nature that one might consider comparable to pregnancy or a physical bearing. Those who had the Spirit of God received it, it came upon them, they could feel it stirring within them, and as the Spirit moved within a person, something came forth, or out of them as a result. It was a creative process, working unto the end of a divine purpose or message, and something was brought forth, because of the work of the Spirit. For this reason, the work of the Holy Spirit was much like a woman who conceives, carries, and gives birth within and from a person.

It is for this reason that it would be the work of the Holy

Spirit involved in the impregnation of Mary. The Spirit's work was creation, spiritual life and breath, and the promise of the church, and thus the Spirit would be involved in the physical creation of Christ in this world. It is the very breath of spiritual life, an aspect of the power of God, that was a vital and active aspect of the incarnation. This makes Isaiah 11 prophetic, showing a specific and unique way that the Spirit would rest upon, within, and through Christ's life, and reflecting His ministry.

A NEW BRANCH [SPROUT; SHOOT; THE MESSIAH] WILL GROW
FROM THE STUMP OF JESSE [KING DAVID'S FATHER; THE MESSIAH WILL RESTORE DAVID'S ROYAL LINE];
A BRANCH WILL COME [SPROUT; *OR* BEAR FRUIT]
FROM HIS ROOTS.
THE SPIRIT OF THE LORD WILL REST UPON HIM [1 SAM. 16:13; MATT. 3:16].
THE SPIRIT WILL GIVE HIM WISDOM AND UNDERSTANDING, GUIDANCE [COUNSEL] AND POWER.
THE SPIRIT WILL TEACH HIM TO KNOW [OF KNOWLEDGE] AND RESPECT [THE FEAR OF] THE LORD.
THIS KING WILL BE GLAD TO [HE WILL GLADLY/WITH DELIGHT] OBEY [REVERE; FEAR] THE LORD.
HE WILL NOT JUDGE BY THE WAY THINGS LOOK [APPEARANCES; THE VISION OF HIS EYES]
OR DECIDE BY WHAT HE HEARS [THE HEARING OF HIS EARS].
BUT HE WILL JUDGE THE POOR HONESTLY [WITH JUSTICE/RIGHTEOUSNESS];
HE WILL BE FAIR [UPRIGHT; JUST; FAIR] IN HIS DECISIONS FOR THE POOR [OPPRESSED; MEEK] PEOPLE OF THE LAND [*OR* EARTH].
AT HIS COMMAND EVIL PEOPLE WILL BE PUNISHED [HE WILL STRIKE THE EARTH WITH THE ROD/SCEPTER OF HIS MOUTH],
AND BY HIS WORDS THE WICKED WILL BE PUT TO DEATH [THE BREATH OF HIS LIPS HE WILL SLAY THE WICKED].
GOODNESS [RIGHTEOUSNESS; JUSTICE] WILL BE LIKE A BELT AROUND HIS WAIST,
AND FAIRNESS [FAITHFULNESS; INTEGRITY] LIKE A BELT AROUND HIS HIPS [WAIST; LOINS]. (Isaiah 11:1-5)

So many amazing things come from the Spirit of God resting upon Christ: wisdom and understanding, counsel and might, knowledge, fear of the Lord, quick understanding, and right judgment. These come when we embrace the Spirit that was present in Christ for ourselves and come to see that right spiritual understanding starts with the origin of right spiritual life. These virtues stir within us and extend out of us, benefiting both those who embrace and carry them and those who receive the benefits of such righteousness as a result. The connection to God, and to creation, lies in the gift of the Spirit, which Christ has, in turn, given to all of us.

Just as the *shekinah* glory brought a feminine counterpart to the divine nature, so too did the work of the Holy Spirit. The feminine Holy Spirit brought something to us that we could easily see, and acknowledge, this side of heaven. It wasn't so much about trying to raise women up above men but about observing the world's operations and recognizing the spiritual realm as a primer for the natural realm. Seeing the world in a male-female perspective, the ancients also saw God in that way and had to embrace a feminine understanding of spiritual things. Power, creativity, life force, and spiritual expressions were often feminine, even if such wasn't so clearly understood. In embracing the Holy Spirit as feminine, the ancients were embracing life as a spiritual principle and recognizing that life comes from the work of women.

Reflections of the feminine nature of the Spirit outside of the Bible

The Holy Spirit is identified as female in several documents (regarded as non-canonical in most canons, but historically relevant) from the earliest of church times.

COME, HOLY NAME OF CHRIST THAT IS ABOVE EVERY NAME;
COME, POWER OF THE MOST HIGH AND PERFECT COMPASSION;
COME, THOU HIGHEST GIFT;
COME, COMPASSIONATE MOTHER;
COME, FELLOWSHIP OF THE MALE;
COME, THOU (F.) THAT DOST REVEAL THE HIDDEN MYSTERIES;
COME, MOTHER OF SEVEN HOUSES, THAT THY REST MAY BE IN THE EIGHTH HOUSE. (Acts of Thomas 2:27)[12]

COME, SILENCE THAT DOST REVEAL THE GREAT DEEDS OF THE WHOLE

GREATNESS;
COME THOU THAT DOST SHOW FORTH THE HIDDEN THINGS
AND MAKE THE INEFFABLE MANIFEST;
HOLY DOVE THAT BEAREST THE TWIN YOUNG;
COME, HIDDEN MOTHER;
COME, THOU THAT ART MANIFEST IN THY DEEDS
AND DOST FURNISH JOY AND REST FOR ALL THAT ARE JOINED WITH
THEE;
COME AND PARTAKE WITH US IN THIS EUCHARIST
WHICH WE CELEBRATE IN THY NAME,
AND IN THE LOVE-FEAST IN WHICH WE ARE GATHERED TOGETHER AT
THY CALL. (Acts of Thomas 5:50)[13]

OPEN, OPEN YOUR HEARTS TO THE EXULTATION OF THE LORD, AND
LET YOUR LOVE ABOUND FROM THE HEART TO THE LIPS.
IN ORDER TO BRING FORTH FRUITS TO THE LORD, A HOLY LIFE; AND TO
TALK WITH WATCHFULNESS IN HIS LIGHT.
RISE UP AND STAND ERECT, YOU WHO SOMETIMES WERE BROUGHT
LOW.
YOU WHO WERE IN SILENCE, SPEAK, FOR YOUR MOUTH HAS BEEN
OPENED.
YOU WHO WERE DESPISED, FROM HENCEFORTH BE LIFTED UP, FOR
YOUR RIGHTEOUSNESS HAS BEEN LIFTED UP;
FOR THE RIGHT HAND OF THE LORD IS WITH YOU, AND HE WILL BE
YOUR HELPER.
AND PEACE WAS PREPARED FOR YOU, BEFORE WHAT MAY BE YOUR
WAR.
HEAR THE WORD OF TRUTH, AND RECEIVE THE KNOWLEDGE OF THE
MOST HIGH.
YOUR FLESH MAY NOT UNDERSTAND THAT WHICH I AM ABOUT TO SAY
TO YOU; NOR YOUR GARMENT THAT WHICH I AM ABOUT TO SHOW YOU.
KEEP MY MYSTERY, YOU WHO ARE KEPT BY IT; KEEP MY FAITH, YOU
WHO ARE KEPT BY IT.
AND UNDERSTAND MY KNOWLEDGE, YOU WHO KNOW ME IN TRUTH;
LOVE ME WITH AFFECTION, YOU WHO LOVE;
FOR I TURN NOT MY FACE FROM MY OWN, BECAUSE I KNOW THEM.
AND BEFORE THEY HAD EXISTED, I RECOGNIZED THEM; AND
IMPRINTED A SEAL ON THEIR FACES.
I FASHIONED THEIR MEMBERS, AND MY OWN BREASTS I PREPARED FOR
THEM, THAT THEY MIGHT DRINK MY HOLY MILK AND LIVE BY IT.
I AM PLEASED BY THEM, AND AM NOT ASHAMED BY THEM.

FOR MY WORKMANSHIP ARE THEY, AND THE STRENGTH OF MY
THOUGHTS.
THEREFORE WHO CAN STAND AGAINST MY WORK? OR WHO IS NOT
SUBJECT TO THEM?
I WILLED AND FASHIONED MIND AND HEART, AND THEY ARE MY OWN.
AND UPON MY RIGHT HAND I HAVE SET MY ELECT ONES.
AND MY RIGHTEOUSNESS GOES BEFORE THEM, AND THEY SHALL NOT
BE DEPRIVED OF MY NAME; FOR IT IS WITH THEM.
PRAY AND INCREASE, AND ABIDE IN THE LOVE OF THE LORD;
AND YOU WHO WERE LOVED IN THE BELOVED, AND YOU WHO ARE
KEPT IN HIM WHO LIVES, AND YOU WHO ARE SAVED IN HIM WHO WAS
SAVED.
AND YOU SHALL BE FOUND INCORRUPT IN ALL AGES, ON ACCOUNT OF
THE NAME OF YOUR FATHER.
HALLELUJAH.
(ODES OF SOLOMON 8:1-22)[14]

A CUP OF MILK WAS OFFERED TO ME, AND I DRANK IT IN THE
SWEETNESS OF THE LORD'S KINDNESS.
THE SON IS THE CUP, AND THE FATHER IS HE WHO WAS MILKED; AND
THE HOLY SPIRIT IS SHE WHO MILKED HIM;
BECAUSE HIS BREASTS WERE FULL, AND IT WAS UNDESIRABLE THAT
HIS MILK SHOULD BE INEFFECTUALLY RELEASED.
THE HOLY SPIRIT OPENED HER BOSOM, AND MIXED THE MILK OF THE
TWO BREASTS OF THE FATHER.
THEN SHE GAVE THE MIXTURE TO THE GENERATION WITHOUT THEIR
KNOWING, AND THOSE WHO HAVE RECEIVED IT ARE IN THE
PERFECTION OF THE RIGHT HAND.
THE WOMB OF THE VIRGIN TOOK IT, AND SHE RECEIVED CONCEPTION
AND GAVE BIRTH.
SO THE VIRGIN BECAME A MOTHER WITH GREAT MERCIES.
AND SHE LABORED AND BORE THE SON BUT WITHOUT PAIN, BECAUSE
IT DID NOT OCCUR WITHOUT PURPOSE.
AND SHE DID NOT REQUIRE A MIDWIFE, BECAUSE HE CAUSED HER TO
GIVE LIFE.
SHE BROUGHT FORTH LIKE A STRONG MAN WITH DESIRE, AND SHE
BORE ACCORDING TO THE MANIFESTATION, AND SHE ACQUIRED
ACCORDING TO THE GREAT POWER.
AND SHE LOVED WITH REDEMPTION, AND GUARDED WITH KINDNESS,
AND DECLARED WITH GRANDEUR.
HALLELUJAH. (Odes of Solomon 19:1-11)[15]

THE DOVER FLEW OVER THE HEAD OF THE MESSIAH
WHO WAS HER HEAD,
AND SHE SANG OVER HIM
AND HER VOICE WAS HEARD. (Odes of Solomon 24:1-2)[16]

AS THE WINGS OF DOVES OVER THEIR NESTLINGS,
AND THE MOUTHS OF THEIR NESTLINGS TOWARDS THEIR MOUTHS,
SO ALSO ARE THE WINGS OF THE SPIRIT OVER MY HEART.
MY HEART CONTINUALLY REFRESHES ITSELF AND LEAPS FOR JOY,
LIKE THE BABE WHO LEAPS FOR JOY IN HIS MOTHER'S WOMB. (Odes of
Solomon 28:1-2)[17]

I RESTED ON THE SPIRIT OF THE LORD, AND SHE LIFTED ME UP TO
HEAVEN;
AND CAUSED ME TO STAND ON MY FEET IN THE LORD'S HIGH PLACE,
BEFORE HIS PERFECTION AND HIS GLORY, WHERE I CONTINUED
GLORIFYING HIM BY THE COMPOSITION OF HIS ODES.
THE SPIRIT BROUGHT ME FORTH BEFORE THE LORD'S FACE, AND
BECAUSE I WAS THE SON OF MAN, I WAS NAMED THE LIGHT, THE SON
OF GOD;
BECAUSE I WAS THE MOST GLORIFIED AMONG THE GLORIOUS ONES,
AND THE GREATEST AMONG THE GREAT ONES.
FOR ACCORDING TO THE GREATNESS OF THE MOST HIGH, SO SHE
MADE ME; AND ACCORDING TO HIS NEWNESS HE RENEWED ME.
AND HE ANOINTED ME WITH HIS PERFECTION; AND I BECAME ONE OF
THOSE WHO ARE NEAR HIM.
AND MY MOUTH WAS OPENED LIKE A CLOUD OF DEW, AND MY HEART
GUSHED FORTH LIKE A GUSHER OF RIGHTEOUSNESS.
AND MY APPROACH WAS IN PEACE, AND I WAS ESTABLISHED IN THE
SPIRIT OF PROVIDENCE.
HALLELUJAH. (Odes of Solomon 36:1-8)[18]

There is a continual theme in these early church writings that
reflects Biblical ideas about the Holy Spirit: the breath of life, the
work of creation, the beckoning and leading us unto the Lord,
the sustainer of life, providing all that is essential to live and
maintain life, and the leader into the truth of our faith, whereby
we find Jesus Christ, waiting for us.

One of the greatest images we have of the Holy Spirit in non-
canonical writings is that of the Regenerator, the catalyst

involved in the powerful work of redemption. To regenerate means to bring to life again, and that is why the ancients saw the Holy Spirit as an active participant in the work of salvation. It was not of the powers of human beings to change, but was the work of the Spirit, leading them through the process of discernment and understanding, bringing them to a new place, a new life, a new understanding of life, rather than just recognizing themselves as belonging to a new religion. It is that precious work of spiritual regeneration that comes through the Holy Spirit that separates the Christian life from general religious practice; it animates; it breathes; it is the power and presence of God, active for our experience, active for our rendering, and coming alive to us through the promise and presence of spiritual renewal.

Debates about the gender of the Spirit[19]

Like all things, the exact nature and gender identity of the Spirit is something that has been of some debate. The question as to where exactly it started isn't easily answered but is somewhat reflected in the conflicts between the east and west churches in early Christianity. In eastern language, including Syriac, the language of the Peshitta (the Bible in the Syrian language), the Holy Spirit is always referred to in feminine terms, and is understood to be feminine, in a literal sense. The Spirit was also spoken of by Aphrahat and Ephraim as feminine in nature, echoing the early writings of Syriac Christianity. The Spirit is consistently seen as a compliment to the Father and the Son, rather than a competition for it. This proves that such a monumental difference in perspective started long before the overt schisms started and also account for the far more mystical nature present in the eastern churches.

In the west, Theolophilus of Antioch and Irenaeus of Lyons both recognized the Holy Spirit with the Wisdom of God, equated as feminine by both. This was not customary but shows early evidence in defense of the Spirit as feminine, with touches of such close enough to the west to impact the western church, in a unique semblance and unity of presence. It is also notable to say that even in the west, the Holy Spirit is almost never depicted as a person (specifically a male person), but is always personified as a dove, which represents a female nature, rather than the male-gender specifications.

In translation, the interpretation of the word "Spirit" into the Latin rendered the word masculine, rather than feminine. It is most likely that in reflecting the attitudes and ideas of culture, considering the Holy Spirit as masculine was a long and hard-fought battle of the west to explain and understand spiritual things through patriarchal ideals. As the Latin version of the Bible was the accepted translation in the west for many centuries, it's not an accident that people also assumed the Holy Spirit fell in line with masculine form. We could call this a conspiracy, but I don't know if it was that deliberate or that it was nothing more than a cultural imposition forced upon a spiritual ideal. The centuries of Christianity that followed see a great deal of cultural absorption upon the spiritual faith, and the result is a decidedly male Trinity, one that lacks female imagery.

I think we almost take the masculine nature – an imposed nature, at that – upon the church – as an assumed, for-granted aspect of our spirituality. It does not make sense that the Holy Spirit would suddenly be assumed to be male when it was, for centuries, assumed to be female. Yet we make the mistake of thinking our concept of spiritual history and identity is accurate, and we just assume that the way the Spirit has been traditionally portrayed in Christianity is, indeed, the way it was always understood. This is not the case, and it does matter that we have ascribed a masculine identity to an aspect of the Godhead that is female in nature.

Does the gender of the Holy Spirit matter?

I believe the identity of the Holy Spirit as feminine matters for a few key reasons. The first, and most obvious reason, being that if the Scriptures have identified the Spirit as feminine, that is something we should recognize and acknowledge. Imposing tradition on translation damages the spiritual realities we are supposed to embrace as believers. It's not right for us to suppose we know more about the Bible than the Scriptures do about themselves, and it is equally wrong for us to avoid things because they make us uncomfortable. The second reason for meaning in the Spirit's identity is to make us uncomfortable and throw us into a state where we must overcome our biases and dislikes as pertain to gender, rather than avoid them and change the nature of the divine. Society dislikes the virtues of women when they are expected to adapt them. Society likes the idea of demure and quiet women, because such is of no threat to men. If we see the work of the Spirit, however, we see a far more balanced viewpoint of women. The quiet, teaching, leading nature of the Spirit also coincides with fire, wind, and water, which have the ability to be some of the most powerful forces on this earth. Women are not all "sugar and spice and everything nice," but have the same power, and same capacity, for gentleness and fire, for security and passion, and for comfort and destruction, as is necessary, depending on the circumstances.

Perhaps the most important reason to properly identify the Holy Spirit by gender is the reality that feminine expression is just as divine in origin as masculine expression, and there is no competition, nor argument, between the two. It is sin that has divided men and women, and sin has dictated the different structural applications we see in male-female interaction. Before the fall in the garden, we do not see Adam, nor Eve, assuming any sort of inherent subordination to one another. Rather, we see Adam and Eve working together, without competition, and without argument. Men weren't above women, and women weren't above men. They were co-existent, equal, and perfect in state. The concept of the Holy Spirit as a divine feminine entity forces us to embrace the reality that everything we have learned about women is wrong from eternity's perspective. If we want to understand the full nature of God and the full nature of the Holy Spirit, we must embrace the feminine, so those attributes can become a part of our active, living faith, as we tap into the never-ending flow of life that is there if we will but receive it for ourselves.

Blessing of the Young Couple Before Marriage (Pascal Dagnan-Bouveret)

CHAPTER EIGHT
The Elect Lady, the Bride of Christ

THEN, EVEN IF I AM DELAYED, YOU WILL KNOW HOW [HOW IT IS NECESSARY] TO LIVE IN THE FAMILY [HOUSEHOLD] OF GOD, WHICH IS THE CHURCH [ASSEMBLY] OF THE LIVING GOD, THE SUPPORT [PILLAR] AND FOUNDATION OF THE TRUTH. WITHOUT DOUBT [OR AND WE ALL AGREE], THE SECRET OF OUR LIFE OF WORSHIP [OR THE TRUTH REVEALED IN OUR FAITH/WORSHIP; THE MYSTERY OF GODLINESS; V. 9] IS GREAT [WHAT FOLLOWS MAY BE FROM AN EARLY CHRISTIAN HYMN]:

HE WAS SHOWN TO US [APPEARED; WAS REVEALED] IN A HUMAN BODY [THE FLESH],
PROVED RIGHT [VINDICATED] IN SPIRIT [OR BY THE SPIRIT],
AND SEEN BY ANGELS.
HE WAS PROCLAIMED TO [AMONG] THE NATIONS [GENTILES],
BELIEVED IN BY [OR IN; THROUGHOUT] THE WORLD,
AND TAKEN UP IN GLORY.
(1 TIMOTHY 3:15-16)

WHEN we talk about the church, we seldom think of the church as a "her." We talk about the church as if it is an "it," with no viable personality or identity its own. This has led us to believe church is nothing more than a building, an impersonal, undynamic gathering of some people who (hopefully) have some things in common in terms of belief and doctrine. We don't connect the church to eternity, and we don't connect the church to us, in a personal way, that impacts the way we perceive our lives and our spirituality. This is a problem when it comes down to understanding our position in the church, because we don't recognize how to be involved and how important being an active part of church life is for each and every one of us. We sit back and debate the finer points, such as can one be saved without church membership, can we have a relationship with Jesus and not go to church, and just how much of church do we need to be saved, endlessly, and without a solution in sight.

There is a certain sadness to this reality, because it does show, inadvertently and often unintentionally, the lack of regard we have for women, and for caretakers in relationships, as such positions have been traditionally held by women. It is evident in church (as much as we say it is this way in the world too), that we do not respect those who labor, work, take care of children, handle daily maintenance, and the general repetitive and difficult tasks that have been much of women's lot throughout the ages. Yet in the church, these things are bestowed upon her as an honor, and we still disregard them. It is thanks to the important call and work of the church that the saints can labor, learn, and function through until Jesus comes back. Without the church, there are no believers; there is none who proclaims the work of Christ; and while salvation would be available, it would not have any long-term, sustaining purpose in the lives of those who figured enough about it to receive it. It is certainly not the church that saves us, but as the church has been saved, the church plays a continuing role in our salvation this side of heaven: maintaining it, teaching us of and from it, working through it, and educating us on everything we need to make it through this life, into the next.

The eternally feminine church

HOWEVER, THE PERFECT VIRGIN STOOD, WHO WAS PREACHING AND SUMMONING AND SAYING:
O YOU SONS OF MEN, RETURN, AND YOU THEIR DAUGHTERS, COME.
AND LEAVE THE WAYS OF THAT CORRUPTOR, AND APPROACH ME.
AND I WILL ENTER INTO YOU, AND BRING YOU FORTH FROM DESTRUCTION, AND MAKE YOU WISE IN THE WAYS OF TRUTH.
BE NOT CORRUPTED NOR PERISH.
OBEY ME AND BE SAVED, FOR I AM PROCLAIMING UNTO YOU THE GRACE OF GOD.
AND THROUGH ME YOU WILL BE SAVED AND BECOME BLESSED. I AM YOUR JUDGE;
AND THEY WHO HAVE PUT ME ON SHALL NOT BE FALSELY ACCUSED, BUT THEY SHALL POSSESS INCORRUPTION IN THE NEW WORLD.
MY ELECT ONES HAVE WALKED WITH ME, AND MY WAYS I WILL MAKE KNOWN TO THEM WHO SEEK ME; AND I WILL PROMISE THEM MY NAME.
HALLELUJAH. (Odes of Solomon 33:5-13)[1]

There isn't much debate about the feminine persona of the church. Picking up where Israel left off, the church stands as God's spouse in this world, as the Bride of Christ to Christians, and as the entity that is here, in this world, to take care of believers, of those who follow Christ, until the time when Christ returns. At the time Christ returns, the church will certainly not cease to be, but will become something else, with a unified purpose in the presence of the Lord.

The work of the church represents a certain level of labor, certainly not the Victorian image of a woman sitting on a couch, somewhere, devoid of human contact. Just as any good mother knows her children need exposure to the world, so too the church takes on this role, emphasizing the necessity of proper equipping so her spiritual children can go forth into the world and have the greatest impact possible on those who will encounter them. She stands, here in this world, not unengaged, but active and ready to take on whatever needs to be addressed. Her husband may not be physically present, but He remains with her and is as much with her spiritually as if He were standing beside of her. In His absence, she performs every duty of maintenance along with governance. She guides and protects, leads and instructs, disciplines and manages, in every possible way, to bring the people of God to the place where they are ready for her husband's return.

This sounds beautiful and poetic, but it dispels many stereotypes while seeming to re-emphasize many notions people have about women in general. The church's role with her children seems to exemplify the best in motherhood, in standing alone without the physical being of a man present, in diligence, in great management, and in handling people. The only problem we see is how negatively people within the church guard and care for her, and often represent her when dealing with the world, and among ourselves. We are so quick to talk about everything wrong in the church – church hurt, church abuse, church mismanagement, church decreases, church problems church issues – we fail to see beyond these issues, to the beautiful, spotless Bride we are to become in the presence of the Lord. We observe human problems and impose them upon an image, upon the feminine Bride of Christ, that is a pure body, one here to do nothing more than the work of God and carry us into eternal life.

No matter how beautiful and eloquent we make the work of the church sound in this world, the church is, herself, a powerful image of women and of all that women can be if they trust themselves to the Lord. Far from the images of traditional marriage and family, we learn through the church that we are valuable, important, and capable, able to choose our relationships, and able to serve a vital function in this world that extends beyond our immediate households and lives. We are here, as Esther was, for such a time as this, and that means every woman who assumes position within the church has the important task of bringing this type to life in a relatable and practical way.

Women as a type of the church

The church is feminine; Eve was a type of the church; and now women, as stock of Eve, all carry a type of the church within us, as the agents who bring forth life in this world. This is a repeated theme throughout the feminine imagery present in the Scriptures and reflects in each and every woman herself. As women are able to carry, birth, and bring forth life, so the church is able to do such in a spiritual sense. The work of the church does not end here, just as it does not end here for women, either. The work of motherhood is anything but demoralizing, even though the world has not seen fit to elevate it, in many cases, above slave status. From the spiritual perspective, the goal of motherhood is not just to bear sons or keep a family lineage alive, but to raise children to adulthood, enabling them to stand as competent, able-bodied representatives of the family and members of society. Contrary to theory, this involves many intricate and intelligent aspects of female work that are not unique, nor exclusive, to men. Any woman who has been a mother, or who has known a mother, knows that women have to do many things very well, as ordered by the spiritual realm, within the natural order. These duties include teaching and instructing children in essential life tasks and issues, helping them to live and discover independence, maintaining daily schedules, correcting bad behavior, discipling unto principles of self-discipline, edify and encourage, provide foundation, and inspire life, all long after a child is physically born. Through the different stages of childhood development, we even find the principle of spiritual rebirth; of being born again, starting over, and finding grace and forgiveness as children falter into the security of their loving parent, with the empowerment and hope to start again.

MY CHILD [SON], LISTEN TO YOUR FATHER'S TEACHING [INSTRUCTION; DISCIPLINE]
AND DO NOT FORGET [NEGLECT] YOUR MOTHER'S ADVICE [INSTRUCTION].
[FOR] THEIR TEACHING [IT] WILL BE LIKE FLOWERS IN YOUR HAIR [A GRACIOUS GARLAND ON YOUR HEAD]
OR A NECKLACE [BEADS] AROUND YOUR NECK. (Proverbs 1:8-9)

I WOULD LEAD YOU AND BRING YOU
TO MY MOTHER'S HOUSE;
SHE IS THE ONE WHO TAUGHT ME. (Song of Solomon 8:2)

"I WILL COMFORT YOU
AS A MOTHER COMFORTS HER CHILD.
YOU WILL BE COMFORTED IN JERUSALEM." (Isaiah 66:13)

JESUS REPLIED, "VERY TRULY I TELL YOU, NO ONE CAN SEE THE KINGDOM OF GOD UNLESS THEY ARE BORN AGAIN."

"HOW CAN SOMEONE BE BORN WHEN THEY ARE OLD?" NICODEMUS ASKED. "SURELY THEY CANNOT ENTER A SECOND TIME INTO THEIR MOTHER'S WOMB TO BE BORN!"

JESUS ANSWERED, "VERY TRULY I TELL YOU, NO ONE CAN ENTER THE KINGDOM OF GOD UNLESS THEY ARE BORN OF WATER AND THE SPIRIT. FLESH GIVES BIRTH TO FLESH, BUT THE SPIRIT GIVES BIRTH TO SPIRIT. YOU SHOULD NOT BE SURPRISED AT MY SAYING, 'YOU MUST BE BORN AGAIN.' THE WIND BLOWS WHEREVER IT PLEASES. YOU HEAR ITS SOUND, BUT YOU CANNOT TELL WHERE IT COMES FROM OR WHERE IT IS GOING. SO IT IS WITH EVERYONE BORN OF THE SPIRIT." (John 3:3-8, NIV)

WHEN JESUS [THEREFORE] SAW HIS MOTHER AND THE FOLLOWER [DISCIPLE] HE LOVED [PROBABLY JOHN HIMSELF] STANDING NEARBY, HE SAID TO HIS MOTHER, "DEAR WOMAN [WOMAN; SEE 2:4], HERE IS [BEHOLD] YOUR SON." THEN HE SAID TO THE FOLLOWER [DISCIPLE], "HERE IS [BEHOLD] YOUR MOTHER." FROM THAT TIME ON, THE FOLLOWER [DISCIPLE] TOOK HER TO LIVE IN HIS HOME. (John 19:26-27)

IF ANYONE BELONGS TO CHRIST, THERE IS A NEW CREATION [THE NEW CREATION HAS ARRIVED; OR THAT PERSON HAS BECOME A NEW CREATION]. THE OLD THINGS HAVE GONE; [LOOK; BEHOLD] EVERYTHING IS MADE NEW [THE NEW HAS COME]! (2 Corinthians 5:17)

PRAISE BE TO [BLESSED BE] THE GOD AND FATHER OF OUR LORD JESUS CHRIST. IN GOD'S GREAT [ABUNDANT] MERCY HE HAS CAUSED US TO BE BORN AGAIN [ANEW; JOHN 3:5–8] INTO A LIVING HOPE, BECAUSE JESUS CHRIST ROSE [OR BY MEANS OF THE RESURRECTION OF JESUS CHRIST] FROM THE DEAD. NOW WE HOPE FOR [OR THIS NEW BIRTH PROVIDES US WITH] THE BLESSINGS GOD HAS FOR HIS CHILDREN [AN INHERITANCE]. THESE BLESSINGS [OR THIS INHERITANCE], WHICH CANNOT BE DESTROYED OR BE SPOILED [CORRUPTED; DEFILED] OR LOSE THEIR BEAUTY, ARE [IS] KEPT IN HEAVEN FOR YOU [MATT. 6:19–21; LUKE 12:33]. GOD'S POWER PROTECTS YOU THROUGH YOUR FAITH UNTIL SALVATION IS SHOWN TO YOU [OR THE COMING OF THE SALVATION THAT IS READY TO BE REVEALED] AT THE END OF [IN THE LAST] TIME. (1 Peter 3:3-5)

This means that women have not only an equal and active role in the church alongside men, they are literal carriers of the church within themselves. Women are a living type, here to live out the message of the life-saving Gospel. It is against God's own nature and type to say that women cannot carry the Gospel message, because they already do. The church herself is feminine, and the natural order of the woman as the life-bearer typifies the spiritual order of the church, and we cannot reject, nor deny, this order. Those who reject the woman the right to speak forth the Word of life do not understand the role of the church in Gospel proclamation, and to reject the woman is to reject the church.

If we want to have a better relationship with the church, we must first strive to have a better relationship with the woman, as the woman is a type of the church. We must lay down hostilities and subordinations, and refrain from the power and control battles that men and women have held from the very beginning. We must lift up and edify the gifts and abilities in women, because we can see those gifts and abilities in the church. Being a part of the church is to embrace something female, both by virtue and authority, and to bring ourselves into a place where we are more comfortable with that which is feminine, as well as acknowledging female authority within our own lives. When we become a part of the church we are becoming a part of a feminine entity, and acknowledge as such with feminine values, such as love and fellowship, that are more powerful and productive in sight of eternity than hatred and power.

The Bridegroom

> *BRIDEGROOM*²
> - *NUMPHIOS.* A BRIDEGROOM
> - ORIGINAL WORD: ΝΥΜΦΊΟΣ, ΟΥ, ὁ
> - PART OF SPEECH: NOUN, MASCULINE
> - TRANSLITERATION: NUMPHIOS
> - PHONETIC SPELLING: (NOOM-FEE'-OS)
> - SHORT DEFINITION: A BRIDEGROOM
> - DEFINITION: A BRIDEGROOM

Some question the validity of the role of the church as a bride because there is limited specific reference to such in the New Testament. The most convincing examination is found in Ephesians 5:22-33, which we examine shortly. There are other references, however, that extend beyond that of the New Jerusalem, spoken of in Revelation (which we will discuss in chapter 10). The most powerful revelation of the church comes through its intimate relationship with Christ, especially where He is portrayed as the Bridegroom.

JESUS ANSWERED, "THE FRIENDS OF THE BRIDEGROOM [*OR* WEDDING GUESTS; CHILDREN OF THE WEDDING HALL] ARE NOT SAD [CANNOT MOURN] WHILE HE IS WITH THEM [JESUS IS REFERRING TO HIMSELF; JOHN 3:29; REV. 19:7]. BUT THE TIME [DAYS] WILL COME WHEN THE BRIDEGROOM WILL BE TAKEN FROM THEM, AND THEN THEY WILL FAST. (Matthew 9:15)

JESUS ANSWERED, "THE FRIENDS OF THE BRIDEGROOM [*OR* WEDDING

GUESTS; CHILDREN OF THE WEDDING HALL] DO NOT FAST WHILE THE BRIDEGROOM IS STILL WITH THEM [JESUS IS REFERRING TO HIMSELF; JOHN 3:29; REV. 19:7]. AS LONG AS THE BRIDEGROOM IS WITH THEM, THEY CANNOT FAST. (Mark 2:19)

JESUS SAID TO THEM, "YOU CANNOT MAKE THE FRIENDS OF THE BRIDEGROOM [OR WEDDING GUESTS; CHILDREN OF THE WEDDING HALL] FAST WHILE HE IS STILL WITH THEM. (Luke 5:34)

THE BRIDE BELONGS ONLY TO THE BRIDEGROOM. BUT THE FRIEND WHO HELPS THE BRIDEGROOM [OR THE BEST MAN] STANDS BY AND LISTENS TO HIM. HE IS THRILLED [REJOICES GREATLY] THAT HE GETS TO HEAR THE BRIDEGROOM'S VOICE. IN THE SAME WAY, I AM REALLY HAPPY [MY JOY IS FULFILLED; IN THIS ANALOGY, JOHN IS THE BEST MAN AND JESUS IS THE BRIDEGROOM]. (John 3:29)

"AT THAT TIME THE KINGDOM OF HEAVEN WILL BE LIKE TEN BRIDESMAIDS [VIRGINS] WHO TOOK THEIR LAMPS AND WENT TO WAIT FOR [MEET] THE BRIDEGROOM. FIVE OF THEM WERE FOOLISH AND FIVE WERE WISE [SENSIBLE; PRUDENT]. THE FIVE FOOLISH BRIDESMAIDS [VIRGINS] TOOK THEIR LAMPS, BUT THEY DID NOT TAKE MORE OIL FOR THE LAMPS TO BURN. THE WISE [SENSIBLE; PRUDENT] BRIDESMAIDS [VIRGINS] TOOK THEIR LAMPS AND MORE OIL IN JARS [FLASKS]. BECAUSE THE BRIDEGROOM WAS LATE [DELAYED], THEY BECAME SLEEPY [DROWSY] AND WENT TO SLEEP.

"AT MIDNIGHT SOMEONE CRIED OUT, 'THE BRIDEGROOM IS COMING [LOOK, THE BRIDEGROOM]! COME AND MEET HIM!' THEN ALL THE BRIDESMAIDS [VIRGINS] WOKE UP AND GOT THEIR LAMPS READY [TRIMMED THEIR LAMPS]. BUT THE FOOLISH ONES SAID TO THE WISE [SENSIBLE; PRUDENT], 'GIVE US SOME OF YOUR OIL, BECAUSE OUR LAMPS ARE GOING OUT.' THE WISE [SENSIBLE; PRUDENT] BRIDESMAIDS ANSWERED, 'NO, THE OIL WE HAVE MIGHT NOT BE ENOUGH FOR ALL OF US [FOR US AND FOR YOU]. GO TO THE PEOPLE WHO SELL OIL AND BUY SOME FOR YOURSELVES.'

"SO WHILE THE FIVE FOOLISH BRIDESMAIDS [THEY] WENT TO BUY OIL, THE BRIDEGROOM CAME. THE BRIDESMAIDS WHO WERE READY WENT IN WITH THE BRIDEGROOM TO THE WEDDING FEAST. THEN THE DOOR WAS CLOSED AND LOCKED [SHUT].

"LATER THE OTHERS CAME BACK AND SAID, 'SIR, SIR, [LORD, LORD] OPEN THE DOOR TO LET US IN.' BUT THE BRIDEGROOM ANSWERED, 'I TELL YOU THE TRUTH, I DON'T KNOW YOU.'

"SO ALWAYS BE READY [STAY AWAKE; BE ALERT; KEEP WATCH], BECAUSE YOU DON'T KNOW THE DAY OR THE HOUR [THE SON OF MAN WILL COME]. (Matthew 25:1-13)

Later in the New Testament, the terminology changes somewhat, but still relates to the same essential imagery:

WHEREFORE, MY BRETHREN, YE ALSO ARE BECOME DEAD TO THE LAW BY THE BODY OF CHRIST; THAT YE SHOULD BE MARRIED TO ANOTHER, EVEN TO HIM WHO IS RAISED FROM THE DEAD, THAT WE SHOULD BRING FORTH FRUIT UNTO GOD. (Romans 7:4, KJV)

I WISH YOU WOULD BE PATIENT WITH ME EVEN WHEN I AM A LITTLE FOOLISH [IN A LITTLE FOOLISHNESS], BUT YOU ARE ALREADY DOING THAT. [FOR] I AM JEALOUS OVER YOU WITH A JEALOUSY THAT COMES FROM GOD [OR GODLY JEALOUSY]. I PROMISED TO GIVE YOU TO CHRIST, AS YOUR ONLY HUSBAND. I WANT TO GIVE YOU AS HIS PURE BRIDE [VIRGIN]. (2 Corinthians 11:1-2)

This imagery is powerful for a few reasons. The first is that the imagery of marriage, betrothal, and promise between God and His people continues through Christ's sacrificial work, bought and wrought for the church, herself. The image of the bridegroom is important, however, because it always points back to Christ, and to a certain level of spiritual union between Christ and His people. Saying that the church was married to Christ and, by proxy, to the people of God, is one that takes on a personal nature, challenging each and every one of us to respond and to live in a certain way. It was more than just about being a group who attended and witnessed a wedding. In the church, we are that wedding; we are that promise; we are the fulfillment of prophecy and connected to eternity, each in our own right.

'[FOR] BY HIS POWER [OR IN HIM] WE LIVE AND MOVE AND EXIST [HAVE OUR BEING; A QUOTATION FROM THE CRETAN PHILOSOPHER EPIMENIDES, FROM ABOUT 600 BC].' [AS] SOME OF YOUR OWN POETS HAVE SAID: 'FOR WE ARE HIS CHILDREN [OFFSPRING; A QUOTATION

FROM ARATUS, A STOIC PHILOSOPHER FROM CILICIA, WHO LIVED ABOUT 315–240 BC].' (Acts 17:28)

The union we have with Christ is more than individualized. We receive that personal connection, that personal intimacy, as we walk with Christ through the work of the church. While some argue that we can have a relationship without the church, such is impossible, because the church is, herself, the Bride of Christ. It is that gathering of believers, all coming together as one, for that union with Him. While we certainly maintain our personal communication with God, we learn how to have that communication as we enter the spiritual connection with the heavenly Bridegroom, Who is Christ. It is through that spiritual identity and union that we find the ultimate fulfillment with Him, and discover just how it is that in Him, we live, and move, and have our being. To better understand this, we must look at marriage, and at the work of the bride, adorned and ready for her husband, present in life and in the church.

The bride

If Christ is the bridegroom and the Bible is full of imagery of the church as Christ's wife, then it only makes sense that the bride of the Bridegroom is the church, herself. Is this imagery relevant, or is it just there to prove a marital relationship in imagery? Surely that is part of it, because such displays commitment, and what is seen ideally as an eternal commitment. Christ didn't just decide to live with the church, or to hang out with her; it was within His choice, and His scope, to marry her, to make that life-long (eternally life-long) commitment to her, and because we are in the church, to make that commitment to us. It proves that God is about more than just our immediate situation, and that eternity is much bigger than the small, little things we go through that sometimes seem bigger than what they might, in view of the eternal, actually be.

Calling the church a bride of Christ also implies the initial excitement of a marital relationship, one that is untainted by the complications and difficulties of later married life. It suggests a purity and an innocence, one where a couple is knowing each other, and can't wait to start that process. That excitement should translate to our relationship with God, but also forces us

BRIDE[3]

- *NUMPHÉ*: A BRIDE, A YOUNG WOMAN
- ORIGINAL WORD: ΝΎΜΦΗ, ΗΣ, ἡ
- PART OF SPEECH: NOUN, FEMININE
- TRANSLITERATION: NUMPHÉ
- PHONETIC SPELLING: (NOOM-FAY')
- SHORT DEFINITION: A BRIDE, DAUGHTER-IN-LAW
- DEFINITION: (A) A BRIDE, YOUNG WIFE, YOUNG WOMAN, (B) A DAUGHTER-IN-LAW.

to challenge of the role of the church in the world. By proxy, it also forces challenge of the role of women in the world. It is generally assumed that what man does is automatically more relevant than the work woman does, and that for the work she does, she should not seek attention, glory, notice, or splendor. Historically speaking, this is exactly how "women's work" has been perceived, and one would think the church's work is unimportant in light of Christ. Yet it is the church that is the bride, and anyone who has ever been to a wedding knows how much attention the bride receives, just for being the bride. It is the bride who stands in splendor, glory, and so everyone notices her. She is not inconspicuous, hiding over in a corner, but does everything she does in front of everyone, as the center of attention. The bride demands attention and demands notice. We cannot, and will not ever, under any circumstances, ignore the bride.

LISTEN TO ME, DAUGHTER; LOOK AND PAY ATTENTION [INCLINE YOUR EAR].

FORGET YOUR PEOPLE AND YOUR FATHER'S FAMILY [HOUSE; GEN. 2:24].

THE KING LOVES [DESIRES; LONGS FOR] YOUR BEAUTY.

BECAUSE HE IS YOUR MASTER [LORD], YOU SHOULD OBEY [BOW YOURSELF BEFORE] HIM.

PEOPLE FROM THE CITY [THE DAUGHTER] OF TYRE HAVE BROUGHT A GIFT [TRIBUTE].

WEALTHY PEOPLE WILL WANT TO MEET YOU [SEEK YOUR FAVOR].

THE PRINCESS [DAUGHTER OF THE KING] IS VERY BEAUTIFUL [ALL GLORIOUS WITHIN].
HER GOWN IS WOVEN WITH GOLD.
IN HER BEAUTIFUL [EMBROIDERED] CLOTHES SHE IS BROUGHT TO THE KING.
HER BRIDESMAIDS [VIRGINS] FOLLOW BEHIND HER,
AND THEY ARE ALSO BROUGHT TO HIM [HER FRIENDS FOLLOW].
THEY COME WITH HAPPINESS AND JOY;
THEY ENTER THE KING'S PALACE. (Psalm 45:10-15)

COME WITH ME FROM LEBANON, MY BRIDE.
COME WITH ME FROM LEBANON,
FROM THE TOP OF MOUNT AMANA,
FROM THE TOPS OF MOUNT SENIR AND MOUNT HERMON.
COME FROM THE LIONS' DENS
AND FROM THE LEOPARDS' HILLS [APART FROM HIM SHE IS IN A DANGEROUS PLACE].
MY SISTER [AN ANCIENT TERM OF ENDEARMENT], MY BRIDE,
YOU HAVE THRILLED MY HEART [DRIVE ME CRAZY];
YOU HAVE THRILLED MY HEART [DRIVE ME CRAZY]
WITH A [ONE] GLANCE OF YOUR EYES,
WITH ONE SPARKLE [JEWEL] FROM YOUR NECKLACE.
YOUR LOVE IS SO SWEET [HOW BEAUTIFUL IS YOUR LOVE], MY SISTER [4:9], MY BRIDE.
YOUR LOVE IS BETTER THAN WINE [MAKES ONE LIGHTHEADED],
AND YOUR PERFUME [THE SCENT OF YOUR OILS] SMELLS BETTER THAN ANY SPICE.
MY BRIDE, YOUR LIPS DRIP HONEY;
HONEY AND MILK ARE UNDER YOUR TONGUE [SENSUOUS LIQUIDS THAT HE WILL EXPLORE].
YOUR CLOTHES SMELL LIKE THE CEDARS OF LEBANON [THE BEST CEDARS].
MY SISTER [4:9], MY BRIDE, YOU ARE LIKE A GARDEN LOCKED UP [SHE HAS NOT BEEN ENTERED BY A MAN],
LIKE A WALLED-IN [SEALED] SPRING, A CLOSED-UP [LOCKED] FOUNTAIN.
YOUR LIMBS [SHOOTS; A BOTANICAL TERM EITHER REFERRING TO THE WOMAN'S LEGS OR HER GENITAL ORGANS] ARE LIKE AN ORCHARD
OF POMEGRANATES WITH ALL THE BEST FRUIT,
FILLED WITH FLOWERS [HENNA; 1:14] AND NARD,
NARD AND SAFFRON [SPICY FLORAL SCENT], CALAMUS [WOODY ODOR],

AND CINNAMON,
WITH TREES OF INCENSE, MYRRH [AROMATIC GUM FROM TREE BARK], AND ALOES [A FRAGRANT WOOD]—
ALL THE BEST SPICES.
YOU ARE LIKE A GARDEN FOUNTAIN—
A WELL OF FRESH [LIVING] WATER
FLOWING [STREAMING] DOWN FROM THE MOUNTAINS OF LEBANON. (Song of Solomon 4:8-15)

I HAVE ENTERED MY GARDEN, MY SISTER [4:9], MY BRIDE.
I HAVE GATHERED MY MYRRH WITH MY SPICE.
I HAVE EATEN MY HONEYCOMB AND MY HONEY.
I HAVE DRUNK MY WINE AND MY MILK [HE ENJOYS PHYSICAL INTIMACY WITH HER]. (Song of Solomon 5:1)

It is an unfortunate fact that, too often, ignoring the bride is exactly what we do. It is not to say the bride is more important than the Bridegroom, but the bride is usually more notable. That is how the church works, especially at this point in spiritual history. The bride is the one who is here, visible and in splendor, for the entire world to see. Jesus is not physically visible currently, but the church herself is. The church is visible in every believer, and that through such vision, and for this reason, it is all the more important we understand the way that marriage mirrors the relationship the church has with Christ.

Marriage as a spiritual type

The Scriptural use of the Bride and Bridegroom language as pertains to Christ and the church awakens us to things easy to understand, as well as things we can relate to, in our spiritual lives. Many of the things we take for granted around us – women, life, relationships, marriage, intimacy, and the joys of life – are also types, or shadows, of other things. Often distorted, marriage is both a type, and a reality. It is something that we can easily identify around us, and that helps us to understand it from a spiritual perspective, as well.

Throughout the ages, marriage has often been interpreted through the lens of literal experience, which means seldom have people embraced the ideal type present therein, and have, instead, sought to reject such based-on living through its reality.

Women, in particular, have often experienced marriage as a punishment for being female rather than a splendor or glory of spiritual experience. This has led to all sorts of difficulty in interpreting marriage in a spiritual context, and coming to understanding the spiritual type of marriage has been often put off in favor of other beliefs and ideals. Yet if we don't understand the type present in marriage, we are missing something key in the work of the church and our relationship with Christ.

Marriage throughout every age (even to the present day) has served more political and social need than those related to emotional, physical, and spiritual issues. Marriage and family serve as slogans and fodder for politicians, selling points for media products, and agencies to preserve bloodlines, finances, dynasties, and familial empires. If we look at history from its true realism, marriage has been used and abused rather than edified. We are deluding ourselves if we believe marriage goes without abuse today. Even though arranged marriage is not an active part of western life, marriage itself still remains under its greatest threat and assault as it is exploited and used to serve an agenda rather than glorify God.

The answer to understanding marriage – and our relationship with Christ – is seeing Biblical understanding of such and recognizing what is present therein in terms of spiritual identity. There is something for us to gain in both type and reality, that has the potential to heal marriage and our relationship with the church, for better understanding of the feminine aspects of marriage and spirituality.

SUBMIT TO ONE ANOTHER OUT OF REVERENCE FOR CHRIST.

WIVES, SUBMIT YOURSELVES TO YOUR OWN HUSBANDS AS YOU DO TO THE LORD. FOR THE HUSBAND IS THE HEAD OF THE WIFE AS CHRIST IS THE HEAD OF THE CHURCH, HIS BODY, OF WHICH HE IS THE SAVIOR. NOW AS THE CHURCH SUBMITS TO CHRIST, SO ALSO WIVES SHOULD SUBMIT TO THEIR HUSBANDS IN EVERYTHING.

HUSBANDS, LOVE YOUR WIVES, JUST AS CHRIST LOVED THE CHURCH AND GAVE HIMSELF UP FOR HER TO MAKE HER HOLY, CLEANSING HER BY THE WASHING WITH WATER THROUGH THE WORD, AND TO PRESENT HER TO HIMSELF AS A RADIANT CHURCH, WITHOUT STAIN OR WRINKLE OR ANY OTHER BLEMISH, BUT HOLY AND BLAMELESS. IN THIS SAME

WAY, HUSBANDS OUGHT TO LOVE THEIR WIVES AS THEIR OWN BODIES. HE WHO LOVES HIS WIFE LOVES HIMSELF. AFTER ALL, NO ONE EVER HATED THEIR OWN BODY, BUT THEY FEED AND CARE FOR THEIR BODY, JUST AS CHRIST DOES THE CHURCH—FOR WE ARE MEMBERS OF HIS BODY. "FOR THIS REASON A MAN WILL LEAVE HIS FATHER AND MOTHER AND BE UNITED TO HIS WIFE, AND THE TWO WILL BECOME ONE FLESH." THIS IS A PROFOUND MYSTERY—BUT I AM TALKING ABOUT CHRIST AND THE CHURCH. HOWEVER, EACH ONE OF YOU ALSO MUST LOVE HIS WIFE AS HE LOVES HIMSELF, AND THE WIFE MUST RESPECT HER HUSBAND. (Ephesians 5:21-33, NIV)

SUBMIT[4]
- *HUPOTASSÓ*: TO PLACE OR RANK UNDER, TO SUBJECT, MID. TO OBEY
- ORIGINAL WORD: ὑποτάσσω
- PART OF SPEECH: VERB
- TRANSLITERATION: HUPOTASSÓ
- PHONETIC SPELLING: (HOOP-OT-AS'-SO)
- SHORT DEFINITION: I PLACE UNDER, SUBJECT TO
- DEFINITION: I PLACE UNDER, SUBJECT TO; MID, PASS: I SUBMIT, PUT MYSELF INTO SUBJECTION.

The book of Ephesians is about understanding the work of the church from eternity past to eternity future. It is a vitally important book for examining the way that the church is not an afterthought or replacement plan within the work of salvation, but that it has been present, in the heart and mind of God, from the original type of the church, found in Eve herself. Yet understanding Ephesians 5 is often buried and muddled under the unfortunate patterns of culture and patriarchy, used to keep women in a certain place and perspective, and used to make marriage a cultural punishment rather than a vindicator and picture of spiritual liberation.

The Bible has long called us to perceive ourselves in picture of eternity. We aren't supposed to look out over our lives and see what we do and what happens to us as a linear, unimportant existence, but as a part of what is happening in a bigger picture. This is to give all aspects of our lives – including our relationships – a priority shift, one that helps us to understand

WIFE[5]
- *GUNÉ:* A WOMAN
- ORIGINAL WORD: ΓΥΝΉ, ΑΙΚΌΣ, ἡ
- PART OF SPEECH: NOUN, FEMININE
- TRANSLITERATION: GUNÉ
- PHONETIC SPELLING: (GOO-NAY')
- SHORT DEFINITION: A WOMAN, WIFE, MY LADY
- DEFINITION: A WOMAN, WIFE, MY LADY.

HUSBAND[6]
- *ANÉR:* A MAN
- ORIGINAL WORD: ἀΝΉΡ, ἀΝΔΡΌΣ, ὁ
- PART OF SPEECH: NOUN, MASCULINE
- TRANSLITERATION: ANÉR
- PHONETIC SPELLING: (AN'-AYR)
- SHORT DEFINITION: A MALE HUMAN BEING, A MAN
- DEFINITION: A MALE HUMAN BEING; A MAN, HUSBAND.

HEAD[7]
- *KEPHALÉ:* THE HEAD
- ORIGINAL WORD: ΚΕΦΑΛΉ, ῆΣ, ἡ
- PART OF SPEECH: NOUN, FEMININE
- TRANSLITERATION: KEPHALÉ
- PHONETIC SPELLING: (KEF-AL-AY')
- SHORT DEFINITION: THE HEAD
- DEFINITION: THE HEAD, MET: A CORNER STONE, UNITING TWO WALLS; HEAD, RULER, LORD.

how God speaks to us on a regular basis through ordinary things and aspects we might never otherwise consider. It's not an easy process, but a life-long one, one that labors and grows, and understands changes through time and space.

If we look at our relationship with God in this manner, it sounds a lot like a marriage, doesn't it? It is not something we complete in one night, nor is it something that is completed within a short period of time. It is a labor, one that develops through love and depth, and (hopefully), as life moves forward, couples gain a better understanding not just of their partner, but of themselves, as well. This is why so much of our spiritual identity relates to marriage and concepts about marriage. As God teaches us about ourselves, it becomes obvious to us that He desires us to engage and relate with Him in a long-term situation that echoes the closeness and intimacies of marriage. God wants to dwell with us daily, live with us, walk with us, and be close to us, one with Him, day in and day out.

So, whenever we start reading about marriage, especially here in Ephesians, we need to hear God speaking to us about what He desires for our relationship with Him. We should hear the desire for spouses to come together in the concept of oneness, as both come from the divine essence that marks spiritual unity. Whenever we enter an earthly marriage, we need to consider what God would desire of us in that situation. The purpose of marriage is not endless bliss, but a long-wrought walk in holiness, one that teaches us about God, ourselves, and ourselves as connected to God. As we learn more about these vital aspects, it helps to bring us to a place where marriage can transform, rather than distort, life, love, and spiritual insight.

What is most important for us to understand in this particular passage is the aspect of submission, which is identified for all believers, and then women, specifically. To understand this principle, we must first understand headship, which is related to ancient societal concepts of financial profitability and decision-making in households. In ancient cultures, women were not allowed to own property. They had no legal power to execute or make decisions, and they were not able to serve as inheritors of familial or marital property upon a male relative's death. This made for interesting attitudes toward women and marriage, as they, too, became a part of a man's estate, regarded as property. This is why slavery is almost always mentioned in connection with headship, as women and slaves were both regarded as property. It does beg to state that we never argue anymore for slavery as a spiritual principle...so why has headship remained as a spiritual concept, rather than a socio-economic issue?

Headship was never a spiritual principle, at least not in the sense that it is often taught in churches today. It was a socio-economic one, based on the political and social climates present in the Greek and Roman cultures of the time. It was how the ancients did business, kept track of property, and maintained their societal status. Until the last century, it was also largely how property was maintained in the west. It wasn't until the early 1980s that clauses of headship in marriage were removed, thus entitling women to make decisions and stand as partners in a marriage, rather than property. Examining this reality, however, should radically alter how we read Ephesians 5:22-33 in a literal sense, because its literal application no longer applies. The Apostle Paul was relating something else through the culture of his day, and this is why we have so much disagreement, confusion, and different opinions about just what it means.

There are a couple of ways we could interpret the injunction of submission in a literal sense, in its original context, but they don't particularly make sense to us now. If we live in a society where women can legally inherit property and are not seen as property themselves, there isn't much to understand as pertains to literal headship, unless we start interpreting headship through the perspective of spiritual, emotional, or financial control. We can draw from it that women should be respectful toward their spouses, but that isn't an extraordinary position and is one that we should exercise in all relationships. If we study the passage, more and more, there are few key things that the Apostle Paul is trying to convey to us about our literal relationships, including:

- We must respect the laws that govern our societies, whether they always support our personal convictions as believers. Inequality between men and women was an unfair aspect of the society in which the first believers lived, but it was a reality for them, day in and day out. There is nothing wrong with social protest, working for and advocating for social change, but while change is not yet in place, we must acknowledge the law, to the best of our ability, understanding and learning about the ways social change and impact are made effectively and with lasting effects.

- We must esteem and acknowledge one another in the Body, not considering ourselves of greater value than another, but respectfully acknowledging one another, consistently and in love, throughout our walk.

- Our social interactions make a huge difference in our spiritual witness. If we act poorly with those we are closest to, such is a negative witness to the greater body of believers and to the world, as a whole. It is unfitting for us to spend our lives at odds, in embitterment, and dislike for one another.

- How we behave at home is just as important as how we behave in the world. Proper love can be shown at home, or it can be lacking. If love lacks at home, such can prove to be problematic. It is important for us to focus on love everywhere in our lives, even in places we might think are private or do not matter.

- Marriage and marital relationships should serve as more than just a political statement. If that is all marriage is to a couple, or to a society, the people in those relationships will suffer.

The spiritual principle present in this passage is the establishment of Jesus Christ as the head, or Lord, of everything – including households, including all believers, and yes, even the church – simply because it is Christ Who is responsible for the church. This means that no earthly person has the power, nor the control, to be a lord, to exercise complete control over people, and that any and all governing positions in this world are for that specified purpose – to implement governance. That is why the Apostle Paul did not encourage an overthrow or complete disruption to the specified social order of his day. He acknowledged it, but there is nothing to suggest that he did not anticipate a time when such social codes would no longer be relevant in ordinary society.

It also means that if we recognize Jesus Christ as the head of all – as the originator of all – that Jesus is above the origination of woman from man, as well, and that Jesus has authority over society, over who is seen as supreme in society, over any ruling or authoritive class, and in the long run, has the full final say over what happens to humanity. By standing as Christians, this is an intense and powerful statement of the Lordship of Christ, far beyond what we might consider when we say "Jesus is Lord." Whenever we utter those words, we are saying that no earthly person has the same right or rule over us, and if Jesus is Lord – that means the secular government, society, our employers, our family members, and yes, in the case of husbands and wives – even husbands – are not Lord.

In light of this, we must recognize what the submission teachings of the New Testament are about: they are not here to implement law, or imply a spiritual inequality or political one for women, but that the statement intended is to establish spiritual and legal authority (in that, in the end, we will have to answer to a higher authority) for Christ, above any and all party on this earth. This prevents evils, abuses, and an improper sense of lordship within the home, and ends the endless competition between men and women as to who is greater, better, or more relevant. Because believers are encouraged to submit one to another as unto Christ, and then the same injunction is repeated for wives, this indicates women are not to interact with husbands in a special context, but in the same practical sense, as she would any other man. A husband is not to be an idol or referred to in terms of superiority or governmental authority (such was customary in days gone by, but indicates something more today, thus making it more of an idolatry than respect), and at the same point, she is to treat him with respect and honor. Just as she would treat someone else, so too she should treat her husband.

This might sound strange, and contrary to what we often hear as pertains to men and women, but it is the reality that the love of God is to permeate our relationships and keep us from esteeming others more than we should, no matter the context of our relationship with that person. One of the biggest complaints I hear as relates to women in the church is that they favor men in their lives, such as the pastor, their father, their sons, their boss, or someone else in the church over their own husbands. There are a variety of differing opinions as to how such a situation should be handled, but the issue itself could be resolved if women were encouraged to view their husbands with the same love and respect they are to show to others in the Christian community. This is a uniquely difficult task within any marriage, as a woman married to a partner sees them from an up-close-and-personal perspective. They know the ins and outs of their partner, the things they do wrong repeatedly, the mistakes they make, and the way that such changes family life. Yet herein lies the most powerful testimonial challenge of any marriage, and for any marriage partner: learning the ins and outs of *agape* love, above and beyond *eros*, which is more a sexual attraction or connection. Marriage is about more than just sex but is about the building up of the love of God within a family, and proving that such is possible.

On the inverse, husbands are expected to exemplify the character of Christ in their marriages, which is an act of submission, even though it's not called that. If we consider the character of Christ in a marriage, then the following is true:

- Men are not to regard themselves as superior to their wives but treat them in equality.

- Husbands are to consider the needs, wants, feelings, thoughts, and perspectives of their wives, and not only think about themselves. This is love.

- Love is not the imposition of abuse, of lording of power, or the restriction or observation of social codes.

- Marriage is not supposed to be about vows, politics, and social bondage, but about the relationship between Christ and the church.

In marriage, we are supposed to see a balance of ideals between male and female, just as we see between Christ and the church. Just as Christ has His purposes, so too does the church. It's not a competition, it doesn't take anything away from the church to acknowledge Christ's purpose, and it doesn't take anything away from Christ to celebrate the church's purpose. The same is true in terms of marriage. It doesn't take anything away from a husband to celebrate a wife, a wife to celebrate her husband, or spouses to mutually recognize and celebrate one another. It's not a competition; it is two agreeing to walk together, unto the end of spiritual representation and personal development.

A great mystery

The most powerful part of Ephesians 5 is often overlooked, in favor of realities rather than shadows. That is the revelation of the more spiritual side of marriage, found later in the chapter:

FOR WE ARE MEMBERS OF HIS BODY. "FOR THIS REASON A MAN WILL LEAVE HIS FATHER AND MOTHER AND BE UNITED TO HIS WIFE, AND THE TWO WILL BECOME ONE FLESH." THIS IS A PROFOUND MYSTERY— BUT I AM TALKING ABOUT CHRIST AND THE CHURCH. (Ephesians 5:30-32)

MYSTERY[8]
- *MUSTÉRION*: A MYSTERY OR SECRET DOCTRINE
- ORIGINAL WORD: ΜΥΣΤΉΡΙΟΝ, ΟΥ, ΤΌ
- PART OF SPEECH: NOUN, NEUTER
- TRANSLITERATION: MUSTÉRION
- PHONETIC SPELLING: (MOOS-TAY'-REE-ON)
- SHORT DEFINITION: ANYTHING HIDDEN, A MYSTERY
- DEFINITION: A MYSTERY, SECRET, OF WHICH INITIATION IS NECESSARY; IN THE NT: THE COUNSELS OF GOD, ONCE HIDDEN BUT NOW REVEALED IN THE GOSPEL OR SOME FACT THEREOF; THE CHRISTIAN REVELATION GENERALLY; PARTICULAR TRUTHS OR DETAILS OF THE CHRISTIAN REVELATION.

Ephesians 5 was never intended to become a marital code for women's conferences, an endless source of contention between men and women, or something to put wives in their place. What it was intended to do was teach us about Christ and the church and use marriage as an illustration for that. The greatest possible mystery of our faith, beyond the resurrection and Second Coming, is the fact that we are members of Christ's body, yet Christ and the church still have a spiritual union, a relationship that is unbound by time and space. Christ and the church are one; they have come together in the mystical union that can be understood to be marriage.

Christ's relationship to the church is a mystery because it doesn't make sense in the natural. Christ has brought us to a place where all of us, male and female, are a part of a feminine entity, one that we do not rightly deserve place therein, in an intimacy with the divine that was never permissible before in history. Through the work of the feminine church, we are held in power, in trust, in spiritual connection, to Christ and one another. We are not just a part of His bride, but as His bride, we are also part of His very body. As the church is one with Him, so, too, are we one with Him. What is impossible in the natural is most possible with the spiritual, and through our place in the church and our union with Christ, we experience that with Him, all things are truly possible (Matthew 19:26, Mark 10:27).

The union of Christ and the church is not something we can easily understand, but it does dispel the notion that the woman or any feminine impression is unsuited for spiritual things. On the contrary, if Eve was created to help Adam, then the church was created to help Christ. Women too, therefore, as types of the church, are here to help in Christ's work and mission. We are appointed for this purpose, for this assistance, for this time and hour, as we represent the beautiful and glorious church through our very selves.

The "Elect Lady"

If you are familiar with the letters of the New Testament, you have probably read 1, 2, and 3 John. Have you ever noticed who the book of 2 John is addressed to?

THE ELDER UNTO THE ELECT LADY AND HER CHILDREN, WHOM I LOVE IN THE TRUTH; AND NOT I ONLY, BUT ALSO ALL THEY THAT HAVE KNOWN THE TRUTH; FOR THE TRUTH'S SAKE, WHICH DWELLETH IN US, AND SHALL BE WITH US FOR EVER. GRACE BE WITH YOU, MERCY, AND PEACE, FROM GOD THE FATHER, AND FROM THE LORD JESUS CHRIST, THE SON OF THE FATHER, IN TRUTH AND LOVE. I REJOICED GREATLY THAT I FOUND OF THY CHILDREN WALKING IN TRUTH, AS WE HAVE RECEIVED A COMMANDMENT FROM THE FATHER. AND NOW I BESEECH THEE, LADY, NOT AS THOUGH I WROTE A NEW COMMANDMENT UNTO THEE, BUT THAT WHICH WE HAD FROM THE BEGINNING, THAT WE LOVE ONE ANOTHER. (2 John 1-5, KJV)

2 John is addressed to a specific woman, identified as the "Elect

Lady." There are many controversies over just who she was, but there are a few theories that stand out, of particular relevance to the theological examinations at hand. The theories are as follows:

- A literal woman, named Cyria, who might have held authority in the early church, perhaps as a congregational pastor.

- A specific congregation within the church.

- The literal universal church, herself.

ELECT LADY[9]
- *KURIA*: A LADY
- ORIGINAL WORD: ΚΥΡΊΑ, ΑΣ, ἡ
- PART OF SPEECH: NOUN, FEMININE
- TRANSLITERATION: KURIA
- PHONETIC SPELLING: (KOO-REE'-AH)
- SHORT DEFINITION: A LADY
- DEFINITION: A LADY; FEMININE OF *KURIOS*, WHICH IS, LORD, MASTER

The name "Cyria" literally means "Lady" or the female equivalent of the word "lord," indicating a certain level of authority or social status within the addressee. It is my personal belief that John is addressing the church, as a whole, because of the terminology implied within the definition of Cyria. As we have already examined earlier in this chapter, the concept of a human being filling the role of a lording authority creates the question of headship within the church, and has the potential to destroy the equality of the saints, found and inherent therein. The position is of a ruler, a governor, or a female lord, one who, as is married to Christ, has that authority over us, and the female entity with that type of leadership would be the greater body, the identity of the church universal. By referring to the church as "lord," the Apostle John is not questioning the Lordship of Christ, but acknowledging the spiritual relationship between Christ and the church, with the church as the spouse, the bride, of Christ. She is not just there by accident, but specifically chosen, specifically appointed, and there in prominence – not just any lady, but an Elect Lady – for the purpose of spiritual work in this world.

The Apostle John goes on to also mention the children of the Elect Lady, or those who are in the faith, a part of the church, participating in their spiritual development as the children of God. Traditionally speaking, caretaking for homes and families and guiding, gathering, and handling children was seen as a female position, so it makes perfect sense the Apostle John would see the work of the church as feminine, and define it in terms of leadership authority. While the people were certainly not literal children, it was the work of the lord, of the church, to keep, guide, and lead these children in this world. That is part of what makes the work so uniquely special, and the address as so important: the church is given the authority on this earth to care for, lead, and tend to the people of God. It is a feminine entity, a female lord, that is left in charge of God's people. This levels the playing field for each and every member of the body, as none of us are more important than another, and understanding such keeps us in check, in command, for the greater good of God's work. Mutual submission from one believer to another is not abstract, because this side of haven, the authority we are given, does not check us as superior, or greater, than to that of the Elect Lady, the church.

It makes the most sense that the Elect Lady is the church, but even if this letter was written to a specific woman who held authority in a community, we can still learn certain things of great importance: women, and female imagery, are important. Women can hold authority, because they all stand as a representation of what the church is, and what the church is to be. Reading these passages and recognizing the evident authority of the church in the New Testament, we cannot easily ignore the fact that the church is female, with full authority. Whenever we fail to elevate our women and recognize them as holding place and position, we are rejecting the authority of the female church. It does not make sense to believe the church is female, and then believe women can't hold position or authority in church. Those who continue to have issues with women in authority ultimately have issues with the church, who is their female leader on earth, and those issues continue to divide the church, because it hits at the heart of the church's positional authority to lead and guide her children.

The two walk together

One of the greatest challenges we face in this world is having the maturity and discipline to walk with others. Human nature is decidedly selfish. In this world, we all know how to put ourselves, our intentions, and our desires first. We like to do for ourselves, and we like others to do for us, as well. This is the very foundation, in many instances, of survival: making sure we have what we need, overlooking and ignoring the concerns and needs of others, and putting ourselves as the primary concern.

The problem with this thinking is that it isn't spiritual; it translates to being insanely selfish. It is, however, the very foundation that our societies and much of our marital interactions are founded upon. We think that we should get married and have children to satisfy our needs, and to satisfy what we feel we need to accomplish, rather than doing what needs to be done to create and experience the stabilities and spiritualities of marriage and family life. The more we approach life like this, the more we approach such upon the church, and create earthly, human problems in an entity that is designed to be spiritual, with a spiritual purpose.

TWO PEOPLE WILL NOT [CAN TWO...?] WALK TOGETHER UNLESS THEY HAVE AGREED TO DO SO [*OR* TO MEET; *OR* ON THE DIRECTION]. (Amos 3:3)

The church walks with Christ in full agreement. They are there for the same purpose, the same goals, and the same ideals. It is not the church that disagrees with Christ, but the people who come to it, burdened and laden down with earthly concepts and embitterments against one another. Here, in this place, God has given us the ability to find refuge in our feminine leader, our spiritual promise, the church. As the church walks with Christ, so we too must find our footing, our place in this feminine, spiritual entity, to walk with Him, ourselves. The sooner we learn how to do this, the better off we will be, and the better able we will be to grow into the full stature of Christ, no longer tossed by the waves, but learning from our Savior and Lord, and His

Bride, the church, our teacher, and our spiritual mother, our Elect Lady and lord, while we live this side of heaven.

Andronicus, Athanasisus of Christianoupolis, and St. Junia (Unknown)

CHAPTER NINE
Female Authority in the Early Church

I ASK [URGE; ENCOURAGE; EXHORT] EUODIA AND SYNTYCHE
[TWO WOMEN IN THE PHILIPPIAN CONGREGATION] TO AGREE IN THE LORD.
AND I ASK YOU, MY FAITHFUL [TRUE; GENUINE] FRIEND [COMPANION; YOKE-PARTNER;
POSSIBLY A PROPER NAME: SYZYGOS], TO HELP THESE WOMEN. THEY SERVED
[STRUGGLED; LABORED] WITH ME IN TELLING THE GOOD NEWS [GOSPEL],
TOGETHER WITH CLEMENT AND OTHERS WHO WORKED WITH ME
[THE REST OF MY COWORKERS], WHOSE NAMES ARE WRITTEN IN THE BOOK OF LIFE
[REV. 3:5; 21:27].
(PHILIPPIANS 4:2-3)

THE principle of authority, or the idea that a certain individual, group, or power has been endowed with the ability to lead and govern, is one that has guided the people of God throughout the ages. Most believers acknowledge that authority, in some form or another, does exist, even if they don't quite agree on how it manifests in subsequent eras or modern eras to come. The most controversial aspect of authority remains, who has it – and who is entitled to have it?

Much of church history has answered the question of authority quite negatively when it comes to women and the exercise of leadership roles in the church. This remains, unfortunately, not just an historical action or issue. While many younger women often argue the year we are in as a criticism of those who do not recognize female church authority, it's safe to say that the year we are in does not seem to be a valid argument when it comes to this most controversial issue. At the writing of this book, the statistics on female leadership in the church remain underwhelming and staggering:[1,2,3]

- Around 10% of American congregations have a female as their senior or only ordained leader. Among mainline Protestants, the percentage is 24%, and among those defined as Evangelicals, the number is only 9%.

- Only two major mainline Protestant denominations have women in their top leadership positions.

- In the extremely liberal Unitarian Universalist Association, women have consistently run for denomination president three years in a row, and no woman has ever won.

- Even though 60% of American Catholics support the ordination of women, the all-male church authorities have made it clear such will never happen.

- The approximate statistics on specific percentages of women in Protestantism within the United Kingdom include: 20% Anglican, 14% Baptist, 3% independent churches, 14% New churches, 17% Pentecostal churches, 38% for smaller denominations, and 40% for the Methodist church.

Through many years visiting churches and working in different denominational settings, I can verify the statistics as accurate. If I am honest, I might even say I've seen more statistics that show lower numbers than the average percentages. It is more disheartening to realize that many denominations that claim to be in favor of female leadership have a casual way of still giving the most solid-performing, largest churches to men, and sending women to pastor, lead, or otherwise handle problem congregations, dying congregations, or regions that are somehow implied to be a waste of male abilities and resources. No matter what the denomination, no matter their claims, and no matter how liberal or forward-thinking a group may claim to be when it comes to women's ordination, women are still regarded as being of lesser value than the men, and the reality is that the statistics on such matters speak for themselves. When it comes to women and authority, there remains many traditional concepts, whether spoken or unspoken, that women are downright unqualified, unable, or not as competent to handle leadership as men.

These realities are evidence in contrast to recognized female authorities (that are not considered feminine, but we shall discuss this further) and defiance when we look over the history of the first-century church. It also assumes the history of Christianity to be consistently anti-female and pro-male, when reality isn't quite this simple. Throughout the history of Christianity, concepts of gender have varied, changed, morphed, returned, and changed again, only to move down to the present day. Concepts on female authority, being female, and being a woman in leadership have always varied, and understanding this is essential, as we delve more deeply into the world of female authority, especially in the early church.

Feminism and Christianity: an essential connection

One of the main points we have examined throughout history is the context of women within society. General society, in every era of history, has always been unfair to women, and has long treated women as if they are irrelevant or inferior. If we look at the experience of women who lived under the Mosaic Law, they were not consistently given the right to make their own decisions or to handle their own relationship with God.

> *VOW*[A]
> - *NEDER*: A VOW
> - ORIGINAL WORD: נֶדֶר
> - PART OF SPEECH: NOUN MASCULINE
> - TRANSLITERATION: NEDER
> - PHONETIC SPELLING: (NEH'-DER)
> - SHORT DEFINITION: VOW

MOSES SAID TO THE HEADS OF THE TRIBES OF ISRAEL: "THIS IS WHAT THE LORD COMMANDS: WHEN A MAN MAKES A VOW TO THE LORD OR TAKES AN OATH TO OBLIGATE HIMSELF BY A PLEDGE, HE MUST NOT BREAK HIS WORD BUT MUST DO EVERYTHING HE SAID.

"WHEN A YOUNG WOMAN STILL LIVING IN HER FATHER'S HOUSEHOLD MAKES A VOW TO THE LORD OR OBLIGATES HERSELF BY A PLEDGE AND HER FATHER HEARS ABOUT HER VOW OR PLEDGE BUT SAYS NOTHING TO HER, THEN ALL HER VOWS AND EVERY PLEDGE BY WHICH SHE OBLIGATED HERSELF WILL STAND. BUT IF HER FATHER FORBIDS HER WHEN HE HEARS ABOUT IT, NONE OF HER VOWS OR THE PLEDGES BY

WHICH SHE OBLIGATED HERSELF WILL STAND; THE LORD WILL RELEASE HER BECAUSE HER FATHER HAS FORBIDDEN HER.

"IF SHE MARRIES AFTER SHE MAKES A VOW OR AFTER HER LIPS UTTER A RASH PROMISE BY WHICH SHE OBLIGATES HERSELF AND HER HUSBAND HEARS ABOUT IT BUT SAYS NOTHING TO HER, THEN HER VOWS OR THE PLEDGES BY WHICH SHE OBLIGATED HERSELF WILL STAND. BUT IF HER HUSBAND FORBIDS HER WHEN HE HEARS ABOUT IT, HE NULLIFIES THE VOW THAT OBLIGATES HER OR THE RASH PROMISE BY WHICH SHE OBLIGATES HERSELF, AND THE LORD WILL RELEASE HER.

"ANY VOW OR OBLIGATION TAKEN BY A WIDOW OR DIVORCED WOMAN WILL BE BINDING ON HER.

"IF A WOMAN LIVING WITH HER HUSBAND MAKES A VOW OR OBLIGATES HERSELF BY A PLEDGE UNDER OATH AND HER HUSBAND HEARS ABOUT IT BUT SAYS NOTHING TO HER AND DOES NOT FORBID HER, THEN ALL HER VOWS OR THE PLEDGES BY WHICH SHE OBLIGATED HERSELF WILL STAND. BUT IF HER HUSBAND NULLIFIES THEM WHEN HE HEARS ABOUT THEM, THEN NONE OF THE VOWS OR PLEDGES THAT CAME FROM HER LIPS WILL STAND. HER HUSBAND HAS NULLIFIED THEM, AND THE LORD WILL RELEASE HER. HER HUSBAND MAY CONFIRM OR NULLIFY ANY VOW SHE MAKES OR ANY SWORN PLEDGE TO DENY HERSELF. BUT IF HER HUSBAND SAYS NOTHING TO HER ABOUT IT FROM DAY TO DAY, THEN HE CONFIRMS ALL HER VOWS OR THE PLEDGES BINDING ON HER. HE CONFIRMS THEM BY SAYING NOTHING TO HER WHEN HE HEARS ABOUT THEM. IF, HOWEVER, HE NULLIFIES THEM SOME TIME AFTER HE HEARS ABOUT THEM, THEN HE MUST BEAR THE CONSEQUENCES OF HER WRONGDOING."

THESE ARE THE REGULATIONS THE LORD GAVE MOSES CONCERNING RELATIONSHIPS BETWEEN A MAN AND HIS WIFE, AND BETWEEN A FATHER AND HIS YOUNG DAUGHTER STILL LIVING AT HOME. (NUMBERS 30:1-16, NIV)

AND SHE MADE A VOW, SAYING, "LORD ALMIGHTY, IF YOU WILL ONLY LOOK ON YOUR SERVANT'S MISERY AND REMEMBER ME, AND NOT FORGET YOUR SERVANT BUT GIVE HER A SON, THEN I WILL GIVE HIM TO THE LORD FOR ALL THE DAYS OF HIS LIFE, AND NO RAZOR WILL EVER BE USED ON HIS HEAD." (1 Samuel 1:11, NIV)

There are a few reasons why these regulations might have existed. Perhaps the most relevant reason why we see such guidelines had to do with the way that God reached out to people within their context and within their culture. Many of these ideals were long-held by various tribes prior to Mosaic Law. In addition, the religious activities, such as vows, were often done by women on their own, rather than making a formal pledge in the temple or one that is done in the presence of a community. As a result, women were not always under formal supervision. Given vows were made for many reasons, the context of a woman making a vow was not seen, nor regarded, in the same way as it was when a man made a vow. The vow a woman made had the potential to threaten home or family life and might easily have upset spheres seen as belonging to women and women's work, so for the sake of continuing cultural identity, the power of the vow went not just to a woman, but to her father or husband, as well. We don't know how often a father or a husband nullified vows made by daughters or wives, or what exactly the context of such was, but to keep the continuity of patriarchy and familial male authority within families, the tribal religion that the ancient Hebrews formed continued to uphold such belief systems within their ranks, whether fair or not. Doing such gave women a certain level of independence, and to keep whatever vows were made within the context of tribal culture, men were given the authority to nullify such vows.

Fathers and husbands only had the right to nullify a vow once they discovered it had been made, which meant a woman did not have to seek out permission to make a vow, to give any notification that she was going to make a vow, and they were not required to tell anyone about the vow, or share that such had been done. It's more than likely that many vows existed throughout Old Testament times without their discovery on the part of a close male relative. While we read the passage and only hear about the power given to the men in the situation, we don't easily read the authority and power given to the women. It seems like the rules were unfair (and maybe to a certain extent they were) but there was much promised to women, even if situations were not always as equal as they might have hoped.

The equity of decision making changed somewhat in Christianity, especially with the advance of spiritual identities and thoughts in the first century. For the first time in her life, a woman was given the ability to make her own decisions in defense of her faith, to make her own vows to God – and they were expected to stick, even in a society that continued to hope her vow did not matter – and women had the spiritual freedom to decide they did not want to marry, they did not want to engage in a life with a man who was not a believer, and they wanted to uphold their own faith. Come hell or high water (or sometimes worse), many of the early female martyrs of the faith encountered both, for no other reason than they decided they would obey God, rather than men, and refuse to submit their lives to the auspices of someone else's guiding.

Even though we do see this spiritual uplifting in the early church, the conflicts between women and society were not as simply resolved as saying we moved from the Old Testament to the New Testament. There is a fundamental understanding within most cultures that either state outright or imply that women do not, or cannot belong to God first. They are thought of as being the property of fathers, husbands, or other men in their lives, and that such creates a conflict as to who a woman is for or what a woman can do. The question of female authority finds itself right here: who does she belong to? If a woman is thought of as belonging to God first, then that means any man in her life must submit to that spiritual order, rather than seeing her as belonging exclusively to himself. This causes conflict, a deep upheaval in the perception of women and their identities, and the conflict has spilled over, through subsequent generations, to general ideas and interactions between men and women throughout Christian history.

The concept that men and women hold an equal status before God might be controversial, but it does originate within Christianity. Feminism might not have been a viable word in the first centuries of Christianity, but it doesn't mean it did not exist. It did, and its existence manifested in three major forms: celibacy and chastity, gender inclusivity, and gender non-binary views, all of which greatly impacted the way that women believed, made decisions, and empowered themselves in the early centuries of Christianity.

Celibacy and chastity

History has always expected women to marry and have families.

That is a part of the cultural norm for women, and was such a natural assumption, the words for "wife" and "woman" were often one word in ancient languages. Making choices about one's own future was not an option for women, and everything about a woman's life, from her choice of mate to her sexual identity, to her reproductive decisions, were already made for her, by a male in her life. Sex and sexuality were a part of this equation, and were done without any choice, any say, or any concept of her own being.

Since marriage was just a natural expectation for women, attitudes about sex and sexuality were intimately attached to a lack of personal choice, a sort of submissive expectation associated with the world. Whether this is right or wrong is not of consequence for what we are talking about, but there was good reason for the women of early Christianity to believe marriage and family would impede their spiritual relationship with God. Being married was seen as a thing of the world, and if they wanted to be a part of something bigger, something eternal, such was seen as a conflict for many of them.

If we are to be honest with ourselves, the way we often handle sex and sexuality in our cultures does present a spiritual conflict, because the two are used as an exchange, instead of as a mutual desire of intimacy. Sex is treated as a reward: If you buy me what I want, if you do what I want, if you marry me the way I want, if I get from you what I want, we can have sex. As part of this bigger game, these messages cause sexual breakdown in relationships, in church as much as out of it. Virginity isn't a "gift" to be handed to the highest or best bidder, we aren't permanently "damaged goods" or "done" because someone has had sex, and having sex or refraining from it does not guarantee a relationship's successes or losses. Too much misunderstanding and too much emphasis on these matters have placed sex and sexuality front and center, as battles for control.

Several women of the early church made a decision: they were going to abandon these worldly ideals and refuse marriage and sex, all together. This might sound extreme, but given their cultural barriers, doing so was the simplest way for them to achieve their spiritual goals; by pursuing exclusively spiritual things. We might not think their perspective was always very balanced, but the point wasn't the specifics of the decision; it was that it was their decision, and they were fully well prepared to uphold that decision, no matter what they faced in their lives.

The decision to refuse marriage and sex, thus refusing to continue a natural lineage, was seen not just as a spiritual decision, but as personal and political ones, as well. By refusing marriage, the women were refusing any association with social submission associated with control, and seeking spiritual liberation, which was associated with freedom. They were not subordinate, but equal in Christ.

Gender inclusivity

Perhaps the most important point of gender inclusion relates to the commendation of women for their service and leadership in the church. Reflecting on the histories and stories of Old Testament women and making a point to recognize women, alongside men for spiritual service, uplifts women. The fact that it is done by the most key figures of the early church makes it that much more amazing, and doing such was no accident. It was the responsibility of these early leaders to clarify the purpose and intent, and they set out to see to it that female leaders were not regarded as less than their male counterparts. In the writings of Paul, the following women are commended, greeted, or mentioned:

- **Phoebe** (Romans 16:1)
- **Priscilla** (Romans 16:3, 1 Corinthians 16:19, 2 Timothy 4:19)
- **Mary** (Romans 16:6)
- **Junia** (Romans 16:7)
- **Tryphena** (Romans 16:12)
- **Tryphosa** (Romans 16:12)
- **Persis** (Romans 16:12)
- **Rufus' mother** (Romans 16:13)
- **Julia** (Romans 16:14)
- **Neresus' Sister** (Romans 16:15)
- **Chloe** (1 Corinthians 1:11)
- **Euodia** (Philippians 4:2)
- **Syntyche** (Philippians 4:2)
- **The women who helped him in the Gospel** (Philippians 4:3)

- **Nympha** (Colossians 4:15)
- **Eunice** (2 Timothy 1:5)
- **Lois** (2 Timothy 1:5)

The role of women in the church is not of as much debate if we understand these passages within a context that isn't hard to understand, nor is it anything that requires great study. These were women of note in their congregations, many of whom are clearly identified as holding positions of authority rather than just as lay members and were commended for the excellent job they were doing. Beyond leadership, this also shows deliberate inclusion of women in the process of church experience and operation. Women were not forced behind a veil or to make their vows in secret but were allowed to stand out loud and in public, both in belief and in service to their Savior. They were included, not excluded, from public spiritual life. This inclusion was despite limited language that referred to mixed groups and audiences by male references (brothers, sons, etc.), a society that seldom received women at all, let alone in any sort of professional or official capacity, and that there were probably many who took issue with the work of women in their respective regions.

Gender non-binary views in early Christianity

Some of the concepts we have about women in terms of their faith and femininity are relatively new in terms of Christian history. While the expectation that women should be married and have families is not new, some of the attitudes we have about women and their dress, attire, emphasis on length of hair or skirts, and concepts about just what is deemed as feminine social behavior or interaction are based in modern-day issues and social constructs. Much of what we understand to be "feminine" exists to deny modern waves of feminism, cultural inclusion, and gender identity. In other words, today being female is designed to counteract what is considered male or somehow outside of traditional gender constructs. Being feminine is deemed as more of what it's not rather than what it is, and the concepts that surround much of this thinking has found a happy home among churchgoers who fear changing times and morals. This response to changing times and ideals is interesting, especially when we note that much of what we define as "feminine" from a Biblical perspective was not considered in years prior.

This becomes especially true in light of the realization that for many centuries of the early church (and in some communities to this day), the expectation of becoming one in the church meant adopting a gender non-binary understanding of life and living. Along with celibacy and chastity, abandoning wealth, and creating environments free from social and societal temptations, we see men and women who desired to pursue the spiritual realm this side of heaven, free from every identity, even that of the restrictions of gender.

The monastic movement began somewhere in the third century with a group of men known as the "Desert Fathers." They were sincere believers who desired to discover a way of living around spiritual asceticism, denying different physiological or psychological desires so they could come to greater spiritual awareness in their own lives. The monastic communities tend to live either alone or with a small community of like-minded believers, practicing extreme forms of self-denial (for example, periods of fasting far longer than normal believers might pursue), long pursuits of prayer, celibacy, the pursuit of spiritual perfection, scholarship and education, and union with the divine. It is believed that through such intense practices, an individual can overcome the selfish and self-existing barriers that keep them from spiritual things and achieve a spiritual unity with God that is otherwise impossible.[5]

Celibacy, living with other believers with the same goals, and focusing on spiritual union meant the men and women who chose to join the monastic movement did so while shedding the confines of their socially recognized gender identities and expectations. Rather than just trying to discipline the flesh, it was the goal of the monastics to try and abandon their flesh, leaving it behind and elevating to a new level of understanding. Naturally, this changed the way they viewed gender, to the point where monastics almost disavowed their gender.

JESUS SAW INFANTS BEING SUCKLED. HE SAID TO HIS DISCIPLES, "THESE INFANTS BEING SUCKLED ARE LIKE THOSE WHO ENTER THE KINGDOM."

THEY SAID TO HIM, "SHALL WE THEN, AS CHILDREN, ENTER THE KINGDOM?"

JESUS SAID TO THEM, "WHEN YOU MAKE THE TWO ONE, AND WHEN YOU MAKE THE INSIDE LIKE THE OUTSIDE AND THE OUTSIDE LIKE THE INSIDE, AND THE ABOVE LIKE THE BELOW, AND WHEN YOU MAKE THE MALE AND THE FEMALE ONE AND THE SAME, SO THAT THE MALE NOT BE MALE NOR THE FEMALE; AND WHEN YOU FASHION EYES IN THE PLACE OF AN EYE, AND A HAND IN PLACE OF A HAND, AND A FOOT IN PLACE OF A FOOT, AND A LIKENESS IN PLACE OF A LIKENESS; THEN WILL YOU ENTER THE KINGDOM." (The Gospel of Thomas, Verse 22)[6]

SIMON PETER SAID TO HIM, "LET MARY LEAVE US, FOR WOMEN ARE NOT WORTHY OF LIFE."

JESUS SAID, "I MYSELF SHALL LEAD HER IN ORDER TO MAKE HER MALE, SO THAT SHE TOO MAY BECOME A LIVING SPIRIT RESEMBLING YOU MALES. FOR EVERY WOMAN WHO WILL MAKE HERSELF MALE WILL ENTER THE KINGDOM OF HEAVEN." (The Gospel of Thomas, Verse 114)[7]

While the Gospel of Thomas remains controversial in the role of Scripture and the early church, one thing it absolutely proves is the way that early eastern Christians often thought. These passages sound horrifying by modern standards, but eastern Christians of the first centuries of Christianity heard them differently. The words echoed a literal unity, one where the male and female became something else, something almost androgynous. This reflected in their dress, their ways of life, and the standards that both men and women would follow the same polity in their rule, with no exceptions.

This gender androgyny was in contrast with the Early Church Fathers, a group of men who were just an assorted group of men who made their views very vocal and very known, often writing or lecturing. They were not all clergy, and some held very scathing views as regarded women:

- "Men should not sit and listen to a woman...even if she says admirable things, or even saintly things, that is of little consequence, since it came from the mouth of a woman." (Origen, *Fragments on 1 Corinthians*)[8]

- "And do you not know that you are (each) an Eve? The sentence of God on this sex of yours lives in this age: the guilt must of necessity live too. You are the devil's gateway: you are the unsealed of that (forbidden) tree: you are the first deserter of the divine law: you are she who persuaded him whom the devil was not valiant enough to attack. You destroyed so easily God's image, man. On account of your desert—that is, death—even the Son of God had to die. And do you think about adorning yourself over and above your tunics of skins?" (Tertullian, *On the Apparel of Women*)[9]

- "...the [female] sex is weak and fickle..." (John Chrysostom, *Homily 9 on First Timothy*)[10]

- "I don't see what sort of help woman was created to provide man with, if one excludes procreation. If woman is not given to man for help in bearing children, for what help could she be? To till the earth together? If help were needed for that, man would have been a better help for man. The same goes for comfort in solitude. How much more pleasure is it for life and conversation when two friends live together than when a man and a woman cohabitate?" (Augustine of Hippo, *The Literal Meaning of Genesis*)[11]

- "...the woman together with her own husband is the image of God, so that that whole substance may be one image; but when she is referred separately to her quality of help-meet, which regards the woman herself alone, then she is not the image of God; but as regards the man alone, he is the image of God as fully and completely as when the woman too is joined with him in one." (Augustine of Hippo, *On the Trinity*)[12]

In this light, it is no wonder that exploring the realms of the gender non-binary in favor of elevating oneself to spiritual levels was most desirable to the women of this era.

Women teaching women

Most of us know about those in the very vocal camp against women's ordination, teaching, preaching, and standing in any sort of authority. It seems like they are everywhere, all the time, trying to make their position known and reverse historical strides women have made in ministry. Much like those who are against women voting, abortion, and other women's issues, the odds of these issues heading in reverse is unlikely, even if they gain a substantial number of followers who support their views. There is a less extreme group, however, that isn't quite as vocal. Since they do side more with those against any form of leadership for women, their positions often assimilate into those who are against any form of leadership. But this is not their position, in its entirety, to be lost. Their position is that it is fine for women to teach other women, it is fine for women to teach children, but it is not fine for women to teach men, or to hold authority over them.

While flawed as a full, substantial argument, the belief that women should teach women is Biblical, even though the requirement for such is not exclusive to women.

DO NOT SPEAK ANGRILY TO [REBUKE; SPEAK HARSHLY TO] AN OLDER MAN, BUT PLEAD WITH [EXHORT; ENCOURAGE] HIM AS IF HE WERE YOUR FATHER. TREAT YOUNGER MEN LIKE BROTHERS, OLDER WOMEN LIKE MOTHERS, AND YOUNGER WOMEN LIKE SISTERS. ALWAYS TREAT THEM IN A PURE WAY [...WITH COMPLETE PURITY]. (1 Timothy 5:1-2)

IN THE SAME WAY, TEACH OLDER WOMEN TO BE HOLY [REVERENT] IN THEIR BEHAVIOR, NOT SPEAKING AGAINST [SLANDERING; GOSSIPING ABOUT] OTHERS OR ENSLAVED TO TOO MUCH WINE [EXCESSIVE DRINKING], BUT TEACHING WHAT IS GOOD. THEN THEY CAN TEACH [TRAIN] THE YOUNG WOMEN TO LOVE THEIR HUSBANDS, TO LOVE THEIR CHILDREN, TO BE WISE [SENSIBLE; SELF-CONTROLLED] AND PURE, TO BE GOOD WORKERS AT HOME [DEVOTED TO HOME LIFE], TO BE KIND, AND TO YIELD [SUBMIT] TO THEIR HUSBANDS. THEN NO ONE WILL BE ABLE TO CRITICIZE [DISCREDIT; MALIGN; BLASPHEME] THE TEACHING GOD GAVE US [WORD OF GOD]. (Titus 2:3-5)

What these passages are actually referring to is the role of "female elders," or women who served in the role of an elder.

> **OLDER WOMEN**[13]
> - *PRESBUTIS:* AN AGED WOMAN
> - ORIGINAL WORD: ΠΡΕΣΒῦΤΙΣ, ΙΔΟΣ, ἡ
> - PART OF SPEECH: NOUN, FEMININE
> - TRANSLITERATION: PRESBUTIS
> - PHONETIC SPELLING: (PRES-BOO'-TIS)
> - SHORT DEFINITION: AN OLD WOMAN
> - DEFINITION: AN OLD WOMAN. RELATED TO PRESBUTEROS, "ELDER; AN ELDER OF A CHRISTIAN ASSEMBLY."

These women were in assistance to the local pastors of a church, poised and prepared for any need which might arise. The work of the elders is a transfer-over from the Old Testament role of the elders, who stood in their stead and assisted in the leadership of the general people with teaching, prayer, community needs, and general spiritual feeding.

The work of any elder, whether male or female is, according to Bible understanding, a part of the appointments, along with bishops and deacons. This means it is not a ministry calling (a work that one is called and established for permanent ministry), but an appointment, a work that one desires to do, seeing the need that exists within a community, and stepping up to handle an assignment that is needed there. While some churches incorrectly teach the role of pastor, bishop, and elder to be interchangeable and, therefore, ordain elders, it is not technically an ordained work.

This doesn't take anything away from the female elders of the New Testament, however. The fact that they were there, and that women should teach other women, is a destruction of patriarchy, all by itself. Even though elders are not an ordained position, they are a leadership role, one that is there for oversight and assistance with a congregation. If women were to be entrusted with the work of eldership, this means they were also of note, and of importance, considered trustworthy, and able and competent to serve as leaders. Whether the women were speaking only to other women, or to the younger men, as well, to provide insight, the contributions of women teaching other women form an important and essential aspect to the spiritual participation of women throughout the ages.

As we spoke of in another chapter, women were uneducated, and under the codes of Judaism that existed in New Testament times, they were prohibited from learning or studying about the law. For women to have opportunity to learn about important matters of the faith, about its context in everyday life, about love and attending to the needs at hand, and yes, even about the social system of the day (because obviously challenging such might put them in harm's way) was a radical thrust into spiritual perspectives and insights. For the first time in history, women were encouraged to be a part of their faith rather than just spectators. Not were they to just take commands, but all women of eligible age were encouraged to find a voice and help out within their respective congregations.

The Scriptures also give evidence for female deacons and overseers, proving women served in all positions of service present in New Testament Christianity:

WITH A CLEAR CONSCIENCE THEY MUST FOLLOW [HOLD ON TO] THE SECRET OF THE FAITH THAT GOD MADE KNOWN TO US [OR GOD'S REVEALED TRUTHS; THE MYSTERY OF THE FAITH; A MYSTERY BEING SOMETHING PREVIOUSLY UNKNOWN BUT NOW REVEALED BY GOD; EPH. 1:9]. TEST THEM FIRST. THEN LET THEM SERVE AS DEACONS IF YOU FIND NOTHING WRONG IN THEM [THEM BLAMELESS]. IN THE SAME WAY, WOMEN [OR WOMEN WHO ARE DEACONS; OR DEACON'S WIVES] MUST BE RESPECTED BY OTHERS [DIGNIFIED]. THEY MUST NOT SPEAK EVIL OF OTHERS [BE SLANDERERS/GOSSIPS]. THEY MUST BE SELF-CONTROLLED [SOBER] AND TRUSTWORTHY [HONEST; FAITHFUL] IN EVERYTHING. (1 Timothy 3:9-11)

I RECOMMEND [COMMEND] TO YOU OUR SISTER PHOEBE, WHO IS A HELPER [OR SERVANT; OR MINISTER; OR DEACON; 1 TIM. 3:11] IN THE CHURCH IN CENCHREA [PHOEBE MAY HAVE BEEN THE MESSENGER CARRYING THIS LETTER]. (Romans 16:1)

Even though there are many who debate the role of women in the church today based on the evidence of women in the New Testament, there is no question that women held leadership positions. This clarifies and explains more controversial passages about women required to be silent or being prohibited from holding any leadership roles, at all. Such was not the case;

there was no across-the-board prohibition on women's leadership. Rather, women were encouraged to properly learn, and be properly taught, what they were to do, and what was to be required of them, before assuming any sort of leadership role in the church. There is nothing wrong with requiring someone to learn before allowing them to assume a leadership position, either male or female. Such wasn't specific to women, but instead, included them in the process, which is a great statement of inclusion for women in Christian leadership.

Profiles of women in the early church

There are more Christian women who have made incredible strides, both in and out of the church, than is reasonable to mention in this chapter. For a look at two hundred and fifty different women who met with these criteria, check out my book, *Surrounded By So Great A Cloud of Witnesses: Women of Faith Who Revolutionized History* (Photini Press, 2018). It is from this book that I am summarizing the history of some of these great women. Here, I will provide a short sampling of a few women who held prominence in the early church, proving that women in leadership is nothing new, but something that has stood since the beginning of the New Testament church.

- **Photini, the woman at the well**: The woman at the well has been labeled and identified as all sorts of things: a harlot, a whore, and the worst kind of sinner – and woman – imaginable. This is because we have frequently divorced our Bible understanding from history, and as a result, we don't know enough about Biblical characters to properly understand them. The woman at the well was baptized as Photini, a name which means "light bearer." Jesus' longest dialogue in the Bible is with her, found in John 4. What we learn of her in John 4 is that she was a Samaritan woman, married multiple times, and now was living with a man to whom she was not married. We don't know exactly what this arrangement was with the man she was living with, as the word for "man" literally just means man, and could have meant anything from living with a male relative, to being a caregiver, to living with someone as a cohabitational arrangement. What we do know is that Photini went out and told everyone about her encounter with Jesus. Tradition takes things a step further, letting us know she converted her five sisters and two nephews, and all of them became leaders in the early church. In the eastern churches, she is known as "equal to the apostles."

- **Mary <u>Magdalene</u>**: Mary Magdalene is an early church figure of much mystique and mystery, largely due to myths that have perpetuated about her throughout the ages. From Pope Gregory I who was the first to claim she was a prostitute to more modern legends about her as the Priory of Sion, Mary Magdalene is one of those women we think we know but just can't wrap our heads around. We don't know much about Mary Magdalene's life, save that she was known for being from Magdala, a city, rather than a male relative's household. She appears to have been well-known and of means, but from what, we honestly don't know. Mary Magdalene is mentioned more than twelve times in the Gospels, and that is more than any names of the male disciples of Christ. She is also the only person mentioned in all four Gospel accounts of the resurrection, as the first person to witness this most important event. As the first apostle of the resurrection, she was the one who was to go and tell others about it, including the male disciples. While there is nothing to suggest that Mary Magdalene was Christ's wife, the mother of his child, or a prostitute, we can see that the role of Mary Magdalene as a church apostle was an important and recognized one, in documents such as The Gospel of Mary.

- <u>**The Four Daughters of Philip the Evangelist**</u>: Mentioned only once in Acts 21:8-9, the four daughters of Philip (Irais, Chariline, Eutychis, and Hermoine) were all unmarried virgins who operated in the prophetic. According to church tradition, the four daughters of Philip were all physicians, learned women endowed with medical knowledge. They offered their medical services free of charge as a witness to lead patients to the Lord.

They spent their lives in constant prayer and service and later became among the earliest martyrs of the church.

- **Lydia**: Lydia is mentioned in Acts 16:14-15 as the first European convert to Christianity, under the ministry of the Apostle Paul. We know she was a businesswoman who specialized in the sale of purple cloth, which was a sign of wealth and luxury in the first century. It was Lydia who offered hospitality to the Apostle Paul and his companions, and they stayed on with her, in her home, for a period of time. When she converted to Christianity, her entire household was baptized and converted as well, and she became their pastor and spiritual leader. Her home became a center of faith for European Christians, and the Apostle Paul returned later to preach and teach in her home.

- **Priscilla**: Priscilla is mentioned in Acts 18:1,18-28, Romans 16:3, 1 Corinthians 16:19, and 2 Timothy 4:19, usually in combination with her husband, Aquilla. She, along with her husband, was a companion of the Apostle Paul and a pastoral leader of the church in Corinth (the church actually met in their home). We best of Priscilla's ministry work in the education of Apollos, who was an influential Jew who needed to know more of Christ. It has been noted that when Priscilla is listed with her husband, her name is listed first. This is unusual for first century practice, and most likely denotes she had a spiritual prominence and importance in the church, over that of her husband.

- **Phoebe**: Mentioned in Romans 16:1-2, Phoebe was a woman who was a deacon or possibly a formalized minister (as the words are interchangeable) in Cenchreae, a village outside of Corinth in Greece. She was introduced to the church in Rome as the Apostle Paul's personal representative. She was commended for her outstanding service, and her work was of great note. She was to be received well, and receive any needed assistance, for she had served faithfully and well.

- **Junia**: Junia comes to us in Romans 16:7, with little fanfare and no attention anywhere else in the New Testament. Yet if you have followed any of the major Christian outlets the past few years, you have probably heard a lot about Junia, and her role as an apostle in the first century. We don't know much about her, save she is mentioned along with Andronicus, who was most likely a male relative. It is evident from her commendation in the Bible that she was acknowledged as an apostle, and church tradition also cites she was also one of the Seventy, sent out in Luke 10:1-10. This tells us that she had a long history with the church, even walking with Christ when He was present on earth. Junia has taken the forefront of patriarchal battles, as some centuries later, Junia's name was changed to Junias in a Roman Catholic push for women to accept monastic roles and subordinate positions to men. The truth resurfaced, however many years later it was, and we now know Junias was Junia, an apostle, serving in the first century, of note and renown even in her day.

- **Apphia**: Mentioned in Philemon 1:2, Apphia was an apostle, listed among the Seventy in Luke 10:1-10. Her primary work was in Colossae, her hometown. It is believed her husband was the Apostle Philemon, the one named after the Apostle Paul's letter where she is mentioned. Tradition states they held church in their house, and that they were martyred during a pagan feast while the saints were gathered in their house to pray.

- **Thecla**: Thecla is a little-known early church figure because her record is not found in the New Testament, but in The Acts of Paul and Thecla, an early church apocryphal document. She was a Christian convert, moved by the preaching and teaching of the Apostle Paul. She desired baptism and wound up baptizing herself! Her experiences with the Apostle Paul (who was her leader) brought her to her own apostolic call, and she pursued the call of the apostle in her own life. She displayed his influence and style in her own ministerial work, and even though she faced a lack of support from her family and financial difficulties, she continued to do the work and saw many miracles. She has been called a role model for young women and is hailed as "the apostle and protomartyr among women." She is also known as an "equal to the apostles" in church traditions.

- **Mariamne**: Another apostle we probably don't recognize by name, Mariamne was the sister of the Apostle Philip, and a companion in the work of both Philip and Bartholomew. She is featured in the apocryphal Acts of Philip, a writing of the early church. Mariamne was of strong faith, known for teaching, baptizing, and leading, even men. She was known as the "Apostolic Virgin," as an influential leader in conversions at Hieropolis. After the Apostle Philip died, Mariamne travelled with the Apostle Bartholomew to India. After he died, she continued in her Gospel work, proclaiming the Gospel throughout Asia minor, all by herself, as an apostle.

The power of the written word

Whenever we talk about the Bible, we probably never think of the Bible as having a gender. Yet like all other Biblical things, the Bible does, itself, have a gender. The very thing we use to subordinate women, uphold patriarchy, offend other people, act unseemly, force views on others, and say women can't do any number of things (including interpret its contents), is feminine.

SCRIPTURE[14]
- *GRAPHÉ*: A WRITING, SCRIPTURE
- ORIGINAL WORD: ΓΡΑΦΉ, ῆΣ, ἡ
- PART OF SPEECH: NOUN, FEMININE
- TRANSLITERATION: GRAPHÉ
- PHONETIC SPELLING: (GRAF-AY')
- SHORT DEFINITION: A WRITING, PASSAGE OF SCRIPTURE, THE SCRIPTURES
- DEFINITION: (A) A WRITING, (B) A PASSAGE OF SCRIPTURE; PLUR: THE SCRIPTURES.

The word for the Bible is the word "Scriptures." The Bible never refers to itself as the "Word" as we frequently call it today, because the word "word" is used in a few different contexts, mostly referring to either spiritual revelation or literal word.

GOD PROMISED THIS GOOD NEWS [GOSPEL] LONG AGO [BEFOREHAND; PREVIOUSLY] THROUGH HIS PROPHETS, AS IT IS WRITTEN IN THE HOLY SCRIPTURES. (Romans 1:2)

UNTIL I COME, CONTINUE TO READ THE SCRIPTURES TO THE PEOPLE [ATTEND/DEVOTE YOURSELF TO THE PUBLIC READING (OF SCRIPTURE)], STRENGTHEN [ENCOURAGE; EXHORT] THEM, AND TEACH THEM. (1 Timothy 4:13)

SINCE YOU WERE A CHILD [INFANT] YOU HAVE KNOWN THE HOLY SCRIPTURES [OR SACRED WRITINGS] WHICH ARE ABLE TO MAKE YOU WISE. AND THAT WISDOM LEADS TO SALVATION THROUGH FAITH IN CHRIST JESUS. ALL SCRIPTURE IS INSPIRED BY GOD [BREATHED OUT BY GOD; GOD-BREATHED] AND IS USEFUL FOR TEACHING, FOR SHOWING PEOPLE WHAT IS WRONG IN THEIR LIVES [REFUTING ERROR; REBUKING], FOR CORRECTING FAULTS, AND FOR TEACHING HOW TO LIVE RIGHT [TRAINING IN RIGHTEOUSNESS]. USING THE SCRIPTURES, [...SO THAT] THE PERSON WHO SERVES GOD [GOD'S PERSON] WILL BE CAPABLE [COMPETENT], HAVING ALL THAT IS NEEDED [FULLY EQUIPPED] TO DO EVERY GOOD WORK. (2 Timothy 3:15-17)

HE WRITES ABOUT THIS [THESE THINGS] IN ALL HIS LETTERS. SOME THINGS IN PAUL'S LETTERS ARE HARD TO UNDERSTAND, AND PEOPLE WHO ARE IGNORANT [UNTAUGHT] AND WEAK IN FAITH [UNSTABLE] EXPLAIN THESE THINGS FALSELY [TWIST/DISTORT THEM]. THEY ALSO FALSELY EXPLAIN [TWIST; DISTORT] THE OTHER SCRIPTURES, BUT THEY ARE DESTROYING THEMSELVES BY DOING THIS [OR WHICH WILL LEAD TO THEIR DESTRUCTION]. (2 Peter 3:16)

This is not to say that the Bible is not God's word, or that God did not inspire the Bible. Nor is it to say that the Scriptures are not a form of divine revelation, or that they do not classify as spiritual "word." What it does mean is that the word for the Bible, the Scriptures, is specifically categorized with its own label and its own identity, within the deposit of revelation God has entrusted through it.

The Scriptures have a long and controversial history, and it is not surprising to say that throughout the history of Christianity, the Bible has taken some pretty complicated hits in terms of its authority and the relevancy of it within the faith. Many of the more traditional churches, including Roman Catholicism and Orthodoxy, place tradition on an equal par with the Scriptures, often nullifying them or controlling how they were understood from a cultural perspective. Treated much like women have always been treated by hostile societies and angry men, she has been misused, abused, abandoned, modified, and treated with a general sense of disrespect.

Yet seeing the relevance of the Scriptures as a feminine entity tie into the respect for the work and presence of women in the early church. Whether such a feminine identity to the word of God was deliberate or accidental, the Scriptures aren't just a general rulebook for good living or a self-help novel. They are the record of our faith, of the experiences our ancestors had with God and the revelation of God to them. They are the very foundation of the authority of our faith, of the realization that God reached out to those of the past, and thus can transform our lives, and the lives of those who receive them, for spiritual empowerment.

The Bible is feminine in identity for one simple reason: it is a book about relationships, social in nature, and all about various interactions, one to another. The need for relationship, connection, and social interaction are all associated with female entity, and the record of the Scriptures connects us to God, to others, to history, and to ourselves, all through the association of spiritual family and the lineage of life. It is this life-giving Word, this spiritual revelation with the power to give life, that maintains its uniquely feminine identity, here to convey an eternal message of life, even in the face of everything that human beings do that is the opposite of life. The Scriptures bring us hope; they bring us truth; they bring us newness of faith, even as we continue to falter, time and time again.

It is also feminine because if we believe the Scriptures to be inspired by God through the Holy Spirit, that means the ancients would have understood the Scriptures to be penned behind-the-scenes by a feminine source. Reflecting that life-giving power, that remains current and eternal from age to age, reflecting the newness and the power to start again, be born again, no matter what time you read – and receive – the life-giving word.

Grace, grace, God's grace

I know I have known a woman or girl or two named Grace in my day, but it never occurred to me that grace is actually of feminine identity in its word origin. It is, and as one of the most powerful concepts present in Christianity, one of the hardest ones to explain and describe, which might be part of why it presents itself as feminine.

BUT GOD'S FREE GIFT [THE GIFT] IS NOT LIKE ADAM'S SIN [VIOLATION; TRANSGRESSION]. [FOR IF] MANY PEOPLE DIED BECAUSE OF THE SIN [VIOLATION; TRANSGRESSION] OF THAT ONE MAN. BUT THE GRACE FROM GOD WAS MUCH GREATER, SINCE MANY PEOPLE RECEIVED GOD'S GIFT OF LIFE [...HOW MUCH MORE DID GOD'S GRACE AND GIFT ABOUND/MULTIPLY TO THE MANY] BY THE GRACE OF THE ONE MAN, JESUS CHRIST [THE DEATH OF THE "ONE" SAVED THE "MANY"; SEE V. 19; IS. 53:11]. (Romans 5:15)

SIN ONCE USED DEATH TO RULE US [JUST AS SIN REIGNED IN DEATH...], BUT GOD GAVE PEOPLE MORE OF HIS GRACE SO THAT GRACE COULD RULE [...SO GRACE WILL REIGN] BY MAKING PEOPLE RIGHT WITH HIM [THROUGH JUSTIFICATION/RIGHTEOUSNESS]. AND THIS BRINGS LIFE FOREVER [ETERNAL LIFE] THROUGH JESUS CHRIST OUR LORD. (Romans 5:21)

IT IS THE SAME NOW. THERE ARE A FEW PEOPLE [IS A REMNANT] THAT GOD HAS CHOSEN BY HIS GRACE. AND IF HE CHOSE THEM BY GRACE, IT IS NOT FOR THE THINGS THEY HAVE DONE [BY WORKS]. IF THEY COULD BE MADE GOD'S PEOPLE BY WHAT THEY DID [WORKS], GOD'S GIFT OF GRACE WOULD NOT REALLY [OR NO LONGER] BE A GIFT. (Romans 11:5-6)

WE ARE WORKING TOGETHER [WITH FELLOW BELIEVERS, OR WITH GOD, OR WITH CHRIST], SO WE BEG [URGE; APPEAL TO; ENCOURAGE] YOU: DO NOT LET THE GRACE THAT YOU RECEIVED FROM GOD BE FOR NOTHING [RECEIVE GOD'S GRACE IN VAIN]. (2 Corinthians 6:1)

BUT HE SAID TO ME, "MY GRACE IS ENOUGH FOR YOU [SUFFICIENT FOR YOU; ALL YOU NEED]. WHEN YOU ARE WEAK, MY POWER IS MADE PERFECT IN YOU [FOR (MY) POWER IS PERFECTED IN WEAKNESS]." SO I AM VERY HAPPY TO BRAG [BOAST] ABOUT MY WEAKNESSES. THEN

CHRIST'S POWER CAN LIVE [RESIDE; *OR* REST] IN ME. (2 Corinthians 12:9)

I MEAN THAT [*OR* FOR; BECAUSE] YOU HAVE BEEN SAVED BY GRACE THROUGH BELIEVING [FAITH]. YOU DID NOT SAVE YOURSELVES; IT WAS A GIFT FROM GOD. IT WAS NOT THE RESULT OF YOUR OWN EFFORTS [WORKS], SO YOU CANNOT [NO ONE CAN] BRAG ABOUT IT [BOAST]. (Ephesians 2:8-9)

Grace is described in many ways: loving-kindness, goodwill, favor, merciful kindness, and even token or benefit. Yet it remains a complicated theological concept because we don't properly or easily understand it. Grace is all it is defined as and more because it's more than just something that we don't deserve or something that is good. Grace is a spiritual condition by which we are given something, freely, without question, from God, Who does not, and is under no obligation, to give it to us. If we don't deserve it, God doesn't have to give it. Grace is a statement of both what God does for us and what we are given, speaking truth about the Giver and the receiver. When we receive His grace, it says something transforming, and changing, about us, as well. God gives us grace, not because we deserve it, but because it is Who He is. When I receive His grace in my life, it brings me to a place where I can receive fully of Who God is, and all God has to reveal to me. Grace is love and forgiveness met in promise, in hope, and in reality.

> *GRACE*[5]
> - *CHARIS*: GRACE, KINDNESS
> - ORIGINAL WORD: ΧΆΡΙΣ, ΙΤΟΣ, ἡ
> - PART OF SPEECH: NOUN, FEMININE
> - TRANSLITERATION: CHARIS
> - PHONETIC SPELLING: (KHAR'-ECE)
> - SHORT DEFINITION: GRACE, FAVOR, KINDNESS
> - DEFINITION: (A) GRACE, AS A GIFT OR BLESSING BROUGHT TO MAN BY JESUS CHRIST, (B) FAVOR, (C) GRATITUDE, THANKS, (D) A FAVOR, KINDNESS.

Women are often considered to be very complicated, hard to figure out, and more than just a little bit mysterious by nature. The most infamous jokes in history are always about men not properly understanding women, their nature, or their movements. People say women tend to do things that men don't understand, but somehow, the result is what was hoped for and desired for. A woman can throw a fit, vow to never speak to someone again, and then move past it in forgiveness and total restoration, as if nothing happened the day before. It's kind of like grace, although grace isn't as unpredictable as we humans can be. We don't understand it, it's not what we deserve, it seems like things should go one way (and they should, rightfully), but as life intervenes, love and forgiveness take over. In a woman, we find the complexity of promise and hope, all in reality. The future meets the past and the present, and as she walks in her shadow as a type of the church and of life, she ushers in something that is beyond beautiful. It walks differently and talks differently, through an air of elegance and poise, in a way that nothing else is quite able to do.

Embracing grace means receiving this incredible revelation of the poise and beauty present in the feminine, present in those women who have embraced their call of God and choose to walk in the power of forgiveness in their own lives. Not everyone always embraces or understands it, many are uncertain of how to receive it, and many more bypass it because they don't know how to handle it. Seeing grace in the light of a good woman who is a bit mysterious, very complex, and knows exactly what is needed, how and when, is just how we can see the work of grace in our own lives. We might not always know what she will do or how she will move, but you can bet that she is the best thing (whether wife, mother, friend, or daughter) that you will ever have in your life.

Love is a girl...love is from God

The Bible doesn't just speak on one type of "love" or one form of what we tend to translate as "love." This is one of the many reasons why we are confused about love, and why in talking about love, we tend to assume that certain types of love are all the same, rather than recognizing they are all very, very different from one another.

> ## LOVE[16]
> - *AGAPÉ:* LOVE, GOODWILL
> - ORIGINAL WORD: ἀΓ'ΑΠΗ, ΗΣ, ἡ
> - PART OF SPEECH: NOUN, FEMININE
> - TRANSLITERATION: AGAPE
> - PHONETIC SPELLING: (AG-AH'-PAY)
> - SHORT DEFINITION: LOVE
> - DEFINITION: LOVE, BENEVOLENCE, GOOD WILL, ESTEEM; PLUR: LOVE-FEASTS.

In the Bible, there are five different types of love (or, shall we say, four different words identified as love) identified:

- **_'Ahab/Eros_**: *'Ahab* is the first instance of love in Scripture. It indicates a drawing, or attraction, to someone or something. It's a bit of a catch-all term, reflecting the primitive nature of its use. The word *eros* is described in the Septuagint (the Greek translation of the Old Testament), especially in the Song of Solomon. It is used to describe sexual attraction, desire, interest, or sexual interest in connection. The word is always used in a sexual context and seeks gratification and pleasure in that context. It's how a man or a woman can say, "I love my wife/husband, but I am not in love with her/him." They are saying that even though they might love them as a person, they are not attracted to them anymore. I connect these two words in their definition because they both refer to a drawing or interest in something. I don't know that I think "love" is a proper translation of these words; I think they are better translated to be "attraction" or "physical desire."

- **_Hesed:_** A term translated as goodness, kindness, faithfulness, or best-known, lovingkindness. It is more than just doing something to do it, but a stirring or root of the prompting to act in love and kindness toward something or someone. It is both a feeling and an action.

- **_Raham/Phileo_**: Two terms used to indicate "brotherly

love" or a strong affection for somebody else. They are more than just being a casual acquaintance of someone but are not sexual or romantic in nature. We could define them both as a platonic, loving friendship, one based on a bond where a friend is "closer than a brother" (Proverbs 18:24). *Raham* describes the characteristics of friendship, while *phileo* describes the love as that of like siblings or among church fellowship.

- ***Storgay***: A Greek word that defines a love for one's relatives, especially in the context of a familial bond. We could define this term as "familial honor."

- ***Agape***: *Agape* is considered the highest form of love. Whenever the Bible speaks of loving God, loving our neighbor, or displaying the love of God to one another (especially in the context of the church, it always speaks of *agape*. It is the divine love, completely spiritual in nature, that seeks the greatest good for everyone involved and is the completeness of unselfish love. In Galatians 5:22, the "love" spoken of in connection with the fruit of the Spirit is *agape*.

When we talk about the love of God, we are talking about *agape*. It is the highest form of love, embodying the highest good and best esteem for others. If I were to explain *agape*, I would say that it is desiring for someone else what we desire for ourselves: nothing more, nothing less. This might sound easy, but when we examine other forms of love and affection, we can easily see why *agape* is difficult. These other alliances: sexual attraction, friendship, familial identity, national pride, and let's just call it what it is, putting ourselves first, all make it so *agape* seems almost impossible. We are so busy identifying things as love that are often confused with it, there's no wonder why we have so much sexual attraction, familial identity, racial identity, esteem for some, and .... And no love.

LOVE IS PATIENT AND KIND. LOVE IS NOT JEALOUS [ENVIOUS], IT DOES NOT BRAG, AND IT IS NOT PROUD [ARROGANT; CONCEITED; PUFFED UP]. LOVE IS NOT RUDE [DISRESPECTFUL], IS NOT SELFISH [SELF-SERVING], AND DOES NOT GET UPSET WITH OTHERS [IS NOT EASILY

PROVOKED/ANGERED]. LOVE DOES NOT COUNT UP [KEEP A RECORD OF] WRONGS THAT HAVE BEEN DONE. LOVE TAKES NO PLEASURE [DOES NOT REJOICE] IN EVIL [WRONGDOING; INJUSTICE] BUT REJOICES OVER THE TRUTH. LOVE PATIENTLY ACCEPTS ALL THINGS [BEARS ALL THINGS; *OR* ALWAYS PROTECTS], ALWAYS TRUSTS [BELIEVES ALL THINGS], ALWAYS HOPES [HOPES ALL THINGS], AND ALWAYS ENDURES [ENDURES ALL THINGS]. (1 Corinthians 13:4-7)

BUT IF SOMEONE OBEYS [KEEPS] GOD'S TEACHING [HIS WORD], THEN IN THAT PERSON GOD'S LOVE [*OR* LOVE FOR GOD] HAS TRULY REACHED ITS GOAL [BEEN FULFILLED/PERFECTED/COMPLETED]. THIS IS HOW WE CAN BE SURE WE ARE LIVING IN GOD [IN HIM]: WHOEVER SAYS THAT HE LIVES [ABIDES; REMAINS] IN GOD MUST LIVE [WALK] AS JESUS LIVED [HE WALKED]. MY DEAR FRIENDS [BELOVED], I AM NOT WRITING A NEW COMMAND TO YOU BUT AN OLD COMMAND YOU HAVE HAD FROM THE BEGINNING [3:23; JOHN 13:34]. IT IS THE TEACHING [WORD] YOU HAVE ALREADY HEARD. (1 John 2:5-7)

THE FATHER HAS LOVED US SO MUCH [SEE WHAT SORT OF LOVE THE FATHER HAS GIVEN US...!] THAT WE ARE CALLED CHILDREN OF GOD. AND WE REALLY ARE HIS CHILDREN [AND WE ARE!]. THE REASON THE PEOPLE IN THE WORLD DO [THE WORLD DOES] NOT KNOW US IS THAT THEY HAVE NOT KNOWN HIM. (1 John 3:1)

THIS IS THE TEACHING [MESSAGE] YOU HAVE HEARD FROM THE BEGINNING: WE MUST LOVE EACH OTHER [AS JESUS HIMSELF TAUGHT: JOHN 13:34–35; 15:12]. DO NOT BE LIKE CAIN WHO BELONGED TO THE EVIL ONE AND KILLED [MURDERED] HIS BROTHER [GEN. 4; JOHN 8:44]. AND WHY DID HE KILL [MURDER] HIM? BECAUSE THE THINGS CAIN DID WERE EVIL, AND THE THINGS HIS BROTHER DID WERE GOOD [RIGHTEOUS; JUST].

BROTHERS AND SISTERS [FELLOW BELIEVERS], DO NOT BE SURPRISED [BE AMAZED; WONDER] WHEN [*OR* THAT; *OR* IF] THE PEOPLE OF THE WORLD HATE [THE WORLD HATES] YOU. WE KNOW WE HAVE LEFT DEATH AND HAVE COME INTO LIFE [PASSED/CROSSED FROM DEATH TO LIFE; JOHN 5:24] BECAUSE WE LOVE EACH OTHER [THE BROTHERS AND SISTERS]. WHOEVER DOES NOT LOVE IS STILL DEAD [ABIDES/REMAINS/CONTINUES IN DEATH]. EVERYONE WHO HATES A BROTHER OR SISTER [FELLOW BELIEVER] IS A MURDERER [BECAUSE THEY HAVE KILLED THAT PERSON IN THEIR HEART; MATT. 5:21–26],

AND YOU KNOW THAT NO MURDERERS HAVE ETERNAL LIFE [ABIDING; REMAINING] IN THEM. THIS IS HOW WE KNOW WHAT REAL LOVE IS: JESUS [HE] GAVE [LAID DOWN] HIS LIFE FOR US [JOHN 15:13]. SO WE SHOULD GIVE [LAY DOWN] OUR LIVES FOR OUR BROTHERS AND SISTERS [FELLOW BELIEVERS; JOHN 15:12]. SUPPOSE SOMEONE HAS ENOUGH TO LIVE [THE WORLD'S POSSESSIONS/GOODS] AND SEES A BROTHER OR SISTER [FELLOW BELIEVER] IN NEED, BUT DOES NOT HELP [CLOSES OFF HIS HEART/COMPASSION FROM HIM]. THEN GOD'S LOVE IS NOT LIVING IN THAT PERSON [HOW DOES GOD'S LOVE ABIDE/REMAIN IN HIM?]. MY CHILDREN [2:1], WE SHOULD LOVE PEOPLE NOT ONLY WITH WORDS AND TALK [IN WORD AND TONGUE], BUT BY OUR ACTIONS AND TRUE CARING [OR BY SHOWING TRUE LOVE THROUGH OUR ACTIONS; IN DEED AND TRUTH]. (1 John 3:11-18)

DEAR FRIENDS [BELOVED], WE SHOULD [LET US] LOVE EACH OTHER, BECAUSE LOVE COMES FROM GOD. EVERYONE WHO LOVES HAS BECOME GOD'S CHILD [BEEN BEGOTTEN/FATHERED BY GOD] AND KNOWS GOD. WHOEVER DOES NOT LOVE DOES NOT KNOW GOD, BECAUSE GOD IS LOVE. THIS IS HOW GOD SHOWED [REVEALED] HIS LOVE TO US: HE SENT HIS ONE AND ONLY SON INTO THE WORLD SO THAT WE COULD HAVE LIFE THROUGH HIM. THIS IS WHAT REAL LOVE IS: IT IS NOT OUR LOVE FOR GOD; IT IS GOD'S LOVE FOR US. HE SENT HIS SON TO DIE IN OUR PLACE TO TAKE AWAY OUR SINS [AS THE ATONING SACRIFICE/PROPITIATION FOR OUR SINS; SEE 2:2].

DEAR FRIENDS [BELOVED], IF GOD LOVED US THAT MUCH [OR IN THIS WAY; JOHN 3:16] WE ALSO SHOULD LOVE EACH OTHER. NO ONE HAS EVER SEEN GOD [GOD THE FATHER; JOHN 1:18], BUT IF WE LOVE EACH OTHER, GOD LIVES [REMAINS; ABIDES] IN [OR AMONG] US, AND HIS LOVE IS MADE PERFECT [IS MADE COMPLETE; COMES TO FULL EXPRESSION] IN US.

[BY THIS] WE KNOW THAT WE LIVE [ABIDE; REMAIN] IN GOD AND HE LIVES [ABIDES; REMAINS] IN US, BECAUSE HE GAVE US [OF; FROM; 3:24] HIS SPIRIT [WE SHARE IN HIS SPIRIT]. WE HAVE SEEN AND CAN TESTIFY [WITNESS; PROCLAIM] THAT THE FATHER SENT HIS SON TO BE [OR AS] THE SAVIOR OF THE WORLD. WHOEVER CONFESSES [ACKNOWLEDGES] THAT JESUS IS THE SON OF GOD HAS GOD LIVING [ABIDING; REMAINING] INSIDE, AND THAT PERSON LIVES [ABIDES; REMAINS] IN GOD. AND SO WE KNOW [HAVE COME TO KNOW] THE

LOVE THAT GOD HAS FOR US, AND WE TRUST [BELIEVE; RELY ON] THAT LOVE.

GOD IS LOVE. THOSE WHO LIVE [ABIDE; REMAIN] IN LOVE LIVE [ABIDE; REMAIN] IN GOD, AND GOD LIVES [ABIDES; REMAINS] IN THEM. THIS IS HOW LOVE IS MADE PERFECT [IS MADE COMPLETE; COMES TO FULL EXPRESSION] IN [*OR* AMONG] US: THAT WE CAN BE WITHOUT FEAR [HAVE BOLDNESS; HAVE CONFIDENCE; 2:28; 3:21; 5:14] ON THE DAY OF JUDGMENT, BECAUSE IN THIS WORLD WE ARE LIKE HIM [PROBABLY REFERRING TO CHRIST, OUR EXAMPLE OF LOVE]. WHERE GOD'S LOVE IS, THERE IS NO FEAR [THERE IS NO FEAR IN LOVE], BECAUSE GOD'S PERFECT LOVE DRIVES OUT FEAR [PERFECT LOVE CASTS OUT FEAR]. IT IS PUNISHMENT THAT MAKES A PERSON FEAR, SO LOVE IS NOT MADE PERFECT [COMPLETE] IN THE PERSON WHO FEARS [FEAR OF PUNISHMENT, NOT AN APPROPRIATE FEAR OF GOD; COMPARE PROV. 1:7; 2 COR. 7:15; PHIL. 2:12].

WE LOVE BECAUSE GOD [HE] FIRST LOVED US. IF PEOPLE SAY, "I LOVE GOD," BUT HATE THEIR BROTHERS OR SISTERS [FELLOW BELIEVERS], THEY ARE LIARS. [FOR] THOSE WHO DO NOT LOVE THEIR BROTHERS AND SISTERS [FELLOW BELIEVERS], WHOM THEY HAVE SEEN, CANNOT LOVE GOD, WHOM THEY HAVE NEVER SEEN. AND GOD GAVE US THIS COMMAND [WE HAVE THIS COMMAND FROM HIM]: THOSE WHO LOVE GOD MUST ALSO LOVE THEIR BROTHERS AND SISTERS [FELLOW BELIEVERS; JOHN 13:34]. (1 John 4:7-21)

Agape sounds like one of those ideals that is nice in concept, but impossible in reality. It doesn't make sense to our natural minds, so we put it out of our thoughts, and in many ways, out of our teaching in the church. We would rather focus on forms of love and affection that don't make us as uncomfortable and don't challenge us as much. Fortunately, and thankfully, *agape* doesn't give up that easily. If it did, we would all be in trouble.

Agape is persistent. *Agape* never gives up. *Agape* hopes, loves, forgives. Oh yeah, and *agape* is feminine.

Some might say it doesn't matter that love is feminine, but I believe it is most relevant. The feminine identity of *agape* is the heart of what it is: it is sacrificial and giving in that sacrifice. Just as women sacrifice to give life, without giving up and through to perseverance, so *agape* perseveres unto spiritual life, unto making it so that we can live into eternity. In order to come into *agape*, we must die to ourselves, and pursue eternal good, eternal life, rather than living for now.

This is not to say that it is easier for women to live in *agape* than men, nor does it specifically mean that God is female, since God is love, as is stated in the Bible (although such would be an interesting argument if someone were to pursue it). Human beings struggle with fallen nature, the flesh, and distorted love, and *agape* is a difficult pursuit for any human, particularly any human who tries to achieve it without God. What the feminine nature of *agape* shows us is a commitment to sacrifice, to unconditional love, to the labor of love present in the sacrifice of bringing life into this world. Through the unconditional love of God, the sacrifice was made for His Son, that eternal life might come into this world. In the action of giving, God sacrificed. Christ sacrificed for us. It proves that in love, there is great sacrifice, and to come to life, sacrifice must be made. Sacrifice must be present in true love, because for life to come forth, for renewal to exist, for that new start to be made, love must produce life.

Gender and church authority and ministry today

Looking back at the gender experiences of the early church plus a few feminine authorities present in the church for all time brings us to a realization of now. If women could stand in leadership authority in the first century, we know there is no question they can do so today. Three of the highest authorities in the church – the Scriptures, grace, and love – are feminine, and remain as such, through all time. Yet in the face of these facts, women still seem to face so much struggle within ministry and our identity as ministers. The question remains: how are we women and in ministry?

There is all sorts of talk today about what it means to be a woman in ministry. We are told, we don't "have to be men" and "we can be a lady, we can be soft." The questions about authority and submission, especially at home, never seem to entirely go away, even in light of evidence that proves submission isn't really for us in church, or in society, as we understand it today. Then we have the flip side of such issues: any woman in ministry technically meets the definition of being somewhat gender queer, and at minimum, gender non-conforming. By being in ministry, women have, from the beginning of the church, challenged gender roles and gender norms. We continue to challenge this today, because ministry has long been a work controversial for women to do. These challenges caused men like the Apostle Paul to rise up and openly state his thanks to the women who had helped and served in ministry. Even though he wasn't into rocking the entire world and changing every societal system in his lifetime, the Apostle Paul recognized his ability to bring change, to foster unity in the church, and to help the women of the church recognize their proper identity in Christ. By inspiring unity, women were inspired to defy the rules, and by proxy, defy the codes of their gender. This remains true, today.

Any time a woman puts on a civic collar shirt or a robe, she puts on a garment traditionally made for a man, wearing "that which pertaineth to a man" (Deuteronomy 22:5) as a minister. Every time she assumes the pulpit, she stands in a place that has excluded her, even though she was clearly included in the very beginning. Each time we interpret the Scriptures, delve into study or scholarship, or teach the word, we are doing something that for centuries refused to make room for us or our gifts. We do not assume the pulpit defined by traditional mores and ideas, or by stereotypes of what we can or cannot do, but by the empowerment of Someone, Something else, something greater than the man who thinks we are unqualified to serve, or the tradition that keeps us down. No matter what society tells us, God has proven to each and every one of us that there is no wrong way to be a woman or live out womanhood.

Many women go into ministry and come out on the other side, not knowing who they are anymore. They keep trying to fall back on a traditional line and thinking of gender identity, when they are in something that, at its core, has always challenged it. Until women in ministry embrace the understanding that ministry is outside traditional gender lines, they will always have the same struggles and problems women have always had. By embracing a bigger sense of God, a different perspective of gender norms, and receiving the newness of life, we have the ability to see how important, and amazing, it is to identify as a woman. Female ideals are at the heart of our faith. Women are at the heart of our faith. In ourselves, we type, and live God's promise. That is a special thing to do, and no matter how much they might try, no one can take it away from us.

The New Jerusalem/Tapestry of the Apocalypse (Unknown)

CHAPTER TEN
Our Eternal Home

BUT OUR HOMELAND [*OR* CITIZENSHIP] IS IN HEAVEN,
AND WE ARE WAITING FOR OUR SAVIOR, THE LORD JESUS CHRIST, TO COME FROM HEAVEN.
BY HIS POWER TO RULE [SUBJECT TO HIMSELF] ALL THINGS, HE WILL CHANGE
[TRANSFORM; TRANSFIGURE] OUR HUMBLE BODIES AND MAKE THEM LIKE
HIS OWN GLORIOUS BODY.
(PHILIPPIANS 3:20-21)

*I*N Genesis, we saw Eve: the type of the church, the mother of all living. In Revelation, we see the church in history and the New Jerusalem, also spoken of as a bride, coming down from heaven as part of the new heavens and new earth. In the beginning, there is a woman; in the end, there is a woman. In the middle, we see many, many women: all of which have a purpose, all of which teach us about something, and all of which lead us to a greater spiritual understanding of God and His purposes for us.

From beginning to end, we see women. Women have a central place in the heart of God, in our faith, in our spirituality. God breathes life into us, and in this earth, women bear life. It is absurd to think women do not have a place in Christian spirituality, just as much as to say women hold a subordinate place. This is why we look so much at female expressions of the divine, of our faith, of our life; because it is not exclusively a man's game. Our faith is here for everyone, for each and every "whosoever" who desires to come forth and receive this eternal promise, God's eternal life.

It is most fitting to end our look at divine feminine expressions to recognize our eternal home, the New Jerusalem which shall appear at the end of time as we understand it, is feminine in identity. This should not come as a huge shock, as many cities in the Bible are identified as being feminine in form. The New Jerusalem is special, however, because it is the only city spoken of as being eternal, of passing from this life into the next. This sets the New Jerusalem aside as a city worth recognizing and studying for our own edification, to see just what makes this city so special, and so amazing.

The book of Revelation and feminine identity

To discuss the New Jerusalem, we must first tap into the work of Revelation, why Revelation is so vitally important to the church, and just what it has to say about the church, which we have already clarified is a feminine entity. The book of Revelation is a beautiful prophetic revelation of the church and the people who are a part of the church, throughout history. Just as the book of Daniel chronicled history for the ancient Israelites, so Revelation chronicles history for the church. Revelation proves that the church shall exist for all time, just as it always has. It proves it will continue to exist, even into the time when Christ shall return and the worldly system, as we understand it, shall be overthrown, and exist no more. Because the book of Revelation is all about the church and church history, that means it contains things past, present and future, and much of its contents are symbolic. We might not easily understand it all, but there are a few things we can clearly see, and some of those images are feminine.

Perhaps the greatest summary of the church, and of the work of the church throughout the ages, is found in Revelation 12:

AND THEN A GREAT WONDER [SIGN; PORTENT; SYMBOLIC DESCRIPTIONS OF HEAVENLY/SPIRITUAL REALITIES] APPEARED IN HEAVEN: A WOMAN WAS CLOTHED WITH THE SUN, AND THE MOON WAS UNDER HER FEET [INDICATING AUTHORITY OR VICTORY; GEN. 37:9], AND A CROWN [A REWARD OF VICTORY] OF TWELVE STARS WAS ON HER HEAD [REPRESENTING THE TWELVE TRIBES OF ISRAEL; THE WOMAN IS A SYMBOL OF THE PERSECUTED PEOPLE OF GOD]. SHE WAS PREGNANT [IN THE WOMB] AND CRIED OUT WITH [LABOR] PAIN, BECAUSE SHE WAS ABOUT TO GIVE BIRTH [TO THE MESSIAH]. THEN ANOTHER WONDER [SIGN; PORTENT; 12:1] APPEARED IN HEAVEN: THERE WAS A GIANT RED DRAGON WITH SEVEN HEADS [REMINISCENT OF THE MANY-HEADED LEVIATHAN REPRESENTING EVIL AND CHAOS, HERE REPRESENTING SATAN; PS. 74:14; IS. 27:1; DAN. 7:1–9] AND SEVEN CROWNS [DIADEMS; ROYAL CROWNS] ON EACH HEAD. HE [OR

IT; THE GREEK MASCULINE PRONOUN CAN REFER TO A PERSON OR THING] ALSO HAD TEN HORNS [SYMBOLS OF STRENGTH AND POWER; DAN. 7:7–8, 20, 24]. HIS TAIL SWEPT A THIRD OF THE STARS OUT OF THE SKY [OR HEAVEN] AND THREW [CAST; HURLED; DAN. 8:10] THEM DOWN TO THE EARTH [REPRESENTING AN EARLY VICTORY AGAINST GOD'S PEOPLE; 12:1]. HE STOOD IN FRONT OF THE WOMAN WHO WAS READY TO GIVE BIRTH SO HE COULD EAT [DEVOUR] HER BABY [CHILD; JESUS THE MESSIAH] AS SOON AS IT WAS BORN. THEN THE WOMAN GAVE BIRTH TO A SON [A SON, A MALE CHILD,] WHO WILL RULE [OR SHEPHERD] ALL THE NATIONS WITH AN IRON ROD [SCEPTRE; 19:15; PS. 2:9]. AND HER CHILD WAS TAKEN UP [OR SNATCHED AWAY; PROBABLY A SYMBOLIC REFERENCE TO THE RESURRECTION, WHERE SATAN'S VICTORY WAS THWARTED] TO GOD AND TO HIS THRONE. THE WOMAN RAN AWAY [FLED] INTO THE DESERT [WILDERNESS] TO A PLACE GOD PREPARED FOR HER WHERE SHE WOULD BE TAKEN CARE OF [NOURISHED; FED] FOR ONE THOUSAND TWO HUNDRED SIXTY DAYS [EQUAL TO THREE AND ONE-HALF YEARS; SEE 11:3]. (Revelation 12:1-6)

WHEN THE DRAGON SAW HE HAD BEEN THROWN [CAST; HURLED] DOWN TO THE EARTH, HE HUNTED FOR [PURSUED; OR PERSECUTED] THE WOMAN WHO HAD GIVEN BIRTH TO THE SON [BOY; MALE]. BUT THE WOMAN WAS GIVEN THE TWO WINGS OF A GREAT EAGLE [OR VULTURE; EX. 19:4; DEUT. 32:10–11; IS. 40:31] SO SHE COULD FLY TO THE PLACE PREPARED FOR HER IN THE DESERT [WILDERNESS]. THERE SHE WOULD BE TAKEN CARE OF [NOURISHED; FED] FOR THREE AND ONE-HALF YEARS [A TIME, TIMES, AND HALF A TIME; 11:2, 3; 13:5; DAN. 7:25; 12:7], AWAY FROM THE SNAKE [SERPENT; GOD WILL SPIRITUALLY NOURISH HIS PEOPLE THOUGH THEY ARE PERSECUTED]. THEN THE SNAKE [SERPENT] POURED [SPEWED; THREW] WATER OUT OF ITS MOUTH LIKE A RIVER TOWARD [AFTER] THE WOMAN SO THE FLOOD WOULD CARRY [SWEEP] HER AWAY [OVERWHELMING WATER SIGNIFIES OVERWHELMING TROUBLE; PS. 18:4; 69:2]. BUT THE EARTH HELPED [RESCUED] THE WOMAN BY OPENING ITS MOUTH AND SWALLOWING THE RIVER THAT CAME [SPEWED; WAS THROWN] FROM THE MOUTH OF THE DRAGON. THEN THE DRAGON WAS VERY ANGRY [FURIOUS; FULL OF WRATH] AT THE WOMAN, AND HE WENT OFF TO MAKE WAR AGAINST ALL HER OTHER CHILDREN [THE REST OF HER SEED/OFFSPRING]—THOSE WHO OBEY GOD'S COMMANDS AND WHO HAVE THE MESSAGE JESUS TAUGHT [OR HOLD FAST TO THEIR TESTIMONY ABOUT JESUS]. (Revelation 12:13-17)

The images of the church used in Revelation 12:1-6 have served as a continual headache for interpreters, mostly because they do not agree on just what the passage is trying to tell us. This means the feminine imagery and its obvious association often go ignored and understated.

In my book, *All That is Seen and Unseen: A Journey Through the Book of Revelation* (Righteous Pen Publications, 2017), I explore the imagery of the woman of Revelation 12 in detail. Revelation chapters 11 and 12 depict the same exact depictions of church history, just with different symbolism. Wanting to get the message across, the imagery is given in a way that as many people as possible could read and understand. In both chapters, we see two prominent figures in God's plan, the numerical figure of 1,260 days, the interaction of heaven and earth, and the presence of Satan, working against the plan God has in place. The people of God are protected, even though they are harassed by the enemy. These parallels point to the imagery of the church as the woman of Revelation 12, protecting and guarding Christ and the Gospel through the attacks of the enemy and the difficulties of this world.

Once again, we see the imagery of the church as proclaiming life, paralleling it with the work of the female to birth and bring forth life. This heralds Jeremiah 31:22, which we spoke of earlier, protecting, embracing, surrounding, and compassing Christ, as the church assumes her role and work as the New Eve. She is not weak or narrow in vision, but a strong, life-giving woman, competent and able to handle any and all that comes her way, as she trusts in her Creator. The church gathers and trains us, preparing us to do the same work – multiply and bring forth something greater as we go forth, recognizing and living through our eternal purpose.

There is also a woman in Revelation that is seen as the ultimate counter opposite of the church, and that is the women of compromise, the harlot, or whore, of Revelation.

THEN ONE OF THE SEVEN ANGELS WHO HAD THE SEVEN BOWLS CAME AND SPOKE TO ME. HE SAID, "COME, AND I WILL SHOW YOU THE PUNISHMENT [JUDGMENT] THAT WILL BE GIVEN TO THE GREAT PROSTITUTE [WHORE], THE ONE SITTING [OR RULING] OVER MANY WATERS [REFERRING TO THE EUPHRATES RIVER AND ITS MANY WATERWAYS (JER. 51:13), OR SYMBOLICALLY TO THE COSMIC FORCES

OF EVIL]. THE KINGS OF THE EARTH SINNED SEXUALLY [PROSTITUTED THEMSELVES; COMMITTED FORNICATION] WITH HER, AND THE PEOPLE OF THE EARTH BECAME DRUNK FROM THE WINE OF HER SEXUAL SIN [PROSTITUTION; FORNICATION; 14:8]."

THEN THE ANGEL CARRIED ME AWAY BY THE SPIRIT [*OR* IN THE SPIRIT] TO THE DESERT [WILDERNESS]. THERE I SAW A WOMAN SITTING ON A RED [SCARLET] BEAST. IT WAS COVERED WITH NAMES AGAINST GOD WRITTEN ON IT [BLASPHEMOUS NAMES], AND IT HAD SEVEN HEADS AND TEN HORNS. THE WOMAN WAS DRESSED IN PURPLE AND RED [SCARLET] AND WAS SHINING [GLITTERING; ADORNED] WITH THE GOLD, PRECIOUS JEWELS, AND PEARLS SHE WAS WEARING. SHE HAD A GOLDEN CUP IN HER HAND, A CUP FILLED WITH EVIL [ABOMINABLE; DETESTABLE] THINGS AND THE UNCLEANNESS OF HER SEXUAL SIN [PROSTITUTION; FORNICATION]. ON HER FOREHEAD A TITLE [NAME] WAS WRITTEN THAT WAS SECRET [A MYSTERY]. THIS IS WHAT WAS WRITTEN:

THE GREAT BABYLON
MOTHER OF PROSTITUTES [WHORES]
AND OF THE EVIL [ABOMINABLE; DETESTABLE] THINGS OF THE EARTH

THEN I SAW THAT THE WOMAN WAS DRUNK WITH THE BLOOD OF GOD'S HOLY PEOPLE [THE SAINTS] AND WITH THE BLOOD OF THOSE WHO WERE KILLED BECAUSE OF THEIR FAITH IN [WITNESSES TO; *OR* MARTYRS FOR] JESUS.

WHEN I SAW THE WOMAN, I WAS VERY AMAZED [GREATLY ASTONISHED; AMAZED WITH GREAT AMAZEMENT]. THEN THE ANGEL SAID TO ME, "WHY ARE YOU AMAZED [ASTONISHED]? I WILL TELL YOU THE SECRET [MYSTERY] OF THIS WOMAN AND THE BEAST SHE RIDES [THAT CARRIES HER]—THE ONE WITH SEVEN HEADS AND TEN HORNS. THE BEAST YOU SAW WAS ONCE ALIVE BUT IS NOT ALIVE NOW [WAS, AND IS NOT; 13:3, 12, 14]. BUT SOON IT WILL COME UP OUT OF THE BOTTOMLESS PIT [ABYSS; 9:1] AND GO AWAY TO BE DESTROYED [ITS DESTRUCTION]. THERE ARE PEOPLE WHO LIVE ON EARTH WHOSE NAMES HAVE NOT BEEN WRITTEN IN THE BOOK [SCROLL] OF LIFE [3:5] SINCE THE BEGINNING [FOUNDATION; CREATION] OF THE WORLD. THEY WILL BE AMAZED WHEN THEY SEE THE BEAST, BECAUSE HE WAS ONCE ALIVE, IS NOT ALIVE NOW, BUT WILL COME AGAIN [WAS, IS NOT,

BUT IS TO COME; IMITATING THE DIVINE TITLE OF THE LAMB (1:18; 2:8) AND GOD (1:4, 8; 4:8)].

"YOU NEED A WISE MIND TO UNDERSTAND THIS. THE SEVEN HEADS ON THE BEAST ARE SEVEN MOUNTAINS [OR HILLS; ROME WAS BUILT ON SEVEN HILLS] WHERE THE WOMAN SITS. AND THEY ARE SEVEN KINGS. FIVE OF THE KINGS HAVE ALREADY BEEN DESTROYED [FALLEN], ONE OF THE KINGS LIVES NOW [IS], AND ANOTHER HAS NOT YET COME. WHEN HE COMES, HE MUST STAY A SHORT TIME. THE BEAST THAT WAS ONCE ALIVE [WAS], BUT IS NOT ALIVE NOW [IS NOT], IS ALSO AN EIGHTH KING. HE BELONGS TO THE FIRST SEVEN KINGS, AND HE WILL GO AWAY TO BE DESTROYED [IS HEADING TO DESTRUCTION].

"THE TEN HORNS [DAN. 7:7–8, 20–25] YOU SAW ARE TEN KINGS WHO HAVE NOT YET BEGUN TO RULE [RECEIVED A KINGDOM], BUT THEY WILL RECEIVE POWER [AUTHORITY] TO RULE WITH THE BEAST FOR ONE HOUR [A SHORT TIME]. ALL TEN OF THESE KINGS HAVE THE SAME [ONE] PURPOSE [INTENTION], AND THEY WILL GIVE THEIR POWER AND AUTHORITY TO THE BEAST. THEY WILL MAKE WAR AGAINST THE LAMB [JESUS], BUT THE LAMB WILL DEFEAT [CONQUER; BE VICTORIOUS OVER] THEM, BECAUSE HE IS LORD OF LORDS AND KING OF KINGS. HE WILL DEFEAT THEM WITH HIS CALLED, CHOSEN, AND FAITHFUL FOLLOWERS [OR THOSE WITH HIM ARE CALLED, CHOSEN AND FAITHFUL]."

THEN THE ANGEL SAID TO ME, "THE WATERS THAT YOU SAW, WHERE THE PROSTITUTE [WHORE] SITS, ARE PEOPLES, RACES [MULTITUDES; CROWDS], NATIONS, AND LANGUAGES. THE TEN HORNS AND THE BEAST YOU SAW WILL HATE THE PROSTITUTE [WHORE]. THEY WILL TAKE EVERYTHING SHE HAS [MAKE HER DESOLATE] AND LEAVE HER NAKED. THEY WILL EAT HER BODY AND BURN HER WITH FIRE [EZEK. 23:25–29]. [FOR] GOD MADE THE TEN HORNS WANT [PUT IT INTO THEIR HEARTS] TO CARRY OUT HIS PURPOSE [INTENTION] BY AGREEING TO GIVE THE BEAST THEIR POWER TO RULE [KINGDOM], UNTIL WHAT GOD HAS SAID COMES ABOUT [THE WORD OF GOD HAS BEEN FULFILLED/COMPLETED]. THE WOMAN YOU SAW IS THE GREAT CITY THAT RULES OVER THE KINGS OF THE EARTH." [WHETHER SYMBOLIZED BY ROME, BABYLON, SODOM OR APOSTATE JERUSALEM, THIS CITY IS ULTIMATELY THE HUMAN WORLD SYSTEM RULED BY SATAN STANDING IN OPPOSITION TO THE CITY OF GOD, THE NEW JERUSALEM.] (REVELATION 17:1-18)

Some might question why I mention the whore of Babylon in this passage, and I am doing so for a simple reason: because it does prove a feminine battle, one between that which is good and that which is bad, but such is accomplished in Scripture without making it a male-female issue. It is not that the whore of Babylon is female and the church is a man, and that women are seen as inherently evil, and men as eternally good. Both images are used just as they are in Proverbs: we see a wise woman and a foolish one, a virtuous woman and one of ill reputation or repute, and both are what they are by their own associations, choices, and decisions. The church has chosen, throughout history, to be the church, to echo the character and desire as the bride of Christ. Every time we make a decision, we choose who we follow, who we love, and who we are to become. The whore of Babylon, following a system that is neither eternal nor godly, has made the decision to compromise herself, for whatever she feels it has to offer.

It's no mistaking then why the New Jerusalem comes out of heaven at the end of Revelation, after the fall of Babylon, splendorous and ready for the saints of all history to take residence therein. It reflects the glory of the church, of those who are unwilling to compromise who they are to be, as they take residence in the Bride, their earthly leader, their spiritual mother, and their promise of eternity. As she was in the beginning, the church is now, and the church will be, to come, radiant and prepared in splendor, ready to take permanent residence in a spiritual, eternal city.

The current Jerusalem

The word Jerusalem technically means "city of peace," although that might be hard to believe, especially from the outside, looking in. One might argue that the physical location of Jerusalem pales in beauty. It has been a city of raucous arguments, territorial fights, religious rantings, wars, and endless debates, at least if you listen to the news. No one can seem to figure out who Jerusalem belongs to, who should live there, who should have it, and it seems like such a decisive place in light of politics and end time events. Since modern-day Israel seized Jerusalem in 1967, there have been an endless number of political events, treaties, and yes, even numerous and detailed

---

JERUSALEM

- *YERUSHALAIM* OR *YERUSHALAYIM*: PROBABLY "FOUNDATION OF PEACE," CAPITAL CITY OF ALL ISR.[1]
- ORIGINAL WORD: יְרוּשָׁלִַם
- PART OF SPEECH: PROPER NAME, OF A LOCATION
- TRANSLITERATION: YERUSHALAIM OR YERUSHALAYIM
- PHONETIC SPELLING: (YER-OO-SHAW-LAH'-IM)
- SHORT DEFINITION: JERUSALEM

- *IEROUSALÉM*: JERUSALEM, THE CAPITAL OF UNITED ISR. AND JUDAH, ALSO A FUTURE HEAVENLY CITY[2]
- ORIGINAL WORD: Ἰερουσαλήμ, ἡ
- PART OF SPEECH: PROPER NOUN, INDECLINABLE
- TRANSLITERATION: IEROUSALÉM
- PHONETIC SPELLING: (HEE-ER-OO-SAL-AME')
- SHORT DEFINITION: JERUSALEM
- DEFINITION: (ARAMAIC FORM), JERUSALEM, THE CAPITAL OF PALESTINE: HENCE JUDAISM, AND ALLEGORICALLY, CHRISTENDOM, THE CHRISTIAN CHURCH.

---

prophetic claims in the years following. It is a city of great intrigue and mystery, and one with so much spiritual significance, it is hard to sort through it all and come out with a clear understanding of what it all means.

The other side of Jerusalem is that it is a diverse city, a center of importance for Judaism, Christianity, and Islam, and Armenians, Christians, Jews, and Muslims all have quarters within the city. People of all different cultures live and work in Jerusalem, and the city has had inhabitants for at least five thousand years. This is an amazing feat, and shows us the powerful diversity of the city, itself. No matter what someone's belief systems may be, everyone can agree there is something special about Jerusalem, and something that draws people there.[3]

The current city of Jerusalem, even with all its issues and

battles, is a type of the New Jerusalem to come. That is why so many are drawn there; that is why the area intrigues people so; that is why people fight over its territory, land, and boundaries. Just as spiritual battle shall stand as a prelude to the advance of the new heavens and the new earth with the New Jerusalem descending from the skies, so all these battles, wars, and fights over the city of peace stand as a type of what must come for us to get to the reality, rather than simply overlook the shadowing promise.

I WILL ALLOW SOLOMON'S SON TO CONTINUE TO RULE OVER [GIVE TO HIS SON] ONE TRIBE SO THAT DAVID, MY SERVANT WILL ALWAYS HAVE A DESCENDANT [LAMP BEFORE ME; POSSIBLY A METAPHOR FOR THE REIGN OF A KING] IN JERUSALEM, THE CITY WHERE I CHOSE TO BE WORSHIPED [PUT MY NAME]. (1 Kings 11:36)

THEN SOLOMON BEGAN TO BUILD THE TEMPLE [HOUSE] OF THE LORD IN JERUSALEM ON MOUNT MORIAH [GEN. 22:2]. THIS WAS WHERE THE LORD HAD APPEARED TO DAVID, SOLOMON'S FATHER. SOLOMON BUILT THE TEMPLE [HOUSE] ON THE PLACE DAVID HAD PREPARED ON THE THRESHING FLOOR OF ARAUNAH [OR ORNAN; 1 CHR. 21:15, 18–28] THE JEBUSITE. (2 Chronicles 3:1)

YOUR GOD SAYS,

"COMFORT, COMFORT MY PEOPLE.
SPEAK KINDLY TO THE PEOPLE OF JERUSALEM [JERUSALEM]
    AND TELL THEM
THAT THEIR TIME OF SERVICE [OR WARFARE] IS FINISHED,
    THAT THEY HAVE PAID FOR THEIR SINS [OR HER SINS ARE PARDONED],
THAT THE LORD HAS PUNISHED JERUSALEM [SHE HAS RECEIVED FROM THE LORD]
    TWICE [DOUBLE] FOR EVERY SIN THEY DID." (Isaiah 40:2)

I, THE LORD, WAS THE FIRST ONE TO TELL JERUSALEM [ZION] THAT THE PEOPLE WERE COMING HOME [OR "LOOK, HELP IS COMING!"; "LOOK, HERE THEY ARE!"].
    I SENT A MESSENGER TO JERUSALEM WITH THE GOOD NEWS. (Isaiah 41:27)

Historically speaking, cities are almost always identified as female because they are identified as a central place of life, analogous to the womb. People live lives, have families, interact with other people, grow and develop as human beings, and house themselves in cities, thus the analogy. Cities also often mirror families in certain respects, as citizens dwell in a city with others, knowing one another's ins and outs, comings and goings, making friends, developing relationships, and continuing on throughout life, much like people do with siblings or close family members. The nature of cities functions around relationships, either healthy or dysfunctional, and as people learn to live and dwell together, they find a certain level of safety, protection, and comfort with one another. Through each and every city, we see the cycles of birth, life, death, and renewal within their walls, all functioning and there to be experienced, over and over again, by its inhabitants.

In the current Jerusalem, which has always prided itself as a city of great diversity, we find all these realities staring us in the face while we await something to come, something that is better. It points us to something else, all the while teaching us about life and hope, and reminding us that God is with us, even if we are unaware of His place in our lives, and even if we don't always easily understand just how God lives and dwells among us by the Spirit.

The dwelling of God

The current, natural city of Jerusalem is also a type of the spiritual dwelling of God within us, because it is spoken of as being the throne of God on earth, housing His glory, the *shekinah* presence of God.

SING PRAISES TO THE LORD WHO IS KING ON MOUNT [DWELLS ON] ZION [THE LOCATION OF THE TEMPLE].
TELL THE NATIONS [AMONG THE PEOPLES] WHAT HE HAS DONE. (Psalm 9:11)

HIS TENT IS IN JERUSALEM [SALEM; SHORTENED NAME OF JERUSALEM];
HIS HOME [ABODE] IS ON MOUNT ZION [Ps. 48]. (Psalm 76:2)

THE LORD HAS CHOSEN JERUSALEM [ZION; THE LOCATION OF THE TEMPLE];
 HE WANTS [DESIRES] IT FOR HIS HOME.
HE SAYS, "THIS IS MY RESTING PLACE FOREVER.
 HERE IS WHERE I WANT TO STAY [WILL SIT/RESIDE BECAUSE I DESIRE IT]. (Psalm 132:13-14)

THE LORD WILL ROAR LIKE A LION FROM JERUSALEM [ROARS FROM ZION];
 HIS LOUD VOICE WILL THUNDER FROM THAT CITY [JERUSALEM],
 AND THE SKY [HEAVENS] AND THE EARTH WILL SHAKE.
BUT THE LORD WILL BE A SAFE PLACE [REFUGE] FOR HIS PEOPLE,
 A STRONG PLACE OF SAFETY [STRONGHOLD] FOR THE PEOPLE [SONS; CHILDREN] OF ISRAEL.
"THEN YOU WILL KNOW THAT I, THE LORD YOUR GOD,
 LIVE ON MY HOLY MOUNT ZION.
JERUSALEM WILL BE A HOLY PLACE,
 AND STRANGERS [FOREIGNERS] WILL NEVER EVEN GO THROUGH IT AGAIN [AS INVADERS]. (Joel 3:16-17)

A MESSAGE FROM [THE WORD OF] THE LORD ALL-POWERFUL [ALMIGHTY; OF HEAVEN'S ARMIES; OF HOSTS] CAME TO ME, SAYING, THIS IS WHAT THE LORD ALL-POWERFUL [ALMIGHTY; OF HEAVEN'S ARMIES; OF HOSTS] SAYS: "I HAVE A VERY STRONG LOVE [AM JEALOUS/ZEALOUS/PASSIONATE] FOR JERUSALEM [ZION; 2:7]. MY STRONG LOVE [JEALOUSY; ZEAL; PASSION] FOR HER IS LIKE A FIRE BURNING IN ME [*OR* WILL MEAN WRATH FOR HER ENEMIES]."

THIS IS WHAT THE LORD SAYS: "I WILL RETURN TO JERUSALEM AND LIVE IN [DWELL IN THE MIDST OF] IT. THEN IT WILL BE CALLED THE CITY OF TRUTH [*OR* FAITHFULNESS], AND THE MOUNTAIN OF THE LORD ALL-POWERFUL [ALMIGHTY; OF HEAVEN'S ARMIES; OF HOSTS] WILL BE CALLED THE HOLY MOUNTAIN [ZION, THE LOCATION OF THE TEMPLE]." (Zechariah 8:1-3)

The concept that God and His presence were "housed" somewhere is analogous to the concept we spoke of with people and a city. Just as cities represented protection, safety, and a certain sense of familial bonding, so did the concept of God as present within a city. It was not uncommon for different ancient gods and goddesses to have seats or altars in certain places, and devotion to those specific deities was a part of the housing, the worship, and the familial sense present in that city. Jerusalem was God's city, a part of the dwelling of His people, their capital, and it was most fitting for His presence to dwell therein, being their deity, and their ruler.

God wants us to understand about the concept of His dwelling, and desires that within the bounds of life, we are able to perceive just how important the concept of embracing His dwelling is in our lives. This is because Jerusalem is not just a type of the New Jerusalem, but of the relationship that we have with God, now. We know that we are temples of the Holy Spirit, of that presence within us, now, as we have become a physical type, ourselves, of that dwelling place.

KNOW YE NOT THAT YE ARE THE TEMPLE OF GOD, AND *THAT* THE SPIRIT OF GOD DWELLETH IN YOU? IF ANY MAN DEFILE THE TEMPLE OF GOD, HIM SHALL GOD DESTROY; FOR THE TEMPLE OF GOD IS HOLY, WHICH TEMPLE YE ARE. (1 Corinthians 3:16-17 KJV)

AND IN HIM YOU TOO ARE BEING BUILT TOGETHER TO BECOME A DWELLING IN WHICH GOD LIVES BY HIS SPIRIT. (Ephesians 2:22, NIV)

This gives us a beautiful picture of what is to come, as the New Jerusalem shall also stand as a living dwelling for the Lord, God, Himself. Just as He is that near to us in this life, so shall He stand in the New Jerusalem, that near, that close, leading and guiding His people. Every single one of us is a type of the New Jerusalem to come, because the divine rests within each of us, through the beautiful and precious Holy Spirit, living within. It gives new meaning to the expression of the Kingdom of God being within us, because it literally, and figuratively, is.

AND WHEN HE WAS DEMANDED OF THE PHARISEES, WHEN THE KINGDOM OF GOD SHOULD COME, HE ANSWERED THEM AND SAID, THE KINGDOM OF GOD COMETH NOT WITH OBSERVATION: NEITHER SHALL THEY SAY, LO HERE! OR, LO THERE! FOR, BEHOLD, THE KINGDOM OF GOD IS WITHIN YOU. (Luke 17:20-21, KJV)

JESUS SAID, "IF THOSE WHO LEAD YOU SAY TO YOU, 'SEE, THE KINGDOM IS IN THE SKY,' THEN THE BIRDS OF THE SKY WILL PRECEDE

YOU. IF THEY SAY TO YOU, 'IT IS IN THE SEA,' THEN THE FISH WILL PRECEDE YOU. RATHER, THE KINGDOM IS INSIDE OF YOU, AND IT IS OUTSIDE OF YOU. WHEN YOU COME TO KNOW YOURSELVES, THEN YOU WILL BECOME KNOWN, AND YOU WILL REALIZE THAT IT IS YOU WHO ARE THE SONS OF THE LIVING FATHER. BUT IF YOU WILL NOT KNOW YOURSELVES, YOU DWELL IN POVERTY AND IT IS YOU WHO ARE THAT POVERTY." (The Gospel of Thomas, Verse 3)[4]

HIS DISCIPLES SAID TO HIM, "WHEN WILL THE KINGDOM COME?"

<JESUS SAID,> "IT WILL NOT COME BY WAITING FOR IT. IT WILL NOT BE A MATTER OF SAYING 'HERE IT IS' OR 'THERE IT IS.' RATHER, THE KINGDOM OF THE FATHER IS SPREAD OUT UPON THE EARTH, AND MEN DO NOT SEE IT." (The Gospel of Thomas, Verse 113)[5]

So often we are looking for what is to come to solve all the world's problems. Yes, a new heavens and new earth will be awesome, and the New Jerusalem to come is beyond imagination. That's part of the reason why we don't properly comprehend what things will be like in the period after the return of Christ; it is beyond comprehension. Whatever the Apostle John saw in his vision was beyond our limited understanding, and yes, it is something to hope for and aspire to see, one day. Still, what we are looking for is within us, if we truly believe God is with us and is dwelling in us through the Holy Spirit. We don't need to seek the whole world to be turned upside down and changed inside out; we need to be the change that has been placed within us, to embrace the realities that are, and stand in eternity today. The Kingdom is within us, meaning the dwelling of God is right here, right now, and the Kingdom is as real today as it will be in the New Jerusalem to come.

Jerusalem's daughters of peace

In the Song of Solomon, we find an interesting reference that is fitting here, in speaking of Jerusalem in connection with women:

[DAUGHTERS] OF JERUSALEM [1:5], PROMISE ME [I ADJURE YOU] BY THE GAZELLES AND THE DEER OF THE FIELD [IN HEBREW SOUNDS LIKE "BY THE (LORD) OF HOSTS" OR "BY GOD ALMIGHTY"] NOT TO AWAKEN

OR EXCITE [AROUSE] LOVE UNTIL IT IS READY [SO DESIRES; LIKELY A WARNING TO THE WOMEN TO WAIT FOR LOVE UNTIL THE RIGHT PERSON COMES ALONG; 3:5; 8:4]. (Song of Solomon 2:7)

[DAUGHTERS] OF JERUSALEM [1:5], PROMISE ME [I ADJURE YOU] BY THE GAZELLES AND THE DEER OF THE FIELD [IN HEBREW SOUNDS LIKE "BY THE (LORD) OF HOSTS" OR "BY GOD ALMIGHTY"] NOT TO AWAKEN OR EXCITE [AROUSE] LOVE UNTIL IT IS READY [SO DESIRES; LIKELY A WARNING TO THE WOMEN TO WAIT FOR LOVE UNTIL THE RIGHT PERSON COMES ALONG; 2:7; 8:4]. (Song of Solomon 3:5)

PROMISE ME [I ADJURE YOU], WOMEN [DAUGHTERS] OF JERUSALEM [1:5], IF YOU FIND MY LOVER, TELL HIM [WHAT SHOULD YOU SAY TO HIM? THAT] I AM WEAK WITH LOVE. (Song of Solomon 5:8)

WOMEN [DAUGHTERS] OF JERUSALEM [1:5], PROMISE [I ADJURE YOU] NOT TO AWAKEN OR EXCITE [AROUSE] LOVE UNTIL IT IS READY [SO DESIRES; LIKELY A WARNING TO THE WOMEN TO WAIT FOR LOVE UNTIL THE RIGHT PERSON COMES ALONG; 2:7; 3:5]. (Song of Solomon 8:4)

One of the most unique things present in the Song of Solomon is its attentive detailing to women and to the forward nature of the women interacting with men and other women in the book. We don't see women as passive or waiting on men in the Song of Solomon, but very direct and upfront about what they are seeking and needing. As we can see from the chapter above, the "daughters of Jerusalem" are specifically charged for a person, but why? According to the Hebrew, the term "daughters of Jerusalem" can refer to any of the following:

- Daughters of Jerusalem (the literal city)
- Young women of Jerusalem (the literal city)
- A personified woman, signifying God's people, such as the church of Jerusalem (found in the literal city or associated with the church in the literal city)
- The sub-cities of Jerusalem or of the larger group of God's people
- The daughters of peace
- The people of God (church) of peace
- The churches of peace

- Us, as the product of the church, standing as vessels of peace

I believe the Song of Solomon is calling on all of the above, with words of advice: to await love, to await it until it arrives. The obvious connotation is literal, but there is a spiritual awareness in it for us, as well. When the love of God, His *agape* love (feminine in nature) awakens us, it changes our entire lives, and our entire perspective. We must await that experience, that knowledge, to have the greatest impact in the world. It is being the living type of the New Jerusalem, as small pictures of it, here and there, ready and prepared to represent the Kingdom in this world, right now. Thus, the Scriptures are speaking to God's women; to His daughters of peace; to His people, His churches, the product of those touched and impacted by His life and His promise, and who are actively living out their faith, in this day and age.

The daughters of Jerusalem are mentioned again, in Luke 23:27-28, this time, in a different context:

A LARGE CROWD OF PEOPLE WAS FOLLOWING JESUS, INCLUDING SOME WOMEN WHO WERE SAD [MOURNING] AND CRYING [WAILING; LAMENTING] FOR HIM. BUT JESUS TURNED AND SAID TO THEM, "WOMEN [DAUGHTERS] OF JERUSALEM, DON'T CRY [WEEP] FOR ME. CRY [WEEP] FOR YOURSELVES AND FOR YOUR CHILDREN.

We can assume Jesus was speaking to literal women of Jerusalem, as He was on the way to the cross, and took note of His female followers, who looked on with sorrow and concern. Jesus' advice to them, however, echoes more of the church within them, and calling them the daughters of Jerusalem connects them to the love they so openly expressed for Christ, Himself. They were to weep for themselves and their own children, for their own repentance. Christ would reign victorious in only a few days' time, and He would have the final victory, once and for all, over suffering and death. Christ was coming with His own Kingdom and His own power, and they were to open themselves to receive it, fully prepared, as daughters of the church, to become daughters of peace in their own right.

The bride, come down from heaven

It's not a big secret that we are being prepared for that time when the heavens and earth shall be made new, even if we don't understand all the details of the eschatology behind it. The New Jerusalem is to be beautiful, is to be glorious, and is beyond any and all measure of imagination.

THEN I SAW A NEW HEAVEN AND A NEW EARTH, FOR THE FIRST HEAVEN AND THE FIRST EARTH HAD PASSED AWAY, AND THE SEA WAS NO MORE. AND I SAW THE HOLY CITY, NEW JERUSALEM, COMING DOWN OUT OF HEAVEN FROM GOD, PREPARED AS A BRIDE ADORNED FOR HER HUSBAND. AND I HEARD A LOUD VOICE FROM THE THRONE SAYING, "BEHOLD, THE DWELLING PLACE OF GOD IS WITH MAN. HE WILL DWELL WITH THEM, AND THEY WILL BE HIS PEOPLE, AND GOD HIMSELF WILL BE WITH THEM AS THEIR GOD. HE WILL WIPE AWAY EVERY TEAR FROM THEIR EYES, AND DEATH SHALL BE NO MORE, NEITHER SHALL THERE BE MOURNING, NOR CRYING, NOR PAIN ANYMORE, FOR THE FORMER THINGS HAVE PASSED AWAY."

AND HE WHO WAS SEATED ON THE THRONE SAID, "BEHOLD, I AM MAKING ALL THINGS NEW." ALSO HE SAID, "WRITE THIS DOWN, FOR THESE WORDS ARE TRUSTWORTHY AND TRUE." AND HE SAID TO ME, "IT IS DONE! I AM THE ALPHA AND THE OMEGA, THE BEGINNING AND THE END. TO THE THIRSTY I WILL GIVE FROM THE SPRING OF THE WATER OF LIFE WITHOUT PAYMENT. THE ONE WHO CONQUERS WILL HAVE THIS HERITAGE, AND I WILL BE HIS GOD AND HE WILL BE MY SON. BUT AS FOR THE COWARDLY, THE FAITHLESS, THE DETESTABLE, AS FOR MURDERERS, THE SEXUALLY IMMORAL, SORCERERS, IDOLATERS, AND ALL LIARS, THEIR PORTION WILL BE IN THE LAKE THAT BURNS WITH FIRE AND SULFUR, WHICH IS THE SECOND DEATH."

THEN CAME ONE OF THE SEVEN ANGELS WHO HAD THE SEVEN BOWLS FULL OF THE SEVEN LAST PLAGUES AND SPOKE TO ME, SAYING, "COME, I WILL SHOW YOU THE BRIDE, THE WIFE OF THE LAMB." AND HE CARRIED ME AWAY IN THE SPIRIT TO A GREAT, HIGH MOUNTAIN, AND SHOWED ME THE HOLY CITY JERUSALEM COMING DOWN OUT OF HEAVEN FROM GOD, HAVING THE GLORY OF GOD, ITS RADIANCE LIKE A MOST RARE JEWEL, LIKE A JASPER, CLEAR AS CRYSTAL. IT HAD A GREAT, HIGH WALL, WITH TWELVE GATES, AND AT THE GATES TWELVE ANGELS, AND ON THE GATES THE NAMES OF THE TWELVE TRIBES OF

THE SONS OF ISRAEL WERE INSCRIBED—ON THE EAST THREE GATES, ON THE NORTH THREE GATES, ON THE SOUTH THREE GATES, AND ON THE WEST THREE GATES. AND THE WALL OF THE CITY HAD TWELVE FOUNDATIONS, AND ON THEM WERE THE TWELVE NAMES OF THE TWELVE APOSTLES OF THE LAMB.

AND THE ONE WHO SPOKE WITH ME HAD A MEASURING ROD OF GOLD TO MEASURE THE CITY AND ITS GATES AND WALLS. THE CITY LIES FOURSQUARE, ITS LENGTH THE SAME AS ITS WIDTH. AND HE MEASURED THE CITY WITH HIS ROD, 12,000 STADIA. ITS LENGTH AND WIDTH AND HEIGHT ARE EQUAL. HE ALSO MEASURED ITS WALL, 144 CUBITS BY HUMAN MEASUREMENT, WHICH IS ALSO AN ANGEL'S MEASUREMENT. THE WALL WAS BUILT OF JASPER, WHILE THE CITY WAS PURE GOLD, LIKE CLEAR GLASS. THE FOUNDATIONS OF THE WALL OF THE CITY WERE ADORNED WITH EVERY KIND OF JEWEL. THE FIRST WAS JASPER, THE SECOND SAPPHIRE, THE THIRD AGATE, THE FOURTH EMERALD, THE FIFTH ONYX, THE SIXTH CARNELIAN, THE SEVENTH CHRYSOLITE, THE EIGHTH BERYL, THE NINTH TOPAZ, THE TENTH CHRYSOPRASE, THE ELEVENTH JACINTH, THE TWELFTH AMETHYST. AND THE TWELVE GATES WERE TWELVE PEARLS, EACH OF THE GATES MADE OF A SINGLE PEARL, AND THE STREET OF THE CITY WAS PURE GOLD, LIKE TRANSPARENT GLASS.

AND I SAW NO TEMPLE IN THE CITY, FOR ITS TEMPLE IS THE LORD GOD THE ALMIGHTY AND THE LAMB. AND THE CITY HAS NO NEED OF SUN OR MOON TO SHINE ON IT, FOR THE GLORY OF GOD GIVES IT LIGHT, AND ITS LAMP IS THE LAMB. BY ITS LIGHT WILL THE NATIONS WALK, AND THE KINGS OF THE EARTH WILL BRING THEIR GLORY INTO IT, AND ITS GATES WILL NEVER BE SHUT BY DAY—AND THERE WILL BE NO NIGHT THERE. THEY WILL BRING INTO IT THE GLORY AND THE HONOR OF THE NATIONS. BUT NOTHING UNCLEAN WILL EVER ENTER IT, NOR ANYONE WHO DOES WHAT IS DETESTABLE OR FALSE, BUT ONLY THOSE WHO ARE WRITTEN IN THE LAMB'S BOOK OF LIFE. (ESV)

From this passage, we get another glimpse of a bride descending from heaven, in all her splendor. Just as the church is a bride because it makes her noticeable and undeniable, the same is true with the New Jerusalem, decked out as a bride, adorned and jeweled. She is not just decked out in jewels and glass to be beautiful, but to be noticeable. She will hold such a sparkle, such a radiance, everyone will have to see and recognize what is happening as God's dwelling place comes down from the great beyond.

Beyond the beauty of the physical city, there is an intrinsic beauty in the New Jerusalem, and all she represents. It is the beauty of eternity; the splendor of what is to come. Just as women are regarded as beautiful of the sexes, so does the New Jerusalem radiate a beauty, all her own, unique and special to her. She is adequate; she is purposed; she is well-equipped, no one can ignore her, nor can anyone deny her.

The radiating beauty of the New Jerusalem reminds each and every one of us of the *shekinah* glory of God, of truth and splendor that sends us running to its interior, to trust the One Who brings it to its beautiful fruition. A union between God and His people, the perfection of the saints becomes relevant – and personal – there in the New Jerusalem. There, in the womb of the city, we find the education, the meeting, and the life we all need, protecting and guiding us, all throughout eternity.

Eternal fellowship

The New Jerusalem is a meeting of heaven and earth, even though we don't exactly understand just how it will happen or what it will look or be like. It doesn't just represent a new replacement of Jerusalem but represents the eternal relationship that we shall have with God and each other. This brings us to the last feminine identity of this book, one that shall last us long into eternity, and that is the principle of fellowship. In the promise of eternal life, so beautifully and eloquently outlined in Revelation, we find the beauty of eternal fellowship, something that will never, ever end.

THEY SPENT [DEVOTED] THEIR TIME LEARNING THE APOSTLES' TEACHING, SHARING [FELLOWSHIP], BREAKING BREAD [THIS MAY REFER TO A MEAL AS IN V. 46, OR TO THE LORD'S SUPPER; LUKE 22:14–20], AND PRAYING TOGETHER. (Acts 2:42)

GOD, WHO HAS CALLED YOU INTO FELLOWSHIP [PARTNERSHIP; RELATIONSHIP] WITH HIS SON, JESUS CHRIST OUR LORD, IS FAITHFUL. (1 Corinthians 1:9)

WE GIVE THANKS FOR THE CUP OF BLESSING [USED IN THE LORD'S

SUPPER], WHICH IS [IS THIS NOT...?] A SHARING [PARTICIPATION; FELLOWSHIP] IN THE BLOOD OF CHRIST. AND THE BREAD THAT WE BREAK IS [IS IT NOT...?] A SHARING [PARTICIPATION; FELLOWSHIP] IN THE BODY OF CHRIST. BECAUSE THERE IS ONE LOAF OF BREAD, WE WHO ARE MANY ARE ONE BODY, BECAUSE WE ALL SHARE THAT ONE LOAF. (1 Corinthians 10:16-17)

[THEREFORE,] DOES YOUR LIFE IN CHRIST GIVE YOU STRENGTH? [IF THERE IS ANY ENCOURAGEMENT IN CHRIST...] DOES HIS LOVE COMFORT YOU? [...IF ANY COMFORT FROM (HIS) LOVE...] DO WE SHARE TOGETHER IN THE SPIRIT? [...IF ANY FELLOWSHIP/SHARING OF THE SPIRIT...] DO YOU HAVE MERCY AND KINDNESS? [...IF ANY MERCY/AFFECTION AND KINDNESS/COMPASSION...] IF SO [...THEN], MAKE ME VERY HAPPY [FULFILL/COMPLETE MY JOY] BY HAVING THE SAME THOUGHTS [BEING LIKE-MINDED/OF ONE MIND], SHARING THE SAME LOVE, AND HAVING ONE MIND [HEART; SOUL] AND PURPOSE [GOAL; MIND]. (Philippians 2:1-2)

BUT IF WE LIVE [WALK] IN THE LIGHT, AS GOD [HE] IS IN THE LIGHT, WE CAN SHARE [HAVE] FELLOWSHIP WITH EACH OTHER. THEN THE BLOOD OF JESUS, GOD'S SON, CLEANSES US FROM EVERY SIN. (1 John 1:7)

FELLOWSHIP[6]
- *KOINÓNIA*: FELLOWSHIP
- ORIGINAL WORD: κοινωνία, ας, ἡ
- PART OF SPEECH: NOUN, FEMININE
- TRANSLITERATION: KOINONIA
- PHONETIC SPELLING: (KOY-NOHN-EE'-AH)
- SHORT DEFINITION: PARTICIPATION, COMMUNION, FELLOWSHIP
- DEFINITION: (LIT: PARTNERSHIP) (A) CONTRIBUTORY HELP, PARTICIPATION, (B) SHARING IN, COMMUNION, (C) SPIRITUAL FELLOWSHIP, A FELLOWSHIP IN THE SPIRIT.

The principle of fellowship, especially in the context we see in Revelation, is not just a matter of visiting one another's church services or coming out when different leaders hold events, although such could be considered an aspect of it. True fellowship is a bond of spiritual love, build on *agape*, that connects us in six main ways: association, communion, communication, distribution, contribution, and intimacy. If we take these things and mix them up, we create the feminine concoction that is fellowship.

- **Association**: Associating with one another is more than just visiting one another's ministries. It is truly being a part of one another's lives and work, sharing one another's joys, concerns, highs, and lows. Through association, we recognize proper order in fellowship, proper authority as it manifests, and respect the gifts and abilities of all. (John 14:26, John 17:21, 1 Corinthians 12:1-30, Galatians 6:2, Hebrews 10:24-25)

- **Communion**: Communion is the literal ordinance of bread and wine or grape juice, reminding us of the Lord's death, until He comes again, in glory. Communion is more than just a sacramental element, however. It is a symbol of unity: unity with God, and unity with those who partake. It is a part of our commitment to God, and our commitment to serve as living types in this world, as we await a time when that which is literally spiritual becomes literally manifest to all. (Matthew 26:26-28, Luke 22:7-38, 1 Corinthians 10:14-33, 1 Corinthians 11:17-34)

- **Communication**: Communication is more than talking to others. It is listening, it is taking in what others say, and it is conveying understanding, rather than just thought or opinion. In communication, we exchange more than ideas; we give a piece of ourselves so that someone else can receive what they need, and vice versa. (Ephesians 4:32, Philippians 4:8, Colossians 4:6, James 1:19, 3 John 1:13-14)

- **Distribution**: Distribution is the proclamation of the message beyond what is immediate or comfortable for us. If we distribute in fellowship, that means we don't just see to it that our own message is shared, but we also share the mutual message of those we fellowship with. We proclaim that which is the Gospel, wherever the Gospel manifests. (Matthew 24:14, Matthew 28:19, Mark 16:15-16, Revelation 11:15)

- **Contribution**: Sometimes we are always the ones who make the overtures, or we always let others come to us. In fellowship, we contribute. We all bring what we have to offer, and we give as much as we take. (Acts 20:35, Hebrews 13:16, James 1:27)

- **Intimacy**: Intimacy is a loaded term that means many things to many people, but the base of intimacy is a loving commitment, one that is shown by making a personal investment in a relationship. We cannot have intimacy if we do not give of ourselves in our relationships, and we cannot have fellowship with God or others if we refuse to invest that part of ourselves that often challenges us to do better, be better, and interact differently than we do with those we hold at arm's length. Intimacy draws us, because that is exactly how God desires to know us. It should be, in the trust of the faith, how we are able to interact with others, as well. (Matthew 6:23-24, Matthew 22:37-40, Romans 12:3, 1 John 4:20)

These six things are a part of fellowship because they teach us about relationship. Sometimes I think we want to say we are a part of the church just to say we are, but we don't make connections as part of our interaction with others. The feminine nature of fellowship is one based on trust, and when people seek to violate that connection, they create distance, detachment, and loss within those who genuinely seek something real and profound. Yet we can't find our place in eternity without fellowship, which means the gentle beckoning of fellowship, the call to interact with others: socially, spiritually, and truthfully, is part of being a believer. It is something we will do in this life as much as we will do it in the next, and we need to learn how to associate, how to function in communion, how to communicate, how to distribute, how to contribute, and how to walk in intimacy, because these are all foundational to the purpose and grace present within the church. We are here to discover the power of this spiritual interaction within this spiritual family that God has placed us to be part of, now and forever.

That is the essence of why fellowship is feminine: it is a social representation of the family unit, which is connected to life, and is connected to women, throughout history. The social intercourse of the church teaches us about spiritual family life, about one to another, about what is real important, and guides and directs us as we navigate relationships through the church world. It's a value that represents life, wholeness, and ultimately growth, things that were the responsibilities of our mothers and foremothers when we were children, for centuries.

We embrace eternal fellowship as we embrace the women of the church, as we embrace the values we were taught by women, growing up (be they our mothers, grandmothers, aunts, sisters, or other prominent women in our lives), when we display the etiquette and characteristics they desired us to have, and when we reach out and interact with others as was their greatest hope. Now in the church, it is the greatest hope of our church mothers today – both the leaders and elders – that we will connect to the body and embrace the fullness of eternal fellowship, preparing for eternity right now, by living in connection with one another and successfully walking with God, right through to all He has for us, forever.

Embracing the feminine now

If there is one major theme I can consider from the founding of this book to the end, it is that we need to embrace the feminine in our lives. For thousands of years, the feminine has been treated as if it is a disposable entity, one that we can live without, and one to degrade. We haven't elevated it to the level it should be, and we certainly have treated women as we treat the feminine: with disregard and unimportance, as a background feature to a main event. It is easy to tell women they shouldn't be angry upset about this, but surely, if men lived with this sort of disregard, no one would tell them they shouldn't be upset. Still, I agree that sitting in anger and embitterment is not going to solve the problems we have, nor is it going to change the way we view women, and the way that we, as women, view ourselves. What will change things is when we stop hiding feminine identities and virtues in the closet, as if they are something to be ashamed of, to avoid and to ignore.

We can see from this book that the identity of the feminine in connection with the divine has always been present with us, and always will be there, guiding and teaching us, leading us, and revealing important things to us about God and our spiritual lives. We must embrace this for ourselves, even if others are resistant to it or refuse to believe it. In all things, we should be conscious of how we speak about spiritual feminine entity, respecting things for what they are, and believing that one day, we shall understand all of these things fully and completely, for ourselves. We must teach our daughters that there is nothing shameful in being female, for they are all types of the church, living and breathing, active and excited. We must teach wives that they are equal to their husbands. We must stop embracing patriarchy as an inherent Christian value and raise up equality and understanding in our day and age. We must make room for those who are different, those who fall outside of the norm, and see God at work in and through them, representing something to us that is more than we have ever considered, comfortably, on our own.

The divine feminine is a part of us, one we cannot divorce without consequence, and one we cannot see as it has been revealed, because she is present from the beginning to the end and in every situation and scene, in between. Maybe the divine feminine isn't always present in the loudest of ways or the ones that always get all the attention, but there she remains: in women of faith, both Old and New Testaments, in the call of women, from Old and New Testament times, to today; in the glory of God; in the names and identities of God; in love, in the Scriptures, in grace, in each and every moment and walk of the church, and the church life; in the New Jerusalem to come, and in the work of eternal fellowship, we find her there, guiding and leading, helping and teaching, and active, engaged, and dedicated, as part of the faith we hold dear. There is nowhere we can go to escape it, nor should we want to.

Christianity is not now, and has never been, an exclusively male dictate, one for men to guide and shape without female input. Those little bits and pieces, revealed to us throughout time immemorial, teach us what it means to be a woman, as much as what it means to be a Christian. If we will only heed and hear, we can see the church become so much more than it is, at current, and watch the women of the church change and flourish, if we are finally able to take the position that is truly for us to have.

REFERENCES

Epigraph
Barker, Elsa. "The Mystic Rose," from *The Oxford Book of English Mystical Verse*, 1917. Public Domain.

Introduction
[1]*The Sibylline Oracles.* http://www.sacred-texts.com/cla/sib/sib05.htm. Accessed April 16, 2018.

Chapter 2
[1]*Strong's Exhaustive Concordance of the Bible*, #2332
[2]Ibid, #1557
[3]Ibid, #1904
[4]Ibid., #3479
[5]Ibid., #7728
[6]Ibid., #1586

Chapter 3
[1]*Strong's Exhaustive Concordance of the Bible*, #7327
[2]Ibid., #5281
[3,4]"Who Was Chemosh?" https://www.gotquestions.org/who-Chemosh.html. Accessed January 15, 2018.
[5]*Strong's Exhaustive Concordance of the Bible*, #1162
[6]Ibid., #2060
[7]Ibid., #1919
[8]Marino, Lee Ann B. *Feminine Perspectives of God: Becoming One New Woman in a Journey Through the Books of Ruth and Esther*. Gastonia, North Carolina: Righteous Pen Publications, 2018. Chapter 8, "Celebrating Female Bravery (and All Who Helped)." pp. 190-191.

Chapter 4
[1]*Strong's Exhaustive Concordance of the Bible*, #5301
[2]Mindel, Nissan. "Miriam." http://www.chabad.org/library/article_cdo/aid/112396/jewish/Miriam.htm/. Accessed January 23, 2018.
[3]"Miriam." https://en.wikipedia.org/wiki/Miriam. Accessed January 24, 2018.
[4]*Strong's Exhaustive Concordance of the Bible*, #4813
[5]Ibid., #1682
[6]Ibid., #2468
[7]Ibid., #451

[8]Mariottini, Claude. "Noadiah the Prophetess." https://claudemariottini.com/2013/09/30/noadiah-the-prophetess/. Accessed February 2, 2018.
[9]"Noadiah, Questionable Prophetess." https://obscurecharacters.com/2014/07/08/a-questionable-prophetess/
[10]*Strong's Exhaustive Concordance of the Bible*, #5129
[11]Ibid., #2403

Chapter 5
[1]*Strong's Exhaustive Concordance of the Bible*, #3068
[2]"Female Images of God in the Bible." http://www.womensordination.org/resources/female-images-of-god-in-the-bible/. Accessed February 6, 2018.
[3]*Strong's Exhaustive Concordance of the Bible*, #410
[4]Ibid., #7706
[5]"El Shaddai." https://en.wikipedia.org/wiki/El_Shaddai. Accessed February 6, 2018.
[6]*Strong's Exhaustive Concordance of the Bible*, #155
[7]Ibid., #8597
[8]Ibid., #6286
[9]Ibid, #3519
[10]Ibid., #3115
[11]Ibid., #1927
[12]Ibid., 145
[13]Ibid., #3367
[14]"Shekinah." https://en.wikipedia.org/wiki/Shekhinah. Accessed March 19, 2018.
[15]Ibid.
[16]Kohler, Kauffman and Blau, Ludwig. "Shekinah." http://www.jewishencyclopedia.com/articles/13537-shekinah. Accessed February 6, 2018.
[17] "Spirit of the Lord." https://en.wikipedia.org/wiki/Shekhinah#Spirit_of_the_Lord. Accessed February 6, 2018
[18]*Strong's Exhaustive Concordance of the Bible*, #2452
[19]Ibid., #2454
[20]Ibid., #8454
[21]Ibid., #1108
[22]Ibid., #4678
[23]Ibid., #5385
[24]Ibid., #5428
[25]Ibid., #2232
[26]Ibid., #2222
[27]Ibid., #4194
[28]Ibid., #8546
[29]Ibid., #2288
[30]Ibid., #3639
[31]Ibid., #5054

Chapter 6
[1]*Strong's Exhaustive Concordance of the Bible*, #3137
[2]Ibid., #1665
[3]Ibid., #4982
[4]Ibid., #5042

Chapter 7
[1]*Timeline 600 B.C.* https://www.packrat-pro.com/timeline/600BC.htm. Accessed February 22, 2018.
[2]*Timeline 400 B.C.* https://www.packrat-pro.com/timeline/400BC.htm. Accessed February 22, 2018.
[3]*Timeline 100 B.C.* https://www.packrat-pro.com/timeline/100BC.htm. Accessed February 22, 2018.
[4]"Female Images of God in the Bible." http://www.womensordination.org/resources/female-images-of-god-in-the-bible/. Accessed February 22, 2018.
[5]*Strong's Exhaustive Concordance of the Bible*, #6918
[6]Ibid., #7308
[7]Ibid., #40
[8]Ibid., #4151
[9]Ibid., #3875
[10]Ibid., #1411
[11]Ibid., #1849
[12]Nettelhorst, R.P. "More Than Just A Controversy: All About The Holy Spirit." http://www.theology.edu/journal/volume3/spirit.htm. Accessed March 1, 2018.
[13]Ibid.
[14]*The Odes of Solomon.* http://gnosis.org/library/odes.htm. Accessed May 16, 2025.
[15]*The Odes of Solomon.* http://gnosis.org/library/odes.htm. Accessed March 21, 2018.
[16]Barnstone, Willis. *The Other Bible: Ancient Alternative Scriptures.* San Francisco, California: HarperSanFrancisco, 1984. pg. 280.
[17]*The Odes of Solomon.* http://gnosis.org/library/odes.htm. Accessed March 21, 2018.
[18]Ibid.
[19]"Gender of the Holy Spirit." https://en.wikipedia.org/wiki/Gender_of_the_Holy_Spirit. Accessed March 21, 2018.

Chapter 8
[1]*The Odes of Solomon.* http://gnosis.org/library/odes.htm. Accessed 3/21/2018
[2]*Strong's Exhaustive Concordance of the Bible*, #3566
[3]Ibid., #3565
[4]Ibid., #5293
[5]Ibid., #1135
[6]Ibid., #435
[7]Ibid., #2776

[8]Ibid., #3466
[9]Ibid., #2962

Chapter 9
[1]"A Quick Question: What Percentage Of Pastors Are Female?" http://hirr.hartsem.edu/research/quick_question3.html. Accessed March 1, 2018.
[2]Sandstrom, Aleksandra. "Women Relatively Rare In Top Positions of Religious Leadership." http://www.pewresearch.org/fact-tank/2016/03/02/women-relatively-rare-in-top-positions-of-religious-leadership/. Accessed March 1, 2018.
[3]"Statistics On Women In Ministry." http://www.eauk.org/church/research-and-statistics/women-in-ministry.cfm. Accessed March 3, 2018.
[4]*Strong's Exhaustive Concordance of the Bible*, #5088
[5]"Monasticism." https://www.britannica.com/topic/monasticism. Accessed March 5, 2018.
[6]Lambdin, Thomas O. *The Gospel of Thomas*. http://www.marquette.edu/maqom/Gospel%20of%20Thomas%20Lambdin. pdf. Accessed March 22, 2018.
[7]Ibid.
[8]"Mysogynist Quotes From Church Fathers And Reformers." http://margmowczko.com/misogynist-quotes-from-church-fathers/. Accessed March 22, 2018.
[9]Ibid.
[10]Ibid.
[11]Ibid.
[12]Ibid.
[13]*Strong's Exhaustive Concordance of the Bible*, #4247
[14]Ibid., #1124
[15]Ibid., #5485
[16]Ibid., #26

Chapter 10
[1]*Strong's Exhaustive Concordance of the Bible*, #3389
[2]Ibid., #2419
[3] "Jerusalem." https://www.britannica.com/place/Jerusalem. Accessed March 8, 2018.
[4]Lambdin, Thomas O. *The Gospel of Thomas*. http://www.marquette.edu/maqom/Gospel%20of%20Thomas%20Lambdin. pdf. Accessed March 22, 2018.
[5]Ibid.
[6]*Strong's Exhaustive Concordance of the Bible*, #2482

ABOUT THE AUTHOR

Dr. Lee Ann B. Marino,
Ph.D., D.Min., D.D.

THESE THAT HAVE TURNED THE WORLD UPSIDE DOWN HAVE COME HITHER ALSO.
(ACTS 17:6, KJV)

DR. LEE ANN B. MARINO, PH.D., D.MIN., D.D. (she/her) is "everyone's favorite theologian" leading Gen X, Millennials, and Gen Z with expertise in leadership training, queer and feminist theology, general religion, and apostolic theology. She has served in ministry since 1998 and was ordained as a pastor in 2002 and an apostle in 2010. She founded what is now Sanctuary Apostolic Fellowship Empowerment (SAFE) Ministries in 2004. Under her ministry heading Dr. Marino is founder and Overseer of Sanctuary International Fellowship Tabernacle (SIFT) (the original home of National Coming Out Sunday) and The Sanctuary Network, and Chancellor of Apostolic Covenant Theological Seminary (ACTS).

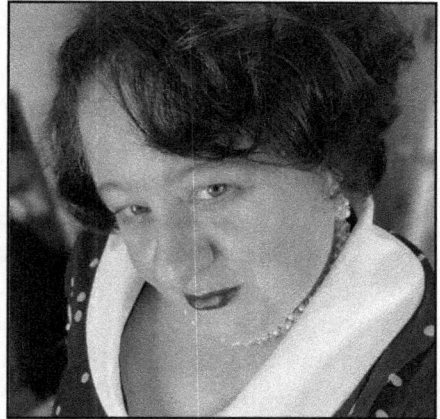

Affectionately nicknamed "the Spitfire," Dr. Marino has spent over two decades as an "apostle, preacher, and teacher" (2 Timothy 1:11), exercising her personal mandate to become "all things to all people" (1 Corinthians 9:22). Her embrace of spiritual issues (both technical and intimate) has found its home among both seekers and believers, those who desire spiritual answers to today's issues.

Dr. Marino has preached throughout the United States, Puerto Rico, and Europe in hundreds of religious services and experiences throughout the years. A history maker in her own right, she has spent over two decades in advocacy, education, and work for and within minority spiritual communities (including African American, Hispanic, and LGBTQ+). She has also served as the first woman on all-male synods, councils, and panels, as well as the first preacher or speaker welcomed of a different race, sexual orientation, or identity among diverse communities. Today, Dr. Marino's work extends to over 150 countries as she hosts the popular *Kingdom Now* podcast, which is in the top 20 percentile of all podcasts worldwide. She is also the author of over 35 books and the popular Patheos column, *Leadership on Fire*. To date, she has had five bestselling titles within their subject matter: *Understanding Demonology, Spiritual Warfare, Healing, and Deliverance: A Manual for the Christian Minister*; *Ministry School Boot Camp: Training for Helps Ministries, Appointments, and Beyond*; *Discovering Intimacy: A Journey Through the Song of Solomon*; *Fruit of the Vine: Study and Commentary on the Fruit of the Spirit*; and *Ministering to LGBTQ+ (and Those Who Love Them): A Primer for Queer Theology* (and its accompanying workbook).

As a public icon and social media influencer, Dr. Marino advocates healthy body image (curvy/full-figured), representation as a demisexual/aromantic, and albinism awareness as a model. Known to those she works with, she is a spiritual mom, teacher, leader, professor, confidant, and friend. She continues to transform, receiving new teaching, revelation, and insight in this thing we call "ministry." Through years of spiritual growth and maturity, Dr. Marino stands as herself, here to present what God has given to her for any who have an ear to hear.

For more information, visit her website at kingdompowernow.org.

www.ingramcontent.com/pod-product-compliance
Lightning Source LLC
Chambersburg PA
CBHW060454090426
42735CB00011B/1987